GERMAN FOR BEGINNERS

ABOUT THE AUTHORS

Charles Duff (1894-1966) had wide experience in the practical use of German. After serving with the French Army as an interpreter, he was employed for many years as Press Officer by the British Foreign Office. Thereafter, he devoted his time to teaching, writing, and translating. He served as lecturer at the Institute of Education, London University, and as Professor of Occidental Languages at Nanyang University.

Mr. Duff pioneered in developing and applying modern methods of teaching foreign languages, using them in classroom work and as a basis for his popular volumes of self-instruction. He wrote and edited many books, including *How to Learn a Language;* and the Barnes and Noble Everyday Handbooks *Spanish for Beginners*, *Italian for Beginners*, and *Russian for Beginners* (with Dmitri Makaroff). He was a contributor to the *Encyclopaedia Britannica*.

Paul Stamford, whose native tongue is German, was educated in Germany where he lived many years both before and since the Second World War. He has translated numerous works from German into English. His practical skill in these languages led to his appointment, first, as an interpreter with the United Nations forces during the war and, later, as translator and interpreter for the Allied Control Commission.

GERMAN
FOR BEGINNERS

by CHARLES DUFF
and PAUL STAMFORD

BARNES & NOBLE BOOKS

A DIVISION OF HARPER & ROW, PUBLISHERS

New York, Hagerstown, San Francisco, London

SECOND EDITION (Revised) 1960

L. C. Catalogue Card Number: 60-10580

ISBN: 0-06-463217-2

This revised American edition published by special arrangement with Charles Duff and Paul Stamford and English Universities Press, Ltd. The original edition entitled *German for Adults* was first issued in Great Britain in 1957.

81 82 83 84   20 19 18 17 16 15 14 13 12

PRINTED IN THE UNITED STATES OF AMERICA

INTRODUCING THE COURSE

THIS is a comprehensive " All-Purposes " Course in German, similar to the Courses in French, Italian, and Spanish in the same series of books, the differences in arrangement and presentation depending on the nature of each language. Like the other Courses, that for German has been prepared on modern principles, evolved from long experience, and is so arranged that it can be used by various categories of adult learners. It is *not* intended for juveniles, but, apart from this, it can be used for self-tuition, private tuition, or class-work. Thus, it can be used by :

(1) Absolute beginners.

(2) Those who already know some German and desire to improve their knowledge. (This includes that large number of people who have studied German at some time but have either forgotten what they learnt or never appreciated its practical applications.)

(3) Those who are interested in the German–Austrian–Swiss contribution to life and culture, and who wish to enjoy or benefit from a first-hand acquaintance with it, either by reading or direct contact. This includes everything that comes under the broad headings of Literature, Drama, Science, Technology, Art, Music, and Philosophy.

(4) Travellers of all kinds and others whose work takes them to the German-speaking countries. They range from holiday-makers to technicians and those engaged in some branch of commerce.

Many who are specially interested in Science, Technology, or Commerce are under the impression that a smattering of German plus some special knowledge of the technical terms of their own subject should be sufficient for their purpose. It does not always work out like that, because the approach to any subject ripens into success only if the normal language of everyday life is fairly well known *first of all*.   Such people should know the elements and foundation material of " All-Purposes " German.   Then " German for Science ", " German for Commerce ", or German for *any* special purpose is merely a matter of adding the special vocabulary of the subject to the basic material that is already known.   Little progress is achieved without a knowledge of German grammar, a well-selected vocabulary, and the rich capacity of German for word-building.

This book, then, contains all that is necessary to make a good foundation, whatever the purpose may be for which the language is required.   In Lesson X hints are given for further study. Specialists, or those studying for entrance to a university, will from that point proceed to deal with the works in German that may be required or set for examination or other purposes.

The Course is divided into ten Lessons, and each Lesson consists of five Sections.   Each of these Sections contains a statement of essential grammar with illustrative examples, and Practice (ÜBUNG) in the grammar and on what has gone before. From Lesson II onwards the learner begins to learn vocabulary and phrases for everyday *Situations*, which forms an important part of the learning process.   From Lesson III onwards he is encouraged to listen to radio broadcasts, which may include television, films, and phonograph records when and where these are available.   Much reading matter is now given, either with interlinear translation or with notes to assist in following the German text.   The reading matter consists of extracts from books and from contemporary newspapers.   From Lesson III all this material is essentially practical, and consists of the kind of German that is used to-day by German speakers in their everyday life.   It shows the grammar " in action ".

A word is necessary about grammar.   German is by its nature an inflected language with a different word-order from English. There can be no evading the grammar required to make it function with reasonable correctness and effect.   The Declensions of Nouns have to be learnt at an early stage, because then they are the most useful words for the learner.   It has to be admitted that there is a point beyond which simplification of these Declensions merely means postponement of learning much that is of immediate practical value, and cannot in the end be avoided. The issue is not evaded. To help the beginner, the Declension of Nouns is presented in stages, and the less important indicated by smaller type. The learner is shown how the Declensions *work*, and this theory is driven home, first by Practice in exercises (ÜBUNG), in the Situations material and in the Reading Matter; and then again by listening to radio broadcasts for speech. Once the theory of the grammar is known, the beginner is advised to concentrate first on reading, which shows the whole mechanism in action.

In working through the Course, the self-taught will make their own pace, but they must always remember that *speech* cannot be learnt from a book, for a book cannot speak! *Speech is learnt by hearing and mimicking*, to begin with; it is perfected by learning from constant listening and practice. German pronunciation presents few difficulties to the English-speaking learner. If the book is used for private tuition or class-work, each teacher makes his own curriculum; a minimum period of one hour is suggested as reasonable to work through a Section.

Mr. Paul Stamford is responsible for the accuracy of the German text. German is his mother tongue, he was educated in Germany, and lived there for many years before and for some time since the Second World War. He was Officer-Interpreter with the Allied Forces and Translator-Interpreter with the Control Commission; and has translated books and a great variety of other matter into German. Otherwise this is a joint collaboration in which the partners worked closely together throughout. We are jointly responsible for the final result, and would be grateful if our attention be drawn (c/o the publishers) to any errors that may be found.

Grateful acknowledgments are due to the publishers, editors and authors of the extracts provided for Reading. Wherever possible acknowledgment is given with the text, though in some cases this has not been found possible. It is hoped that this collective acknowledgment will be acceptable. To the Aufbau-Verlag, Berlin, our thanks are due for their kind permission to use the extracts from *Der Streit um den Sergeanten Grischa*,* and to the Verlag Oeffentliches Leben for those from *Till Eulenspiegel*. Finally, we thank our own publishers and printers for their patient collaboration in making this book clear and attractive typographically.

CHARLES DUFF
PAUL STAMFORD

* Published in England by Hutchinsons as *The Case of Sergeant Grischa*, excellently translated from the German by Eric Sutton.

TABLE OF CONTENTS

PART I: First Principles

LESSON I

LESSON II

PART II : The Framework of the Language

LESSON V

WHY LEARN GERMAN?

Because :

It is one of the important languages of the modern world.

It is spoken by over 80,000,000 people—in Germany, Austria, Switzerland—and by many millions elsewhere in Europe, as well as in America, sometimes as their mother-tongue, or, alternatively, as their second language.

It is akin to English, being a member of the same group of languages and having thousands of words which resemble English words.

It is a particularly useful language for those interested in science, technology, or commerce. In some branches of science and technology the German-speaking countries are second to none.

It has a fine literature, classical and modern, especially in lyrical poetry. In this literature are represented some of the world's greatest minds.

In works of non-fiction, and in reliable reference and text-books on almost every subject, German excels.

It is necessary for those who wish to travel outside the beaten track of tourists in Germany, Switzerland, and Austria, and will often be understood in parts of Holland, the Scandinavian countries, Yugoslavia, Czechoslovakia, and Hungary, where English would draw a blank.

It is worth learning for itself alone, being an interesting inflected language with a rich vocabulary, and often providing the key to the earliest writings in Old English (also called Anglo-Saxon).

GERMAN FOR BEGINNERS

PART I

FIRST PRINCIPLES

> To learn a language it is not enough to know so many words. They must be connected according to the particular laws of the particular language.
>
> *Jespersen*

HOW TO STUDY

1. Take one Section or part of a Lesson at a time. First read it through carefully in order to *understand* everything. When it is understood, and not before, learn the principles, words, and examples, and be sure you *know how they work*.

2. Next go on to the Practice. Whenever you feel it necessary, go over it more than once. Never proceed to the next Section until you know what has gone before.

3. When a Lesson has been finished, go over it again from time to time. Never fail to revise those parts of which you are doubtful.

4. Declensions and conjugations are best learnt by constant revision and practice—practice in grammar, reading, and with " Situation Material ".

5. After Lesson III you should listen as often as possible to Radio Broadcasts. This trains the ear to German sounds.

6. PRACTICE, whether as " set " Practice on Grammar, or as Reading Material, or as Listening to Radio, or as speaking with German speakers: this is the road to success.

7. Never miss an opportunity of *hearing German spoken*.

8. If your progress is not as rapid as you would like it to be, be neither impatient nor dismayed.

NEVER MIND SLOW PROGRESS SO LONG AS YOU KEEP GOING!

LESSON I

§ 1. *The Alphabet—Der Umlaut* (¨)*—Vowels and Their Sounds—Diphthongs—Practice*

THE German alphabet consists of the same twenty-six letters as the English, the only differences being that **a, o, u,** and **au** are sometimes printed **ä, ö, ü,** and **äu,** and the combination **ß** is used to represent the German double letter **sz.**

THE ALPHABET: The names of the German letters are shown in the following table.

LETTERS	GERMAN NAMES	LETTERS	GERMAN NAMES
A—a	**ah**	P—p	**pay**
B—b	**bay**	Q—q	**koo**
C—c	**tsay**	R—r	**err**
D—d	**day**	S—s	**ess**
E—e	**ay**	T—t	**tay**
F—f	**eff**	U—u	**oo**
G—g	**gay**	V—v	**fow**
H—h	**haa**	W—w	**vay**
I—i	**ee**	X—x	**iks**
J—j	**yot**	Y—y	**ipsilon**
K—k	**kaa**	Z—z	**tsett**
L—l	**ell**	ä	**a-Umlaut**
M—m	**emm**	ö	**o-Umlaut**
N—n	**enn**	ü	**u-Umlaut**
O—o	**oh**	äu	**au-Umlaut**

The Roman letters shown above are used in this book. Most reading matter in German is now being printed in this kind of type. However, a few current writings and many of the classical books found in libraries are printed in the Gothic alphabet shown on page 307. (There is also a German script alphabet for handwriting, shown on page 309, but in Germany the American-British script has been widely adopted.)

3

Der Umlaut (¨): There are no accent marks (such as, for example, those in French), but the diaeresis (¨) is used to modify the sounds of **a, o, u,** and the diphthong **au,** so that when written **ä, ö, ü,** and **äu** they must be pronounced in the manner described below. They are then called **a-, o-, u-, au- Umlaut** (or modified **a, o, u, au**), and the sign represents an *e*, now omitted.

VOWELS AND THEIR SOUNDS: Vowels are either long or short.

A vowel is long in German:
1. When it is doubled.
2. When it comes before **h.**
3. In **i** followed by **e (ie).**
4. Before a single consonant that is followed by another vowel.

Examples: 1. **das Haar,** the hair. 2. **der Sohn,** the son. 3. **wieder,** again. 4. **eben,** even.

A vowel is short:
1. When it comes before two or more consonants.
2. In the endings **-el, -er,** and **-en.**
3. In prefixes such as **be-, ge-, ver-, zer-.**
4. The letter **e** at the end of a word.

Examples: 1. **besser,** better. 2. **der Finger,** finger. 3. **beschreiben,** to describe. 4. **die Katze,** cat.

The vowels are pronounced as follows:

Long **a** like English *a* in *far, father*: **der Vater,** father; **schlafen,** sleep; **der Name,** name.

Short **a** like English *a* in *art, what*: **der Mann,** the man; **bald,** soon; **also,** therefore.

Long **e** like French *é* (or *ê* in *fête*): **der Esel,** the ass; **lesen,** read; **zehn,** ten.

Short **e** like *e* in *set, bet*: **wenn,** when, if; **setzen,** sit.

Long **i** like *i* in *machine*: **mir,** me: **das Fieber,** the fever; **Amerika,** America.

Short **i** like *i* in *wing, miss, sit*: **das Kind,** the child.

Long **o** like *o* in *no, stove*: **der Sohn,** the son; **der Ofen,** the stove.

Short **o** like *o* in *omit, obey:* **kommt,** comes; **der Morgen,** morning.

Long **u** like *u* in *rude*: **das Blut,** the blood; **schlug,** struck; **zu,** to.

Short **u** like *u* in *pull*: **das Pfund,** the pound; **unser,** our; **die Mutter,** Mother.

Modified:

Long **ä** like *a* in *gate*: **das Mädel,** girl (colloq.); **der Bär,** bear.

Short **ä** like German short **e: die Hände,** the hands; **hätte,** had.

Long **ö** rather like *ea* in *earth*, or French *eu* in *deux* or in *le feu*: **das Öl,** the oil.

Short **ö** is the same sound, shorter: **die Hölle,** hell; **könnte,** could.

Long **ü** like the French *û* in *sûr*, Scots *u* in *gude*: **die Übung,** the practice.

Short **ü** is the same sound, shorter: **der Müller,** the miller.

When **Y** is used as a vowel, it is pronounced like German **i.**

DIPHTHONGS:

ai, ei are almost like English *ai* in *aisle* or *ei* in *height*, or *i* in *fine*: **der Mai,** *May* (month); **mein,** *mine*. (**ay, ey** pronounced the same, but are only to be found in some surnames and foreign words.)

au is like *ou* in *house*, but in German the **a** and **u** sounds blend to make a stronger sound like *ahoo* said quickly: **das Haus,** the house; **die Frau,** the lady, woman.

äu like *oy* in *boy*: **die Häuser,** the houses.

eu the same as **äu: neu,** new; **neun,** nine; **heute,** to-day.

ie is strictly not a diphthong, and is pronounced like long **ë.**

PRACTICE

English-speaking people have more difficulty in pronouncing German vowels than the Scots, Welsh, or Irish, because, generally speaking, the latter pronounce their own vowels clearly and "pure" like Italian vowels. With the exception of German short **-e** at the end of a word or in the endings **-el, -en, er,** all German vowels, especially the long ones, must be given a good, clear sound.

First learn to distinguish between long and short vowels, and go over the words given to illustrate them several times, paying at this stage more attention to vowels than to consonants. Do not yet attempt to memorize the words or their meanings—at least until the pronunciation of the consonants is known. If at all possible, get someone who speaks German well to go over the vowels and illustrative words a few times, and *mimic* the pronunciation.

§ 2. *Pronunciation of Consonants—Double Consonants and Other Sounds—Stress or Tonic Accent—Practice—List of Words— Note on Resemblance*

CONSONANTS: The Consonants are pronounced as in English, with the following exceptions:

b at the end of a word is English *p*: **der Dieb,** the thief.

d at the end of a word is English *t*: **das Kind,** the child.

g is always pronounced hard as in English *go*: **gehen,** to go.*

h is silent after a vowel in a syllable; otherwise, it is aspirated:

der Sohn, the son   **hundert,** hundred
die Hand, the hand   **fähig,** capable

j English *y*: **jung,** young.

k is pronounced before *n*: **der Knabe,** the boy.

*A soft **g,** as in English *age*, occurs in some foreign derivatives: **der Ingenieur,** the engineer.

r is a much stronger sound than English *r*. It may be either trilled with the tip of the tongue (as is done in Spanish or Italian) or produced by vibrating the uvula against the back of the tongue, like the sound made in gargling: **rot,** red; **das Grab,** the grave.

s at the beginning of a word, sounds like our *z*; also before and between vowels = English *z*

> **sein,** to be   **die Rose,** the rose

Single **s** is never like *s* in *some, sing.*

s at the end of a word = English *ss*: **das Haus,** the House.

v = English *f*: **der Vater,** the father.

w = English *v*: **das Wasser,** the water.   **ss** = English *ss*.

z = English *ts* as in *cats*: **der Tanz,** the dance; **der Zug,** the train.   *Note:* *tz* has the same sound: **die Katze,** the cat.

DOUBLE CONSONANTS AND OTHER SOUNDS:

ck = *k*.

ch has no equivalent in English.   After unmodified **a, o, u,** and **au** it is a guttural like Scottish *ch* in *loch* or Irish *gh* in *lough*.   Thus: **hoch,** high; **das Buch,** the book; **das Dach,** the roof.   Otherwise it is a palatal sound: **ich,** I; **die Dächer,** the roofs; **welcher,** who, which.   This sound resembles a well-sounded *h* in such words as *Hugo, huge*.   **chs** = *ks*: **das Wachs,** the wax.

ph = *f* as in English.

pf both letters are sounded: **das Pferd,** the horse.

qu = *kv*: **die Quelle,** the well.

sz (printed ß in Gothic, ß in Roman) always sounds like English *ss*: **der Kuß,** the kiss.

sch = English *sh*: **Herr Schmidt,** Mr. Smith.

sp, st at the beginning of a word = English *shp-, sht-*: **sprechen,** to speak; **stehen,** to stand.

-ti- in the ending **-tion** = English *tsee*.   Thus: **die Nation,** the nation.

th = *t*: **das Theater,** the theatre.

-ng, -nger as in *sing, singer*: **der Ring,** the ring; **der Finger,** finger.

STRESS OR TONIC ACCENT: In words of more than one syllable there is always a syllable more heavily stressed than the other or others. This is usually the first or " root " syllable. Thus: **háben,** to have; **Fräúlein,** Miss.

Exceptions: (1) Words beginning with inseparable prefixes (Lesson VI, §1) are stressed on the syllable immediately following the prefix. Thus: **schréiben,** to write; **beschréiben,** to describe. (2) Words consisting of two indeclinable words (Adverbs, Prepositions) have the stress on the second. Thus: **daráuf,** thereon. (3) Words from foreign languages have the stress as in the language from which they come. Thus: **das Regimént,** the regiment.

PRACTICE

It is highly important at the outset to achieve at least a passable pronunciation. A really good pronunciation can be achieved only by practice and by listening to good speakers. If at all possible, the beginner should have the help of a good speaker, for preference one whose mother-tongue is German. The equivalents given above are based on English sounds, and must be regarded as mere approximations. Strictly, no English vowel is the exact equivalent of a German vowel, because all German vowels are "pure". German pronunciation is more clear-cut, more definite, and without the vagueness, slurring, and the half-sounding of consonants which is too often found in English speech. Good German speakers make full use of their vocal apparatus, and the best rule for the foreign learner is to observe, listen carefully, and mimic their way of speaking.

In §§ 1 and 2 the learner has been given a number of German words, with their meanings, to illustrate the sounds of the language. They are now given, without their meanings, in the order in which they appeared. Go over them, slowly at first, referring back where necessary for pronunciation or meaning, until they can be pronounced clearly and without difficulty.

LIST OF WORDS

das Haar—der Sohn—wieder—eben—besser—der Finger—beschreiben—die Katze—der Vater—der Mann—der Esel—wenn—das Fieber—das Kind—der Ofen—der Morgen—das Blut—das Pfund—das Mädel —der Bär—die Hände—das Öl—die Hölle—die Übung —der Müller—der Mai—mein—das Haus—die Frau— die Häuser—neun—heute—der Dieb—gehen—hundert—die Hand—fähig—jung—der Knabe—rot—das Grab—sein—die Rose—das Wasser—der Tanz—der Zug—hoch—das Buch—das Dach—ich—die Dächer— welcher—das Wachs—das Pferd—die Quelle—der Kuß—Herr Schmidt—sprechen—stehen—die Nation —das Theater—der Ring—haben—das Fräulein— schreiben—darauf—das Regiment

NOTE ON RESEMBLANCE: The German and English languages belong to the same group of languages: the Germanic branch of the Indo-European " family ". Hence, there is a large number of words in the two languages which resemble one another, often with little or no difference in form or meaning. This makes the learning of many German words easy for the English-speaking learner.

Note that all Nouns are written with a capital letter in German.

§ 3. *Inflection: Declension—The Four Cases—Articles:* **DER** *and* **EIN**—*Possessive Adjectives—Demonstrative Adjectives— New Words and Phrases—Practice*

Grammarians call German a " synthetic " language. By this they mean that it is characterized by the combination of simple words or elements of words into compounds or complex words. It prefers to express a complex notion by compounded or variable words instead of with a number of distinct words. English, by contrast, is an " analytical " language. Instead of expressing changes of meaning in a word by changes of its ending or by combining it with another word or words, it prefers to make a liberal use of particles—minor parts of speech, usually short and unchangeable.

INFLECTION: In German the forms of certain words are changed to express different grammatical meanings or relations. This takes place in Articles, Nouns, Adjectives, and Pronouns, and their inflections or changes in endings are called *Declension*. When it takes place in Verbs it is called *Conjugation*. These Inflections will be dealt with under their different headings in the Lessons.

THE FOUR CASES: There are four cases in German: Nominative, Genitive, Dative, Accusative. Articles, Nouns, Adjectives, and Pronouns have these four cases, which are indicated by declension.

The **Nominative** case indicates the *subject*, or initiator, of action or speech. The Nominative is the *doer*.

The **Genitive** indicates the *possessor* of something.

The **Dative** indicates the *recipient* of something: the indirect object of speech or action.

The **Accusative** indicates the person or thing *directly affected* by the action. It is used for direct object.

Thus:

            I   GAVE MARY'S HAT   TO   ALICE
Cases: *Nom.*   *Gen.*   *Acc.*   *Dat.*

The Nominative answers the question WHO? WHAT?
The Genitive answers the question WHOSE? OF WHAT?
The Dative answers the question TO WHOM? TO WHAT?
The Accusative answers the question WHOM? WHAT?

Declension of German Articles, Nouns, Adjectives, and Pronouns varies not only in accordance with case, but also with gender and number. That of Articles, Adjectives, and Pronouns is fairly regular, and it is fixed, so that learning these declensions is not difficult. But the declension of Nouns is more troublesome. It has a number of variations, and there are exceptions to many of the rules which ingenuity has devised. Nevertheless, even with Nouns there are certain principles which, if known, will save the learner much time and worry.

The declensions of Articles, Adjectives, and Pronouns must be known thoroughly.

ARTICLES—**DER,** *the:* The words *the* and *a, an* are called "articles". The former is the definite article, the latter the indefinite. The articles are declined in German and have the four cases Nominative, Genitive, Dative, and Accusative in each gender in the singular and *the* in the plural. *A, an* have no plural, by their nature. **DER,** *the,* is declined as follows:

	Singular			Plural All	
Cases	Masc.	Fem.	Neuter	genders	
Nominative	**DER**	**DIE**	**DAS**	**DIE**	*the*—Subject
Genitive	**DES**	**DER**	**DES**	**DER**	*of the*—Possessive
Dative	**DEM**	**DER**	**DEM**	**DEN**	*to the*—Object, indirect
Accusative	**DEN**	**DIE**	**DAS**	**DIE**	*the*—Object, direct

It is best to learn these by the gender and the plural. Thus: **DER, DES, DEM, DEN—DIE, DER, DER, DIE—DAS, DES, DEM, DAS.** Plural: **DIE, DER, DEN, DIE.** Know them thoroughly before proceeding.

INDEFINITE ARTICLE—**EIN,** *a, an, one :* It is important at this stage to become familiar with the endings of these words in their various cases, because those endings are similar, not only in the indefinite article **EIN,** *a, an, one,* and in its pronoun **EINER, EINE, EINES,** but also, as will be seen, in other words, especially adjectives. Take **EIN,** *a, an :*

	Masc.	Fem.	Neuter	
Nominative	**EIN**	**EINE**	**EIN**	a, an
Genitive	**EINES**	**EINER**	**EINES**	of a
Dative	**EINEM**	**EINER**	**EINEM**	to a
Accusative	**EINEN**	**EINE**	**EIN**	a

POSSESSIVE ADJECTIVES: The following Possessive Adjectives, and also **KEIN**, are declined in the same way as **EIN** but have a plural:

Masc.	Fem.	Neuter	Plural	
MEIN	**MEINE**	**MEIN**	**MEINE**	my
DEIN	**DEINE**	**DEIN**	**DEINE**	thy, your (sing.)
SEIN	**SEINE**	**SEIN**	**SEINE**	his, its
IHR	**IHRE**	**IHR**	**IHRE**	her
UNSER	**UNS(E)RE**	**UNSER**	**UNS(E)RE**	our
EUER	**EU(E)RE**	**EUER**	**EU(E)RE**	your (plural)
IHR	**IHRE**	**IHR**	**IHRE**	their
IHR	**IHRE**	**IHR**	**IHRE**	your (polite formal)
KEIN	**KEINE**	**KEIN**	**KEINE**	not any, not one, no

Declension of Plural

Nominative	**KEINE**
Genitive	**KEINER**
Dative	**KEINEN**
Accusative	**KEINE**

The singular of all these words is declined like **EIN,** the plural like **KEINE.** Thus:

	Masc.	Fem.	Neuter	Plural
Nominative	**MEIN**	**MEINE**	**MEIN**	**MEINE**
Genitive	**MEINES**	**MEINER**	**MEINES**	**MEINER**
Dative	**MEINEM**	**MEINER**	**MEINEM**	**MEINEN**
Accusative	**MEINEN**	**MEINE**	**MEIN**	**MEINE**

DEMONSTRATIVE ADJECTIVES: Although articles have been considered as separate parts of speech, and it is convenient in learning German to continue to do so, they are really adjectives. There are similarities in the declension of adjectives and the articles, and especially in the demonstrative adjectives such as **DIESER,** *this,* **JENER,** *that.* **JEDER,** *every, each,* **MANCHER,** *many (a),* **SOLCHER,** *such (a),* **WELCHER,** *which (one).* All these are declined like **DER,** *the.*

Cases	Singular Masc.	Fem.	Neuter	Plural— All Genders	
Nom.	**DIESER**	**DIESE**	**DIESES**	**DIESE**	this, these
Gen.	**DIESES**	**DIESER**	**DIESES**	**DIESER**	of this, these
Dat.	**DIESEM**	**DIESER**	**DIESEM**	**DIESEN**	to this, these
Acc.	**DIESEN**	**DIESE**	**DIESES**	**DIESE**	this, these

Words Already Given in §1 and §2

der Bär, bear
der Esel, ass, jackass
der Finger, finger
der Junge (also, **der Knabe),** boy
der Mai, May
der Mann, man
der Morgen, morning
der Ofen, stove
der Sohn, son
der Vater, father

die Frau, woman
die Hand, hand
die Hände, hands
die Katze, cat
die Übung, drill, practice

kommen, to come
kommt, comes

gehen, to go
geht, goes

wenn, if, when
wieder, again

das Blut, blood
das Fieber, fever
das Haus, house
die Häuser, houses
das Kind, child
das Mädchen (Mädel,) girl
das Öl, oil

eben, even
heute, to-day
jung, young
neun, nine
rot, red

The preceding words should be memorized.

New Words and Phrases

der Freund, friend

die Freundin, friend (girl)
die Toilette, lavatory
das Postamt, Post Office

Herr, Mr., Sir
Frau, Mrs.
Fräulein, Miss

wer ? Who ?   **was ?** What ?   **wo ?** Where ?
ja, yes   **nein,** no
hier, here   **da, dort,** there
er, he
sie, she } **ist,** is **kommt,** comes   **nicht,** not
es, it

bitte, please (also *pardon* when something has not been heard)

danke, thanks, thank you

guten Morgen, good morning; **guten Tag,** good day
guten Abend, good evening; **gute Nacht,** good night

Practice: ÜBUNG

Note : Translations in all Practice material are literal and follow the word-order of German, which often differs from the English.

WER IST DA?
Who is there ?
HIER IST DER SOHN.
Here is the son.
SEIN VATER KOMMT HEUTE.
His father comes to-day.
ER IST MEIN FREUND.
He is my friend.
WO IST SEINE FRAU?
Where is his wife ?
SIE IST NICHT HIER.
She is not here.
KOMMT SIE HEUTE?
Does she come to-day ?
NEIN, SIE KOMMT HEUTE NICHT.
No, she does not come to-day.
IST DIE FRAU IHRE FREUNDIN? *
Is the woman your friend ?

* **-IN** = feminine ending. **Freund** = friend (male). **Freundin** = friend (female).

NEIN, SIE IST NICHT MEINE FREUNDIN.

No, she is not my friend.

IST DAS MÄDEL JUNG?

Is the girl young?

JA, ES * IST JUNG.

Yes, she is young.

GUTEN MORGEN, FRÄULEIN.

Good morning, Miss.

IST HIER DAS POSTAMT?

Is here the Post Office?

NEIN, HERR SCHMIDT, HIER IST KEIN POSTAMT. ES IST DORT.

No, Mr. Smith, here is no Post Office.   It is there.

DANKE! GUTEN ABEND, MEIN FRÄULEIN.

Thanks.   Good evening, Miss.

WER IST DIESER MANN HIER?

Who is this man here?

WER, BITTE?

Pardon, who?

JENER HERR DORT.

That gentleman there.

ER IST MEIN VATER.

He is my father.

KOMMT DER JUNGE WIEDER?

Does the boy come again?

JA, ER KOMMT HEUTE WIEDER.

Yes, he comes to-day again.

UNSER HAUS IST ROT.

Our house is red.

DIE KATZE IST JUNG.

The cat is young.

IST BLUT ROT?

Is blood red?

JA, ES IST ROT.

Yes, it is red.

WO IST DIE TOILETTE, BITTE?

Where is the lavatory, please?

* **ES** to agree with **das Mädel** (neuter).

SIE IST DORT, FRAU SCHMIDT.
It is there, Mrs. Smith.

WELCHER ESEL KOMMT DA ?
Which jackass is coming there ?

ER IST KEIN ESEL.
He is no jackass.

GUTE NACHT, MEIN FREUND !
Good night, my friend !

§ 4. *Nouns: Gender—Safest Rule—For Reference—Rule for Compound Nouns—Visualization—Practice— Numbers—Words and Phrases—How to Practice— Practice*

A Noun is a word which names some person, place, thing, or state. Thus: *a man, the church, a table, the sweetness—man, church, table, sweetness*, are Nouns.

GENDER: There are, in German as in English, three genders: masculine, feminine, and neuter. But the gender of German Nouns does not always follow the simplicity of nature like that of English Nouns. Often it does not correspond to sex, as in:

DAS WEIB, the woman   **DAS MÄDCHEN,** the girl
DAS FRÄULEIN, the young lady, Miss

Nevertheless, the names of most men and male animals are masculine in German, and also the names of most women and female animals are feminine.

DER MANN, the man;   **DIE FRAU,** the woman, lady
DER HAHN, the rooster;   **DIE HENNE,** the hen
DER HUND, the dog;   **DIE HÜNDIN,** the bitch

But the names of things are not necessarily neuter. They can be masculine, feminine, or neuter.

Safest Rule: Because of the doubt English-speaking people often have as to the gender of German Nouns, the safest rule is:

LEARN THE APPROPRIATE ARTICLE WITH EVERY GERMAN NOUN

der TISCH, the table   **die SCHRIFT,** the writing
das BUCH, the book

For Reference: It is helpful to remember the following:

MASCULINE are—

(1) Male human beings and animals.

(2) The names of the days of the week, the months, the seasons, and the points of the compass. Thus:

der Montag, Monday   **der Februar,** February
der Sommer, summer

(3) Stones:

der Stein, stone   **der Marmor,** marble

(4) Many Nouns derived from Verbs and ending in **-ER, -EL.** Thus:

der Flieger, flyer; from **fliegen,** to fly
der Flügel, wing; also from **fliegen**

(5) Nouns ending in **-IG, -ICH, -ING, -LING.** Thus:

der Käfig, cage   **der Rettich,** radish
der Sperling, sparrow

Note: **der Mond,** moon.

FEMININE are—

(1) Female human beings and animals.

(2) Most trees, flowers, small animals, insects. Thus:

die Eiche, oak   **die Tulpe,** tulip
die Biene, bee

(3) Most two-syllable words ending in **-E.** Thus:

die Seite, page   **die Sonne,** sun
die Gabe, gift

(4) Nouns ending in **-EI, -HEIT, -KEIT, -IN, -SCHAFT, -UNG, -IE, -IK, -ION, -TAT, -TUR** (the last five mostly of foreign origin). Thus:

die Partei, party   **die Klugheit,** prudence
die Freundschaft, friendship   **die Ironie,** irony
die Kultur, culture
die Lektion, lesson

NEUTER are—

(1) Names of countries and towns. Thus:

das Kanada, Canada   **das Deutschland,** Germany

Exceptions: **die Türkei,** Turkey
die Schweiz, Switzerland

(2) Names of metals. Thus:

das Gold, gold

(3) Verbs used as Nouns, all ending in **-EN** (corresponding to the English gerund). Thus:

das Singen, singing

(4) All diminutives ending in **-CHEN, -LEIN.** Thus:

das Hündchen, puppy   **das Fräulein,** young lady

(5) Letters of the alphabet:

das A; das Z

(6) Most Nouns beginning with the prefix **GE-.** Thus:

das Gespräch, conversation
das Gebirge, range of mountains

(7) Most Nouns in **-TUM, -NIS.** Thus:

das Altertum, antiquity   **das Ereignis,** event

RULES FOR COMPOUND NOUNS: Every compound Noun takes the gender of its last component. Thus:

die TASCHE, pocket; **das TUCH,** cloth; **das TASCHENTUCH,** handkerchief

VISUALIZATION: It is important once you have learned to pronounce German properly, to get into the habit of *thinking* in that language as quickly as possible. Thus, there is no need for you to say over the English of the phrase **,, Guten Morgen "** once you know what it means and how and when to use it. *You think it in German.* It will still not be quite possible for you to do this with every word, but the habit is one which can and must be developed. Thus, when you think of **der Bruder** you will no doubt immediately think of *"brother"*. But there is another way, and a better one, of learning the words for persons and things that are "picturable", those of which you can form a picture in your mind. This is visualization, and you must never miss an opportunity of using it. As each word is being memorized, try to form in the mind a visual image (picture) of the thing, or an association of the idea. So, with **das Weib, das Mädchen, das Fräulein,** you think of *woman, girl, young lady.* And similarly of **der Mond, die Sonne, das Kind:** *moon, sun, child.*

PRACTICE

Turn back to the List of Words on page 9, and go over them, trying to visualize those whose meanings you know. And similarly with all other words that have been met so far. At first you may be able to visualize only the concrete, but soon you will find that visualization can be applied to many other words. Take, for example, **die Freundschaft,** which represents an abstract idea. Conjure up in your mind some " friendship " of your own, and remember **die Freundschaft** by it. It may be a little difficult at first, but, if you persist, you cannot fail to benefit. The practice is well worth while, and there is no limit to it. It teaches you to *think in German* instead of learning by translation.

In future: turn back from time to time and, visualizing, go over words and phrases—until they become second nature.

NUMBERS:

EIN, EINS	ZWEI	DREI	VIER	FÜNF
1	2	3	4	5

Learn these numbers, if possible without thinking of their English equivalents, and by looking at the figures. **EINS** is used in counting. **EIN** is used when it comes before a Noun: **EIN MANN,** *a (one) man.*

Words and Phrases

From List on page 9 :

der Tanz, dance   **die Rose,** rose   **das Wasser,** water
der Zug, train   **die Katze,** cat   **das Dach,** roof
der Kuß, kiss   **die Quelle,** well   **die Dächer,** roofs
der Ring, ring   **die Nation,** nation   **das Theater,**
                                              theatre
                                      das Grab, grave

New Words and Phrases :

der Mond, moon   **die Sonne,** sun   **kalt,** cold
                die Uhr, time   **warm,** warm
ich bin, I am   **die Blume,**   **groß,** big
Sie sind, you are   flower   **klein,** small
sie sind, they are   **die Blumen,**   **BIN ICH ?** = Am
                flowers   I ?
                ich habe, I have   **IST ER ?** Is he ?
und, and   **er,** he ⟩**IST,** is   **HAT ER ?** Has
aber, but   **sie,** she ⟩   he ?
                es, it ⟩**HAT,** has   **HABEN SIE ?**
langsam, slow   **Sie haben,** you   Have you ?
langsamer,   have; **sie haben,**
  slower   they have

Wieviel ? How much ?
Wie viele ? How many ?
Wie viele Finger haben Sie ? How many fingers have you ?
Ich habe fünf Finger. I have five fingers.
Was ist dies ? What is this ?
Es ist eine Blume. It is a flower.
Wie viele Blumen haben Sie ? How many flowers have you ?
Ich habe vier Blumen. I have four flowers.
Ist es kalt ? Is it cold ?
Nein, es ist warm. No, it is warm.
Ist die Katze groß ? Is the cat big ?
Nein, sie (*she*) **ist klein.** No, she's small.
Sprechen Sie englisch ? Do you speak English ?

Ja, ich spreche englisch, aber ich spreche nicht deutsch.
Yes, I speak English but I don't speak German (speak not German).

Verstehen Sie ? Do you understand ?

Ich verstehe es nicht. I don't understand it.

Wieviel Uhr ist es ? What time is it ?

Es ist ein Uhr. It is one o'clock.

Es ist zwei Uhr. It is two o'clock.

How to Practise: If a teacher, or a friend who speaks German well, is available, it will be possible with the Words and Phrases given to make many other conversational sentences. If no such help is available, you should try to construct some new sentences by yourself. The main object is practice, so that words can be learned *in action*, and not just as lists. This is important.

THIS METHOD OF PRACTICE SHOULD BE USED UNTIL YOU ARE QUITE FAMILIAR WITH MOST OF THE WORDS AND PHRASES IN EACH SECTION AND LESSON. CONSTANT REVISION DRIVES THEM HOME.

Practice: ÜBUNG

If the English translation of some of the sentences given for practice, or some of the sentences themselves, seem rather simple or naïve, this is because the material you know is still limited, and at this stage literal and not free translation best explains the German. *It is the German text that is important.* The English is merely an aid.

GUTEN MORGEN, HERR SCHMIDT.
Good morning, Mr. Schmidt.

ES IST HEUTE KALT, ABER DIE SONNE IST WARM.
It is cold to-day, but the sun is warm.

BITTE SPRECHEN SIE LANGSAM.
Please speak slowly.

ICH VERSTEHE DEUTSCH NICHT GUT.

I do not understand German well.

WIE VIELE HÄNDE UND FINGER HABEN SIE?

How many hands and fingers have you?

ICH HABE ZWEI HÄNDE UND JEDE HAND HAT FÜNF FINGER.

I have two hands and each hand has five fingers.

KOMMEN DER JUNGE UND DAS MÄDEL HEUTE?

Come the boy and the girl to-day? (i.e. Do the boy and girl come to-day?)

JA, SIE KOMMEN HEUTE WIEDER.

Yes, they come to-day again.

SIE SIND SCHON HIER.

They are already here.

IST DIES IHR BUCH? NEIN, DAS IST NICHT MEIN BUCH.

Is this your book? No, that is not my book.

ICH HABE KEIN BUCH.

I have no book.

IST DIESER MANN SEIN VATER? JA, ER IST SEIN VATER.

Is this man his father? Yes, he is his father.

IST DAS WASSER WARM?

Is the water warm?

NEIN, DAS WASSER IST NICHT WARM, ES IST KALT.

No, the water is not warm, it is cold.

WIE VIELE HÄUSER SIND DA?

How many houses are there?

HIER SIND DREI HÄUSER.

Here (there) are three houses.

DIESES HAUS IST GROSS, ABER DAS DACH IST KLEIN.

This house is big, but the roof is small.

IST DIE ROSE ROT?

Is the rose red?

JA, DIESE BLUME IST ROT.

Yes, this flower is red.

DIE FRAU HAT BLUMEN.

The woman has flowers.

WIE VIELE BLUMEN HAT SIE?

How many flowers has she?

SIE HAT VIELE BLUMEN.

She has many flowers.

HAT SIE EINEN RING?

Has she a ring?

NEIN, DIESE FRAU HAT KEINEN RING.

No, this lady has no ring.

ICH HABE EINEN HUND UND EINE KATZE, ·ABER KEINEN ESEL.

I have a dog and a cat but no donkey.

DIE SONNE IST WARM, ABER DER MOND IST KÄLT.

The sun is warm, but the moon is cold.

SIND SIE GROSS? *

Are you tall?

JA, ICH BIN GROSS, ABER MEINE FRAU IST KLEIN.

Yes, I am tall, but my wife is small.

§ 5. *Adjectives : Rules for Declension—Numbers : Practice—Practice (General)*

An Adjective is a word used to describe the quality or nature of a Noun.

RULES FOR DECLENSION: German Adjectives are declined. The following three possibilities arise.

I. The Definite Article precedes the Adjective which is followed by a Noun;

II. The Indefinite Article or a Possessive Pronoun precedes it, followed by a Noun;

III. The Adjective stands alone with the Noun.

The declension varies slightly in the three cases:

Note: **GROSS** = groß. In capital letters ß is printed **SZ** or, more commonly, **SS**.

I. When the Definite Article precedes the Adjective which is immediately followed by a Noun, all cases of the Adjective take **-EN** except the following:

Singular	Masc.	Fem.	Neuter
Nominative	-E	-E	-E
Accusative		-E	-E

Thus:

Singular

the good man

N. **DER GUTE MANN**
G. **DES GUTEN MANNES**
D. **DEM GUTEN MANN(E)**
A. **DEN GUTEN MANN**

the good woman

DIE GUTE FRAU
DER GUTEN FRAU
DER GUTEN FRAU
DIE GUTE FRAU

the good child

N. **DAS GUTE KIND**
G. **DES GUTEN KINDES**
D. **DEM GUTEN KIND(E)**
A. **DAS GUTE KIND**

Plurals

N. **DIE GUTEN MÄNNER,**   **FRAUEN, KINDER**
G. **DER GUTEN MÄNNER,**   **FRAUEN, KINDER**
D. **DEN GUTEN MÄNNERN,** **FRAUEN, KINDERN**
A. **DIE GUTEN MÄNNER,**   **FRAUEN, KINDER**

Thus: **DIESER GUTE MANN**, this good man
       DIESES GUTEN MANNES, etc.

For declension of these Pronouns, see pp. 12-13.

II. When an Adjective is preceded by the Indefinite Article **EIN, EINE, EIN,** or when it is preceded by one of the Possessive Pronouns **MEIN,** *my*; **DEIN,** *thy*; **SEIN,** *his, its*; **IHR,** *her*; **UNSER,** *our*; **EUER,** *your* (plural); **IHR,** *your* (polite, formal; possessive of **SIE,** *you,* polite, formal); and **KEIN,** *no, not any,* the endings are:

	Masc.	*Fem.*	*Neuter*
Nominative	**-ER**	**-E**	**-ES**
Accusative	**-EN**	**-E**	**-ES**

All other cases and the plural end in **-EN**. Thus:

N. **EIN GUTER MANN**   **EINE GUTE FRAU**
G. **EINES GUTEN MANNES**   **EINER GUTEN FRAU**
D. **EINEM GUTEN MANN(E)**   **EINER GUTEN FRAU**
A. **EINEN GUTEN MANN**   **EINE GUTE FRAU**

    N. **EIN GUTES KIND**
    G. **EINES GUTEN KINDES**
    D. **EINEM GUTEN KIND(E)**
    A. **EIN GUTES KIND**

Similarly:

Singular

N. **KEIN GUTER MANN,** no good man
G. **KEINES GUTEN MANNES**
D. **KEINEM GUTEN MANN(E)**
A. **KEINEN GUTEN MANN**

Plural

N. **KEINE GUTEN MÄNNER, FRAUEN, KINDER**
G. **KEINER GUTEN MÄNNER, FRAUEN, KINDER**
D. **KEINEN GUTEN MÄNNERN, FRAUEN, KIND-ERN**
A. **KEINE GUTEN MÄNNER, FRAUEN, KINDER**

III. When there is no Article and no Possessive Pronoun of those listed in II, then the Adjective is declined like **DIESER** (page 13), except that **-EN** is preferred to **-ES** in the Genitive singular of the masculine and neuter. Thus:

Singular

	Masc. good tree	*Fem.* red flower	*Neuter* good bread
N.	**GUTER BAUM**	**ROTE BLUME**	**GUTES BROT**
G.	**GUTEN BAUMES**	**ROTER BLUME**	**GUTEN BROTES**
D.	**GUTEM BAUM(E)**	**ROTER BLUME**	**GUTEM BROT(E)**
A.	**GUTEN BAUM**	**ROTE BLUME**	**GUTES BROT**

Plural

Masc. good trees	Fem. red flowers	Neuter good bread (loaves)
N. **GUTE BÄUME**	**ROTE BLUMEN**	**GUTE BROTE**
G. **GUTER BÄUME**	**ROTER BLUMEN**	**GUTER BROTE**
D. **GUTEN BÄUMEN**	**ROTEN BLUMEN**	**GUTEN BROTEN**
A. **GUTE BÄUME**	**ROTE BLUMEN**	**GUTE BROTE**

However, when a German Adjective does not immediately precede a Noun or Pronoun (that is, when it is used as a predicate), there is no declension at all; it remains invariable.

Thus:

Der Mann ist gut.   The man is good.
Er ist gut.   He is good.
Die Kinder sind gut.   The children are good.

IT WILL BE NECESSARY TO REVIEW THE DECLENSION OF ADJECTIVES, UNTIL THE FORMS HAVE BECOME FAMILIAR. I and II are the most frequently used, and must be known well.

NUMBERS:

SECHS 6	**SIEBEN** 7	**ACHT** 8	**NEUN** 9	**ZEHN** 10

As suggested on page 19, learn these numbers by looking at the figures. You should then know 1-10, which will enable you to do simple sums:

$$2 + 1 = 3 \quad \text{zwei und eins ist drei}$$
$$3 + 1 = 4 \quad \text{drei und eins ist vier}$$
$$4 + 2 = 6 \quad \text{vier und zwei ist sechs}$$
$$7 + 2 = 9 \quad \text{sieben und zwei ist neun}$$
$$6 + 4 = 10 \quad \text{sechs und vier ist zehn}$$

gleich (or **ist**), equals   **weniger,** less, minus

With these words and the numerals, you can go a little further. Thus:

$$10-6=4 \quad \text{zehn weniger sechs ist vier}$$
$$7-4=3 \quad \text{sieben weniger vier ist drei}$$
$$7-2=5 \quad \text{sieben weniger zwei ist fünf}$$

Practise doing these little sums with 1–10 for at least half an hour, or until you can do them easily, with as little effort as it would cost you in English. It is important to practise in this way with numbers, because it is one more step towards fluency. *It teaches you to think in German, which must always be your goal.*

PRACTICE: ÜBUNG

Das kleine Kind der schönen Frau ist hier.
The small child of the beautiful woman is here.
Wo ist die gute Mutter des kleinen Knaben?
Where is the good mother of the small boy?
Ist der Sohn eines großen Mannes gut?
Is the son of a great man good?
Nicht alle Söhne großer Männer sind groß.
Not all sons of great men are great.
Mancher gute Freund hat kein schönes Haus.
Many a good friend has not a beautiful house.
Was haben Sie in Ihrer Hand?
What have you in your hand?
Ich habe sechs rote Rosen in meiner Hand.
I have six red roses in my hand.
Geben Sie dem kleinen Mädel die roten Blumen.
Give the little girl the red flowers.
Die Frau hat drei große Ringe an ihren schönen Händen.
The woman has three big rings on her beautiful hands.
Geben Sie bitte den schönen Blumen kaltes Wasser.
Give please the beautiful flowers cold water.
Die zwei kleinen Katzen spielen mit dem jungen Hund.
The two little cats play with the young dog.
Ich habe hier fünf warme Brote.
I have here five warm (loaves of) bread.

Geben Sie dem guten Knaben zwei Brote und dem schönen Mädel drei.

Give the good boy two (loaves of) bread and the beautiful girl three.

In dem großen Garten sind zehn kleine Bäume.

In the big garden are ten small trees.

Da sind nicht viele.

There are not many.

Ist das Dach des weißen Hauses rot?

Is the roof of the white house red?

Ja, es ist ein weißes Haus mit einem roten Dach.

Yes, it is a white house with a red roof.

Wie geht es Ihnen, Herr S.?

How are you, Mr. S.?

Danke, es geht mir gut.

Thanks, I am well (*literally:* It goes to me well).

Aber meiner lieben Frau geht es nicht gut.

But my dear wife is not well.

Das tut mir leid, mein lieber Freund.

I am sorry, my dear friend.

Und wie geht es Ihrem kleinen Sohn?(Ihrem = to your.)

And how is your little son?

Es geht ihm sehr gut. (ihm = to him.)

He is very well.

Das freut mich.

I am glad of that (*literally:* That " joys " me).

Geben Sie bitte diese schönen roten Rosen Ihrer Tochter.

Give please these beautiful red roses to your daughter.

Mit Vergnügen.

With pleasure.

Wieviel Uhr ist es?

What is the time?

Es ist neun Uhr.

It is nine o'clock.

Auf Wiedersehen!

Good-bye!

LESSON II

§ 1. Declension of Nouns—Masculine Nouns: Group I— The "Situation"—Travel: Passports, Baggage, etc.— Numbers—Practice

THE declension of German Nouns presents difficulties for the English-speaking learner, no matter how the subject is approached. Nevertheless, certain general principles (to be found on pages 55 and 58) will lighten the beginner's task.

It will be useful, moreover, to remember at the very beginning that virtually all German Nouns form their plural in one of the following five ways:

1. By retaining the same form as the singular or sometimes by placing an *Umlaut* on the stem vowel. (Cf. English *one sheep, five sheep*.) Example: **der Garten, die Gärten.**

2. By adding **-e** to the singular and placing an *Umlaut* on the stem vowel where possible. Example: **die Maus, die Mäuse.** (Note that the English cognate *mouse, mice* also changes its stem vowel in the plural.)

3. By adding **-er** to the singular and placing an *Umlaut* on the stem vowel. Examples: **das Lied, die Lieder; das Faß, die Fässer** (barrels).

4. By adding **-(e)n** to the singular. (Cf. English *the child, children*.) Examples: **die Nummer, die Nummern** (numbers); **die Schallplatte, die Schallplatten** (phonograph records).

5. By adding **-s** to the singular. This method is used only in the case of some Nouns of foreign origin. Examples: **das Auto, die Autos; das Aspirin, die Aspirins.**

29

The basic rule is that the *gender of the German Noun must be known* before its declension is attempted. Hence the importance of always learning the Noun with its correct Article, which shows the gender.

For the purpose of declension, the German Nouns are first classified in accordance with their genders: Masculine, Feminine, and Neuter, and Nouns of each gender then fall into groups in accordance with the number of syllables and the ending of the nominative singular. Consequently:

MEMORIZE THE MODEL DECLENSION, THE RULES FOR EACH GROUP, AND THE MAIN EXCEPTIONS. Note, however, that some students can learn German Noun declensions readily by memorizing the Genitive and Plural forms of each Noun as they encounter it. If you are in this group, you need not memorize the following rules concerning the various classes of German Nouns, but you would still do well to study the rules carefully and use them for reference.

DECLENSION: MASCULINE NOUNS

There are five groups of Masculine Nouns.

Group I. The first group comprises Masculine Nouns ending in **-EL, -EN,** and **-ER.** These Nouns add **s** in the Genitive Singular and **n** in the Dative Plural; all other forms remain unchanged. The Nouns of this group are declined like **der Diener,** (man)-servant:

Singular	Plural
N. **der DIENER,** servant	N. **die DIENER,** the servants
G. **des DIENERS,** the servant's	G. **der DIENER,** of the servants
D. **dem DIENER,** to the servant	D. **den DIENERN,** to the servants
A. **den DIENER,** the servant	A. **die DIENER,** the servants

The majority of the Nouns in group I do *not* modify root vowels **a, o, u.**

Here is the list, for reference, of those Nouns which modify the root vowels **a, o, u,** in the plural to: **ä, ö, ü,** respectively.

der ACKER, acre	**der Laden,** shop
der APFEL, apple	**der Mantel,** cloak
der BODEN, ground, floor	**der Nagel,** nail
der BOGEN, arch	**der Ofen,** stove
der BRUDER, brother	**der Sattel,** saddle
der Faden, thread	**der Schade(n),** damage
der GARTEN, garden	**der Schnabel,** beak
der Graben, ditch	**der Schwager,** brother-in-law
der HAFEN, harbor	**der VATER,** father
der HAMMER, hammer	**der VOGEL,** bird
der HANDEL, trade	

Those in capitals should be memorized now, the others later.

Example:

Singular	*Plural*
N. **der Bruder**	**die Brüder**
G. **des Bruders**	**der Brüder,** *etc.*

There are two minor exceptions in Masculine Nouns of group I:

1. A few Nouns ending in **-er** or **-el** take **-n** throughout the plural:

> **der BAUER, des BAUERS, die BAUERN,** farmer(s)
>
> **der Gevatter, des Gevatters, die Gevattern,** godfather(s)
>
> **der VETTER, des VETTERS, die VETTERN,** cousin(s)
>
> **der Muskel, des Muskels, die Muskeln,** muscle(s)
>
> **der PANTOFFEL, des PANTOFFELS, die PANTOFFELN,** slippers
>
> **der Stachel, des Stachels, die Stacheln,** thorn(s)

2. The following Masculine Nouns can end in either **-E** or **-EN,** but otherwise follow the model declension:

der Fels(en), rock
der Funke(n), spark
der Haufe(n), heap
der Same(n), seed
der Wille(n), will

der FRIEDE(n), peace
der GLAUBE(n), belief
der NAME, name
der Schreck(en), terror

General Rule: In memorizing Nouns, always learn the nominative singular, genitive singular, and nominative plural. From these, all other cases can be made. This will be seen as you learn.

THE "SITUATION": On page 18 you have learnt about Visualization as an important help in memorizing words. Of at least equal importance is *using situations in every-day life* as a means of learning everyday words, phrases, and idioms (see page 310). Life largely consists of situations, and here we shall try to make use of those most likely to be of practical value to the learner. But he need not limit himself to those for which the necessary material in words and phrases is given here. *He must try to work in as much as possible of everything he has learnt in previous Lessons and Sections.* In this way both knowledge of words and phrases, and flexibility in their use, comes by practice. Continue with Visualization in learning new words, and take as much advantage as possible of the material given with each Lesson under the heading of a common situation. Here is the first:

TRAVEL: *Passports, Baggage, etc.*

die Auskunft, information
der Paß, passport
die Pässe, passports
das Visum, visa
das Konsulat, Consulate
der Konsul, Consul
die Reise, journey, trip
eine Reise nach, a trip to . . .
Deutschland, Germany
die Schweiz, Switzerland

Österreich, Austria
der Träger, porter
das Abteil, compartment
das Gepäck, luggage
das Handgepäck, hand luggage
der Koffer, trunk, suitcase
der Omnibus, bus
das Auto, automobile, car
der Autobus, bus

direkt, direct
die Zeit, time
nehmen, to take
nehmen Sie, take . . .
ich nehme, I take
nehme ich? do I take?
tragen, to carry
tragen Sie, carry . . .
ich trage, I carry
trage ich? do I carry?
brauchen, to require
Sie brauchen, you require
ich brauche, I need

brauche ich? do I need?
fahren, to travel
ich fahre, I travel
fahren Sie? do you travel?
Um wieviel Uhr? At what time?
um . . . Uhr, at . . . o'clock
heute, to-day
morgen, to-morrow
der Morgen, morning
heute Morgen, this morning
der Abend, evening
heute Abend, this evening

NUMBERS:

11 **ELF**   12 **ZWÖLF**   13 **DREIZEHN**
14 **VIERZEHN**   15 **FÜNFZEHN**

Continue learning the numbers as suggested on pages 19 and 26, and practice accordingly.

PRACTICE: **ÜBUNG**

AUF DEM DEUTSCHEN KONSULAT
At the German Consulate

Kann ich hier Auskunft haben?
Can I have information here?
Ja, bitte? *
Yes, please?
Brauche ich einen Paß?
Do I need a passport?
Ja, Sie brauchen einen Paß.
Yes, you need a passport.
Und ein Visum?
And a visa?

* **BITTE** (literally = *I beg you*) can be used in various ways which these "Situations" will indicate practically. Here it means "*Please go ahead*", or "*Please state your requirements*".

Nein, Sie brauchen kein Visum für Deutschland.
No, you do not need a visa for Germany.
Wann fahren Sie?
When do you travel?
Ich fahre heute Abend um elf Uhr.
I travel this evening at 11 o'clock.
Hier ist der Paß meiner Frau.
Here is the passport of my wife.
Sie fährt morgen in die Schweiz.
She travels to-morrow to Switzerland.
Braucht sie ein Visum für diese Reise?
Does she need a visa for this journey?
Nein, sie braucht kein Visum für solch eine Reise.
No, she does not need a visa for such a trip.
Wieviel Gepäck haben Sie?
How much luggage have you?
Ich habe sehr viel Gepäck.
I have very much luggage.
Ich nehme mein Handgepäck ins Abteil.
I('ll) take my hand luggage into the compartment.
Ich kann mein großes Gepäck nicht tragen.
I cannot carry my large luggage.
Es sind sieben Koffer.
There are seven trunks.
Ich gebe sie einem Träger.
I('ll) give them to a porter.
Fahren Sie mit dem Omnibus oder dem Autobus?
Do you travel by bus or coach?
Ich fahre mit dem Autobus.
I travel by coach.
Wieviel Zeit haben Sie für die Reise nach Deutschland?
How much time have you for the journey to Germany?
Ich habe vierzehn Tage für die Reise.
I have a fortnight (= fourteen days) for the trip.
Ich danke Ihnen für die gute Auskunft.
I thank you for the good information.
Wir tun das gern.
We do that willingly.

§ 2. Masculine Nouns contd.—Groups II to V—Practice
— Note on Practice—TRAVEL: The Railway Station

MASCULINE NOUNS—*contd. from page* 32

Group II: Nouns ending in **-E,** with plural **-N.**

DER BOTE, messenger	**DIE BOTEN,** messengers
DES BOTEN	**DER BOTEN**
DEM BOTEN	**DEN BOTEN**
DEN BOTEN	**DIE BOTEN**

Exception: **DER KÄSE,** *cheese*; Genitive Singular, **des KÄSES**; Plural, **DIE KÄSE.**

Note: Similarly declined, although lacking the **-e** of the nominative singular (in some of them optional) are:

der Bär, bear	**der MENSCH,** man
BURSCH(-E), fellow	**Mohr,** Moor
Christ, Christian	**Narr,** fool
Fürst, prince	**Ochs(-e),** ox
Fink(-e), finch	**Pfau,** peacock
Geck, fool	**Prinz,** prince
GESELL(E), partner	**Spatz,** sparrow
Graf, count	**Sproß,** sprout
Held, hero	**TOR,** fool
HERR, Mr., gentleman	**Vorfahr,** ancestor
Hirt(e), herdsman	

Thus: **Der MENSCH** (human being), **des MENSCHEN, dem MENSCHEN, den MENSCHEN**; Pl. **die MENSCHEN.**

Note: To avoid confusion **DER HERR** takes **-N** throughout in the singular and **-EN** in the plural. Thus: **Herr, Herrn, Herrn, Herrn;** plural **die Herren,** etc.

Group III: mostly Nouns of one syllable.

(*a*) With modification in the plural, as:

der BALL, ball, sphere	**DIE BÄLLE,** the balls
des BALLES	**DER BÄLLE**
dem BALLE	**DEN BÄLLEN**
den BALL	**DIE BÄLLE**

(b) Without modification in the plural.

Certain Masculine Nouns of one syllable do *not* modify in the plural, but follow **DER TAG**, declined as follows:

der **TAG**	die Tage
des Tages	der Tage
dem Tage	den Tagen
den Tag	die Tage

Short lists of Masculine monosyllabic Nouns and several other Nouns not modified in the plural:

der **Aal**, eel	der **LACHS**, salmon
ABEND, evening	**LAUT**, sound
Amboß, anvil	**Leichnam**, corpse
ARM, arm	**Luchs**, lynx
BESUCH, visit	**MONAT**, month
Docht, wick	**Pfad**, path
DOM, cathedral	**PUNKT**, point, dot
ERFOLG, success	**SCHUH**, shoe
Flur, hall, passage	**STOFF**, stuff, material
Forst, forest	**STRAND**, beach
GOLF, gulf	**TAG**, day
GRAD, degree	**Thron**, throne
HUND, dog	**Versuch**, attempt

Group IV: This group includes a small number of monosyllabic Masculines; in the plural they modify the root vowel *if possible*, and add **-er.**

der **Mann**, the man	die **Männer**, the men
des **Mannes**	der **Männer**
dem **Manne**	den **Männern**
den **Mann**	die **Männer**

Nouns declined like **der Mann** include:

GEIST, spirit, ghost	**Strauch**, bush, shrub
GOTT, God	**WALD**, wood, forest

Disyllabic Masculines in Group IV modify the second syllable, thus:

der **IRRTUM**, error	die **IRRTÜMER**, errors
Vormund, guardian	**Vormünder**, guardians

Exception: **der Bösewicht**, villain, **die Bösewichter**, villains. (May also form plural die Bösewicht*e*.)

Group V: This still smaller group of Masculine Nouns takes **-en** (or **-n**) in the plural, without modification of vowels:

der Staat, state	**die Staaten,** states
des Staates	**der Staaten**
dem Staate	**den Staaten**
den Staat	**die Staaten**

Nouns declined like **der Staat** include:

der Dorn, thorn	**der SEE,** lake
Lorbeer, laurel	**Sporn** (pl. **-en**), spur
Mast, mast	**Strahl,** beam, ray
NACHBAR, neighbour	**Untertan,** subject (of a
SCHMERZ, pain	state)

and Nouns of foreign origin ending in **-OR,** such as:

der DOKTOR   des DOKTORS   die DOKTOREN, doctor (-s)

Practice: ÜBUNG

From now onwards, some of the Practice material is given in German only. This means that in it only words already known are used. A translation is provided when the material tends to be more difficult.

Die Arme und Hände des Burschen sind groß. Der Hund ist ein Geselle des Menschen. Die Untertanen des Grafen sind gute Christen. Ich gebe den Spatzen und Finken Wasser. Der Kopf des Bären ist groß. Sind dies* die roten Bälle des Knaben? Die Erfolge des Tages sind nicht groß.

Geben Sie dem Manne seine Schuhe. Die Abende des Monats sind lang. Am Strande des Sees sind viele Orte. In dem Dome sind Männer und Frauen. Gute Geister kommen am Tage. Narren und Toren sind Nachbarn im Staate. Die Wälder und Seen sind groß. Zwei kleine Irrtümer. Alle Abende hat er Schmerzen. Die Doktoren kommen zu ihm.

Es ist in der Hand Gottes. Die Würmer im Walde sind klein. Wir haben drei Hunde, aber keine Katzen. Der Stoff des Schuhes ist gut. Das Wort hat drei Laute. Das A in Bälle hat zwei Punkte. Die Götter geben den Menschen große Reichtümer.

* Short form preferred with singular or plural forms of **SEIN**

Note on Practice

With the " Situation Material " under the heading " Travel " already given and now continued, together with what is learnt of grammar and the German words used to teach it, the learner should be able to make up a variety of sentences relating not only to the situation in question but also to others. It is a matter of exercising the ingenuity. This kind of Practice can become a habit, and often proves to be more effective than "set" exercises. From now onwards you must use the "Situation Material" that will be given in each Lesson to the best effect: it helps to drive home everything that has been learnt as well as the new matter under each heading.

AT THE END OF EACH LESSON REVIEW PRACTICE MATERIAL INCLUDING " SITUATIONS " GIVEN IN PREVIOUS LESSONS. DO THIS THROUGHOUT THE COURSE.

Travel : **DIE EISENBAHN,** *The Railway*

der Bahnhof, station

die Fahrkarte ⎫
das Billett ⎬ ticket

die Fahrkarten ⎫
die Billette ⎬ tickets

die Rückfahrkarte, return ticket

der Fahrkartenschalter, booking-office

der Wartesaal, waiting-room

der Bahnsteig, platform

die Sperre, barrier

der Zug, train

der Schnellzug, express train

der Personenzug, passenger train

der Güterzug, goods train

der Wagen, coach

der Schlafwagen, sleeper

der Speisewagen, restaurant car

das Raucherabteil, smoking compartment

das Nichtraucherabteil, non-smoker

der Sitzplatz, seat

der Eckplatz, corner seat

der Fensterplatz, window seat

die Platzkarte, seat ticket

die Toilette, lavatory

erste Klasse, first class

zweite Klasse, second class

dritte Klasse, third class

die Abfahrt, departure

die Ankunft, arrival

die Abgangszeit, time of departure

der Kellner, waiter

der Schaffner, conductor, guard

einen Platz reservieren, to reserve a seat

kosten, to cost

was kostet ? How much does it cost ?

eine Fahrkarte lösen, to buy a ticket	**Die Türe schließen,** to close the door
warten, to wait	**Nicht hinauslehnen!** Don't lean out!
Einsteigen! Take your seats!	**Die Fahrkarten, bitte!** Tickets, please!

16 **SECHZEHN**   17 **SIEBZEHN**   18 **ACHTZEHN**
19 **NEUNZEHN**   20 **ZWANZIG**   21 **EINUND-**
                                            ZWANZIG

Wir kommen zum Bahnhof. We come to the station. (= *We're coming.*)

Wo löse ich eine Fahrkarte? Where do I get a ticket?

Der Schalter ist dort. The ticket window is there.

Geben Sie mir bitte zwei Fahrkarten erster Klasse nach Hamburg. Give me please two tickets first class to Hamburg.

Wieviel kostet eine Rückfahrkarte zweiter Klasse? How much is a return ticket second class (cost)?

Achtzehn Mark. 18 DM. (See page 69.)

Wo ist der Schnellzug nach Hamburg? Where is the express for H.?

Er ist auf Bahnsteig sechs. It is at platform 6.

Bitte, reservieren Sie mir einen Eckplatz. Please reserve me a corner seat.

Es tut mir leid, wir haben keine Eckplätze frei. I am sorry, we have no corner seats free.

Wir hätten gern zwei Fensterplätze. We should like to have two window seats.

Gepäckträger, tragen Sie bitte meine zwei Koffer an die Sperre. Porter, carry please my two trunks to the barrier.

Ich nehme meinen Handkoffer ins Abteil. I('ll) take my (hand) suit-case into the compartment.

Um wieviel Uhr geht der Zug? At what time does the train go?

Der Zug geht um vier Uhr. The train goes at four o'clock.

Ich muß eine halbe Stunde warten. I must wait half an hour.

Wir gehen in den Wartesaal. We('ll) go into the waiting-room.

Der Schaffner : Bitte einsteigen und die Türen schließen!
The conductor: Please take your seats and close the doors!

Dieses ist ein Raucherabteil. This is a smoking compartment.

Darf ich das Fenster öffnen? May I open the window?

Wo ist die Toilette ? Where is the lavatory?

Jeder Wagen hat zwei Toiletten. Each coach has two lavatories.

Gibt es einen Speisewagen in diesem Zug ? Is there a diner in this train ?

Kellner, bringen Sie die Speisekarte bitte! Waiter, bring the menu card please.

Der Schaffner kommt und kontrolliert die Billette. The conductor comes and inspects the tickets.

Ankunft und Abfahrt der Züge stehen im Fahrplan.
Arrival and departure of the trains are in the time-table.

Note: These sentences, you will notice, begin to be more practical. They are the sort of sentences which help you to "get around". But they serve other purposes: they are helping you to become accustomed to the German *way of thinking*. If you can learn these sentences now, you are learning the use of words, the Declensions, the German word-order as well as a practical vocabulary that is essential in everyday life.

Therefore, from now onwards, once you *understand* what is given in the **Übung,** go on and *learn* what is given in "Situation Material". Until you come to the Reading Material, concentrate on Situations.

§ 3. *Feminine Nouns: Groups I, II, and III—Numbers —Practice—Travel: By Boat*

DECLENSION: FEMININE NOUNS

The declension of the German Feminine Nouns is much simpler than that of the Masculine Nouns. There are only three groups, with few exceptions to the model declensions.

General Rule: *Feminine Nouns never change in the Singular*.

Group I. This group comprises the majority of Feminine Nouns of more than one syllable. They form the plural by adding **-n** or **-en,** with no modification of root vowels. They are conveniently subdivided as follows:

(*a*) Nouns ending in **-e** add **-n** in the plural.

die **BLUME,** flower	die **BLUMEN,** flowers
der **BLUME**	der **BLUMEN**
der **BLUME**	den **BLUMEN**
die **BLUME**	die **BLUMEN**

(*b*) Nouns ending in **-el** or **er** add **-n** in the plural.

die **NADEL,** needle	die **NADELN,** needles
die **FEDER,** feather, pen	die **FEDERN,** feathers, pens

Note: **die MUTTER,** *mother*; **die TOCHTER,** *daughter*, are exceptions in that they modify in the plural: **die MÜTTER, die TÖCHTER.**

(*c*) Nearly all other Feminine Nouns of more than one syllable take **-en** in the plural. Among them are all with the endings **-EI, -HEIT, -KEIT, -IN, -SCHAFT, -UNG, -ION, -TAT,** and **-UR.**

Examples:

die **PARTEI,** party; die **PARTEIEN,** parties
die **KRANKHEIT,** illness; die **KRANKHEITEN**
die **LÖSUNG,** solution; die **LÖSUNGEN**
die **KULTUR,** culture; die **KULTUREN**

Exceptions: Group I

Feminine Nouns ending in **-IN** double the **-N-** in the plural; **die Königin,** queen; **die Königinnen,** etc.

Feminine Nouns in **-NIS** and **-SAL:**

die **KENNTNIS,** knowledge *plural:*	die **KENNTNISSE**
	der **KENNTNISSE**
	den **KENNTNISSEN**
	die **KENNTNISSE**

However, the majority of Nouns ending in **-NIS** and **-SAL** are Neuter.

Group II. This group comprises Feminine Nouns of one syllable which take **-E** and modify in the plural.

die HAND, hand; **die HÄNDE,** hands
der HÄNDE
den HÄNDEN
die HÄNDE

Reference list of Feminine Nouns like **die HAND:**

die **ANGST,** anxiety	die **Laus,** louse
Axt, axe	**LUFT,** air, breeze
*****BANK,** bank, bench	**LUST,** pleasure
Braut, fiancée	**MACHT,** power
BRUST, breast, chest	**Maus,** mouse
FAUST, fist	**NACHT,** night
FRUCHT, fruit	**NOT,** need, necessity
Gans, goose	**Nuß,** nut
Gruft, vault, tomb	**Sau,** sow
HAUT, skin	**SCHNUR,** cord, string
Kluft, cleft, gap	**STADT,** city, town
KRAFT, strength	**WAND,** wall
KUH, cow	**WURST,** sausage
KUNST, art, trick	**Zünft,** guild

* **die BANK,** *the bank* (*for money*), has plural **die BANKEN.**

Only those in capitals need be memorized at this stage. The others are of less frequent occurrence.

Group III. This group comprises Feminine Nouns of one syllable which take **-EN** and do not modify in the plural. There are only a few of these Nouns.

die FRAU, woman, lady; **die FRAUEN,** ladies, *etc., throughout.*

Reference list of Feminine Nouns declined like **die FRAU:**

die **BURG,** castle	die **SAAT,** seed
FAHRT, journey	**SCHRIFT,** writing
FLUCHT, flight	**TAT,** deed, act
Fracht, freight	**Tracht,** load, costume
Jagd, hunting, chase	**TÜR,** door
Last, load	**UHR,** hour, time
PFLICHT, duty	

Numbers:

20 **ZWANZIG**	26 **SECHSUNDZWANZIG**
21 **EINUNDZWANZIG**	27 **SIEBENUNDZWANZIG**
22 **ZWEIUNDZWANZIG**	28 **ACHTUNDZWANZIG**
23 **DREIUNDZWANZIG**	29 **NEUNUNDZWANZIG**
24 **VIERUNDZWANZIG**	30 **DREISSIG**
25 **FÜNFUNDZWANZIG**	

Continue to practice with numbers as on page 26.

Practice: **ÜBUNG**

Die Töchter der Mütter haben Blumen in den Händen. Die Eichen sind Bäume des Waldes. Wie viele Bänke sind in den Gärten? Der Bauer hat zweiundzwanzig Gänse und vierundzwanzig Kühe. In den Läden gibt es Nadeln und Federn. Die drei Parteien dieses Staates. Die vielen Schönheiten der Städte des Landes. Die Tätigkeiten der Menschen sind gut. Die Tochter hat viele Freundschaften. Deutschland, England und die Schweiz sind Nationen. Der König und die Königin machen Besuche. Die Mutter und ihre Freundinnen sind hier. Nicht alle Lösungen sind gut. Mit seinen Kenntnissen der Literatur und der Kunst. Singen und Malen sind schöne Künste. Die kalten Lüfte in den Nächten. Die Macht der Staaten ist groß. Er ist in Nöten. Das Haus hat vier Wände. In dem Laden sind viele Würste. Wie viele Türen sind im Dome? Er hat große und kleine Pflichten. Wir kommen auf den Fahrten zu den Burgen in den Wäldern. Was kosten diese zwei Uhren? Diese Uhr * kostet siebzehn Mark und jene zwölf. Siebzehn und zwölf sind neunundzwanzig. Die Früchte und die Saaten der Äcker sind gut.

* **die Uhr** = *clock, watch,* and is also used for time (see pages 21 and 67).

Travel: *By Boat*—die **SEEREISE,** *Ocean trip*

reisen, to travel
das Reisen, travel
das Schiff, ship
der Fahrplan, time-table
der Dampfer, steamship, steamer
bekommen, to obtain
Wo bekomme ich? Where do I obtain?
ich möchte . . . I should like, I want . . .
essen, to eat
ich möchte essen, I'd like to eat
das Deck, deck
die Decke, decks
das Oberdeck, top (upper) deck
das Unterdeck, lower deck
die Kabine, cabin
die Kabinen, cabins
Gibt es? Is there?
Es gibt There is . . .
Gibt es ein Promenadendeck? Is there a promenade deck?
der Kapitän, captain
der Ingenieur, engineer
der Zahlmeister, purser
der Offizier, officer
die Offiziere, officers

an Bord, on board
ich möchte eine Deckkabine haben, I'd like to have a deck cabin
ich möchte an Bord essen, I'd like to eat on board
Zeigen Sie mir . . ., show me . . .
ich kann, I can . . .
Kann ich . . .? Can I . . .?
Kann ich eine andere Kabine haben? Can I have another cabin?
die Bar, bar
das Restaurant, restaurant
der Liegestuhl, deck-chair
die Überfahrt, crossing
die Nordsee, North Sea
England, England
Deutschland, Germany
Österreich, Austria
die Schweiz, Switzerland
die Vereinigten Staaten, the United States
der Amerikaner, the American
der Engländer, Englishman
der Deutsche, German
der Österreicher, Austrian
der Schweizer, Swiss
(ab)fahren, to sail (see page 182, Prefix **ab.**)

Wann fährt das Schiff ab? When is the ship sailing?
Der Dampfer fährt um drei Uhr ab. The steamer sails at three o'clock.
Wo ist meine Kabine? Where is my cabin?

Haben Sie eine Deckkabine erster Klasse? Have you a
deck cabin first class?

**Ich möchte einen Liegestuhl auf dem Promenadendeck
haben.** I should like to have a deck-chair on the promenade
deck.

Es ist eine gute Überfahrt durch den Kanal. It is a good
crossing of (through) the English Channel.

Ist die Bar geöffnet? Is the bar open?

Die Bar im Unterdeck ist geschlossen. The bar on the
lower deck is closed.

Kann ich den Kapitän sprechen? Can I speak to the captain?

Nein, Sie können den Kapitän nicht sprechen. No, you
cannot speak to the captain.

Kann ich einen anderen Offizier sprechen? Can I speak
to another Officer?

Ja, der Zahlmeister ist hier. Yes, the purser is here.

Ist ein Arzt an Bord? Is there a doctor on board?

Der Arzt ist ein Engländer. The doctor is an Englishman.

**Dieses Schiff fährt durch die Nordsee direkt nach
Deutschland.** This ship goes across (through) the North
Sea direct to Germany.

§ 4. *Neuter Nouns, Declension—Groups I, II, and III—
Numbers—Practice—Travel: By Air*

DECLENSION: NEUTER NOUNS

Group I: Endings **-EL, -EN, -ER,** and diminutives
-CHEN, -LEIN. This group corresponds to Group I
of the Masculines (see page 31) and, in fact, is declined
in exactly the same way.

das FENSTER, window   Plural: **die FENSTER,** windows
des FENSTERS   **der FENSTER**
dem FENSTER   **den FENSTERN**
das FENSTER   **die FENSTER**

One neuter Noun in **-ER** modifies in the plural:

das KLOSTER, monastery; **die KLÖSTER**

Included in this considerable group are all Verbs used as Nouns, and by their nature they have no plural:

das SINGEN, singing   **das LAUFEN,** running

Group II: Nearly all other Neuter Nouns of more than one syllable are declined like **das METALL,** *metal*. Thus:

das METALL, metal	**die METALLE,** metals
des METALLES	**der METALLE**
dem METALL	**den METALLEN**
das METALL	**die METALLE**

Into this group also come Neuter Nouns ending **-NIS** and **-SAL.** (For Feminine Nouns with **-NIS** ending see Exceptions, page 41.) The only difference in declension is that Feminines do not change in the singular, but Neuters take **-ES** in the Genitive Singular. Both Feminines and Neuters take **-SE** in the plural.   Thus:

das Geheimnis, secret	*plural :* **die GeheimnisSE**
des Geheimnisses	**der Geheimnisse**
dem Geheimnis	**den Geheimnissen**
das Geheimnis	**die Geheimnisse**

And similarly, Neuter Nouns ending in **-SAL, -MAL :**

das Schicksal, destiny; **des Schicksals; die Schicksale**
das Grabmal, tomb; **des Grabmals; die Grabmale,** tombs

Note :

die Trübsal, affliction; *plural* **die Trübsale**

and it is also neuter:

das Trübsal, des Trübsals, die Trübsale

Exceptions in group II are Neuters ending in **-TUM** or with the prefix **GE-.** Neuters ending in **-TUM** modify that syllable and add **-ER.** The others modify the root syllable if possible, and add **-ER.**

das Herzogtum, duchy	*plural :* **die HerzogtümER**
das Gemach, room, flat	**die GemächER**
Gemüt, mind, temper	**die GemütER**
Geschlecht, sex	**die GeschlechtER**
Gesicht, face	**die GesichtER**
Gespenst, ghost	**die GespenstER**
Gewand, garment	**die GewändER**

Group III. Neuter Nouns of one syllable are subdivided into three categories according to the ending they take in the plural.

(*a*) Monosyllables forming the plural by adding **-er** and with modification of the root vowel.

das RAD, wheel	**die RÄDER,** wheels
des RADES	**der RÄDER**
dem RADE	**den RÄDERN**
das RAD	**die RÄDER**

(*b*) Monosyllables ending in **-r** add **-e** in the plural; no modification.

das Jahr, year	**die Jahre,** years
des Jahres	**der Jahre**
dem Jahre	**den Jahren**
das Jahr	**die Jahre**

Declined like **das Jahr** are the following:

das Haar, hair	**das Paar,** pair
Heer, army	**Rohr,** reed, tube
Meer, sea	**Tier,** animal
Moor, moor	**Tor,** gate

Note the following miscellaneous neuter monosyllables which are declined in the same way:

das BEIN, leg	**die BEINE,** legs
des BEINES	**der BEINE**
dem BEINE	**den BEINEN**
das BEIN	**die BEINE**

das BOOT, boat	**das RECHT,** right
BROT, bread	**Reh,** doe, deer
DING, thing	**SCHAF,** sheep
Fell, hide	**SCHIFF,** ship
GIFT, poison	**SCHWEIN,** pig
Los, lot	**STÜCK,** piece
Netz, net	**WERK,** work
PFERD, horse	**Zelt,** tent
REICH, kingdom	**Ziel,** aim

(*c*) A few Neuter monosyllables like **das BETT.**

das BETT, bed	**die BETTEN,** beds
des BETTES	**der BETTEN**
dem BETTE	**den BETTEN**
das BETT	**die BETTEN**

das HEMD, shirt	**das OHR,** ear

and note :

das HERZ, heart	**die HERZEN**
des HERZENS	**der HERZEN**
dem HERZEN	**den HERZEN**
das HERZ	**die HERZEN**

Declined similarly are the following three Nouns ending in **-e**:

das AUGE, eye	des Auges	*plural*:	die AUGEN, eyes
das ENDE, end	des ENDES		die ENDEN, ends
*das ERBE, heritage	des ERBES		*no plural*

*der Erbe, heir, *plural* die Erben

As a general rule, Nouns ending in **-e** are either Masculine (Group II, page 35) or Feminine (Group I, page 41).

PRACTICE: ÜBUNG

Die Fenster des Klosters sind offen. Es gibt hier zwei Klöster. Das Kommen und Gehen der Jahre. Der Mai ist die Zeit des Reisens. Der Wagen hat vier Räder. Die roten Haare des Kindes. Die Tore des Gartens. Pferde und Ochsen sind Tiere. Die Beine des Rosses sind lang. Die Heere der Staaten sind groß. Das Wasser im Boote ist kalt. Er ist in vielen Dingen gut. Haben wir diese Rechte ? Die guten Werke der Menschen. In jenem Zelte sind zwei Schweine. Der Esel hat große Ohren. Wie viele Hemden sind hier ? Er ist am Ende seines Zieles. Ist sie in den Gemächern ? Das warme Blut des Herzens. Die roten Gesichter der Knaben. Die schönen Augen des Mädchens. Er hat keine Geheimnisse. Welche Schicksale haben die Menschen ?

NUMBERS:

30 **DREISSIG—EINUNDDREISSIG—ZWEIUND-DREISSIG,** etc.

40 **VIERZIG—EINUNDVIERZIG—NEUNUND-VIERZIG**

50 **FÜNFZIG—ZWEIUNDFÜNFZIG—SECHSUND-FÜNFZIG . . .**

Continue to Practice with numbers 1-50 as suggested on pages 19 and 26.

TRAVEL: *By Air*—das Reisen im Flugzeug

das Flugzeug, airplane	starten, to take off
der Flieger, aviator (flier)	die Landung, landing
der Flugplatz, aerodrome	die Wasserlandung, sea
der Flughafen, airport	landing

fliegen, to fly
fliegen über, to fly over
der Flugzeugführer, pilot
der Fahrgast, air passenger
gehen, to go
Gehen wir? Do we go?
Gehen wir direkt nach Hamburg? Do we go direct to Hamburg?
Geht das Flugzeug nach...? Does the plane go to ...?
am besten, the best way, manner
fahren, to travel (by something)
die Fahrt, journey
ich fahre, I travel
wir fahren, we travel
fahren wir? do we travel?
Sie fahren, you travel
eine Tasse Tee, a cup of tea
eine Tasse Kaffee, cup of coffee
dürfen, to be allowed to
ich darf, I am allowed (to)
Darf ich? Am I allowed (to)?
nehmen, to take

mitnehmen, to take with
Wieviel Gepäck darf ich mitnehmen? How much baggage am I allowed to take with me?
Wo sind wir jetzt? Where are we now?
wechseln, to change
Darf ich meinen Platz wechseln? Can I (am I allowed to) change my place?
Was kostet die Fahrt nach ...? What does the journey to ... cost?
hin und zurück, there and back
Was für ein ...? What kind of ...?
Was für ein Flugzeug ist es? What kind of a plane is it?
Wir sind. Sind wir? We are. Are we?
Wann landen wir? When do we land?
Ich kann nichts sehen. I can see nothing.

Kommen wir hier zum Flughafen? Do we get here to the airport?

Ja, fahren Sie immer geradeaus. Yes, keep driving straight ahead.

Ich möchte mit dem nächsten Flugzeug nach Berlin fahren. I should like to travel on (with) the next plane to Berlin.

Fliegt dieses Flugzeug direkt nach Berlin oder macht es eine Zwischenlandung? Does this plane fly direct to Berlin or does it make an intermediate landing?

Es landet in Hannover und geht nach Aufenthalt von einer Stunde weiter.   It lands in Hanover and goes on after a stop of one hour.

Wie viele Fahrgäste haben in diesem Flugzeug Platz?   How many passengers can be seated in this plane?

Es faßt zweiundzwanzig Fahrgäste und hat vier Mann Besatzung.   It takes twenty-two passengers and has a crew of four.

Der Flugzeugführer sitzt im Führersitz.   The pilot is sitting in the cockpit.

Sie dürfen Ihr Gepäck nicht in die Kabine nehmen.   You may not take your luggage into the cabin.

Wir bringen es für Sie in den Gepäckraum.   We('ll) take it for you into the luggage hold.

Bekommen wir im Flugzeug Erfrischungen?   Do we get refreshments on the plane?

§ 5. *Compound Nouns, Declension— Unusual Plurals— Two Plurals— Numbers—General Practice with Declensions—Travel: By Car or Bus—General Rules— Table of Declensions for Reference*

Hundreds of Compound Nouns can be made from simple Nouns by putting together one or more independent simple words.   For example:

> **der Nebel,** mist, fog; **das Horn,** horn: **das NEBEL-HORN,** fog-horn
>
> **das Werk,** work; **die Halle,** hall, shed: **die Werkhalle,** work shed

The gender is always that of the last Noun.

Rule: A Compound Noun in German has the stress on the first Noun, takes the gender of the last Noun, and *only the last Noun is declined*:

DER ÁPFELBAUM, apple tree	**DIE ÁPFELBÄUME,** apple trees
DES ÁPFELBAUMES	**DER ÁPFELBÄUME**
DEM ÁPFELBAUM	**DEN ÁPFELBÄUMEN**
DEN ÁPFELBAUM	**DIE ÁPFELBÄUME**

When the first Noun ends in **-E**, it is usual to insert **-N** for euphony:

die Blume, flower; **der Garten,** garden: **der BLUMEN-GARTEN,** flower garden

Compounds with **-MANN** have plural in **-LEUTE,** -people. Thus:

DER EDELMANN, noble-man	**DIE EDELLEUTE,** noble-men, etc.
DER HAUPTMANN, cap-tain	**DIE HAUPTLEUTE**
DER HANDELSMANN, tradesman	**DIE HANDELSLEUTE**
DER KAUFMANN, mer-chant	**DIE KAUFLEUTE**
DER SEEMANN, seaman	**DIE SEELEUTE**

Note : **die Staatsmänner,** statesmen; **die Dienstmänner,** street porters.

UNUSUAL PLURALS: Certain Compound Nouns do not have the plural form expected. These either (*a*) add another kind of plural ending such as **-erein** or **-keiten,** or (*b*) add the plural form of another word. Here are some examples:

(*a*) **der Betrug,** fraud, deception   *plural :* **die Betrügereien**
    der Streit, strife, struggle   **die Streitigkeiten**
    der Zank, dispute   **die Zänkereien**

(*b*) **der TOD,** death; **die TODESFÄLLE,** cases of death; **die TODESARTEN,** kinds of death
    der FRIEDEN, peace; **die FRIEDENSSCHLÜSSE,** peaces, conclusions of peace
    die Gunst, favour; **die Gunstbezeigungen,** favours, signs of favour
    das UNGLÜCK, misfortune; **die UNGLÜCKSFÄLLE,** cases of misfortune

IRREGULAR PLURALS: Note the following:

    das KAPITAL, capital   *plural :* **die KAPITALIEN**
    das HOSPITAL, hospital   **die HOSPITÄLER**
    das REGIMENT, regiment   **die REGIMENTER**

TWO PLURALS: Many German Nouns have more than one meaning in the singular. This meaning is usually clear from the context or from what follows. But there are usually two different plurals for such words, some of which are in common use and should be known.　A list is given for reference:

Singular	*Plurals*
das Band, bond (of blood, friendship), tape	**die Bande,** bonds (of blood, etc.) **Bänder,** tapes, bandages
die BANK, bank, bench	**die BÄNKE,** benches **BANKEN,** banks (for money)
das DING, thing, gadget	**die DINGE,** things (in general)
der LADEN, shutter, shop, store	**die LADEN,** shutters **LÄDEN,** shops, stores
das LAND, land, country	**die Lande,** lands (*unusual*) **LÄNDER,** countries
dàs LICHT, light, candle (the material)	**die Lichte,** lights (candles) **LICHTER,** lights (flames *or* lights seen)
das TUCH, cloth in general, piece of cloth	**die Tuche,** cloth materials **TÜCHER,** pieces of cloth
das WORT, word (in particular, or in general)	**die WORTE,** words (*in a sentence*) **WÖRTER,** words (*in a vocabulary* or *dictionary*)

NUMBERS:

60	**SECHZIG**	100	**HUNDERT**
70	**SIEBZIG**	200	**ZWEIHUNDERT**
80	**ACHTZIG**	300	**DREIHUNDERT**
90	**NEUNZIG**	1000	**TAUSEND**

450　**VIERHUNDERTUNDFÜNFZIG**

797　**SIEBENHUNDERTSIEBENUNDNEUNZIG**

If a date:　　　　　1957

NEUNZEHNHUNDERTSIEBENUNDFÜNFZIG

If a number:

EINTAUSENDNEUNHUNDERTSIEBENUND-FÜNFZIG

2000　**ZWEITAUSEND**　　10,000　**ZEHNTAUSEND**

die NULL, zero　　　　　　**die NULLEN,** zeros

You are now equipped to deal with cardinal numbers.

SOME GENERAL PRACTICE WITH THE DECLENSIONS

Test yourself with this Practice.　It will show you where revision may be necessary.

In unserem Garten gibt es schöne Blumen. Die Apfelbäume des Gartens sind groß. Er hat zwei Bücher in den Händen. Die Seiten des Buches sind weiß. Die Söhne gehen mit dem Vater und die Töchter mit der Mutter. Die Plätze auf den Bänken sind hart. Das Geld ist in den Banken. Er sagt viele Dinge mit wenigen Worten. Im Wörterbuche stehen Tausende von Wörtern. Die Fenster und Türen des Hauses. Wieviele Bilder sind an den Wänden des Raumes? Die Lichter des Autos. Die Räder des Wagens. Es gibt viele Tiere im Walde. Die Federn des Vogels sind schön. Er gab den Spatzen und Finken Wasser. Geben Sie den Gänsen und Hühnern Brot. Die Ochsen und Pferde arbeiten für den Menschen. Die Saaten des Sommers und Winters. Die Geschäfte des Kaufmanns gehen gut. Die braunen Schuhe des jungen Burschen. Die Mädchen haben Blumen in den Haaren. Hunde und Katzen sind keine Freunde. Am Ufer des Meeres sind Häuser. Ich gebe dem Boten einen Brief. Fahren Sie mit dem Zuge? Ich sehe mit den Augen. Die fünf Finger der Hand. Die kleinen Hunde spielen mit den Bällen. Die Dörfer und Städte der großen Länder. Die Schiffe fahren auf dem Wasser. Die Tage des Monats und die Monate des Jahres. Ich trinke keinen kalten Tee. Nehmen Sie die schönen Äpfel. Er arbeitet viele Stunden am Tage. Das Flugzeug fährt nicht in der Nacht. Die kalten Lüfte der Nächte.

TRAVEL: *By Car or Bus*

der Omnibus, bus
der Autobus, bus,
der Kraftwagen⎱automobile,
das Auto⎰ car
das Nummernschild,
  license plate
das Licht, light
die Lichter, lights

die Reifenpanne, punctured
  tire
aufpumpen, to pump up,
  inflate
die Luftpumpe, pump
der Führerschein,
  driver's license
richtig, right, properly
das Liter, litre

das Öl, lubricating oil
das Benzin, gasoline
der Benzintank, gas tank
die Garage, garage
der Kühler, radiator
die Bremse, brake
das Steuerrad, steering-wheel
der Vergaser, carburetor
das Ersatzteil, spare part
der Volkswagen, people's car
füllen, to fill
Füllen Sie den Kühler, fill the radiator
Füllen Sie den Benzintank, fill the gas tank
brauchen, to need
ich brauche, I need
ich brauche vier Liter Benzin, I need 4 litres of gasoline
reinigen, to clean
reinigen Sie bitte, please clean

schmieren, to grease
schmieren Sie die Federn, grease the springs
waschen, to wash
waschen Sie, wash (*Imp.*)
der Sitz, seat
die Sitze, seats
der Führersitz, driver's seat
der Kofferraum, place for luggage, trunk
die Reparatur, repairs
fertig, ready
funktionieren, to function
es funktioniert nicht, it doesn't work
kontrollieren, to examine
Kontrollieren Sie bitte, please examine
die Tankstelle, gas station
Garage über Nacht für den Wagen, garage overnight for the car

Fahren Sie selbst? Do you drive yourself?
Nein, meine Frau sitzt am Steuer. No, my wife is (sits) at the wheel.
Sie hat einen Führerschein. She has a driving licence.
Ich habe nicht genügend Benzin. I have not sufficient gas.
Wo ist die nächste Tankstelle? Where is the next gas station?
Ich brauche zehn Liter Benzin, und füllen Sie auch den Kühler. I need 10 litres of gas; also fill the radiator.
Die Handbremse funktioniert nicht richtig. The hand brake does not work properly .
Wollen Sie sie bitte einmal kontrollieren. Will you please just examine it.
Haben Sie einige Ersatzteile bei sich? Have you some spare parts with you?

Ja, einen Ersatzreifen. Yes, a spare tire.
Dieses ist eine Einbahnstraße. This is a one-way street.
Sie müssen nach rechts abbiegen. You must turn to the right.
Komme ich hier auf die Hauptverkehrsstraße? Do I get here to the main road?
Hier ist eine Umleitung. Here (there) is a detour.
Achtung! Bahnübergang. Attention! Level crossing.
Wo kann ich parken? Where can I park?
Sehen Sie dort die Verkehrslichter? Do you see there the traffic lights?
Da ist eine Straßenkreuzung. There's a street crossing.
Links davon ist ein Parkplatz. To the left of it.(therefrom) is a parking lot.
Der Lastwagen vor uns fährt langsam. That truck in front of us travels slowly.
Überholen wir ihn. Let us overtake it.
Schalten Sie den dritten Gang ein. Switch to the third gear.
Die Höchstgeschwindigkeit ist achtzig Stunden-Kilometer. Speed limit is 80 km.p.h.
Die Autobahn ist für Radfahrer verboten. The super highway is prohibited for cyclists.

Some General Rules

The following is a summary of the general rules of declension which have been given and applied in this Lesson.

1. Masculine Nouns with their Nominative Singular ending in **-E** add **-N** in all other inflections, singular and plural.

der Jude, Jew   **die Juden**
des Juden   **der Juden**
dem Juden   **den Juden**
den Juden   **die Juden**

2. Masculine Nouns other than those ending in **-E** and all Neuter Nouns add **-s** in the Genitive Singular.

der Garten, garden   **der König,** king
des Gartens   **des Königs**

TABLE OF DECLENSIONS OF NOUNS BY GROUPS

MASCULINES	FEMININES	NEUTERS
I. Endings -el, -en, -er. *No* change in plural:	I. Nouns of more than one syllable—	I. Endings -el, -en, -er. *No* change in plural:
der Diener die Diener des Dieners der Diener dem Diener den Dienern den Diener die Diener	(*a*) ending -e add -n in plural: die Blume die Blumen der Blume der Blumen der Blume den Blumen die Blume die Blumen	das Fenster die Fenster des Fensters der Fenster dem Fenster den Fenstern das Fenster die Fenster
II. Ending in -e; take -n in plural:	(*b*) ending -el or -er; add -n in plural: die Nadel die Nadeln (throughout)	II. Nearly all other polysyllables take -e in plural:
der Bote die Boten des Boten der Boten dem Boten den Boten den Boten die Boten	(*c*) Nearly all other polysyllables add -en in plural: die Lösung die Lösungen (throughout)	das Metall die Metalle des Metall(e)s der Metalle dem Metall den Metallen das Metall die Metalle

III. Monosyllables which take -e in plural with or without modification:

der Ball	die Bälle
des Balles	der Bälle
dem Ball(e)	den Bällen
den Ball	die Bälle

IV. Monosyllables which take -er and modify in plural:

der Mann	die Männer
des Mannes	der Männer
dem Mann(e)	den Männern
den Mann	die Männer

V. Monosyllables which take -en in plural without modification:

der Staat	die Staaten
des Staates	der Staaten
dem Staat(e)	den Staaten
den Staat	die Staaten

II. Monosyllables which take -e in plural and modify vowel:

die Hand	die Hände
der Hand	der Hände
der Hand	den Händen
die Hand	die Hände

III. Monosyllables which take -en in plural and do not modify:

die Frau	die Frauen
der Frau	der Frauen
der Frau	den Frauen
die Frau	die Frauen

III. Monosyllables—

(a) take -er and modify in plural:

das Rad	die Räder
des Rades	der Räder
dem Rad(e)	den Rädern
das Rad	die Räder

(b) ending in -r add -e in plural; no modification:

das Jahr	die Jahre
des Jahres	der Jahre
dem Jahre	den Jahren
das Jahr	die Jahre

(c) a few that take -en in plural:

das Bett	die Betten
des Bettes	der Betten
dem Bette	den Betten
das Bett	die Betten

SOME GENERAL RULES—*contd.*

3. The Accusative Singular of All Neuter Nouns is the same as the Nominative.

das Buch, book	**das Atom,** atom
des Buches	**des Atoms**
dem Buche	**dem Atom**
das Buch	**das Atom**

4. Feminine Nouns never vary in the Singular.

die Leiter, ladder	**die Frau,** woman
der Leiter	**der Frau**
der Leiter	**der Frau**
die Leiter	**die Frau**

5. The Nominative, Genitive, and Accusative of all plurals are alike.

die Tische, tables	**die Städte,** cities
der Tische	**der Städte**
den Tischen	**den Städten**
die Tische	**die Städte**

6. The Dative Plural of *all* Nouns ends in **-N.**

7. Only the final component of a compound Noun is declined, and it always follows its own declension. (See page 51.)

Note: When the Nominative and Genitive Singular and the Nominative Plural of any Noun are known, all other cases can be formed from the table on pages 56-57. The required cases are usually shown in a dictionary thus: der Fluß **(-es, ̈e);** die Nadel **(-, -n);** das Wort **(-es, ̈er** or **-e).**

LESSON III

§ 1. *Comparison of Adjectives—Irregular Comparisons—Practice —The Customs:* **das Zollamt**—*Listening to Radio— Reading*

SEE page 23 for declension of Adjectives—the same rules apply to their comparatives and superlatives. Most German Adjectives can be used as Adverbs. Thus **GUT** = *good* and *well*, though there is also **WOHL**, the Adverb for *well*.

Monosyllables with root vowel **a, o,** or **u** may modify, but those with **au** never modify. Thus:

> **ALT,** old; **ÄLTER,** older; **ÄLTEST,** oldest
> **LAUT,** loud; **LAUTER,** louder; **LAUTEST,** loudest

Note : The **-E** in the superlative is usually dropped except in words which end in a hissing sound: **-s, -ß, -z, -sch.** Thus:

> **ARM,** poor; **ÄRMER,** poorer; **ÄRMST,** poorest

But:

> **HEIß,** hot; **HEIßER,** hotter; **HEIßEST,** hottest

Adjectives which end in **-EL,-EN, -ER** drop the **-E** of those endings in the comparative. Thus:

> **EITEL,** vain; **EITLER,** vainer; **EITELST,** vainest

DECLENSION OF COMPARATIVES AND SUPERLATIVES: The general rule is that both comparatives and superlatives are declined like other Adjectives. Thus:

> **DER ALTE MANN,** the old man
> **DER ÄLTERE MANN,** the older man
> **DER ÄLTESTE MANN,** the oldest man

59

But when the superlative is not followed by a Noun, expressed or understood, another form with **AM** (= **an dem**) is used:

DIE BLUMEN SIND *AM* SCHÖNSTEN. The flowers are at their most beautiful.

Strictly, this is an adverbial form (see Lesson VI, § 5). This form ending in **-(E)STEN** preceded by **AM** (= *at the*) is always used when the superlative is used predicatively or adverbially. Thus:

KALT, KÄLTER, der, die, das KÄLTESTE = when used attributively
AM KÄLTESTEN = predicatively

Modification : (*a*) Adjectives of more than one syllable do not modify. Thus:

LANGSAM, slow; **LANGSAMER,** slower; **der, die, das LANGSAMSTE,** the slowest

(*b*) The following monosyllables do not modify, those in capitals being in common use:

bunt, bright, colourful	**RUND,** round
FALSCH, false	**SANFT,** soft
FLACH, flat	**satt,** satiated
FROH, merry	**schlaff,** slack
hohl, hollow	**SCHLANK,** slender
kahl, bald	**schlapp,** limp
KLAR, clear	**STOLZ,** proud
knapp, scanty	**STUMM,** silent, dumb
lahm, lame	**toll,** mad
matt, languid	**VOLL,** full
NACKT, naked	**WAHR,** true
rasch, quick	**zahm,** tame
roh, raw, rough	**zart,** tender

IRREGULAR COMPARISONS:

Positive	*Comparative*	*Superlative*
BALD, soon	**EHER,** sooner	**EHESTE,** soonest
GERN, willingly	**LIEBER,** rather	**LIEBSTE,** most willing
GROSS, big	**GRÖSSER,** bigger	**GRÖSSTE,** biggest
GUT, good	**BESSER,** better	**BESTE,** best

Positive	Comparative	Superlative
HOCH, high	**HÖHER,** higher	**HÖCHSTE,** highest
NAHE, near	**NÄHER,** nearer	**NÄCHSTE,** nearest
VIEL, much	**MEHR,** more	**MEISTE,** most
WENIG, little, small	**WENIGER** or **MINDER,** smaller, less	**WENIGSTE** or **MINDESTE,** smallest, least

And note:

HÖCHSTENS, at most   **NÄCHSTENS,** at an early
WENIGSTENS, at least   date

All the other superlatives in the list can have the form **AM** and the ending **-(E)STEN.** Thus: **AM BESTEN, AM GRÖSSTEN,** etc.

THAN is expressed by **ALS:**

> **Mein Freund ist ärmer ALS ich.** My friend is poorer than I.

AS . . . AS = **SO . . . WIE.** Thus:

> **Mein Freund ist SO groß WIE ich.** My friend is as tall as I.

NOT SO . . . AS = **NICHT SO . . . WIE.** Thus:

> **Er ist NICHT SO alt WIE ich.** He is not so old as I.

MORE, BETTER, LESS THAN . . . = **MEHR ALS...**
                                                        BESSER ALS...
                                                        WENIGER ALS...
                                                              etc.

ALL THE . . . = **DESTO . . .**
SO MUCH THE . . . = **UM SO . . .** Thus:

> **DESTO BESSER,** all the better
> **UM SO KÄLTER,** so much the colder

Note that **FRÜHER,** the regular comparative of **FRÜH,** *early*, often becomes the comparative of **BALD,** *soon*. Thus:

> **Er kam FRÜHER als sein Bruder.** He came sooner than his brother.

GERN, *willing(-ly)*, usually has **AM LIEBSTEN** for superlative :

> **Er spielt am liebsten Fußball.** He plays football most willingly (= *for preference, or with greatest pleasure*).

PRACTICE: **ÜBUNG**

Er ist größer als sein Bruder, aber sein Vater ist der größte. Ist die Tochter schöner als ihre Mutter ? Er ist so alt wie ich. Das jüngste Kind der Familie. Die Tage sind länger als die Nächte. Das Wasser ist kälter als die Luft. Die wärmere Luft des Raumes. Der Zug fährt schneller als das Auto; das Flugzeug fährt am schnellsten. Er geht so langsam wie ich. Sprechen Sie bitte lauter und klarer! Dieser Bursche ist schlanker als jener. Der Hahn ist stolzer als das Huhn.

Dieses ist der höhere Berg, aber er ist nicht der höchste. Ich gehe zum ältesten Mann des Dorfes. Geben Sie mir schönere Blumen. Ist dieses das leichtere Brot ?—Nein, es ist so schwer wie jenes. Juli ist der heißeste Monat des Jahres. Ist dieses das kleinere Stück ? Nein, es ist das größere.

Essen Sie Äpfel gern ? Ich esse Nüsse lieber. Aber Kirschen esse ich am liebsten. Geht es Ihnen heute besser ? Ja, es geht mir gut. Kommen Sie bald wieder ? Ich komme eher als ich sagte. Hat er viel Geld ? Er hat mehr Geld als ich. Aber sein Freund hat am meisten. Ist die nächste Übung schwerer als diese ? Nein, sie ist nicht so schwer wie diese. Desto besser! Ich habe heute viel Zeit. Aber ich habe morgen weniger Zeit. Im nächsten Monat habe ich die meiste Zeit.

The Customs : das Zollamt

persönliche Sachen, personal effects

getragene Sachen, worn (used) effects

zahlen, to pay

die Ferien (pl.), holiday(s)

die Durchreise, transit journey

ich gedenke, mich nur zwei Wochen aufzuhalten, I expect to stay only two weeks

die Bescheinigung, certificate

die Summe, sum (of money)

die Ordnung, regulation

Haben Sie außerdem noch etwas? Have you anything else?

im Lande bleiben, to stay in the country

verzollen, to declare

etwas zu verzollen, anything to declare

zollpflichtig, subject to duty

für meinen eignen Bedarf, for my own use

der Zoll, duty

der Beamte, (Customs) officer

Wieviel Zoll habe ich zu zahlen? How much duty have I to pay?

die Geschäftsreise, business trip

das Muster, die Muster, sample(s)

die Devisen, currency

die Devisenkontrolle, currency control

gültig, valid

der Zollschein, customs clearance

das Empfehlungsschreiben, credential

wie lange? how long?

Der Zollbeamte: **Sind dieses alle Ihre Koffer?** *The customs officer :* Are these all your suit-cases?

Der Fahrgast: **Ja, und außerdem habe ich eine Handtasche.** *The passenger :* Yes, and apart from that I have a hand-bag.

Der Beamte: **Haben Sie etwas zu verzollen?** *The Officer :* Have you anything to declare?

F.: **Ich habe nur meine persönlichen Sachen und ein paar kleine Geschenke.** I have only my personal effects and a few small presents.

B.: **Wir werden sehen. Öffnen Sie bitte diesen Koffer hier.** We shall see. Please open this case here.

F.: **Sind diese Zigaretten zollpflichtig?** Are these cigarettes dutiable?

B.: **Nein, hundert Zigaretten sind zollfrei.** No, 100 cigarettes are duty free.

F.: **Aber für Spirituosen ist Zoll zu zahlen.** But for spirits duty must be paid.

B.: **Sind Sie auf einer Geschäftsreise?** Are you making a business trip?

F.: **Nein, ich mache eine Ferienreise.** No, I am making a holiday journey.

B.: **Haben Sie Devisen bei sich? Kommen Sie bitte mit zur Devisènkontrolle.** Have you foreign currency with you? Please come along to the currency control.

F.: **Erhalte ich eine Bescheinigung über die Geldsumme?** Do I get a certificate about the sum of money?

B.: **Nun ist alles in Ordnung. Sie können wieder in den Zug einsteigen.** Now everything is all right. You can board the train again.

LISTENING TO RADIO: READING

You may now usefully begin to listen to radio broadcasts in German, though you must not yet expect to understand very much of what you hear. Never mind! Even if at first you understand nothing but the simplest words, you will soon find yourself becoming accustomed to the sound and sounds of spoken German. Then you may be surprised to discover how many words you can pick up and, little by little, as you continue with the Course, more and more will be understood. This is a valuable training: because you will in time be "taking in" the German, understanding it—and without translation. This practice in thinking in German takes you well on the way to fluency in speaking.

For stations broadcasting in German, refer to page 231. Begin with simple broadcasts such as News Bulletins (**Die Nachrichten**) and Weather Forecasts (**Der Wetterdienst**). From now you will also read matter in normal German such as is to be found in newspapers, reviews, and in that written by certain authors. Here is an example of what is meant:

READING

Es war an einem heißen Tag am Luzerner See. Ein Mann mit Koffern rannte auf die Landungsbrücke zu. Er wollte das Schiff unbedingt noch erreichen.

Zwei Meter Wasser waren zwischen Dampfer und Brücke. Der Mann mit den Koffern nahm allen Mut zusammen. Er lief . . . er sprang . . . er landete an Bord.

„ Uff! " rief er erlöst, „ das wäre geschafft! "

Der Kapitän des Schiffes beglückwünschte ihn zu dem Sprung.

„ Aber es wäre nicht nötig gewesen," fügte er hinzu. „ Dies ist nicht das Schiff, das abfährt,—es ist das Schiff, das gerade anlegt."

LITERAL TRANSLATION: It was on a hot day by the Lake of Lucerne. A man with suit-cases ran to the landing bridge. He very much wanted to reach the boat.

Two meters of water were between steamer and bridge. The man with the suit-cases summoned all his courage. He ran . . . he jumped . . . he landed on board.

" Gosh," he exclaimed relieved, " that's done! "

The ship's captain congratulated him on his jump.

" But it would not have been necessary," he added. " This is not the boat that's leaving, it's the boat that is just arriving."

Note : In the Reading you will often find words not hitherto met. Note their meanings and learn as many as you can.

§ 2. *Numbers : Cardinal, Ordinal, Fractions—Learning to use the Numbers—The Time—Practice—Money and Exchange— Reading :* **WIEDERERKENNEN**

You already know the cardinal numbers, but they are listed here to help in learning ordinals and fractions, which are derived from them. Then you will learn to tell the time, which will provide useful practice. The numbers must be known well, as they are indispensable.

Cardinal Numbers	Ordinal Numbers		Fractions	
0 null				
1 eins	der erstTE	1st		
2 zwei (*gen.* zweier)	zweiTE	2nd	ein halb	$\frac{1}{2}$
3 drei (*gen.* dreier)	dritTE	3rd	dritTEL	$\frac{1}{3}$
4 vier	vierTE	4th	vierTEL	$\frac{1}{4}$
5 fünf	fünfTE	5th		
6 sechs	sechsTE	6th		
7 sieben	siebenTE	7th		
8 acht	achTE	8th		
9 neun	neunTE	9th		
10 zehn	zehnTE	10th		
11 elf				
12 zwölf				
13 dreiZEHN			-TEL	
14 vierzehn				
15 fünfzehn	-TE, th			
16 sechzehn				
17 siebzehn				
18 achtzehn				
19 neunzehn				
20 zwanzig	zwanzigSTE		ein zwanzigSTEL	
21 einundzwanzig	} -STE, th			
22 zweiundzwanzig				
30 dreißig	dreißigSTE, th			
31 einunddreißig				
40 vierzig				
45 fünfundvierzig				
50 fünfzig				
53 dreiundfünfzig				
60 sechzig				
64 vierundsechzig				
70 siebzig	-STE, th		-STEL	
76 sechsundsiebzig				
80 achtzig				
87 siebenundachtzig				
90 neunzig				
98 achtundneunzig				
100 hundert				
1000 tausend				

1957 = neunzehnhundertsiebenundfünfzig
3 + 5 = 8: drei und fünf ist acht
      or : drei und fünf gleich acht (gleich, *equals*)
12 − 7 = 5: zwölf weniger sieben ist fünf (weniger, *less*)

LEARNING THE NUMBERS: As already indicated, do not learn the numbers in German by associating them with their English equivalents. Learn them, first by saying them over in tens, and from 20 onwards repeating each number in full: **einundzwanzig, zweiundzwanzig, dreißig, einunddreißig, zweiunddreißig,** etc. When the words are well known, begin to do little sums in mental addition:

$2 + 5 = 7$: **zwei und fünf ist sieben**
$3 + 6 = 9$: **drei und sechs ist neun**
$9 + 3 = 12$: **neun und drei ist zwölf**
$12 + 4 = 16$: **zwölf und vier ist sechzehn**

and then:

$8 - 2 = 6$: **acht weniger zwei ist sechs**
$19 - 8 = 11$: **neunzehn weniger acht ist elf**

You will, of course, realize that this is carrying a stage farther what has already been emphasized: that it is better to learn new German words by associating them with the ideas they represent rather than with their English equivalents. The principle is an important one, first because it cuts out the process of translation, which is a barrier to learning; and, second, because it teaches you to think direct in German. Your goal throughout must be to learn to *think in German.*

Note : The word **EINS** is used for *one* only when it is not followed by another number. Thus, in counting you say: **EINS, ZWEI, DREI.** And : **DREIHUNDERTUNDEINS** = 301.

The Time : **DIE UHR**

Wieviel Uhr ist es ? What time is it ?
Können Sie mir die genaue Zeit sagen ? Can you tell me the exact time ?
ES IST DREI UHR. It is three o'clock.

I. **ES IST 3 UHR 15** or II. **ES IST (EIN) VIERTEL (AUF) VIER**

3 Uhr 30   **HALB VIER**
3 Uhr 45   **DREIVIERTEL VIER**

3 Uhr 5   **FÜNF MINUTEN**
                                      NACH DREI
3 Uhr 50   **ZEHN MINUTEN**
                                      VOR VIER

I and II illustrate the German way of telling the time. I is similar to ours, as when we say 3.15 instead of "*a quarter-past three*". I is an exact method and easy to learn, but not so commonly used as II. In the latter the half-hours are considered as being half-way towards the next hour, and the quarters are reckoned as *on* (**AUF**) "*towards*" the next hour. The (**EIN**) and (**AUF**) are omitted in everyday speech, and one says: **ES IST VIERTEL VIER** or one can say **ES IST VIERTEL NACH DREI.**

a.m. = **VORMITTAGS,** in the forenoon
p.m. = **NACHMITTAGS,** in the afternoon
UM WIEVIEL UHR? At what time, o'clock?
UM DREI UHR. At three o'clock.
UM DREI UHR NACHMITTAGS. At three o'clock
in the afternoon.

(**DES**) **MORGENS,** in the   (**DES**) **NACHMITTAGS,** in
morning   the afternoon
(**DES**) **ABENDS,** in the even- (**DES**) **NACHTS,** at night
ing

PRACTICE: **ÜBUNG**

Das Jahr hat dreihundertfünfundsechzig Tage.
The year has 365 days.
Vierundfünfzig und fünfundzwanzig ist neunundsiebzig,
    54 + 25 = 79.
Einhundert(und)drei weniger acht ist fünfundneunzig, 103
    − 8 = 95.
**Dreihundertvierundvierzig und einhundert(und)elf ist vier-
hundertfünfundfünfzig,** 344 + 111 = 455.
Sechstausendsiebenhundertundneunzig, 6,790.
Wann gehen Sie zur Arbeit?
When do you go to work?

Um halb acht Uhr morgens.
At half-past seven in the morning.
Mein Zug fährt zehn Minuten vor acht.
My train goes (at) ten minutes to eight.
Und abends nehme ich den Zug um fünf Uhr zwölf.
And in the evening I take the train at 5.12.
**Um zehn Uhr vormittags trinke ich eine Tasse Kaffee
und um dreiviertel vier nachmittags eine Tasse Tee.**
At ten o'clock in the morning I drink a cup of coffee and at a
quarter to four in the afternoon a cup of tea.
Ich arbeite sieben und eine halbe Stunde.
I work seven and a half hours.

Money : **GELD**

Germany : 1 **Deutsche Mark** (DM) = 100 **Deutsche Pfen-
nige** (Dpf)
Dpf 100 = DM 1
Switzerland : 1 **Frank** (Fr.), unit of currency
Fr. 1 = 100 **Rappen** (or *centimes*, a word also
used)
Austria : 1 **Schilling** (Sch.) = unit of currency
Sch. 1 = 100 **Groschen** (Gr.)

(*Note :* Germany formerly also used **der Taler** (coin) =
3 **Mark**; and **der Groschen** = 10 **Pfennige**. These words
are found in reading.)

das Geld, money	**der Zehnmarkschein,** 10-DM bill
das Papiergeld, paper money	
die Banknote ⎫ bank-note	**die Pfundnote,** pound note
der Geldschein ⎭	**die Dollarnote,** dollar note
das Kleingeld, change	**das Bargeld,** cash
das Geldstück, coin	**der Kurs,** rate of exchange
das Zehnpfennigstück, 10-Dpf coin	**ausländisches Geld,** foreign money
das Zweimarkstück, 2-mark piece	**der Kreditbrief,** letter of credit

einwechseln, to change
abheben, to draw money
einlösen, to cash
der Reisescheck, travellers' cheque

die Zweigstelle, branch office
der Direktor, manager
unterschreiben, to sign

Having learnt the numbers, how to tell the time, and about money, you can now make up all kinds of useful sentences, especially if you know the following:

Amerika, America	**amerikanisch**	**ein Amerikaner,** an American
England, England	**englisch**	**ein Engländer,** Englishman
Deutschland, Germany	**deutsch**	**ein Deutscher**
		zwei Deutsche
Österreich, Austria	**österreichisch**	**ein Österreicher**
		zwei Österreicher
die Schweiz, Switzerland	**schweizerisch**	**ein Schweizer**
		zwei Schweizer
Schottland, Scotland	**schottisch**	**ein Schotte**
		zwei Schotten
Irland, Ireland	**irisch**	**ein Irländer, der Ire**

In the Bank : AUF DER BANK

Ich möchte Reiseschecks eintauschen. I'd like to cash travellers' cheques.

Sie sind Engländer und haben englische Reiseschecks? You're an Englishman and have English travellers' cheques ?

Ja. Wie ist der Kurs für das Pfund? Yes. What's the rate of exchange for the pound ?

Sie bekommen heute elf Mark fünfundsiebzig Pfennig für das englische Pfund. You get to-day 11 marks 75 pfennigs for the English pound.

Geben Sie mir bitte Deutsche Mark für fünf Pfund. Give me please German marks for five pounds.

Das macht: Achtundfünfzig Mark und fünfundsiebzig Pfennig. That makes: 58 marks and 75 pfennigs.

Ich möchte auch eine Zehn-Dollarnote einwechseln. I'd like to change also a ten-dollar note.

Der Kurs für den amerikanischen Dollar ist vier Mark zehn. The rate of exchange for the American dollar is 4 marks 10.

Sie bekommen zusammen einundvierzig Mark. You receive altogether 41 marks.

Geben Sie mir bitte etwas Kleingeld. Please give me some change.

Hier sind einige Zwanzigmarkscheine, etwas Silbergeld und ein paar Zehn- und Fünf-Pfennigstücke. Here are some twenty-mark bank-notes, a little silver money, and a few ten- and five-pfennig pieces.

Bitte unterschreiben Sie hier. Please sign here.

Wann schließen Sie? When do you close?

Um halb fünf (Uhr). At half-past four.

READING

WIEDERERKENNEN

Als ein neuer Gast den Speisesaal eines Hotels betrat, blickte ein Mann, der beim Mittagessen saß, mit einem Lächeln auf, und sagte:

„ Ah, guten Tag, guten Tag, mein Freund. Erinnern Sie sich nicht, daß wir uns hier vor ein oder zwei Wochen trafen? "

Der Eingetretene sah den Stammgast mit leerem Blick an und sagte: „ Verzeihen Sie! Aber ich denke nicht, daß ich Sie kenne."

„ Wohl möglich," entgegnete der andere. „ Denn eigentlich kenne ich Sie auch nicht. Aber ich erkenne jenen Regenschirm wieder."

„ Wie kann denn das sein, mein lieber Mann? " antwortete der neue Gast. „ Als ich vor vierzehn Tagen hierherkam, hatte ich gar keinen Schirm."

„ Natürlich nicht," sagte der Stammgast. „ Aber ich hatte einen."

Translation:

RECOGNITION

When a newcomer entered the dining-room of a hotel, a man who was having a meal looked up with a smile and said :

" Ah, good day, good day, my friend—don't you remember, we met here a week or two ago ? "

The newcomer looked blankly at the diner and said, " Pardon me, but I don't think I know you."

" Well, that's possible," replied the other, " because I don't really know you either. But I do recognize that umbrella."

" How can it be, my dear man ? " answered the newcomer. " When I came here a fortnight ago, I had no umbrella."

" Of course not," said the diner, " but I had one."

§ 3. *Numbers : Miscellaneous Forms and Uses—Weights and Measures—The Date—Practice—Finding the Way—Reading*
Mein alter Onkel

EIN is fully inflected: before a Noun like the Indefinite Article, standing alone like **DIESER. Wieviel haben Sie? EINEN, -E, -ES. HUNDERT** and **TAUSEND** are also used as nouns with plurals in **-E** (dative plural **-EN**). A Noun following must then be in the genitive or be preceded by **VON,** *of.* Thus:

> **HUNDERTE VON MENSCHEN,** hundreds of men
> **der Hundertste,** the hundredth

DIE MILLION, EINE MILLION, *a million,* is a Noun and follows the rules for Nouns. **Eine Millionste,** *a millionth.*

ZWEI and **DREI** have endings **-ER** (Genitive) and **-EN** (Dative) when *not* preceded by an Article or Possessive Adjective which shows the case. Thus:

> **DIESER ZWEI FREUNDE,** of these two friends
> **DER ZWEI FREUNDE,** of the two friends
> **ZWEIER FREUNDE,** of two friends
> **DREIER FREUNDE,** of three friends

Note that the Ordinal Numbers are formed by adding **-TE** up to 19th, and **-STE** after 19th. Irregulars: **der ERSTE,** *first*, and **der DRITTE,** *third*. Only the last element in a compound ordinal takes the ending:

725th = **SIEBENHUNDERTFÜNFUNDZWAN-ZIGSTE**

Full numbers in German are written close up; large numbers are grouped in threes, spaced or with full stops (but not divided by commas as in English). Decimal points are written with a comma. Thus: 25 760 for our 25,760; and 7,5 for our 7.5. And: 7 560 312 for our 7,560,312.

The ending **-TEL — TEIL,** *part*.

Ein Viertel, a fourth part, a quarter (= **ein Vier-teil**)

Numeral Adverbs are formed by adding **-MAL,** *time-s*:

EINMAL, once, etc.　　　　　**ZWEIMAL,** twice
ACHTMAL, eight times

Ordinal Adverbs can be formed by adding the suffix **-NS** to the ordinal numbers:

ERSTENS, ZWEITENS, DRITTENS, VIERTENS u.s.w.,*
firstly, secondly, thirdly, fourthly, etc.

Variative Numerals denoting " kinds of " are formed by adding the suffix **-ERLEI** to the cardinals:

EINERLEI, one kind of　　　　**ZWEIERLEI,** two kinds of

And note the indefinites:

ALLERLEI, all kinds of　　　　**SOLCHERLEI,** such like
VIELERLEI, many kinds of　　　**MANCHERLEI,** several kinds of

Multiplicatives denoting " *-fold* " are formed by adding the suffix **-FACH** to the cardinals. Thus:

EINFACH, single, simple　　　　**ZWEIFACH,** twofold
ZEHNFACH, tenfold, etc.

Note: **VIELFACH,** *manifold*. These vary like Adjectives.

HALB, *half*, and **GANZ,** *whole*, are Adjectives, usually with an Article.

EIN HALBER TAG, a half day　　**EIN HALBES JAHR,** a half
DER GANZE TAG, the whole　　　year
day　　　　　　　　　　　　**DIE GANZE ZEIT,** the whole
DAS GANZE JAHR, the whole　　time
year

Note the Noun:

DIE HÄLFTE, the half
DIE HÄLFTE DES APFELS, the half of the apple
DREI TAGE UND EIN HALBER, three and a half days, three days and a half *or, more common* **DREI UND EIN HALBER TAG**

* u.s.w. = **und so weiter** = et cetera.　　**weiter** = further

ANDERTHALB, meaning *one and a half*, is followed by a nominative plural.   Thus:

> **ANDERTHALB TAGE, ANDERTHALB MONATE,** one and half days, months

WEIGHTS AND MEASURES: Masculine and Neuter Nouns denoting weight or measure after cardinal numbers remain invariable, and " *of* " before a following Noun is omitted in German. Thus:

> **EIN GLAS WASSER,** a glass of water
> **ZWEI GLASS WEIN,** two glasses of wine
> **DREI PFUND ZUCKER,** three pounds of sugar
> **SIEBEN FUSS HOCH,** seven feet (or foot) high

But Feminine Nouns in **-E** are put in the plural:

> **ZWEI FLASCHEN WEIN,** two bottles of wine
> **DREI TASSEN TEE,** three cups of tea

Weights and Measures : Equivalents

1 **Kilometer** = 1093 yards or about 0·62 of a mile	
1 mile (1760 yards) = 1 **Meile** = 1609 **Meter**	
1 **Meter** = 39·4 inches	1 yard = 91·4 **Zentimeter**
1000 **Meter** = 1 **Kilometer**	100 **Zentimeter** = I **Meter**
1 **Liter** = 1·76 or about 1¾ pints	1 gallon = 4·54 (4½) litres
5 **Liter** = 1 gallon + 0·80 pints	1 pint = 0·56 = more than ½ **liter**
1 **Kilogramm** = about 2¼ lbs. = 1000 **Gramm**	
100 **Gramm** = 3·53 oz. or about 3½	
1 **Pfund** = 500 **Gramm** = ½ **Kilogramm** (a continental pound)	
1 **Zentner** = 100 **Pfund** = 50 **Kilogramm**	

The Date : **das Datum**

1. **DER WIEVIELTE IST HEUTE?**
2. **DEN   WIEVIELTEN   HABEN WIR HEUTE?**

} What is the date to-day ?

Answer :

1. **ES IST DER ERSTE, DER ZWEITE, DER DRITTE, u.s.w.**   It is the first, second, third, etc.

Or :

2. WIR HABEN DEN ERSTEN, DEN ZWEITEN, DEN DRITTEN, u.s.w.

English " *of* " is omitted in the phrase " *in the month of* " :

IM MONAT JUNI, in the month of June

Note the following :

AM SIEBENTEN JULI, on the seventh of July
DEN DRITTEN JANUAR, the third of January
IM JAHRE 1957, in the year 1957
DEN ZWEITEN JANUAR 1958, the 2nd January 1958
DEN 10ten MÄRZ, 10th March

The Date on a Letter : **Den 4. Dezember 1956.** Note that a full stop is written after the 4. **Den 6. Juli 1957. Den 14. März 1958.** And that there is no comma after the month.

Days of the Week, Months, Seasons

Sonntag, Sunday	**Donnerstag,** Thursday
Montag, Monday	**Freitag,** Friday
Dienstag, Tuesday	**Samstag ***
Mittwoch, Wednesday	**Sonnabend †** } Saturday

Months of the Year

Januar	**Juli**
Februar	**August**
März	**September**
April	**Oktober**
Mai	**November**
Juni	**Dezember**

Seasons

Der Frühling, Spring	**Der Herbst,** Autumn
Der Sommer, Summer	**Der Winter,** Winter

* In South Germany, Austria, and Rhineland.   † Elsewhere.

Practice: ÜBUNG

In den Bäumen sind viele Hunderte von Vögeln.
In the trees (there) are many hundreds of birds.
Der Staat mit Tausenden von Soldaten.
The state with thousands of soldiers.
Tausend ist eine Eins mit drei Nullen.
Thousand is a one with three zeros.
Diese zwei Knaben sind jung.
These two boys are young.
Das Auto der zwei Männer ist hier.
The car of the two men is here.
Die Freundschaft dreier Mädchen ist schön.
The friendship of three girls is beautiful.
Der wievielte ist heute?
What date is it to-day?
Heute ist der siebenundzwanzigste Juli.
To-day is the twenty-seventh of July.
Der einunddreißigste Dezember ist der letzte Tag des Jahres.
The thirty-first of December is the last day of the year.
Eine halbe Stunde.
Half an hour.
Eine viertel Stunde.
A quarter of an hour.
Drei viertel Stunde.
Three quarters of an hour.
Ein achtel.   Ein sechzehntel.   Ein zweiunddreißigstel =
An eighth.   A sixteenth.   A thirty-secondth.
Haben Sie diese Übung einmal gelesen?
Have you read this practice once?
Nein, ich lese sie dreimal.
No, I read it three times.
Geben Sie mir bitte zweierlei Käse.
Please give me two kinds of cheese.
Die Mutter kauft vielerlei Dinge.
The mother buys many sorts of things.

Er erzählt allerlei Geschichten.
He tells all sorts of stories.

Er ist ein einfacher Mann.
He is a simple man.

Ich habe es dreifach bezahlt.
I have paid it three times over.

Er gab mir die Hälfte seines Brotes.
He gave me half of his bread.

Ich schlafe die ganze Nacht.
I sleep all night.

Sie ist halb so reich wie er.
She is half as rich as he.

Der Zug fährt anderthalb Stunden.
The train travels one and a half hours.

Wir haben zwei und eine halbe Stunde gewartet.
We have waited two and a half hours.

Der Vater trank drei Glas Bier, seine Frau zwei Tassen Tee und der Sohn ein Glas Limonade.
The father drank three glasses of beer, his wife two cups of tea, and the son a glass of lemonade.

Sie kauft ein halbes Pfund Kaffee, zwei Pfund Zucker und drei Kilogramm Kartoffeln.
She buys half a pound of coffee, two pounds of sugar, and three kilograms of potatoes.

Das nächste Dorf ist sechs Kilometer von der Stadt.
The next village is six kilometres from the town.

Wie groß sind Sie?
How tall are you?

Ich bin ein Meter zweiundsiebzig.
I am 1 metre 72 cm.

Er hat vier und einen halben Meter Stoff.
He has four and a half metres of material.

Das Insekt ist anderthalb Zentimeter (1,5 cm.) lang.
The insect is one and a half centimetres (1.5 cm.) long.

Ein Liter ist etwa ein und drei viertel englische „ Pints ".
A litre is about one and three-quarters (of an) English pint.

Ich brauche sieben Liter Benzin.
I need seven litres (of) petrol.

Der Mann bringt vier Zentner Kohlen.
The man is bringing four hundredweights of coal.
Welches Datum hat der Brief?
What date has the letter ?
Mittwoch, den 19. September 1956.
Wednesday, the 19th of September, 1956.
Sein Freund kommt Sonntag, den 5. August.
His friend comes (on) Sunday, the 5th of August.
Diese Karte aus Österreich ist von Montag, den 7. Januar 1957.
This card from Austria is (dated) (of) Monday, the 7th of January, 1957.
Im Winter ist es kälter als im Sommer.
In winter it is colder than in summer.
Die Tage des Frühlings sind schöner als jene des Herbstes.
The days of (the) spring are more beautiful than those of (the) autumn.
Der Monat Oktober hat einunddreißig Tage.
The month of October has thirty-one days.
Die sieben Tage der Woche vergehen schnell.
The seven days of the week pass quickly.

Finding the Way

der Laden, shop
die Läden, shops
das Geschäft (pl. **-e**), business,
das Postamt, Post Office
die Buchhandlung, bookseller's
die Apotheke, chemist's, pharmacy
das Automobilgeschäft, car-dealer's
das Hutgeschäft, hat shop
der Obstladen, fruit shop
die Photohandlung, photo supplies store
das Papiergeschäft, stationer's
der Zigarrenladen, tobacconist's
der Schuhmacher, shoemaker
der Schneider, tailor
das Konsulat, consulate
britisch, British
die Botschaft, Embassy
die Gesandtschaft, Legation

die Handelskammer, Chamber of Commerce
das Rathaus, town hall
der Arzt, doctor, physician
der Zahnarzt, dentist
der Optiker, optician
das Schuhgeschäft, shoe shop
das Warenhaus, department store
der Weg nach, the way to
der kürzeste Weg nach, the shortest way to
die Karte, map
der Führer, guide book
Wie lange dauert es? How long does it take?
zu Fuß gehen, to go on foot
einen Wagen (Taxi) nehmen, to take a taxi

mit dem Omnibus fahren, to go by bus
die Haltestelle, stop, stopping-place
das Opernhaus, opera house
umsteigen, to change bus, tram, train
den Weg zeigen, to direct
Wo ist das britische Konsulat, bitte? Where is the British Consulate, please?
der Halteplatz für Autotaxen (Taxis), Taxicab rank
mit der Straßenbahn fahren, to go by tram
die Untergrundbahn, underground railway
die Endhaltestelle, terminus
geradeaus, straight on
rechts, to the right
links, to the left

Ist dies der direkte Weg nach dem Rathaus? Is this the direct way to the Town Hall?
Ja, gehen Sie nur geradeaus. Yes, merely go straight on.
Es ist nicht weit. It is not far.
Sie können zu Fuß gehen. You can go on foot.
Wie lange dauert es? How long does it take?
Etwa eine Viertelstunde. About a quarter of an hour.
Auf dem Marktplatz sind viele Läden und Geschäfte. At the market place (there) are many shops and businesses.
Wo ist hier eine gute Buchhandlung? Where is there a good bookshop hereabouts?
In der zweiten Straße nach links. In the second street to the left.
Ich möchte einen Führer der Stadt Berlin haben. I'd like to have a guide to the City of Berlin.

Können Sie mir den kürzesten Weg zum Postamt zeigen?
Could you show me the shortest way to the Post Office?

Nehmen Sie die Straßenbahn! Take the tram.

An der nächsten Ecke ist eine Haltestelle. On the next corner there's a stop.

Wie komme ich zur britischen Botschaft? How do I get to the British Embassy?

Am besten fahren Sie mit der Untergrundbahn. The best is (for) you (to) go by subway.

Sie müssen am Opernhaus umsteigen. You must change at the Opera House.

Sie können auch mit dem Omnibus zur Endhaltestelle fahren. You can also travel by bus to the terminus.

Vor dem Bahnhof ist eine Haltestelle für Autotaxen. In front of the station is a taxicab rank.

Bitte bringen Sie mich zur deutschen Handelskammer. Please take me to the German Chamber of Commerce.

READING

Mein alter Onkel

Mein alter Onkel ist ein komischer Mann.

Warum, was ist mit ihm los?

Er hat einen ungewöhnlichen Pulsschlag—sechzig in der Minute.

Das ist in der Tat ein ungewöhnlicher Zufall.

Sehen Sie, ohne die Hilfe einer Uhr kann er die Zeit für das Kochen der Eier zum Frühstück zuverlässig angeben: drei Minuten. Er kann beim Boxen genau auszählen, wenn einer K.O. ist.

Wirklich?

Auch als ich ihn letzte Woche photographierte, konnte er mir die exakten Belichtungszeiten angeben. Er zählte seinen Puls: drei, vier, fünf . . . und es waren stets drei, vier, fünf Sekunden.

Was für ein Vorteil! Da braucht er keine Uhr mehr. Und ich hoffe, er schenkt Ihnen seine schöne goldene Uhr, bevor sein Puls aufhört zu schlagen.

LITERAL TRANSLATION : *My old uncle is a strange man.*
Why, what's the matter with him ?
He has an unusual pulse beat—sixty to the minute.
That is indeed an unusual coincidence.
Look, without the help of a clock he can time accurately the boiling
of eggs for breakfast : three minutes.   He can count (the seconds) in
boxing when one is K.O.
Really ?
Also when I took a photograph of him last week, he could give (tell)
me the exact exposure periods.   He counted his pulse, three, four,
five . . . it was always three, four, five seconds.
What an advantage !   He does not need a watch any more.   And
I hope he will give you his beautiful golden watch before his pulse ceases
to beat.

§ 4. *Geographical Names and Adjectives : List for Reference—* *Practice—The Post Office—Reading* **Ein Postbote**

As a general rule, the names of countries are neuter, and they
are used without an Article.   But note the exceptions:

die Tschechoslowakei, Czecho-   **die   Niederlande,**   the
slovakia   Netherlands
die Schweiz, Switzerland   **die Türkei,** Turkey

Note : These *always* have the article:

> **Sind Sie in der Schweiz gewesen?**   Have you been in
> Switzerland ?
> **Nein, aber ich werde in die Schweiz gehen.**   No, but
> I shall go to Switzerland.

Note :

> **der Deutsche,** the German (man) ⎱pl. **die Deutschen**
> **die Deutsche,** the German (woman)⎰
> **ein Deutscher** and **eine Deutsche,** pl. **Deutsche**

This is declined like an Adjective with **der** or **die, ein** or **eine**
(see pages, 11, 24).
The Adjective is **deutsch,** an exception to the general rule
that all Adjectives of nationality end in **-ISCH.**   They are all
written with a *small* letter.   Only when they become Nouns is a
capital letter used: **ein Deutscher,** *a German.*

When **GANZ** and **HALB** are used without an article before geographical names, they are not declined. With an article, they are declined:

> **ganz England,** the whole of England (all England)
> **halb London,** the half of London (half London)

but : **das ganze England** and **das halbe London.**

Note :

> **die Vereinigten Staaten,** The United States
> **die Union der Sozialistischen Sowjetrepubliken,** The Union of Socialist Soviet Republics. (Usually referred to as **die Sowjetunion,** *the Soviet Union.*)

> **das Vereinigte Königreich,** The United Kingdom
> **der Weltteil Europa,** the continent of Europe

The feminine of names of inhabitants of countries is formed by adding **-IN** to the name, or by changing **-E** to **-IN:**

> **Der Jugoslawe, die Jugoslawin,** the Jugoslav (man), (woman)

GEOGRAPHICAL NAMES, ADJECTIVES OF NATIONALITY, etc.

The Continents : **Die Erdteile**

Name	*Adjective*	*Inhabitant*
Afrika	**afrikanisch**	**Afrikaner (-in)**
Amerika	**amerikanisch**	**Amerikaner (-in)**
Asien	**asiatisch**	**Asiate (Asiatin)**
Australien	**australisch**	**Australier (-in)**
Europa	**europäisch**	**Europäer (-in)**

Note the following :

> **das Mittelländische Meer,** the Mediterranean Sea
> **die Nordsee,** the North Sea
> **der Kanal,** the Channel
> **die Ostsee,** the Baltic

der **Atlantische Ozean,** the Atlantic Ocean
das **Nördliche Eismeer,** the Arctic Ocean
der **Stille Ozean,** the Pacific Ocean

Country	Adjective	Inhabitant
Belgien, Belgium	belgisch	**Belgier**
Bulgarien, Bulgaria	bulgarisch	**Bulgare**
Dänemark, Denmark	dänisch	**Däne**
Deutschland, Germany	deutsch	**Deutsche**
England, England	englisch	**Engländer**
Finnland, Finland	finnisch	**Finne**
Frankreich, France	französisch	**Franzose**
Griechenland, Greece	griechisch	**Grieche**
Holland, Holland	holländisch	**Holländer**
Irland, Ireland	irisch	**Irländer** or **Ire**
Italien, Italy	italienisch	**Italiener**
Jugoslawien, Jugoslavia	jugoslawisch	**Jugoslawe**
die Niederlande, Netherlands	niederländisch	**Niederländer**
Norwegen, Norway	norwegisch	**Norweger**
Österreich, Austria	österreichisch	**Österreicher**
Polen, Poland	polnisch	**Pole**
Portugal, Portugal	portugiesisch	**Portugiese**
Preußen, Prussia	preußisch	**Preuße**
Rumänien, Roumania	rumänisch	**Rumäne**
Rußland, Russia	russisch	**Russe**
Sachsen, Saxony	sächsisch	**Sachse**
Schottland, Scotland	schottisch	**Schotte**
Schweden, Sweden	schwedisch	**Schwede**
die Schweiz, Switzerland	schweizerisch	**Schweizer**
Spanien, Spain	spanisch	**Spanier**
die Tschechoslowakei, Czechoslovakia	tschecho-slowakisch	**Tscheche**
die Türkei, Turkey	türkisch	**Türke**
Ungarn, Hungary	ungarisch	**Ungar**

This list is for reference. Geographical words are omitted from the Vocabulary at the end of the book.

PRACTICE: **ÜBUNG**

Schreiben Sie einen Brief nach Deutschland?
Are you writing a letter to Germany?
Nein, ich schreibe nach der Schweiz.
No, I am writing to Switzerland.
Schweden und Norwegen sind europäische Länder.
Sweden and Norway are European countries.

Die Sowjetunion ist halb europäisch und halb asiatisch.
The Soviet Union is half European and half Asiatic.

Deutsches Bier und französische Weine sind gut.
German beer and French wines are good.

Fahren Sie durch Belgien und Frankreich in die Schweiz?
Are you travelling through Belgium and France to Switzerland?

Nein, ich fahre im Flugzeug über Deutschland nach Österreich.
No, I'm travelling by 'plane over Germany to Austria.

Drei Italiener und zwei Spanier sind in diesem Hotel.
Three Italians and two Spaniards are in this hotel.

Sind auch Französinnen und Engländerinnen da?
Are there also French and English ladies?

Nein, aber einige Griechinnen und Türkinnen.
No, but (there are) some Greek and Turkish women.

Nur Europäer und keine Amerikaner und Amerikanerinnen.
Only Europeans and no Americans and American women.

Italien, Griechenland und die Türkei liegen am Mittelländischen Meer.
Italy, Greece, and Turkey are situated on the Mediterranean Sea.

Sind die Russen und Polen Freunde? Nicht immer!
Are the Russians and Poles friends? Not always!

Der Kanal ist zwischen England und Europa.
The Channel is between England and Europe.

Schiffe fahren von den Vereinigten Staaten von Amerika über den Atlantischen Ozean nach ganz Europa.
Ships go from the United States of America over the Atlantic Ocean to the whole of Europe.

Im Nördlichen Eismeer ist es kalt.
It is cold in the Arctic Ocean.

Ich gebe diese Blumen der schönen Schottin.
I'm giving these flowers to the beautiful Scottish girl.

Er sprach mit drei jungen Österreichern.
He spoke to three young Austrians.

Ich lese das Buch eines klugen Iren.
I'm reading the book of an intelligent Irishman.

Guter dänischer und holländischer Käse.
Good Danish and Dutch cheese.
Zürich ist eine Stadt in der Schweiz.
Zurich is a town in Switzerland.
Hamburg ist eine deutsche Stadt an der Nordsee.
Hamburg is a German town on the North Sea.
Belgrad ist die Hauptstadt Jugoslawiens.
Belgrade is the capital of Jugoslavia.

The Post Office

das Postamt, post office
die Hauptpost, General Post Office
der Brief, letter
die Briefe, letters
das Paket, parcel
die Pakete, parcels
die Briefmarke, stamp
die Briefmarken, stamps
Briefe ins Ausland, letters for abroad
der eingeschriebene Brief, registered letter
das Porto, postage
die Postanweisung, postal order
die gewöhnliche Post, ordinary post
die Luftpost, air mail
durch Eilboten, by express
die Drucksache, printed matter
als Postpaket, by parcel post
das Zuschlagporto, extra postage
der Inhalt, contents
die Zustellung, delivery

die Versicherung, insurance
Übergewicht haben, to exceed (have overweight)
der Bestimmungsort, destination
der Briefträger, postman
Porto bezahlt, prepaid
unvollständige Adresse, incomplete address
der Empfänger, addressee
das Formular (-e), form(s)
das Telegrammformular, telegram form
der Schalter, office window
Zu welchem Schalter gehe ich? To which window do I go?
ein Telegramm aufgeben, to send a telegram
postlagernde Briefe, letters in *Poste Restante*
einschreiben, to register
erwarten, to expect
ich erwarte, I expect
BEI = c/o (care of); at, near
der Briefumschlag, envelope
die Postkarte, postcard

Inland, interior, inland
Ausland, foreign, abroad
die Einschreibegebühr, registration fee
der Postdirektor, postmaster
die Quittung, receipt
der Absender, sender
die Unterschrift, signature
fortgehen, to go out (of post)

Geht dies heute abend ab? Will this go out this evening, to-night?
ich möchte . . . I want . . .
zerbrechlich, fragile
verderblich, perishable
Wo bekommt man Postanweisungen ausgezahlt? Where are postal orders cashed?

Ich möchte vier Briefmarken zu zwanzig Pfennig, drei zu vierzig Pfennig und sechs Postkarten haben. I should like to have four stamps of 20 dpf., three of 40 dpf. and six post cards.

Ist dieses der Schalter für eingeschriebene Briefe? Is this the office window (counter) for registered letters?

Ich möchte diesen Brief durch Eilboten senden, und dieses ist ein Luftpostbrief ins Ausland. I'd like to send this letter by express, and this is an air mail letter for abroad.

Ihr Brief hat Übergewicht. Your letter has (is) overweight.

Sie müssen doppeltes Porto zahlen. You must pay double postage.

Die Adresse des Empfängers ist unvollständig. The address (of the addressee) is incomplete.

Bitte unterstreichen Sie den Bestimmungsort. Please underline the destination.

Geht die Post noch heute abend ab? Will the mail go out again to-night?

Ich habe hier zwei kleine Pakete und einige Drucksachen. I have here two little parcels and some printed matter.

Sind in diesem Paket zerbrechliche oder verderbliche Sachen? Are (there) in this parcel fragile or perishable things?

Ja, ich möchte sie versichern. Yes, I'd like to insure them.

Die Versicherung des Paketes kostet drei Mark. The insurance of the parcel costs three marks.

Die Einschreibegebühr ist fünfzig Pfennig. The registration fee is 50 dpf.

Hier ist Ihre Quittung. Here is your receipt.

Ich möchte ein Telegramm nach London aufgeben. I should like to send a telegram for (to) London.

Gehen Sie zu dem dritten Schalter. Go to the third (office) window.

Sie bekommen dort Telegrammformulare. You'll get telegram forms there.

Ich erwarte postlagernde Briefe. I expect letters in *poste restante*.

Die Briefumschläge von Drucksachen müssen offen bleiben. The envelopes of printed matter must remain open.

Sie kosten weniger Porto als gewöhnliche Briefe. They cost less postage than ordinary letters.

Wo bekomme ich diese zwei Postanweisungen ausgezahlt? Where do I get these two postal orders cashed?

READING

EIN POSTBOTE

Ein Postbote öffnete seine Lohntüte und fand, daß darin zwanzig Mark zuviel waren. Da seine Frau einen neuen Hut haben wollte und er dafür kein Geld hatte, gab er ihr die 20 Mark und sagte nichts im Büro. Als er in der nächsten Woche seine Lohntüte bekam, fand er, daß darin 20 Mark weniger waren. Sofort ging er ins Büro und meldete den Irrtum.

„ Ja, wirklich," sagte der Kassierer. „ Aber wie ist es mit den 20 Mark, die Sie letzte Woche zuviel erhielten? "

Der Postbote wurde sehr ärgerlich und erwiderte: „ Ich lasse mir einen Irrtum einmal gefallen. Aber ich wende mich dagegen, wenn so etwas zwei Wochen hintereinander vorkommt." —Der Kassierer weigerte sich zu zahlen.

Als der Postbote es seiner Frau erzählte, sagte sie: „ Das macht nichts! Ich habe meinen neuen Hut, und du kannst dem Kassierer dafür danken."

LITERAL TRANSLATION : *A postman opened his pay-packet one week and found that there were DM 20 too many. As his wife wanted a new hat and he had no money for it, he gave her the 20 marks and said nothing about them in the office. Next week when he got his pay-packet, he found that it was 20 marks short. Immediately he went to the office and told them of the error.*

" Yes, indeed," said the cashier, " but how about the 20 marks too much that you received last week? "

The postman was very angry and replied : " I don't mind a mistake once, but I won't have this sort of thing two weeks running." The cashier refused to pay.

When the postman told his wife, she said : " It doesn't matter. I have my new hat, and you can thank the cashier for it."

Note on Reading : You will have noticed that, in the Reading Matter, there are words which have not been met before. Note their meaning from the translation. You must *read the German text several times* once you know the meaning as given in the literal translation. This helps to drive home all that you have learnt.

§ 5. *Structural Words and their Uses—Tenses of Verbs : Past and Present—Past Participles—Simple Word-order—Practice—Hotel and Lodging—Reading :* **TILL EULENSPIEGEL**

There is a large number of words which may be called " structural " because one or more of them will be found in almost any sentence. They help out the other words with structure in regard to meaning. Such English words are *be, not, for, to,* etc., and they may come within any grammatical definition. This is a rather vague category of words, and the term is used merely for convenience and not for a grammatical purpose. You have already met many such words in German and, as they are highly important, they may now be reviewed and expanded. They must be well known, with their uses. For example:

SEIN, to be   **ich bin, er IST, Sie sind**
HABEN, to have   **ich habe, er HAT, Sie haben**
WERDEN, to become—used to form the future:

     ich werde sein, I shall be
     er wird haben, he will have
     Sie werden haben, you will have

NICHT, not

> **Sie werden nicht haben**

MAN, one, somebody, people, they

A very useful little word, corresponding to French *on* in *on dit* = *they say, people say.* Thus:

> **MAN HAT KEINE ZEIT,** one has no time
> **MAN SAGT SO,** they say so

See also Lesson IV, § 5.

SELBST, *self* in an emphatic sense:

> **sie selbst,** herself
> **er selbst,** himself

ALL, *all,* invariable before a masculine or neuter singular adjective of possession:

> **ALL MEIN GELD,** all my money
> **BEIDE,** both: **BEIDE FRAUEN,** both ladies

ABER, but
AN, on, upon
AUF, on
AUS, out of
BEI, at, near, by
DA, there
FORT, forth, away
HIER, here
JA, yes
MIT, with

NACH, towards, *also* after
NEIN, no
NICHTS, nothing
ODER, or
UND, and
WEG, away
ZU, to, towards
ZURÜCK, back
ZUSAMMEN, together

All these are important words, and the list could be expanded even from those already given in the Lessons up to now. But sufficient have been listed here to enable you to recognize a " structural " word, so that whenever you meet what you may consider to be a new one, you must memorize it. Such words turn up again and again in speech and in reading matter.

TENSES OF VERBS: You have already been using the Present Tense of many Verbs: **haben,** *to have.* *Present Tense :* **ich habe,** *I have,* etc. But every Verb has a Past Tense—the Past of **haben** is **ich hatte** and the Past of **SEIN** is **ich war.** These are Verbs which change their " root " vowel and are sometimes called " irregular ", but the term " Strong Verb " is a better one for them. The regular or " Weak " Verbs do not change the vowel in the Past Tense: **LOBEN,** to praise

Present Tense	*Past Tense*
ich LOBE, I praise	**ich lobTE,** I praised
er LOBT, he praises	**er lobTE,** he praised
wir LOBEN, we praise	**wir lobTEN,** we praised
Sie LOBEN, you praise	**Sie lobTEN,** you praised
sie LOBEN, they praise	**sie lobTEN,** they praised

PAST PARTICIPLES: The above are simple tenses, but when we say *I have praised,* this is a compound tense and here " *praised* " is a Past Participle, which in German would be **GElobT** (most German Past Participles have the prefix **GE-**). You have already met many Past Participles and will meet many more. As in English, the German Past Participle can be used as an Adjective. For example, **VERLOREN** is the Past Participle of **VERLIEREN,** *to lose* (the prefix **VER-** does not have **GE-** before it). So one says **das verlorenE Buch,** *the lost book* (**-E** is the appropriate Adjectival ending). **Ich habe gelobt,** *I have praised*.

SIMPLE WORD-ORDER: You cannot fail to have noticed that the Word-order in German sentences often differs from that in English. You must pay careful attention to German Word-order, for which there are fixed rules which can be learnt and must be applied. Here is the order for simple straightforward (direct) sentences:

I	II		II	III
SUBJECT	MAIN VERB	or	AUXILIARY	OBJECT
ich	**habe**			**das Buch**
I	have			the book

When there is a compound tense as *I have had*, *had* (the Past Participle) comes LAST:

ich habe das Buch gehabt, I have had the book

But often there is an object Pronoun, as in the sentence: *I have given him the book.*

him is indirect object, *book* is direct object.

In German this indirect object Pronoun (as in English) comes before the direct, but the Past Participle still goes last:

ich habe ihm das Buch gegeben, I have him the book given

This is enough for the moment. You will remember what you have observed, that in a question the Verb comes first and then the subject:

Habe ich das Buch? Have I the book?
Habe ich das Buch gegeben? Have I given the book?
Habe ich ihm das Buch gegeben? Have I given him the book?

PRACTICE: **ÜBUNG**

Wo sind wir?
Where are we?
Wir sind im Zimmer.
We are in the room.
Ist Ihre Mutter hier?
Is your mother here?
Nein, sie ist nicht hier.
No, she is not here.
Haben Sie sie gesehen?
Have you seen her?
Ja, ich habe sie heute gesehen.
Yes, I have seen her to-day.
Wird Ihr Freund morgen kommen?
Will your friend come to-morrow?
Er wird morgen nicht kommen.
He will not come to-morrow.

Wann wird er hier sein?
When will he be here?
Er wird nächste Woche hier sein.
He will be here next week.
Werden wir viel Arbeit haben?
Shall we have much work?
Nein, wir werden nicht viel Arbeit haben.
No, we shall not have much work.
Hat man das gehört?
Has one heard that?
Man hat es nicht gehört.
They have not heard it.
Man fährt mit dem Zug.
People travel by train.
Ich bin selbst gekommen.   (*Note:* **bin,** *not* **habe.**)
I myself have come.
Haben Sie selbst das Paket getragen?
Have you yourself carried the parcel?
Wir selbst werden dies machen.
We ourselves shall do (make) this.
Sie selbst hat es ihm gesagt.
She herself has said it to him.
Ich gebe all mein Geld weg, aber ich gebe nicht alle meine Briefe.
I give away all my money, but I do not give all my letters.
Ich habe beide Männer gesehen.
I have seen both men.
Er hat mir nichts gesagt.
He has said nothing to me.
Wann werden Sie zurück sein?
When will you be back?
Ist das Haus groß oder klein?
Is the house big or small?
Die Mutter kommt mit dem Kind.
The mother comes with the child.
Wir gehen zusammen zu dem Lehrer.
We are going together to the teacher.

Der Ball liegt bei dem Stein.
The ball lies by (near) the stone.
Hier und da ist ein Baum.
Here and there is a tree.
Auf der Brücke ist eine Bank.
On the bridge is a bench.
Er schläft nach der Arbeit.
He sleeps after work.
Wir lobten die Mädchen.   We praised the girls.
Haben Sie auch den Knaben gelobt? Have you also
praised the boy?
Nein, wir haben ihn nicht gelobt.
No, we have not praised him.
Er verlor seine Uhr.
He lost his watch.
Wo hat er sie verloren?
Where has he lost it?
Er hat es nicht gesagt.
He has not said (it).
Wir werden ihn fragen.
We shall ask him.
Warum haben Sie ihn nicht heute morgen gefragt?
Why have you not asked him this morning?
Ich fragte ihn zweimal, aber er hat keine Antwort gegeben.
I asked him twice, but he has given no answer.
Wann haben Sie den Brief bekommen?
When did you get the letter?
Ich habe ihn schon lange gehabt.
I have had it already (a) long (time).

Hotel and Lodging

das Hotel, hotel
die Pension, boarding-house
das Zimmer, room
das Schlafzimmer, bedroom
mit Bad, with bath
im Zentrum, center (of a
town or city)

ein größeres
ein kleineres } **Zimmer,**
ein billigeres
bigger, smaller, cheaper—
room
der Vorname, Christian
name

das Geburtsdatum, date of birth

der Geburtsort, place of birth

der Familienname, surname

die Nationalität, nationality

ausfüllen, to fill up

Füllen Sie das Formular aus, fill up the form

der Sitz, seat, chair

der ständige Wohnsitz, permanent address

ein Einzelzimmer, single room **(mit einem Bett)** with one bed

ein Doppelzimmer mit zwei Betten, a double room with two beds

ich möchte das Zimmer sehen, I'd like to see the room

teuer, expensive

billig, cheap

die Nummer, number (of room)

das Badezimmer, bathroom

der Speisesaal, dining-room

wecken, to call, awaken

stören, to disturb

der Schlüssel, key

die Treppe, stairs

mit warmem und kaltem Wasser, with hot and cold water

ohne Verpflegung, without meals

die Bedienung, service

Prozent, per cent

in Ordnung, ready, in order

das Anmeldeformular, registration form

außerhalb der Stadt, outside the town

für eine Nacht, für eine Woche, for a night, week

der Fahrstuhl, lift, elevator

die Sachen, belongings

warten, to wait

Herein! Come in!

zumachen, to shut

die Schuhe putzen, to clean shoes

Sie finden einige gute Hotels am Bahnhof und im Zentrum der Stadt. You (will) find some good hotels at the station and in the center of the town.

Ich möchte ein Einzelzimmer haben. I'd like to have a single room.

Hier ist ein größeres Zimmer mit Bad. Here is a larger room with bath.

Wir haben auch kleinere und billigere Zimmer. We also have smaller and cheaper rooms.

Alle unsere Schlafzimmer sind mit warmem und kaltem

Wasser. All our bedrooms have (are with) warm and cold water.

Sie können auch ein Zimmer ohne Verpflegung haben. You can also have a room without meals.

Hier ist der Schlüssel. Here is the key.

Die Nummer Ihres Zimmers ist 12. The number of your room is 12.

Wir berechnen zehn Prozent für Bedienung. We charge ten per cent for service.

Der Fahrstuhl ist links von der Treppe. The lift is (to the) left of the stairs.

Wollen Sie morgens geweckt werden? Do you want to be called in the morning?

Ja, bitte, um (ein) viertel vor acht. Yes, please, at a quarter to eight.

Möchten Sie Tee im Zimmer haben? Would you like to have tea in your room?

Nein, ich komme in den Speisesaal. No, I'll come to the dining room.

Stellen Sie Ihre Schuhe vor die Tür. Put your shoes outside (in front of) the door.

Der Diener wird Ihre Schuhe putzen. The servant will clean your shoes.

Herein! Come in!

Störe ich? Do I disturb (you)?

In the Reading which follows, the meaning of every word is given as near to it as possible. Note all new words. When the passage is understood read the German over several times.

READING: From **TILL EULENSPIEGEL**

Als Till Eulenspiegel noch ein kleiner Junge war und
When Till Eulenspiegel was still a small boy and
nicht viel von der Art der Leute wußte, da ging er eines
did not know much of the nature of (the) people, he went one
Tages mit seinem Vater Klaus über Land. Sie hatten
day with his father Claus into the country. They had

ihren Esel bei sich; denn sie wollten Mehl von einer
their ass with them; for they wanted to fetch flour from a
Mühle holen. Der Graue trabte daher auch noch ganz
mill. The grey (ass) trotted along still quite
unbelastet zwischen ihnen.
unburdened between them.

Da spotteten die Leute, denen sie begegneten, und
Then the people jeered, whom they met, and
sagten: „ Seht die beiden Narren. Sie haben einen Esel
said, " Look the two fools. They have an ass
mit sich, könnten reiten, aber gehen zu Fuß.
with them, (they) could ride, but go on foot."

Eigentlich haben die Leute recht, dachte sich Till und
Really the people are right, thought Till and
setzte sich auf den Esel. Als aber nun wieder Leute
seated himself on the ass. But when now again people
vorüberkamen, waren die auch nicht zufrieden. Sie
passed these too were not content. They
schimpften Till einen faulen Schlingel, der seinen alten
called Till a⋅ lazy rascal who lets his old
Vater laufen lasse.
father walk.

Flugs stieg Till vom Esel; denn er dachte, die Leute
Quickly Till got off the ass; for he thought the people
möchten wohl recht haben. Statt dessen ritt nun Vater
might well be right. Instead now father
Klaus auf dem Grautier.
Claus rode on the grey animal (ass).

[Contd. on page 103.

LESSON IV

§ 1. *Personal Pronouns : Table—Forms of Address—Reflexive Pronouns and* **SELBST**—*Agreement of Pronouns—Practice —In the Hotel or Boarding-house—Reading :* **TILL EULEN-SPIEGEL**—*contd.*

A PRONOUN is a word used to take the place of a Noun. It is a " substitute word ". Thus: " He gave *it* to me "—*it* is a Pronoun taking the place of some Noun, *me* also is a Personal Pronoun, the indirect object of *gave*. The Pronouns in German are declined and, once learnt, are not difficult to use.

Many of the Pronouns in the list below have already been met, and it is now advisable to learn them all. Most of them are in everyday use. It is perhaps also advisable to refer to page 10 for the use of the cases: they are even more important in the Pronouns than in Nouns, *and must be well known.*

TABLE OF PERSONAL PRONOUNS

Person	Nominative	Genitive	Dative	Accusative
1	**ICH,** I	**MEINER,** of me	**MIR,** to me	**MICH,** me
2	**DU,** thou	**DEINER,** of thee	**DIR,** to thee	**DICH,** thee
3	**ER,** he (it)	**SEINER,** of him (it)	**IHM,** to him	**IHN,** him
	SIE, she (it)	**IHRER,** of her	**IHR,** to her	**SIE,** her
	ES, it	**SEINER,** of it	**IHM,** to it	**ES,** it
Plural				
1	**WIR,** we	**UNSER,** our, of us	**UNS,** to us	**UNS,** us
2	**IHR,** you (ye)	**EUER,** of you	**EUCH,** to you, ye	**EUCH,** you, ye
3	**SIE,** they	**IHRER,** of them	**IHNEN,** to them	**SIE,** them
Note :	**Sie,** you *	**Ihrer,** of you	**Ihnen,** to you	**Sie,** you

* In English the Pronouns *thou* and *ye*, Second Person Singular and plural, are no longer used. We always say *you* = **Sie.**

97

In German there are three forms of address, only one of which need ever be used by the foreigner unless there is some very good reason otherwise. This is the form **Sie,** which is the Third Person Plural **sie,** but written with a capital **S** to distinguish it. **Sie,** *you,* takes the same form of the Verb as **sie,** *they.* Thus:

Sie sind, you are   **Sie haben,** you have
sie sind, they are   **sie haben,** they have

Sie, *you,* is the polite form used in everyday intercourse among German-speaking people. The safest rule for the stranger is to use it, at all events until he knows the language well, and always unless he feels sure that he will not cause offence or laughter by using one of the other two forms given below.

The familiar form **DU** in the singular (plural **IHR**) is used to address animals, close friends, relations, children, the Deity. It is also used in poetry and in the solemn language of religion and prayer. The plural **IHR** is often used by speakers addressing an audience.

Hence, in this book **Sie,** *you,* is used throughout, but in some of the Reading and in the treatment of Verbs the forms for **DU** and **IHR** will be given for the sake of completeness. This is the easiest way to learn those forms, and one day the learner will no doubt wish to read German poetry, especially lyrical poetry, and German literature in general, in which all three forms may be found.

AGREEMENT OF PRONOUNS: Care must be taken to use Pronouns in the genders and cases corresponding to those of the objects to which they refer:

Wo ist der Vater? ER ist nicht hier.
Wo ist die Mutter? SIE ist hier.
Wo ist das Kind? ES ist dort.

Haben Sie meinen Stock? Ich habe IHN. *Masc.*: I have IT.
Haben Sie die Blume? Ich habe SIE. *Fem.*: I have IT.

Note this idiomatic use :

Wer ist es?   Who is it?
Ich bin ES.   It is I.
Er ist ES.   It is he.
Wer war es?   Who was it?
Sie war ES.   It was she.

And :

Ich bin krank und mein Bruder ist ES auch.   I am ill
and my brother is (it) also.
ES WAR EINMAL EIN MANN . . .   There was once
a man . . .

PRONOUNS WITH REFLEXIVE VERBS: When the action of a
Verb is referred back to the subject (Nominative), the Verb is
called a Reflexive Verb (for which see Lesson VI, § 4), and such
Verbs require a Pronoun object (Accusative).   Such Pronouns
are often called Reflexive Pronouns.   In English they are
expressed by *-self*, as in *I wash myself, you wash yourself*, etc.
Such Verbs are more frequent in German than in English (see
page 194).   In German the accusatives of the first person
(**MICH**, singular, **UNS**, plural) and of the second person
(**DICH**, singular, **EUCH**, plural) are used as Reflexive Pronouns of the first and second persons, respectively; and **SICH**
is used as the reflexive of **SIE**, *you*, and for all genders, singular
and plural, of the third person.   Thus:

ich wasche MICH, I wash myself
du wäschst DICH, thou washest thyself
er wäscht SICH, he washes himself
wir waschen UNS, we wash ourselves
ihr wascht EUCH, you (ye) wash yourselves
sie waschen SICH, they wash themselves

And :

Sie waschen sich, you wash yourself

The word **SELBST**, as noted on page 89, **also meaning** *self*
is used only to emphasize any Personal Pronoun:

ich SELBST, I myself
er selbst hat es getan, he himself has done it
Sie selbst, you yourself

Do not confuse **SELBST** with the reflexive.   Compare the
following:

er tötete SICH, he killed himself (reflexive)
er SELBST tötete den Hund, he himself killed the dog

SELBST placed in front of a Noun or Pronoun expresses
even.   Thus:

SELBST ICH WASCHE MICH, even I wash myself
SELBST SEINE MUTTER LOBT IHN NICHT,
even his mother does not praise him

Practice: **ÜBUNG**

Wo ist *das* Geld ?—*Es* ist nicht hier.
Sind *die* Kinder hier ?—*Sie* sind hier.
Ist *der* Bote gekommen ?—*Er* ist gekommen.
Wo ist *die* Tochter ?—*Sie* ist im Garten.
Haben Sie *den* Vater gesehen ?—Ich habe *ihn* gesehen.
Gibt er Ihnen *das* Buch ?—Er gibt *es mir.*
Mein Kind, bringst du *das* Brot ?—Ja, Mutter, ich bringe *es
dir.*
Hat *der* Knabe *seine* Schuhe ?—*Er* hat *sie.*
Hat das Mädchen *seinen* Ring ?—*Es* hat *ihn.*
Trägt *die* Frau *ihren* Hut ?—*Sie* trägt *ihn.*
Gibt *die* Mutter *ihrem* Kind einen Kuß ?—*Sie* gibt *ihm* einen
Kuß.
Geben *die* Männer *dem* Pferd *das* Wasser ?   *Sie* geben *es ihm.*
Haben *Sie es mir* gesagt ?—Ich habe *es Ihnen* nicht gesagt.
Bekommen *wir unsere* Äpfel ?—*Ihr* bekommt *eure* Äpfel.

Ich freue *mich* über das Bild, aber mein *Freund* freut *sich* nicht
darüber.

Wir alle freuen *uns*, Sie zu sehen. Meine *Mutter* freut *sich* auch.

Freuen *sich die Jungen* auch? *Das* kleine Kind freut *sich*.

Erinnern *Sie sich meiner?*—Ja, *ich* erinnere *mich Ihrer* gut.
(Do you remember me?—Yes, I remember you well.)

Meine Tochter erinnert sich Ihrer nicht.
(My daughter does not remember you.)

Die kleinen Katzen waschen sich selbst.
(The little kittens wash themselves.)

Wir waschen uns jeden Tag.
(We wash ourselves every day.)

In the Hotel or Boarding-house : **Im Hotel oder in der Pension**

die Diele, lounge
die Flasche, bottle
die Wärmflasche, hot-water bottle
der Blick, glance, gleam
der Augenblick, moment
warten Sie einen Augenblick, wait a moment
der (die) Kassierer(-in), cashier
das Frühstück, breakfast
das Mittagessen, midday meal, lunch
das Abendessen, evening meal, dinner, supper
einberechnet, including
klingeln, to ring (for)
die Klingel, bell
die Nachtklingel, night bell
die Wäsche, laundry
die Besorgung, message

abreisen, to leave
Ich bitte um die Rechnung. I'd like to have the bill
das Kopfkissen, pillow
die Seife, soap
das Tuch, cloth
das Handtuch, towel
treffen, to meet
ich treffe, I meet
treffen wir uns, let us meet
bringen, to bring
bringen Sie mir . . . bring me . . .
das Zimmermädchen, chambermaid
der Portier, hall-porter
der Nachtportier, night porter
in einem Hotel absteigen, to stay at a hotel

der Bote, messenger

ich bitte um . . . I should like . . .

Heute abend werde ich abreisen. I shall be leaving this evening

Wann muß ich mein Zimmer verlassen? When must I vacate my room?

Jetzt gehe ich schlafen. I'm going to bed now

ich soll, I must (a duty)

soll ich? must I?

bezahlen, to pay

ich bezahle, I pay

Wo soll ich meine Rechnung bezahlen? Where shall I pay my bill?

ich fahre von hier nach . . . I'm going from here to . . .

bei, at, with

bei Ihnen, with you

zuviel, too much

berechnen, to charge

Sie berechnen zuviel. You're charging too much

Geben Sie mir, give me

die Rechnung, bill

die quittierte Rechnung, receipted bill

schicken, to send

die Post, mail

Bitte schicken Sie meine Post nach . . . Please send my mail to . . .

wiederkommen, to return

ich hoffe, I hope (**hoffen,** to hope)

ich werde bald wiederkommen, I'll soon return

Auf Wiedersehen! Till we meet again. (*Au revoir.*)

Wann sind die Mahlzeiten hier im Hotel? When are the mealtimes (here) in the hotel?

Das Frühstück ist von halb acht bis neun Uhr. Breakfast is from half past seven till nine o'clock.

Auf Wunsch können Sie es schon früher haben. If you wish you can have it (already) earlier.

Das Mittagessen wird um ein Uhr im Speisesaal serviert. Lunch is served at one o'clock in the dining-room.

Abendessen gibt es von 7 bis 8 Uhr 30. Evening meals from 7 to 8.30.

In Ihrem Zimmer ist eine Klingel; klingeln Sie bitte, wenn Sie etwas wünschen. In your room (there) is a bell; ring please if you want anything.

Das Zimmermädchen wird Ihnen sofort Seife und ein sauberes Handtuch bringen. The chambermaid will at once bring you soap and a clean towel.

Ich möchte gern ein anderes Kopfkissen haben. I'd like to have another pillow.

Würden Sie mir bitte auch eine Wärmflasche bringen! Would you bring me please also a hot-water bottle.

Ist im Hotel ein Herr Schmidt abgestiegen? Is (there) a Mr. Schmidt staying at the hotel?

Einen Augenblick, bitte! A moment please.

Ich will einmal nachsehen. I'll just have a look.

Er ist in der Vorhalle; Sie können ihn dort treffen. He is in the lounge; you can meet him there.

Ich werde morgen abreisen. I shall leave to-morrow.

Wann muß ich dann mein Zimmer verlassen? When must I (then) vacate my room?

Um Mittag. At midday.

Geben Sie mir bitte die Rechnung. Give me the bill please.

Ich glaube, Sie haben zuviel für das Zimmer berechnet. I believe you have charged too much for the room.

Entschuldigen Sie bitte! Pardon me!

Da ist ein kleiner Fehler unterlaufen. There is (occurred) a little mistake.

Wollen Sie Ihre Hotelrechnung in bar bezahlen? Do you want to pay your hotel bill in cash?

Der Kassierer wird Ihnen eine quittierte Rechnung geben. The cashier will give you a receipted bill.

Wie hat es Ihnen bei uns gefallen? How did you like it with us?

Es hat mir bei Ihnen ausgezeichnet gefallen. I liked it very much (with you).

Kommen Sie bald wieder. Come again soon.

Auf Wiedersehen! Au revoir!

READING: **TILL EULENSPIEGEL**—*contd.*

Die nächsten, an denen sie vorüberkamen, fingen nun
The next ones whom they passed (by) started now
erst recht zu schelten an: „ Der große, gesunde Kerl setzt
all the more to chide : " The big, healthy fellow sits

sich auf den Esel. Aber den kleinen, schwachen Jungen
on the ass. But he lets the small weak boy
läßt er hinterherlaufen."
trail behind."

Da wollte nun Till es allen recht machen und stieg zu
Then Till wanted to make it right to all and climbed up
seinem Vater auf den Esel. Jetzt fingen die Leute jedoch
next to his father on the ass. Now, the people, however, started
erst richtig an, mit den Fingern auf sie zu zeigen. „ Seht
properly to point (with the) fingers at them. " Look
die beiden Bauernlümmel," sagten sie, „ die Tierquäler
at the two peasant ruffians," they said, " the tormentors
setzen sich beide auf den mageren Esel und scheren sich
of animals seat themselves both upon the thin (skinny) ass and don't
nicht um das arme Tier."
care for the poor animal."

„ Da bleibt uns nur noch eines," sagte Till zu seinem
" There remains only one thing," Till said to his
Vater, „ wir müssen absteigen und den Esel tragen."
father, " We must get off and carry the ass."
Und so machten sie es. Da hielt man sie denn alle drei
And so they did. Now, one took them all three
für Esel und rechte Narren. Eulenspiegel aber hatte
for asses and proper fools. Eulenspiegel thus
entdeckt, daß man es den Leuten nicht recht machen kann,
discovered that one cannot make it right for (the) people
wie immer man es treibt.
whatever one does. [Contd. on page 109.

§ 2. *Relative Pronouns : Declension—Agreement—Word-order :*
*Rule in Relative Clauses—***DER JENIGE***—Practice—Food*
—Menu, etc.—Reading : **TILL EULENSPIEGEL***—contd.*

A Relative Pronoun is one which refers to some Noun which
has gone before, and it also connects two statements which
together form a sentence. Thus:

The house in *which* I live is a good one.
The house *that* Jack built.

The girl *whom* I saw with you yesterday.
The boy *whose* pencil was lost.

Which, that, whom, and *whose* are Relative Pronouns.

In English we also can say: *The house Jack built. The girl I saw with you yesterday.* This is quite usual in our everyday speech, in which the Relative Pronoun is often omitted. In German the Relative is *never* omitted, and therefore it is important to know these Pronouns and how to use them.

There are two main forms in German for the English Relative Pronouns *who, which,* and *that.* They are: **DER** and **WELCHER,** which are declined as follows:

	Masc.	*Fem.*	*Neuter*	*Plural :* *All genders*
N.	**DER,** who, which	**DIE,** who, which	**DAS,** that, which	**DIE,** who, which, that
G.	**DESSEN**	**DEREN**	**DESSEN**	**DEREN,** whose, of which
D.	**DEM**	**DER**	**DEM**	**DENEN,** to whom, to which
A.	**DEN**	**DIE**	**DAS**	**DIE,** whom, which, that
N.	**WELCHER**	**WELCHE**	**WELCHES**	**WELCHE,** who, that
G.	**DESSEN**	**DEREN**	**DESSEN**	**DEREN** etc.
D.	**WELCHEM**	**WELCHER**	**WELCHEM**	**WELCHEN**
A.	**WELCHEN**	**WELCHE**	**WELCHES**	**WELCHE**

Note that **DER** is declined like the Demonstrative Pronoun **DER** and not like the Definite Article. See page 11 and page 111. **WELCHER** differs from the Adjective **WELCHER** only in the Genitive. **DER** is more commonly used than **WELCHER.**

The German Relative agrees in gender and number with the Noun to which it refers. Thus:

DER KNABE, DER ...	**DER KNABE, WELCHER ...**	The boy who ...
DIE BLUME, DIE ...	**DIE BLUME, WELCHE ...**	The flower which, that ...
DAS MÄDCHEN, DAS ...	**DAS MÄDCHEN WELCHES ...**	The girl who ...

Note that in German there is a comma after the subject (nominative), though not necessarily so in English. Not only must the relative sentence in German be within commas, but the gender and case of the antecedent (**der Knabe, die Blume, das Mädchen**) and of the relative depends (as in English) each on its function in its own part of the sentence. Thus:

Das Mädchen, DAS an der Tür ist, ist meine Schwester. The girl who is at the door is my sister.

Die Frau, DEREN Hut verloren ging, ist meine Mutter. The lady whose hat got lost is my mother.

Word-order in relative sentences (clauses) : It will be seen that " *who is at the door* ", " *whose hat is lost* " become " *who at the door is* " and " *whose hat lost got* " in German.

Rule : AFTER THE RELATIVES **DER** AND **WELCHER** THE VERB IS PLACED AT THE END OF THE SENTENCE.

This rule covers simple straightforward sentences. When there is a compound tense of a Verb, made with, for example, an auxiliary + a Past Participle, in German the Past Participle comes first in these relative sentences, and the auxiliary at the end. Thus:

DIE FRAU, WELCHE IHREN HUT VERLOREN HAT, IST HIER. The lady who has lost her hat is here.

HIER IST DIE BLUME, DIE ICH GESEHEN HABE. Here is the flower (that) I have seen.

Word-order in a German sentence will be dealt with more fully in Lesson IX, § 4. Meantime, strict attention must be given to what is said above.

DERJENIGE, meaning *this one, the one, the one which, that,* is a useful and common antecedent for the relative when there is no Noun as an antecedent. Thus:

DERJENIGE, DER HIER IST, IST MEIN BRUDER.
This one ⎫
The one ⎭ who is here is my brother.

It is fully declined as follows:

	Masc.	Fem.	Neuter	All genders
N.	DERJENIGE	DIEJENIGE	DASJENIGE	DIEJENI-GEN
G.	DESJENIGEN	DERJENIGEN	DESJENIGEN	DERJENI-GEN
D.	DEMJENIGEN	DERJENIGEN	DEMJENIGEN	DENJENI-GEN
A.	DENJENIGEN	DIEJENIGE	DASJENIGE	DIEJENI-GEN

Note that the Article in this compound word follows the normal declension of the Article, and -jenige the declension of an Adjective (see page 24).

Practice: ÜBUNG

Der Bote, der den Brief bringt, ist hier. Wo ist der Mann, den Sie gesehen haben? Der Garten, dessen Tor offen ist, ist schön. Der Hund, dem der Mann Wasser gibt, ist krank. Bringt er das Buch, welches ich haben will? Das Mädchen, dessen Hände kalt sind, geht in das Haus. Das Schiff, mit dem (or : welchem) er fährt, kommt von London.

Die Frau, die er liebt, ist reich. Die Tasse, aus welcher er trinkt, ist schön. Ist dieses die Freundin, die er erwartet? Die Bank, auf der (or : welcher) er sitzt, ist rot. Die Vögel, welche singen, sind auf dem Dach. Wir haben keine Zimmer, deren Wände rot sind. Die Mütter, deren Kinder gut sind, sind glücklich. Die Schuhe, in denen er geht, sind braun. Menschen, welchen es nicht gut geht, sind unglücklich. Sind dieses die Dinge, die er haben will?

Ist dieses der Zug, mit dem Ihr Bruder kommt?—Es ist derjenige, mit dem er kommt. Diejenige, die ich gesehen habe, ist seine Schwester. Dasjenige, das ich haben möchte, kann ich nicht bekommen. Diejenigen, die Gutes tun, sind zu loben. Ich sah denjenigen, dem ich das Geld gab. Sind dieses die Blumen, welchen Sie Wasser gegeben haben? Nein, es sind nicht diejenigen, denen ich es gegeben habe.

Food—Menu, etc.*

die Speisekarte, menu
der Tee, tea
der Kaffee, coffee
die Tasse, cup
die Tasse Tee, Kaffee, cup of tea, coffee
die Butter, butter
das Brot, bread
das Ei, egg; die Eier, eggs
gekocht, boiled
hart gekochtes Ei, hard-boiled egg
weich gekochtes Ei, soft-boiled egg
die Spiegeleier, fried eggs
das Rührei, scrambled egg
Rühreier auf Toast, scrambled eggs on toast
verlorenes Ei, poached egg
der Speck, bacon
Eier und Speck , bacon and eggs
geröstetes Brot, toast (also Toast)
der Schinken, ham
die Schokolade, chocolate
die Sahne, cream
der Tisch, table
zweimal Tee, tea for two
Wir möchten einen Tisch für zwei Personen. We'd like a table for two
einmal Kaffee, coffee for one

(das) Brötchen und Butter, roll and butter
Herr Ober! Waiter!
der Oberkellner, head waiter
Danke, no thank you (at table)
der Pfeffer, pepper
reichen Sir mir bitte . . . please pass me the . . .
der Haferbrei, porridge
das Omelett, omelette
Bitte, nehmen Sie das weg. Please remove this
das Messer, knife
die Gabel, fork
der Löffel, spoon
der Teller, plate
bedienen, to serve
schnell, quickly
Bedienen Sie uns schnell, serve us quickly
die Portion, portion
Bitte. Ja, bitte. Yes, please
das Salz, salt
bestellen, to order
bestellt, ordered
Das habe ich nicht bestellt. I didn't order it
die Milch, milk
Das stimmt nicht. That's not correct
Kann ich mit (dative) . . . sprechen? Can I speak to . . .?

* See also pages 114, 223.

Herr Ober, wir möchten einen Tisch für drei Personen.
Waiter, we should like to have a table for three.

Geben Sie mir bitte die Speisekarte. Give me the menu,
please.

Ich möchte einmal Schinken und Eier, und Toast. I'd
like ham and eggs for one, and toast.

**Für meine Frau bringen Sie zwei weich gekochte Eier,
Brötchen und Butter.** For my wife, bring two soft boiled
eggs, rolls and butter.

**Für das Kind Haferbrei mit Milch und eine Schokolade
mit Sahne.** For the child porridge with milk and chocolate
with cream.

Wollen Sie auch ein Omelett? Do you want an omelette
too?

Danke! No, thanks.

Bedienen Sie uns bitte schnell. Serve us quickly, please.

Nehmen Sie das Rührei auf Toast weg. Take away the
scrambled egg on toast.

Wir haben es nicht bestellt. We have not ordered it.

**Wollen Sie mir bitte noch ein Messer und einen Löffel
geben.** Will you give me please another knife and a spoon.

Reichen Sie mir bitte Pfeffer und Salz. Please pass me
(the) pepper and salt.

Bringen Sie zweimal Kaffee, Herr Ober! Waiter, bring
coffee for two, please!

Hier ist die Rechnung. Here is the bill.

Stimmt es? Is it correct?

Nein, das stimmt nicht. No, that's not correct.

READING: **TILL EULENSPIEGEL**—*contd.*

Schon war Eulenspiegel ein rechter kleiner Schelm
Already Eulenspiegel had become quite a little rascal
geworden und trieb allerlei Unfug, da zogen seine Eltern
and got up to (committed) all kinds of mischief, when his parents
von Kneitlingen in das Magdeburgische nach Saaldorf,
moved from Kneitlingen to Saaldorf in the Magdeburgh (County),

nicht weit von Helmstedt.   Dort war Tills Mutter her
not far from Helmstedt.   There Till's mother was from
und sie wohnten nun in einem Haus an dem Flüßchen
and they lived now in a house by the little river
Saal.   Hier starb sein guter Vater, und Eulenspiegel
Saal.   Here his good father died, and Eulenspiegel
blieb mit seiner verarmten Mutter allein. Obwohl Till
remained alone with his impoverished mother.   Although Till
nun schon bald sechzehn Jahre alt war, hatte er doch
was by now nearly sixteen years of age, he had
noch kein rechtes Handwerk gelernt, nur Kunststücke,
not yet learnt a proper trade, only tricks
wie sie umherziehende Gaukler können.
(such) as travelling jugglers know.

Das Haus an der Saal, in dem Eulenspiegel mit seiner
The house by the Saal, in which Eulenspiegel lived with his
Mutter wohnte, hatte in seinem spitzen Dachgiebel einen
mother,   had   under   its   pointed   gable   (roof)   a
Bodenraum.   Dort spannte Till ein Seil und lernte
loft.   There   Till   put   up   a   rope   and   learnt
heimlich darauf zu laufen; denn seine Mutter wollte es
secretly to walk on it; for his mother would not
nicht leiden.
allow it.

[Contd. on page 117.

Note: Words will sometimes be found in the Reading which are not given in the Vocabulary at the end of the book. That Vocabulary is intended for general purposes, not for this special reading, in which less useful words are often met.

3. *Interrogative Pronouns*—**WAS FÜR EIN . . .?**—*Possessive Pronouns : Formation*—*Practice*—*In the Restaurant : Dishes — Cartoon — Reading :* **TILL EULENSPIEGEL** —*contd.*

The Interrogative Pronouns ask questions and are declined. They are: *Who? What? Which (one)?* = **WER? WAS? WELCHER? WER** and **WAS** are declined as follows:

Nominative	**WER?** Who?	**WAS?** What
Genitive	**WESSEN?** Whose?	**WESSEN?** Of what?
Dative	**WEM?** To whom?	**WEM?** To what?
Accusative	**WEN?** Whom?	**WAS?** What?

WELCHER is declined like **DIESER.** Thus:

			Plural :
Masc.	*Fem.*	*Neuter*	*All genders*
N. **WELCHER**	**WELCHE**	**WELCHES**	**WELCHE** Which?
G. **WELCHES**	**WELCHER**	**WELCHES**	**WELCHER** Of which?
D. **WELCHEM**	**WELCHER**	**WELCHEM**	**WELCHEN** To which?
A. **WELCHEN**	**WELCHE**	**WELCHES**	**WELCHE** Which?

WER IST DIESER MANN? Who is this man?

WESSEN BUCH IST ES? Whose book is it?

WEM GEHÖRT DAS BUCH? To whom does the book belong?

WEN SAHEN SIE? Whom did you see?

WAS SAGEN SIE? What do you say?

WESSEN FREUEN SIE SICH? Of what are you pleased?

WEM GIBT ER NACH? To what does he give in?

WAS IST GESCHEHEN? What has happened?

Welcher = *which*, of two or more:

WELCHER MANN IST DORT? Which man is there?

WELCHE DAME MEINEN SIE? Which lady do you mean?

HIER SIND DREI BÜCHER. WELCHES WOLLEN SIE? Here are three books. Which one do you want?

What kind of (a) . . . ? is expressed by the interrogative phrase **WAS FÜR EIN** . . . ? The **EIN** is declined in the ordinary way. Thus:

1. **WAS FÜR EIN MANN IST IHR BRUDER?** What kind of a man is your brother?
2. **WAS FÜR EIN MÄDCHEN IST SEINE SCHWESTER?** What kind of a girl is his sister?
3. **WAS FÜR EINE FRAU IST SEINE MUTTER?** What kind of a lady is his mother?
4. **WAS FÜR EINEM KIND HABEN SIE DAS GELD GEGEBEN?** To what kind of a child have you given the money?
5. **WAS FÜR EINEN BOTEN HAT ER GESANDT?** What kind of a messenger has he sent?

Note **einEM** and **EinEN,** dative and accusative, after the Verbs **gegeben** and **gesandt.**

The corresponding plural is formed: **WAS FÜR WELCHE . . .** Thus:

WAS FÜR WELCHE TIERE GIBT ES IM WALDE? What kinds of animals are in the wood?

In answering these questions, the Adjective or Adjectives follow their usual declension (see page 24). Thus:

1. **Er ist ein GUTER.** He is a good (man). (*Masc.*)
2. **Es ist ein GUTES.** It is a good (one). (*Neut.*)
3. **Sie ist EINE GUTE.** It is a good (one). (*Fem.*)
4. **EinEM GUTEN.** To a good (one). (*Dative case.*)
5. **EinEN GUTEN.** A good (one). (*Accusative case.*)

Note well that in each reply the Article and Adjective follow the gender and case of the Noun in the question.

FORMATION OF POSSESSIVE PRONOUNS: These, which must not be confused with the Possessive Adjectives (for which see page 12) are formed from the Possessive Adjectives in the following ways:

I. By adding **-ER, -E, -ES** to the possessive Adjectives, as **meinER, meinE, meinES.**

II. By prefixing the Definite Article and adding **-E,** as **Der meinE, die meinE, das meinE.**

III. By prefixing the Definite Article and adding **-IGE,** as **der meinIGE, die meinIGE, das meinIGE.**

Thus:

Ist das Ihr Hut? Is it (that) your hat?

1. **Ja, es ist MEINER.** Yes, it is mine. *No Article.*
2. **Ja, es ist DER MEINE.** Yes, it is mine. *With Article.*
3. **Ja, es ist DER MEINIGE.** Yes, it is mine. *With Article.*

Table : *Possessive Adjectives and Pronouns*

Personal Pronouns	Possessive Adjectives	Possessive Pronouns I	II	III
ICH, I	**MEIN,**[1] my	**MEINER,**[2] mine	der **MEINE**[3]	der **MEINIGE**[4]
DU, thou	**DEIN,** thy	**DEINER,** thine	**DEINE**	**DEINIGE**
ER, he	**SEIN,** his	**SEINER,** his	**SEINE**	**SEINIGE**
SIE, she	**IHR,** her	**IHRER,** hers	**IHRE**	**IHRIGE**
ES, it	**SEIN,** its	**SEINER,** its	**SEINE**	**SEINIGE**
WIR, we	**UNSER,** our	**UNSRER,** ours	der **UNSERE**	der **UNSRIGE**
IHR, you, ye	**EUER,** your	**EURER,** yours	**EURE**	**EURIGE**
SIE, they	**IHR,** their	**IHRER,** theirs	**IHRE**	**IHRIGE**
Sie, you	**Ihr,** your	**Ihrer,** yours	der **Ihre**	der **Ihrige**

[1] **MEIN, DEIN,** etc., are declined like **EIN,** see page 11.

[2] **MEINER,** etc., are declined like **DIESER,** see page 13.

[3] **DER MEINE,** etc., die meine, das meine. **des meineN,** etc., der meineN, des meineN. *Pl.* { die meinen and **-N** throughout

[4] **DER MEINIGE,** die meinige, das meinige. *Pl.* die meinigeN, and **-N** throughout.

Remember that the difference between a Possessive Adjective and a Possessive Pronoun is that the former stands in front of an existing Noun and the latter stands *instead* of a Noun. The Adjective *qualifies*, the Pronoun *replaces*. Thus:

mein Bruder und seine Schwester, my brother and his sister

But:

mein Bruder und seiner, my brother and his (brother)

or

mein Bruder und der seine.

Practice : **ÜBUNG**

Wer ist jener Herr ?—Es ist Herr Schmidt. Wessen Hund läuft da ?—Es ist der (Hund) des Nachbarn. Wem hat er das Geld gegeben ? Wen treffen Sie heute abend ? Welcher Mann ist gekommen ?—Der alte ist gekommen. Welchen Boten haben Sie geschickt ?—Den schnellsten. Welchem Knaben hat er Geld gegeben ?—Er hat es dem guten gegeben. Welche Frau sehen Sie ?—Ich sehe die schöne. Welche Tiere sind im Garten ?—Die jungen sind darin. Welchen Kindern bringt er Geschenke ? Er bringt den guten die Geschenke. Welche Filme haben Sie gesehen ?—Ich habe die neusten gesehen. Die Städte welcher Länder kennen Sie ?—Ich kenne die Haupstädte der meisten. Was für ein Tag ist heute ?—Heute ist ein schöner (Tag). Was für einen Hut wünschen Sie ?—Ich wünsche einen schwarzen. Was für einem Menschen hat er das Brot gegeben ? —Er hat es einem armen gegeben. Was für welche Gedanken hat sie ?—Sie hat keine bösen. In was für welchen Zeiten leben wir ?—In unruhigen. Was für welche Leute haben Sie besucht ? —Ich habe freundliche besucht. Ist dies Ihr Buch ?—Es ist meines. Sind das Ihre Schuhe ?—Nein, es sind nicht die meinen *or* . . . nicht die meinigen. Ist dieses sein Sohn ?—Ja, es ist der seine. Hat sie ihren Schirm zurückbekommen ?—Ja, sie hat den ihrigen zurückbekommen. Gibt er den Zucker seinem Hund oder meinem ? Sind unsere Kinder im Garten oder sind es die Ihrigen ? Wessen Ball ist dies ?—Der Knabe sagt, es ist seiner; aber seine Schwester sagt, es ist ihrer. Hat das Kind dieses seinem Vater gesagt ?—Nein, es hat das nicht seinem Vater sondern dem meinen gesagt.

In the Restaurant : Dishes

das Restaurant, restaurant
die Speisekarte, menu
die Weinkarte, wine list

die Vorspeisen, hors d'œuvres
die Tomate, tomato
der Salat, salad

der geräucherte Lachs, smoked salmon
die Sardinen, sardines

die Suppe, soup
die legierte Suppe, thick soup
die Bouillon, clear soup

der Fisch, fish
die Forelle, trout
die Scholle, plaice
die Krabbe, crab
der Hering, herring
der Hummer, lobster
die Austern, oysters

das Geflügel, poultry
das Huhn, fowl, hen
das Hühnchen, spring chicken

gebraten, roast
gekocht, boiled

der Rinderbraten, roast beef
das Hammelfleisch, mutton
das Kotelett, cutlet
das Schweinekotelett, pork chop
das Kalbfleisch, veal
das Hammelkotelett, mutton cutlet
das Lammkotelett, lamb cutlet, chop
der Hammelbraten, roast mutton
der Schweinebraten, roast pork
auf dem Rost gebraten, grilled
im Ofen gebraten, gebacken, roasted

die Tunke, sauce
die Zitrone, lemon
das Olivenöl, olive oil
der Essig, vinegar

die Kartoffeln, potatoes

die Salzkartoffeln, boiled potatoes
die Bratkartoffeln, fried potatoes
das Gemüse, vegetables
die Erbsen, peas
die Bohnen, beans
der Kohl, cabbage
der Weißkohl, white cabbage
der Rotkohl, red cabbage
die Pilze, mushrooms
der Spargel, asparagus
die Zwiebel(n), onion(s)
der Reis, rice
der Blumenkohl, cauliflower

der Kopfsalat, lettuce salad
der Kartoffelsalat, potato salad
der Eisalat, egg salad

der Käse, cheese
der Rahmkäse, cream cheese

die Nachspeise, dessert
das Obst, fruit
eine Flasche, a bottle of
das Wasser, water
das Eiswasser, iced water
das Bier, beer
dunkles Bier, dark beer, stout
die Limonade, lemonade
das Mineralwasser, mineral water

essen, to eat
trinken, to drink
Ich habe Hunger } I am hungry
Ich bin hungrig

Herr Ober, geben Sie mir bitte die Speisekarte. Waiter, please give me the menu.

Welche Vorspeise wünschen Sie? What kind of hors d'œuvre do you want?

Ich möchte Fisch haben. I'd like to have fish.

Wir haben heute frische Forelle, Scholle und Hummer. We have to-day fresh trout, plaice, and lobster.

Die Bouillon ist nicht heiß genug. The clear soup is not hot enough.

„Herr Ober, warum sind die Portionen in
Ihrem Bahnhofsrestaurant so klein?" —
„Damit die Gäste ihren Zug nicht versäu-
men, mein Herr!"

Bringen Sie mir einen Teller legierte Suppe. Bring me a plate of thick soup.

Ich möchte Kalbfleisch mit Bratkartoffeln essen. I'd like (to eat) veal with fried potatoes.

Bedaure, das steht heute nicht auf der Karte. Sorry, that is to-day not on the menu.

Wollen Sie Hühnchen haben? Do you want spring chicken?

Nein, bringen Sie mir Schweinebraten und Salzkartoffeln. No, bring me roast pork and boiled potatoes.

Welches Gemüse wünschen Sie? What vegetables do you want?

Ich esse gern Blumenkohl, Erbsen und Bohnen. I like (to eat) cauliflower, peas, and beans.

Sie können auch Pilze mit Zwiebeln und Reis haben. You can have also mushrooms with onions and rice.

Reichen Sie mir bitte die Tunke. Please pass me the sauce.

Hier ist Essig und Öl für den Kopfsalat. Here is vinegar and oil for the lettuce.

Was wünschen Sie als Nachspeise? What do you want as dessert?

Bringen Sie Käse und eine Flasche Bier. Bring cheese and a bottle of beer.

Ich möchte etwas Obst haben. I'd like to have some fruit.

Herr Ober, zahlen! Waiter, I want to pay.

Hier ist Ihre Rechnung. Here is your bill.

Zahlen Sie bitte an der Kasse. Pay at the cashier's please.

READING: **TILL EULENSPIEGEL**—*contd.*

Aber seine Mutter erwischte ihn, als er gerade auf dem
But his mother caught him just as he danced on the
Seil tanzte. Da nahm sie einen großen Knüppel und
rope.   She   took   a   big   stick   and
wollte ihn durchwalken. Unser Till jedoch wischte flink
wanted to beat him (well). Our Till however quickly slipped
aus der Bodenluke und setzte sich auf den Dachfirst. Und
out of the attic window and sat down on the top of the roof. And
dorthin konnte ihm natürlich seine gute Mutter nicht
there(to)   his   good   mother   naturally   could   not
folgen. Das machte Till so übermütig, daß er bei
follow him.   That made Till so daring that on the
nächster Gelegenheit sein Seil aus der Bodenluke über
next occasion he fastened his rope from the attic window across
den Fluß, zur Bodenluke des Hauses am andern Ufer
the river to the attic window of the house on the other
spannte. Natürlich sammelte sich bald allerlei Volk an,
bank.   Of course, all kinds of people soon assembled,

jung und alt, um Eulenspiegels Künsten zuzusehen. Das
young and old, to watch Eulenspiegel's tricks. That
ärgerte nun seine Mutter sehr. Darum schlich sie heim-
angered his mother very much. Therefore she sneaked secretly
lich auf den Boden, nahm ein Messer und schnitt das Seil
to the attic, took a knife and cut through the
durch. So fiel Till unter dem Gelächter der Leute in die
rope. So Till fell into the Saal, amid the laughter of the
Saal.
people.

Besonders die Bauernjungen lachten ihn aus und
Especially the peasant boys laughed at him and
riefen, daß er das Baden wohl nötig gehabt hätte. Das
shouted that he probably had needed a bath badly. The
kalte Bad störte unsern Till nicht, aber die dummen
cold bath did not disturb our Till, but the silly remarks
Reden. So nahm er sich vor, es ihnen heimzuzahlen.
(did). So he made up his mind to pay it back to them.

[*Contd. on page* 123.

§ 4. *Demonstrative Pronouns —* **DERSELBE and DERJEN-
IGE—DERJENIGE—DAS—SOLCHER—**Contractions
with **DA—**Practice—Drinks—Reading : **TILL EULEN-
SPIEGEL—**contd.

Demonstrative Pronouns are those which demonstrate, point
out, or draw attention to something. *This* house, *that* dog—
here the words *this* and *that* are in the nature of Adjectives,
because they are followed by a Noun. But when we say *this*
(one), *that* (one), and *one* is understood, *this* and *that* are Demonstrative Pronouns.

The principal Demonstrative Pronouns are:

Masc.	Fem.	Neuter	All genders
DIESER, this one	**DIESE**	**DIESES**	**DIESE,** these (ones)
JENER, that one	**JENE**	**JENES**	**JENE,** those (ones)

Masc.	*Fem.*	*Neuter*	*All genders*
SOLCHER,	**SOLCHE**	**SOLCHES**	**SOLCHE,**
such (a one)			such (ones)
DERSELBE,	**DIESELBE**	**DASSELBE**	**DIESELBEN,**
the same (one)			the same (ones)

and:

DERJENIGE—DIEJENIGE—DASJENIGE,   *the   one* (*that*) with Plural ending in **-EN** throughout: **DIEJENIGEN,** etc.

DIESER, JENER, and **SOLCHER** are declined like the Adjective **DIESER** (for which see page 13).

DERSELBE and **DERJENIGE** are declined as if they were two words with each part declined.   Thus:

Masc.	*Fem.*
DERSELBE	**DIESELBE**
DESSELBEN	**DERSELBEN**
DEMSELBEN	**DERSELBEN**
DENSELBEN	**DIESELBE**

Neuter	*Plural :* *All genders*
DASSELBE,	**DIESELBEN**
DESSELBEN	**DERSELBEN**
DEMSELBEN	**DENSELBEN**
DASSELBE	**DIESELBEN**

For the declension of **DERJENIGE,** see page 107.

DER also is used as a Demonstrative Pronoun, and then it is regarded as a contracted form of **DERJENIGE.** In such a use it is declined like **DER** when used as a Relative Pronoun (for which see page 105). Both **DERJENIGE** and **DER** as demonstratives express the idea of *the one, that, he, she, it.*

That, these, those are very often expressed by the word **DAS,** which then remains indeclinable whatever the gender or number of the Noun which it replaces. Thus:

Wer ist es? Who is it?
DAS ist mein Vater. THAT is my father.
DAS ist meine Mutter. THAT is my mother.
DAS ist mein Kind. THAT is my child.

Similarly, **DIES,** indeclinable, expresses *this (one), these (ones)*:

WESSEN HUT IST DIES? Whose hat is this?
DERJENIGE MEINES BRUDERS. The one of my brother. My brother's.

Or simply: **DER MEINES BRUDERS.**

Note: When **SOLCHER, -E, -ES,** Plural **-E,** meaning *such a,* is followed by a Noun, the **EIN** is placed first:

EIN SOLCHER MANN, such a man
EINE SOLCHE FRAU, such a woman
EIN SOLCHES MÄDCHEN, such a girl

But if the **EIN** be placed after, **SOLCHER** becomes **SOLCH** and is then indeclinable:

SOLCH EIN MANN—SOLCH EINE FRAU—SOLCH EIN MÄDCHEN

CONTRACTIONS WITH **DA,** *there*: With certain Prepositions (for which see Lesson VIII, § 1) the Adverb **DA** is used to form compound words which are in the nature of Demonstrative Pronouns. For example, **DARAUF,** *thereon,* **DARÜBER,** *over it (thereover),* etc. Thus:

WO IST ES? *Where is it?*
DARAUF, *thereon, on that* (indicating, say, *a table*).
ICH HOFFE DARAUF. I hope so (because the Verb **HOFFEN,** *to hope,* is followed by **AUF** when it means *to hope in (something)*). This usage will be dealt with more fully under Prepositions.

PRACTICE: **ÜBUNG**

Wollen Sie dieses Brot?—Nein, ich möchte jenes Brot.

Die Hand dieser Frau ist schön. Der Bart jenes Mannes ist grau.

Am ersten Tage dieses Jahres. Die langen Stunden jener dunklen Nächte.

Sind diese Äpfel gut ? Ja, aber jene Äpfel sind noch besser.

Er sagt dieses und jenes *or* Er sagt dies und das.

Haben Sie diese schönen Bilder gesehen ?

Er trägt immer dieselben braunen Schuhe.

Er sagt oft solche Dinge.—Tun Sie dasselbe ?

Er geht mit demjenigen, der zuerst kommt.

Ist es das Werk desjenigen Künstlers, der nur eine Hand hat ?

Wohnen Sie in diesem großen Haus ? Nein, ich wohne in jenem kleinen Häuschen.

Er lobt diejenigen Schüler, die viel arbeiten.

Ich höre solche Worte selten.

Wo haben Sie solch einen schönen Hut gesehen ?

Wir haben ein solches Glück heute gehabt.

Ich gebe solch einem faulen Burschen keinen Pfennig.

Wer ist dieser Knabe ?—Das ist mein Freund.

Ist dies Ihr Mantel ?—Nein, das ist derjenige meines Vaters.

Fräulein, ist das Ihre Handtasche ?—Nein, es ist die meiner Freundin.

Sind dies Ihre Hemden ?—Nein, es sind diejenigen meines Dieners.

Mit welchen Kindern haben die Ihrigen gespielt ?—Meine Kinder haben mit denen des Nachbars gespielt.—Waren es nicht die des Bürgermeisters ?

Ist der Teller auf dem Tisch ?—Ja, er steht darauf.

Sprechen Sie von dem Schicksal des Kapitäns ? Ich spreche davon.

Drinks

eine Tasse Tee, a cup of tea

das Kännchen Tee, pot of tea

die Untertasse, saucer

die Kaffeekanne, coffee-pot

die Sahnenkanne, cream jug

die Zuckerdose, sugar bowl

ein Glas Milch, glass of milk

der Kaffee verkehrt, milk with a dash (of coffee)

schwarzer Kaffee, black coffee

(der) Kaffee mit Zucker und Sahne, coffee with sugar and cream

der Eiskaffee, iced coffee

schwach, weak

stark, strong

die Zitronenlimonade, lemon squash

helles Bier, light beer
das Seidel, tankard
der Apfelmost, cider
der Wein, wine
der Weißwein, white wine
der Rotwein, red wine
der Rheinwein, hock
der Aperitif, *apéritif*, appetizer
der Cognac, cognac
der Likör, liqueur
Whisky und Soda, whiskey and soda
der Wacholder, gin
der Cocktail, cocktail

der Sekt, champagne
der Bordeaux, claret
das Sodawasser, soda water
heiße Schokolade, hot chocolate
die Orangeade, orange squash
das Eis, ice
Gefrorenes, ice-cream
das Erdbeereis, strawberry ice
das Himbeereis, raspberry ice
der Durst, thirst
Ich habe Durst⎱ I am thirsty
Ich bin durstig⎰

Ich habe großen Durst.   I am very thirsty.

Ist eine Tasse Tee oder schwarzer Kaffee besser gegen den Durst? Is a cup of tea or black coffee better against thirst?

Ich nehme ein Glas kalte Milch, und Sie?—Kaffee verkehrt. I('ll) take a glass of cold milk, and you?—Coffee with Milk with a dash (of coffee).

In dieser Untertasse ist etwas Wasser. In this saucer (there) is some water.

Entschuldigen Sie, ich besorge sofort eine andere. Excuse, me, I'll get another one immediately.

Bringen Sie mir ein Seidel helles Bier.   Will you bring me a tankard of light beer.

Wie wäre es mit einem Likör oder einem Glas Rheinwein? How about a liqueur or a glass of hock?

Nein, dann nehme ich lieber ein Gläschen Wacholder. No, I'd rather (take) a small glass of gin.

Können wir auch eine halbe Flasche Sekt haben? Can we also have a half bottle of champagne?

Es gibt hier Eiskaffee und heiße Schokolade. There's (here) iced coffee and hot chocolate.

Auch Gefrorenes und Limonaden für Kinder, die keinen Wein haben dürfen. Also ice-cream and lemonades for children who must not have (any) wine.

Sie können auch eine Flasche Apfelmost trinken. They can drink also a bottle of cider.

Bringen Sie uns eine Portion Erdbeereis und zwei Portionen Himbeereis. Bring us one portion of strawberry ice and two portions of raspberry ice.

READING: **TILL EULENSPIEGEL**—*contd.*

So zog nun eines Tages unser Till wiederum das Seil
So now one day our Till fastened again the rope
von seinem Hausgiebel hinüber zu des Nachbarn Dach,
from his house-gable across to the neighbor's roof,
auf der anderen Seite des Flüßchens. Bald sammelte
on the other side of the little river. Soon enough
sich genug Volk, jung und alt; denn sie dachten sich ganz
people gathered, young and old, for they thought quite rightly
recht, hier werde es wohl Kurzweil geben. Till versprach
there would be some entertainment. Till now promised
nun den Jungen ein schönes Kunststück, wenn sie ihm
the boys a nice trick if each of them
dazu jeder den linken Schuh geben würden. Alle waren
would give him for it his left shoe. All were
begierig, dies Stück zu sehen, und zogen eifrigst die
curious to see this piece and they took off eagerly the(ir)
linken Schuhe aus. Die Alten halfen ihnen dabei. Es
left shoes. The old ones assisted them in it. There
waren nahezu zwei Schock, an die hundertzwanzig Schuhe,
were nearly six score, about one hundred and twenty shoes
die Eulenspiegel da erhielt. Die meisten davon sahen sich
which Eulenspiegel thus received. Most of them looked very much
überaus ähnlich. Diese linken Schuhe zog nun Eulen-
alike. Eulenspiegel hung all these left shoes
spiegel alle auf eine lange Schnur und stieg damit auf das
on a long string and climbed with them on the

Seil. Alle standen da und gafften mit offenem Mund
rope. All stood there and gaped up with open
hinauf. Sie dachten, die Sache würde nun recht beginnen.
mouths. They thought the spectacle would now begin properly.

[*Contd. on p.* 130.

§ 5. *Indefinite Pronouns—***MAN** *and Others—Words both Adjectives and Pronouns—Use of* **ALL(-E)**—*Everyday Phrases
with* **ALLE**—*Practice—***CAFÉ: BIERHALLE**—*Reading :*
TILL EULENSPIEGEL—*contd.*

INDEFINITE PRONOUNS: There is a group of frequently recurring words which, for convenience, are called Indefinite Pronouns. They are " indefinite " because they have no expressed
antecedent Noun. Those in capitals are in constant use in
everyday speech:

MAN, *one, somebody, people, they*—it corresponds to the
French word *on* as in *on dit* = *people say*, " *they say* ", " *it is
said* ". **MAN** can be used only as subject and is indeclinable.
Man sagt = *they say*.

EINANDER, one another	**gar nichts,** nothing at all
JEDERMANN, everybody	**SELBST,** self (*emphatic*); *also*
JEMAND, anybody, somebody	**selber**
NIEMAND, nobody	**irgend jemand,** anybody at
ETWAS, something	all
NICHTS, nothing	**irgend etwas,** anything at all

JEDERMANN has **-S** in the genitive singular but is otherwise indeclinable:

JEDERMANN WAR DORT, everybody was there
ER IST JEDERMANNS FREUND, he is everybody's
friend

JEMAND and **NIEMAND** have **-S** in the genitive singular
and may sometimes have **-EM** in the dative and **-EN** in the
accusative:

IST DIES JEMANDS BUCH. Is this somebody's
book?

ER SAGT NIEMANDEM GUTEN MORGEN. He bids nobody good morning.

ER HAT NIEMAND(-EN) GELOBT. He has praised nobody.

SELBST and **selber** do not change, nor do some of the others in the above list: **man, etwas, nichts, einander.**

EINANDER is often compounded with Prepositions:

miteinander, with one another ⎫
gegeneinander, against one another ⎬ **einander** and compounds are indeclinable
füreinander, for one another ⎭

Of all these words **MAN** is the most useful: not only does it fill the place of *one, they, somebody, people, we* in such sentences as:

We don't say that. **Man sagt das nicht.**
Somebody told him so. **Man erzählte ihm so.**
People never do such things. **Man tut solche Dinge nie.**
One knows it very well. **Man weiß es sehr wohl.**
They believe so in France. **Man glaubt so in Frankreich.**

but it can be used to form the passive of Verbs in innumerable instances. Thus, instead of saying *I have been praised*, we can say: **Man hat mich gelobt**—*One has praised me.* Similarly: **Man hat mich gefragt, ob . . .** *I have been asked whether . . .*

Words Which Are both Adjectives and Pronouns: There is an important group of words which fulfil both these functions. The commonest are:

ALL, -ER, -E, -ES, *Plural* **ALLE,** all
BEIDE, both
VIELE, many
WENIGE, few

ALL as an Adjective needs care in use, because it can be either variable or invariable. It is invariable before a masculine or neuter Possessive Adjective in the singular:

ALL MEIN GELD, all (of) my money

Otherwise it is variable: (1) It may follow a Noun, and then it agrees with the Article or Demonstrative Adjective:

Die Mädchen alle, all the girls; **Jene Jungen alle,** all those boys

(2) The definite Article is omitted after it:

alle Mädchen, all the girls; **alle Knaben,** all the boys

(3) It agrees with a feminine Demonstrative or Possessive Adjective:

alle seine Blumen, all his flowers; **alle ihre Blumen,** all her flowers; **alle diese Blumen,** all these flowers

(4) An Adjective which follows it is declined like **GUTE, -EN** (see page 24):

alle guten Knaben, all good boys

Note the following everyday phrases:

ALLE TAGE, every day
ALLE ZWEI TAGE, every second day
ALLE ACHT TAGE, every eight days, etc.
WIR ALLE, SIE ALLE, all of us, of them (*or* you)

and note:

DIE GANZE NACHT, all night (*i.e.,* the whole night)

BEIDE, *both,* as an Adjective follows the Declension of the defining word, thus:

DIE BEIDEN SCHWESTERN, both sisters
SEINE BEIDEN SCHWESTERN, both his sisters

VIELE, *many,* and **WENIGE,** *few,* like the plural of **GUTE** on page 24.

VIELE GUTE MÄNNER, many good men
WENIGE GUTE FRAUEN, few good women

Practice: ÜBUNG

Man spricht davon. Man erzählt uns. Man sagt solche Dinge nicht.

Was man hört, das glaubt man gern. Hat man Sie gefragt?

Jemand hat an die Tür geklopft. Ist jemand da? Hier ist niemand.

Ich habe jemanden gesehen. Er gibt jedem etwas.

Haben Sie mit niemandem darüber gesprochen?—Ich habe es niemandem erzählt.

Kann ich es irgend jemandem geben? Wünschen Sie irgend etwas?

Jedermann weiß es. Das ist nicht jedermanns Sache.

Gesundheit ist etwas, das man jedermann wünscht.

Ich habe hier für jeden etwas. Nichts davon ist wahr.

Er hat heute gar nichts getan. Man glaubt ihm kein Wort.

Ich habe es selbst gehört. Hat man Sie erkannt? Niemand hat mich erkannt.

Die Freunde lieben einander. Oft streiten die Menschen miteinander um nichts.

Die beiden Wagen fahren gegeneinander.

Aller Anfang ist schwer. Alle Menschen sind Brüder. Er will alles oder nichts.

Mit all seinem Geld kann er das Land nicht kaufen. Alle meine Briefe sind hier.

Die Mutter hat allen ihren Kindern zu essen gegeben. Die Katze hat alle ihre vier Füße im Wasser. Beide Hunde sind krank. Haben Sie mit den beiden Schwestern getanzt? Meine beiden Hände sind kalt. Er kennt sie alle beide schon lange. Wir alle freuen uns sehr. Es ist nicht alle Tage Sonntag. Die Ferien haben uns allen gut getan. Er hat eine ganze Flasche Wein getrunken. Ich habe ihn den ganzen Monat nicht gesehen. In der ganzen Stadt ist kein Hotel frei. Viele kleine Vögel sitzen in dem Baum. Ich schicke Ihnen das Bild mit vielen guten Wünschen. Man trifft hier wenige junge Mädchen. Dieses ist die Insel mit den wenigen sicheren Häfen und den vielen großen Schiffen.

Café : Bierhalle : Wirtschaft

Lassen Sie uns ein Café oder eine Wirtschaft aufsuchen, wo wir einen guten Trunk haben können. Let's find a Café or pub where we can have a good drink.

Ich denke, da ist eine beim Rathaus. I think there's one near the Town Hall.

Ja, da ist eine gute. Yes, that's a good one.

Da sind wir. Nun, Hans, was wollen Sie zu trinken haben? Here we are. Well, Hans, what will you have to drink?

Ich möchte eine Orangeade. I'd like an orange squash.

Ich will ein Glas Dunkelbier haben. I'm going to have a glass of dark beer.

Herr Ober, bringen Sie uns eine Orangeade und ein Glas Dunkelbier. Waiter! Bring us an orange squash and a glass of dark beer.

Haben Sie heute die Zeitung gelesen? Have you read the newspaper to-day?

Nein. Aber ich habe eine hier. No. But I have one here.

Gibt es etwas Neues? Is there any news?

Was passiert in England? What is happening in England?

Nicht viel. Außer daß es an ein paar Orten regnet. Nothing much. Except that in a few places it's raining.

Schön daß wir gutes Wetter für unsere Ferien haben. It's good that we're having nice weather for our holiday.

Wie gefällt Ihnen diese Stadt? How do you like this town?

Sie gefällt mir sehr gut. I like it very much.

Sie waren schon früher einmal hier, nicht wahr? You were here before, weren't you?

Ja, vor langer Zeit. Sie hat sich verändert. Yes, a long time ago. It has changed.

Zum bessern oder schlechtern? For the better or worse?

Zum bessern, denke ich. For the better, I think.

Jedermann scheint sehr glücklich und geschäftig. Everybody seems very happy and busy.

Wo wohnen Sie? Where are you staying?

Ich wohne in einer netten Pension. I'm staying in a nice boarding-house.

Ist sie bequem? Is it comfortable?

Sie ist sehr bequem und nicht teuer. It's very comfortable and not dear.

Ist das Essen gut? Is the food good?

Das Essen ist ausgezeichnet. Und es gibt eine Menge. The food is excellent. And there's plenty of it.

Ich kenne die Besitzerin. Sie ist eine gute, ordentliche Frau. I know the owner. She's a good honest woman.

Sie wohnen hier, nicht wahr, Hans? You live here, don't you, Hans?

Ja. Ich bin Berliner, aber ich liebe diese Stadt mehr als Berlin. Yes. I'm a Berliner, but I like this town better than Berlin.

Sind Sie schon lange hier? Have you been long here?

Seit 1954. Since 1954.

Denken Sie, hier zu bleiben? Do you think you'll stay here?

Gerade jetzt habe ich eine gute Stelle, und das paßt mir. Just now I have a good job, and it suits me.

Ich möchte hier leben. I'd like to live here.

Das Postamt ist nicht weit von hier, nicht wahr? The Post Office is not far from here, isn't it?

Es ist ganz nahe. Wollen Sie hingehen? It's quite close. Do you want to go there?

Später am Tage. Ich will einen Luftpostbrief abschicken. Later in the day. I want to send an air (mail) letter.

Schön, lassen Sie uns noch ein Glas trinken und dann gehen. Well, I think we'll have another drink and then go.

Ja. Herr Ober! Dasselbe nochmal. Yes. Waiter! The same again.

Dies Bier ist gut. Wie ist Ihre Orangeade? This beer is good. How's your orange squash.

Vortrefflich. Gerade richtig. Excellent. Just right.

Haben Sie die Neuigkeit über Marlene Dietrich gesehen? Have you seen the news about Marlene Dietrich?

Nein. Was ist mit ihr los? No. What's happened to her?

Sie ist gerade in London und mag auch nach Deutschland kommen. She's in London just now and may be coming to Germany.

Sie ist Amerikanerin, nicht wahr? She's American isn't she?

Ja, aber sie ist natürlich in Deutschland geboren. Yes, but of course she was born in Germany.

Gut. Ich denke, wir gehen nun, was? Well, I think we may go now, don't you?

Kommen Sie! Die Zeit vergeht. Come along. Time is getting on.

Um wieviel Uhr essen Sie zu Mittag? What time do you have lunch?

Kurz nach zwölf Uhr. Soon after midday.

Das ist ziemlich früh, nicht wahr? That's rather early isn't it?

Ja, aber ich will nachher einen Spaziergang machen. Yes, but I want to go for a walk afterwards.

Hier ist das Postamt. Kann ich Ihnen helfen? Here's the Post Office. Can I help you?

Kommen Sie mit. Ich brauche Ihre Hilfe. Come with me. I need your help.

Ihr Deutsch wird alle Tage besser. Your German get's better every day.

Es freut mich, daß Sie so denken. I'm glad you think so.

There are some words in the above which have not already been given. Go over this "Situation" a few times until you know them all. First cover the English and try to remember it; then cover the German and do your best to remember it.

READING: **TILL EULENSPIEGEL**—*contd.*

Zwar hätte mancher gerne erst seinen Schuh wieder
Indeed, many a one would have wished first to have his shoe
gehabt. Aber vorläufig schwang sie Eulenspiegel an der
back. But by now Eulenspiegel swung them on the
Schnur vom Seil, drehte und wendete sich, als wenn
string from the rope, turned round and round as if (in)
Wunder was für ein lustig Stücklein käme.
wonder what kind of a gay performance would come next.
Dann aber stand er plötzlich still, schnitt eine Grimasse
Then suddenly he stood still, pulled a face
und sagte : „ Jeder gebe gut Obacht, damit jeder seinen
and said : " Everybody pay good attention that each one (may) see
Schuh sehe und dann auch den richtigen finde." Damit
his own shoe and find the right one." Thereupon
schnitt er die Schnur durch, und die Schuhe purzelten
he cut the string and the shoes tumbled
auf die Erde zwischen Haus und Ufer. Jedermann
to the ground between house and river bank. Everyone
stürzte herzu, die Jungen und die Alten. Viele Hände
jumped at them, the young and the old ones. Many hands
griffen nach den herumliegenden Stiefeln. Der eine rief :
grabbed for the scattered shoes. (The) one called out:

„ **Der da, der ist mein.“ Und der andere schrie : „ Du**
" *That one, that's mine.*" *And the other one cried:* "*You*
lügst, es ist der meine.“ So langten sie einander in die
lie, it's mine." *So they started to fight*
Haare * und prügelten sich. Erst rauften sich die Jungen,
and beat one another. First the boys scuffled,
lachten, weinten, wälzten sich miteinander. Dann kamen
laughed, cried, rolled over each other. Then the
auch die Alten in Hitze, teilten erst den Jungen Backen-
old ones also got heated, (and) first boxed the ears of the young-
streiche aus. Dann prügelte sich jeder mit jedem.
sters. Finally everybody beat everybody else.

Eulenspiegel aber saß auf dem Seil und lachte : „ Erst
But Eulenspiegel sat upon his rope and laughed: " *First*
war ich daran. Nun seid ihr es.“ Damit schlüpfte er in
it was I. Now it's you." *Then he slipped into*
die Bodenluke und ließ sich nicht mehr sehen.
the attic and was not seen any more.

Vier Wochen konnte er sich nicht aus dem Hause
For four weeks he could not dare to leave the house.
wagen. Er saß in der Stube und flickte fleißig Schuhe
He sat in his room and industriously mended shoes
für die Helmstedter Bürger. Seine Mutter aber, die nicht
for the Helmstedt citizens. But his mother, who did not
wußte, was es mit dem Fleiß für eine Bewandtnis hatte,
know what was the cause of his industry,
freute sich sehr.
was extremely pleased.

  * **einander in die Haare langen,** an idiom meaning *to start fighting*
one another.

ENDE

PART II

THE FRAMEWORK OF THE LANGUAGE

> Language is nothing but a set of human habits, the purpose of which is to give expression to thoughts and feelings . . . linguistic intercourse takes place not in isolated words as we see them in dictionaries, but by means of connected communications, chiefly in the form of sentences.
>
> *Jesperson*

HOW TO STUDY PART II

1. In general, follow the advice given on page 2. for Part I. This applies especially to self-taught learners.

2. Pay particular attention to the Reading Matter. Always read it over once or twice *before looking at the translation* and do your best to make sense of it. Then read the translation *to make sure of the sense*. Next, go over it once very carefully, comparing text and translation, until you know every meaning. Make a list of new words. Finally, read over the German text without thinking of the English, so that you are thinking in German.

MAKE A POINT OF GOING BACK OVER ALL READING MATTER UNTIL YOU ARE QUITE CONFIDENT THAT YOU CAN READ AND UNDERSTAND IT ALL WITHOUT DIFFICULTY.

3. Take the grammar easily. Do not proceed until you understand. Revise constantly. Memorize all new words and all examples.

4. Never forget that language does not consist of grammar or of isolated words, but of connected communications, chiefly in the form of sentences. These sentences represent *habits of speech*. The Reading Matter exemplifies them in a form you can study at your leisure. By listening to Radio, you hear them in rapid action.

GRAMMAR IS THEORY—READING AND RADIO LISTENING PROVIDE THIS THEORY IN PRACTICE.

LESSON V

A VERB is a word that tells what *is* or what is *done* ; the part of speech expressing *being* or *action*. The Verb and the Noun are the most important words in the language.

As will be seen, there are different kinds of Verbs, and each kind will be treated separately. But there are certain principles which apply to large groups of Verbs or generally. Although on pages 136-40 will be found the full treatment of all parts of a typical Verb for reference, the beginner will find that, for most practical purposes, it is necessary to know *thoroughly* only the six parts stated below. The full Verb should be learnt little by little until each part can be recognized and its meaning known immediately. It will be found that German Verbs follow certain easily recognizable principles.

ESSENTIAL PARTS OF THE VERB WHICH MUST BE KNOWN

I. *The Infinitive :* This names the action without indicating the doer, as in English *to praise, to speak, to write.* In German it ends in **-N** or **-EN** :

LOBEN, to praise   **SPRECHEN,** to speak
SCHREIBEN, to write   **ÄNDERN,** to change

The Infinitive is often used as a Noun : **das Schreiben,** *the writing.*

II. *The Present Indicative :* The Indicative (Mood) indicates *assertion* or *enquiry*, in all its Tenses. In English we have

135

three forms for the Present Tense Indicative : *I praise, I do praise, I am praising*—all of them expressed by only one form in German : **ICH LOBE.** And : **LOBE ICH,** *do I praise?*

III. *The Simple Past or Imperfect Tense*, corresponds to the English : *I praised, I did praise, I was praising :* in German **ICH LOBTE.**

IV. *The Simple Future Indicative*, formed in English with *will* or *shall* and in German with **WERDEN** (literally *to become*) as in : **ICH WERDE LOBEN,** *I shall praise.* (Note that the Infinitive is always used in this sense after **werden.**)

V. *The Imperative*, which gives a command. In German it is the same as the Infinitive followed by **Sie** for the Second Person Plural, which is the form most commonly used :

LOBEN SIE ! Praise !   **SPRECHEN SIE !** Speak !

VI. *The Participles, Present and Past :* These are adjectival words formed from the Verb but maintaining the verbal relation to other words (in a statement). In English they end in *-ing* (present) and in regular Verbs *-ed* (past) as in *praising, praised.* In German the equivalent endings are **-END, -T,** but in German there is in the Past Participle also the prefix **GE-.** Thus :

LOBEND, praising   **GELOBT,** praised

Of these the Past Participle is used to form Compound Tenses, as **ICH HABE GELOBT,** *I have praised.* The Present Participle is very often used as an Adjective : **das sprechende Kind,** *the talking child.*

Rule : If the Infinitive, the Imperfect, and the Past Participle are known, all other parts of a regular or " Weak " Verb can be formed. You will find later that this applies to *all* Verbs.

I. TABLE OF THE SIMPLE AUXILIARY VERBS

Infinitive :

habEN, to have	**seiN,** to be	**werdEN,** to become

Present Participle :

habEND, having	**seiEND,** being	**werdEND,** becoming

Past Participle:

| **GEhabT,** had | **gewesen,** been | **geworden,** become |

Present Indicative:

ich habE, I have	**ich bin,** I am	**Ich werde,** I become
du haST	**du biST**	**du wirST**
er, sie, es haT	**er isT**	**er wird**
wir habEN	**wir sind**	**wir werdEN**
ihr habT	**ihr seid**	**ihr werdET**
sie habEN	**sie sind**	**sie werdEN**

Imperfect:

ich hatTE, I had	**ich war,** I was	**ich wurdE,** I became
du hatTEST	**du warST**	**du wurdEST**
er hatTE	**er war**	**er wurdE**
wir hattEN	**wir warEN**	**wir wurdEN**
ihr hatTET	**ihr warT**	**ihr wurdET**
sie hattEN	**sie warEN**	**sie wurdEN**

Present Perfect:

| **ich habe gehabt,** I have had, etc. | **ich BIN gewesen,** I have been, etc. | **ich bin geworden,** I have become, etc. |

Pluperfect:

| **ich hatte gehabt,** I had had, etc. | **ich war gewesen,** I had been, etc. | **ich war geworden,** I had become, etc. |

Future:

| **ich werde haben,** I shall have, etc. | **ich werde sein,** I shall be, etc. | **ich werde werden,** I shall become, etc. |

Conditional:

| **ich würde haben,** I would have, etc. | **ich würde sein,** I would be, etc. | **ich würde werden,** I would become, etc. |

There are two more tenses:

Future Perfect: **ICH WERDE GEHABT HABEN,** I shall have had
Past Conditional: **ICH WÜRDE GEHABT HABEN,** etc.

But these are not greatly used.   The auxiliaries are irregular.

II. THE REGULAR OR " WEAK " VERB **LOBEN**

Infinitive:	**lobEN,** to praise	
Present Participle:	**lobEND,** praising	
Past Participle:	**GElobT,** praised	
Present Tense:	**ich lobE,** I praise	**wir lobEN**
	du lobST	**ihr lob(e)T**
	er lobT	**sie lobEN**

Imperfect:	ich lobTE, I praised	wir lobTEN
	du lobTEST	ihr lobTET
	er lobTE	sie lobTEN

Compound Perfect: **ich habe gelobt,** I have praised, etc.
ich hatte gelobt, I had praised, etc.

Future: **ich werde loben,** I shall praise, etc.

Conditional: **ich würde loben,** I would praise, etc.

As most of these forms have already been met, they are not difficult to learn in these TABLES. What follows should drive home the principles on which the German Verb is based.

The Tables should be studied, especially that of the " Weak " Verb **LOBEN,** particularly endings in large type, so that regularly formed Tenses will be known. Certain principles have been referred to on page 135. Of these the following should be known, as they refer to nearly all " Weak " Verbs. German Verbs are either Weak or Strong.

A Strong Verb forms the Imperfect and often the Past Participle by a vowel-change of the " root ". For Strong Verbs see pages 163 to 165. Also Lessons VI and VII.

The ROOT *of a Verb* is found by dropping the **-N** or **-EN** of the Infinitive. Thus **LOB-** from **LOB-EN. SING-** from **SING-EN,** *to sing.*

SINGEN is a *Strong Verb* because the Imperfect is **(ich) SANG.**

A *Weak Verb* forms its Imperfect by adding **-TE** or **-ETE** to the Root. Thus **LOBEN, (ich) LOBTE.** These are also called regular Verbs.

The Past Participles of both Strong and Weak Verbs have the prefix **GE-** before the Past Participle. Thus:

GELOBT, praised   **GESUNGEN,** sung

The principal parts of these two Verbs are: **LOBEN, LOBTE, GELOBT** and **SINGEN, SANG, GESUNGEN.** From these other Tenses are formed.

FORMATION OF TENSES: This should be studied with the help of the Tables. (For Subjunctive, see page 153.)

The three Simple Auxiliary Verbs **HABEN, SEIN,** and

WERDEN are so called because they help to form Compound Tenses of other Verbs; and **WERDEN** is used to form the Passive of *all* Verbs. Verbs of movement take **SEIN** to form Compound Tenses: **ICH BIN GEGANGEN.** See page 158. Otherwise **HABEN** is used.

ALL WEAK VERBS—*To form the Present Tense Indicative :* Drop the **-EN** of the Infinitive (i.e., find the Root) and add:

First Person Singular : **-E**
Second   „   „   **(e)ST**
Third   „   „   **(e)T**
First   „   Plural: **-EN**
Second   „   „   **-T**
Third   „   „   **-EN**

To form the Imperfect or Simple Past : To the Root add: **-TE, -TEST, -TE, -TEN, -TET, -TEN. Ich lobTE,** etc.

To form the Simple Future : Use the Present Tense of **WERDEN** with the Infinitive of the Verb:

ich WERDE LOBEN, I shall praise
du WIRST LOBEN, thou wilt praise
er WIRD LOBEN, he will praise, etc.

Verbs ending in **-IEREN,** such as **STUDIEREN,** *to study,* are conjugated regularly like a Weak Verb except that their Past Participles do not require **GE-.**

ich studierE, I study
ich studierTE, I studied
ich habe studierT, I have studied

Otherwise to form the Past Participle : Prefix the Root with **GE-** and add **-T** to it. Thus: **GElobT,** *praised.* The Past Participle is used to form Compound Tenses:

ich habe GElobT, I have praised

The Present Participle : Always formed by adding **-END** to the root. Thus: **lobEND.**

It is inadvisable to proceed until these simple principles have been mastered. With them, these Tenses of all Weak Verbs can be formed. There is only one other Tense which need be known at this stage—the Conditional. As these Tenses are constantly recurring in simple speech, they are of essential importance.

THE CONDITIONAL TENSE. The simple Conditional of all Verbs is formed by using the Past Subjunctive of **WERDEN** with the Infinitive of the main Verb. Thus:

> **ich würde loben, I should praise, etc.**
> **du würdest loben**
> **er würde loben**
> **wir würden loben**
> **ihr würdet loben**
> **sie würden loben**

PRACTICE: **ÜBUNG**

Ich liebe meinen Vater. Das Kind liebt seine Mutter. Der Vater und die Mutter lieben ihre Kinder. Lieben Sie Ihre Schwester? Wir lieben unsere Freunde. Der Lehrer lobte den Schüler. Er hat gut gearbeitet. Wir werden morgen auch arbeiten.

Werden Sie heute kommen?—Nein, ich habe keine Zeit.

Ist der Bote hier gewesen? Er ist nicht hier gewesen.

Hat die Frau ihren Schirm? Sie hat ihn gehabt. Hatte er das Buch in der Tasche?—Er hatte es nicht.

Wir hatten gestern Besuch. Wer war da? Unsere alten Freunde waren da. Werden sie morgen wiederkommen? Nein, aber ich werde zu ihnen gehen.

Der Knabe ist groß geworden. Wir hatten ihn lange nicht gesehen. Haben Sie Ferien gehabt?—Ich habe noch keine gehabt. Ich war nicht zu Hause, als er mich besuchte. Wo war er gewesen, als wir gekommen waren? Ich würde froh sein, ihn zu treffen.

Haben Sie ihn gefragt? Ich werde ihn morgen fragen.

Er lebt jetzt in Deutschland; früher hat er in Amerika gelebt; und er wird nächstes Jahr in der Schweiz leben. Wieviele Menschen wohnen in diesem Hause? Wohnt der Doktor hier? Er wohnte hier früher einmal. Was wird seine Frau sagen? Das was sie immer gesagt hat. Wir haben ihn oft gefragt. Hören Sie etwas? Ich hörte nichts. Sie hatten es vor langer Zeit gehört.

Es regnet heute. Es hat gestern geregnet. Wird es morgen regnen?

Im Herbst werden die Äpfel reif. Werden sie in diesem Jahr reif werden?

Würde er ihn gefragt haben? Ich hatte es gehofft. Aber sie würde dieses nicht erwartet haben.

Er blickte mich fragend an. Ich habe ihm keine Antwort gegeben. Er lernte die Übung spielend. Die spielenden Kinder sind im Garten. Der Knabe hatte einen lebenden Fisch im Glas.

Werden Sie bald fertig sein? Ich werde mit der Arbeit heute fertig werden. Man wird oft nach seinem Namen gefragt. Wurden Sie auch gefragt?—Ja, ich bin oft gefragt worden. Wir werden Sie nicht wieder fragen.

Der Mann war sehr alt geworden. Wir werden alle älter werden. Ich würde gern auch klüger werden. Dann werden alle Menschen Sie loben.

READING: **DIE LORELEI**
Von Heinrich Heine

German lyrical poetry lends itself admirably to help the foreign learner in learning the language. Most of it is simple and straightforward, and much of it has been set to music for singing. **DIE LORELEI** is a good example. First go over each line with the literal translation until you know what each word means. Then read the German over several times until you have grasped it all. Finally, try to learn it, verse by verse, until you can say it all over by heart without reference to the text.

Die Lorelei

Ich weiß nicht, was soll es bedeuten,
Daß ich so traurig bin;
Ein Märchen aus alten Zeiten,
Das kommt mir nicht aus dem Sinn.

Die Luft ist kühl und es dunkelt,
Und ruhig fließt der Rhein;
Der Gipfel des Berges funkelt
Im Abendsonnenschein.

Die schönste Jungfrau sitzet
Dort oben wunderbar,
Ihr goldnes Geschmeide blitzet,
Sie kämmt ihr goldnes Haar.

Sie kämmt es mit goldnem Kamme,
Und singt ein Lied dabei;
Das hat eine wundersame,
Gewaltige Melodei.

Den Schiffer im kleinen Schiffe
Ergreift es mit wildem Weh;
Er schaut nicht die Felsenriffe,
Er schaut nur hinauf in die Höh'.

Ich glaube, die Wellen verschlingen
Am Ende Schiffer und Kahn;
Und das hat mit ihrem Singen
Die Lorelei getan.

TRANSLATION: I do not know what it must mean/That I am so sad;/A legend (tale) from olden times,/That comes (gets) not out of my mind (*i.e.*, I cannot forget).

The air is cool and dusk falls,/And softly flows the Rhine;/The peak of the mountain glitters/In the evening sunshine.

The loveliest maiden sits/Up there wonderfully,/Her golden jewellery flashes,/She combs her golden hair.

She combs it with golden comb,/And withal sings a song;/That has a wondrous/powerful melody.

The boatman in his little skiff/It seizes with frantic grief ;/He looks not at the ridge of rock,/He looks only upwards.

I believe, the waves engulf/In the end (both) boatman and boat ;/ And that with her singing/The Lorelei (maiden) has done.

Die Lorelei : a rock in the Rhine. Heinrich Heine, a lyric and satiric poet, journalist, and critic (1797–1856). This ballad has been set to music and is a famous folk-song. If possible, get somebody to sing it for you, and you should learn the melody. You may be able to get a phonograph record of it.

LISTENING TO RADIO : Reminder : you should listen as much as possible to Radio Broadcasts in German. See page 231 for Wave-lengths. By now, you should be able to get the gist of much that you hear. Listening to Radio is excellent Practice for the ear, as you will hear different voices and various kinds of speech. Never be dismayed if at times you understand nothing or next to nothing. This can happen to us all at times in our own language ! Facility in understanding comes with increasing knowledge and practice.

§ 2. *The Six Auxiliaries of Mood—Conjugations—*ZU *with the Infinitive—Practice—Cycling, Hiking, Camping—Continuous Reading :* **Hans im Glück**

There are in German six important Verbs (usually called " Auxiliaries of Mood " because of their nature), which are fully conjugated. They are important because of their constant recurrence in speech and writing. The full range of their use is complicated and is best learnt by practice and experience. But their basic significance, meanings, and use can be known for most everyday purposes. First their basic meanings will be considered. The six Verbs are :

DÜRFEN, to be permitted to

> This Verb denotes *permission* (from somebody) to do something, also a *right* or *liberty* to do it, without dictates or obligation.

> **DARF ICH RAUCHEN?** May I smoke?

KÖNNEN, to have the power to do something, the physical ability

Thus:

> **ICH KANN SCHNELL LAUFEN,** I can (am physically able to) run quickly.

MÖGEN, to have the inclination, liking

Often with the idea of plausibility or probability.

> **ICH MAG KRANK SEIN,** (I feel that) I may be ill.
> *Or :* It may be that I'm ill.

MÜSSEN, to be under compulsion to

There is an idea of necessity, obligation.

> **Ich muß zu Bett gehen.** I (really) must go to bed
> **Das Kind muß es tun.** The child must do it

SOLLEN, to be under moral constraint to

> **Sie sollen nicht herkommen!** You shall not come here.
> **Du sollst nicht stehlen.** Thou shalt not steal. (*Biblical commandment.*)

WOLLEN, to will, wish to

Differs from **SOLLEN** in that it indicates the will or desire of the subject, whereas **sollen,** even when in the first person, implies the will of *another*. Thus:

> **Ich soll fahren,** I must (am constrained to) travel
> **ICH WILL fahren,** I want to travel

All six Auxiliaries of Mood take **HABEN** to form the Compound Tenses. **ICH HABE gedurft, gekonnt, gemocht, gemußt, gesollt, gewollt.**

They do *not* take **ZU** before an infinitive: **Er soll nicht kommen.**

After an Infinitive an old form of the Past Participle exactly like the Infinitive is used.

> **Er hat nicht kommen wollen.** He has not wanted to come.

These Verbs will often come into the Practice and Reading as we proceed. Once their basic meanings are known, and these are the most frequently used, other variant uses are best learnt from practice and reading.

The Six Auxiliaries of Mood are conjugated fully, and only the Present Indicative presents any difficulty: Thus:

	DÜRFEN	KÖNNEN	MÖGEN	MÜSSEN	SOLLEN	WOLLEN
ich	DARF	KANN	MAG	MUß	SOLL	WILL
du	DARFST	KANNST	MAGST	MUßT	SOLLST	WILLST
er	DARF	KANN	MAG	MUß	SOLL	WILL
wir	DÜRFEN	KÖNNEN	MÖGEN	MÜSSEN	SOLLEN	WOLLEN
ihr	DÜRFT	KÖNNT	MÖGT	MÜßT	SOLLT	WOLLT
sie	DÜRFEN	KÖNNEN	MÖGEN	MÜSSEN	SOLLEN	WOLLEN

Imperfect Indicative

ich DURFTE   KONNTE   MOCHTE   MUßTE   SOLLTE   WOLLTE

Past Participles

GEDURFT	GEKONNT	GEMOCHT
GEMUßT	GESOLLT	GEWOLLT

These forms of the Past Participle exist and are sometimes seen in print though rarely heard in speech. *The old form, similar to the Infinitive, is generally used.* Thus:

ER HAT NICHT FAHREN KÖNNEN. He has not been able to travel.

The regular form with **GE-** should be used when there is no second Infinitive, that is, when the Auxiliary of Mood is used by itself and for its own meaning. Thus:

ER HAT ES NICHT GEKONNT. He has not been able to.

which might be used in reply to the question: **Hat er fahren können?**

It will be observed that the Auxiliary of Mood is placed *last*, after the principal Verb. See Word-order, pages 90 and 281.

These rules apply to the other Auxiliaries of Mood, which are always used without **ZU,** *to.*

ZU with the Infinitive: The Infinitive is used with **ZU** excepting with these Auxiliaries of Mood, **WERDEN** to form the future tense, and a small group of other Verbs. The commonest are:

FÜHLEN, to feel	**LASSEN,** to let, leave
GEHEN, to go	**LEHREN,** to teach
HEIßEN, to be named	**LERNEN,** to learn
HELFEN, to help	**MACHEN,** to make
HÖREN, to hear	**SEHEN,** to see

Ich lasse ihn sprechen. I let him speak.
Ich sah ihn kommen. I saw him come.
Ich hörte ihn singen. I heard him sing.
Ich werde zurückkommen. I shall come back.
Ich lerne deutsch sprechen. I learn to speak German.

After all other Verbs and statements, the Infinitive is preceded by **ZU**. Thus:

ICH WÜNSCHE NACH HAUSE ZU GEHEN. I want to go home.
ICH HATTE KEINE ZEIT ZU LERNEN. I had no time to learn.

Practice: ÜBUNG

Darf ich zu Ihnen kommen?—Sie dürfen zu mir kommen. Kann Ihr Hund hoch springen?—Mein Hund kann nicht hoch springen. Das Mädchen mag gerade schlafen. Die Pferde mögen hungrig sein. Müssen wir in die Schule gehen?—Ja, Kinder, ihr müßt * jetzt in die Schule gehen. Soll ich das Fenster schließen?—Sie sollen das Fenster nicht schließen. Wohin wollen Sie fahren?—Ich will nach Hamburg fahren. Kann ich Ihnen helfen?

Durfte er das tun?—Er durfte den Wein nicht trinken. Konnten Sie die schweren Koffer tragen?—Ich konnte sie nicht tragen. Der Diener mußte sie holen. Mochte er sie gern tragen?—Er tat es gern. Sollte die Tochter der Mutter helfen? —Sie sollte ihr helfen. Wollten Sie einen Brief schreiben?— Ich wollte gerade einen schreiben.

* ihr müßt, when speaking to children.

Wir haben in das Land reisen dürfen. Die Pferde haben den Wagen nicht ziehen können. Ich hatte die Übung nicht machen wollen. Hat er so schnell gehen müssen? Hat sie die Wahrheit sagen sollen?—Sie hat das nicht gewollt. Er hat das auch nicht gemocht.

Werden wir mit dem Auto fahren können?—Nein, Sie werden zu Fuß gehen müssen. Wohin soll ich den Brief bringen?—Wollen Sie ihn bitte zur Post bringen. Wird er die Übung gekonnt haben? Er wird sie wahrscheinlich nicht gekonnt haben. Ich habe letzten Monat in England bleiben müssen; aber jetzt habe ich nach Deutschland fahren können. Werden Sie morgen abreisen wollen?

Ich sehe ihn in das Haus treten. Lassen wir es ruhig geschehen! Lernt das Kind laufen? Er lehrte den Knaben lesen. Wir helfen ihm das Rätsel lösen. Machen wir ihn besser arbeiten. Hörten Sie ihn diese Worte sagen? Sie gehen heute nachmittag spazieren.

Wünschte er, eine Tasse Tee zu trinken? Sie brauchen den Koffer nicht selbst zu tragen. Ich glaubte ihn früher schon gesehen zu haben. Er hoffte, noch zwei Tage in der Stadt bleiben zu können. Wir haben gesagt, es gern tun zu wollen. Hatte er versprochen, Ihnen das Geld zu geben? Wir freuen uns, die Kinder spielen zu sehen.

Cycling, Hiking, Camping

radfahren ⎫
radeln ⎭ to cycle
das Radeln, cycling
das Fahrrad, cycle
wandern, to hike
das Wandern, hiking
lagern, to camp
das Lager, camp
die Ausrüstung, outfit
das Kettenschloß, padlock
der Schlüssel, key
die Pumpe, pump

das Werkzeug, tool
der Schraubenschlüssel, spanner
der Gepäckträger, carrier
der Reifen, tyre
das Reparaturmaterial, repair outfit
die Panne, puncture, burst
die Lampe, lamp
die Taschenlampe, pocket torch
das Zelt, tent

ein Zelt aufschlagen, to pitch a tent

der Rucksack, rucksack

der Schlafsack, sleeping-bag

die Thermosflasche, thermos flask

die Karte, map

die Wegekarte, road map

übernachten, to spend the night

die Herberge, inn, lodging

die Jugendherberge, youth hostel

das Gerät, utensil

die Kochgeräte, cooking-utensils

die Wanderkleidung, hiking clothes

suchen, to seek, look for

die Sonnenbrille, sun-glasses

der Spirituskocher, spirit-stove

der Brennstoff, fuel

die Unterkunft, shelter, lodging

die Erfrischungen, refreshments

der Hof, farm

der Landwirt; der Bauer, farmer

die Lebensmittel, groceries

Zwei Freunde auf der Wanderung. Two friends on a hiking tour.

A. **Wir wollen drei Tage wandern.** We want to hike for three days.

    Werden wir die ganze Zeit radeln? Shall we cycle all the time?

B. **Unsere Fahrräder und die Ausrüstung für das Wandern sind bereit.** Our bicycles and (the) outfit for (the) hiking are ready.

A. **Haben wir Pumpe, Schraubenschlüssel und Reparatur-material im Rucksack?** Have we the pump, spanners, and repair outfit in the rucksack?

B. **Vergessen wir nicht, die Lampe und einen Ersatzreifen mitzunehmen.** Let's not forget to take the lamp and a spare tyre.

A. **Ich hoffe, wir werden keine Panne haben.** I hope we shall not have a puncture.

B. **Unsere Wanderkleidung ist ausgezeichnet.** Our hiking clothes are excellent.

A. **Ich habe das Zelt fürs Übernachten auf meinem Gepäckträger.** I have the tent on my carrier for (spending) the night.

B. **Ich nehme die beiden Schlafsäcke.** I'm taking the two sleeping-bags.

A. **Wer soll den Spirituskocher und den Brennstoff tragen?** Who shall carry the spirit-stove and the fuel?

B. **Ich habe die Thermosflasche und die Kochgeräte eingepackt.** I have packed the thermos flask and the cooking-utensils.

A. **Hoffen wir, daß wir Unterkunft in der Jugendherberge finden werden.** Let's hope that we shall find shelter in the youth hostel.

B. **Auf der Wegekarte sehe ich, daß hier in der Nähe ein Hof ist.** I see on the road map that there is a farm in the vicinity.

A. **Vielleicht können wir bei dem Bauern frische Milch und Lebensmittel bekommen.** Perhaps we can get fresh milk and foodstuff from the farmer.

B. **Dort im Walde können wir unser Zelt aufschlagen und übernachten.** There in the wood we can pitch our tent and spend the night.

CONTINUOUS READING   Grimm's **MÄRCHEN**

HANS IM GLÜCK: JACK IN LUCK

Hans hatte seinem Herrn sieben Jahre gedient. Da
Jack had served his master seven years. He
sprach er zu ihm: „ Herr, gebt mir nun meinen Lohn!
then spoke to him: " Master, give me my wage(s)!
Ich möchte jetzt wieder zu meiner Mutter zurück!"
I'd like (to go) back now to my mother."

„ Du hast mir treu und ehrlich gedient," sagte der Herr,
" You have served me loyally and honestly," the master said,
„ du sollst auch einen guten Lohn bekommen!" Dabei
"you shall also get a good reward!" Thereupon
gab er ihm einen Klumpen reinen Goldes, der so groß
he gave him a lump of pure gold, which was as large

war wie sein Kopf. Hans war sehr erfreut, zog sein
as   his   head.   Jack   was   very   pleased,   pulled   his
Tüchlein aus der Tasche, wickelte den Goldklumpen
handkerchief from his pocket, wrapped therein the lump of gold,
hinein, hob ihn auf die Schulter und trat den Weg nach
lifted   it   on   his   shoulder   and   started   (on   the)   the   way
Hause an.
home.

Als er auf der Landstraße wanderte, kam ein Reiter auf
As   he   wandered   along   the   highway,   a   horseman   trotted
ihn zugetrabt, der frisch und munter im Sattel eines
towards   him   who   sat   fresh   and   gay   in   the   saddle   of   a
brauen Pferdes saß. Als der Reiter an ihm vorüberkam,
brown   horse.   When   the   horseman   went   past   him,
sagte Hans so vor sich hin: „ Ja, ja, was ist doch das
Jack   said   to   himself: " Yes,   yes,   what   a   fine
Reiten für eine schöne Kunst. Man sitzt dabei im Sattel
art   indeed   riding   is.   One   sits   (thereby)   in   the   saddle
wie auf einem Polsterstuhl und kommt doch schnell
as   on   an   upholstered   chair   and   yet   travels   quickly
weiter, ohne daß man seinen Fuß an einen Stein stößt und
without   knocking   one's   foot   against   a   stone   and
sich die teuern Sohlen abläuft.“
using up (the) expensive soles."

Der Reiter hörte die Worte. Er hielt seinen Gaul an
The   man   on   horseback   heard   the   words.   He   stopped   his   horse
und rief: „ Ei, Hans, warum läufst du denn zu Fuß und
and   called   out : " Eh,   Jack,   why   do   you   go   on   foot   and
reitest nicht? “
not   ride? "

[*Contd. on page* 156.

Note: The Brothers Grimm (Jacob Ludwig Karl 1785–1863 and
Wilhelm Karl 1786–1859) published in 1812–15 the first edition of their
world-famous **Kinder- und Hausmärchen,** a collection of folk-tales,
some of them taken down from the tellers, others found in old manu-
scripts, others from printed books. For the first time a considerable
body of German folklore was made available to the reading public, and
many of the stories have since become a part of European literature. In
English they are usually known as *Grimm's Fairy Tales,* but the German

title is much more comprehensive. They are excellent reading for foreign learners because of the simplicity of their language and the easily understood ideas. See page 293 for a text.

§ 3. *The Imperative—Word-order : Place of* **NICHT**—*The Inter-rogative of Verbs—The Subjunctive Mood : Formation and Use of Present and Imperfect—Practice—Radio and Amuse-ments—Continuous Reading :* **Hans im Glück**

THE IMPERATIVE OF VERBS : The simplest and most common form of the Imperative has already been mentioned (page 136), and this should always be used in speaking or writing. It is formed by placing the Pronoun **Sie** (*you*, usual Second Person Plural) after the form for the Infinitive, which is the same as the ordinary First and Third Persons Plural of the present Indicative. Thus :

LOBEN Sie ihn! Praise him!
LOBEN WIR IHN! Let us praise him!
GEHEN WIR JETZT! Let us go now!

The Imperative is sometimes formed with the Verb **LASSEN,** *to let, to allow,* followed by the Infinitive of the main Verb. Then **LASSEN** becomes a kind of auxiliary :

LASSEN SIE IHN HEREINKOMMEN! Let him come in!

ZU *is not used with* **LASSEN.**

The familiar form **Lobe ihn!** is easily recognizable, but need not be used by the foreigner.

THE NEGATIVE OF VERBS : **NICHT,** *not.* (1) In simple tenses with direct statements it is placed immediately *after the Verb*:

ICH HABE NICHT, I have not
ich bin nicht, I am not
ich werde nicht, I do not become
ich lobe nicht, I do not praise

(2) In all other circumstances **NICHT** is placed :
  (*a*) AFTER the direct object (accusative) as in—
    ICH HABE IHN NICHT GELOBT.   I have not praised him
    ICH HABE IHN NICHT GESEHEN.   I have not seen him
    ICH HABE ES NICHT GESAGT.   I have not said it.

AFTER an Adverb of time, as in—

ICH HABE ES GESTERN NICHT GEFUNDEN. I
have not found it yesterday

(*b*) BEFORE an Adverb of place or manner—

ER KAM NICHT HIERHER. He did not come here
ER WOHNT NICHT HIER. He does not live here

BEFORE a word on which emphasis is laid—

Ich will nicht Soldat werden. I will not (*i.e.*, do not
wish to) become a soldier

But—

Ich will Soldat nicht werden, ich bin es. I do not
want to become a soldier, I am one.

These rules are rather arbitrary, and one often finds that they are not
followed strictly. Latitude is permissible to the native speaker or
writer, but the foreigner is well advised to keep to this definite order
until the language is well known. See also Word-order, pages 90, 281.

NIE, NIEMALS, *never*, follow the same rules as **NICHT.**

THE INTERROGATIVE OF VERBS : (1) When there is a Personal
Pronoun, place it after the main Verb. Thus:

HABEN SIE EINEN BLEISTIFT? Have you a pencil ?
RAUCHEN SIE? Do you smoke ?

(2) When there is no Pronoun, the Noun is placed after the
Verb. Thus:

SPRICHT IHRE SCHWESTER DEUTSCH? Does your
sister speak German ?
IST HERR SCHMIDT ZU HAUSE? Is Mr. Schmidt at
home ?

THE SUBJUNCTIVE MOOD : The Mood of a Verb is the form
in grammar which denotes style or manner of statement. The
Indicative Mood, as we have seen on page 135, indicates assertion
or enquiry. The Imperative Mood gives a command. The
Subjunctive Mood, broadly, indicates *doubt* or *condition*. It
usually expresses a *wish, request, possibility, probability, sup-
position*; and it is used after certain Verbs and Conjunctions.
There is a tendency for the Subjunctive to fall into disuse, and,
except for the Subjunctive of **WERDEN,** it is possible to express

most of the common ideas of everyday life without using it. But, as it is often met in reading, it should be recognized.

REGULAR FORMATION OF THE PRESENT AND IMPERFECT SUBJUNCTIVE: The Present Subjunctive is formed by adding to the Root: **-E, -EST, -E, -EN, -ET, -EN.** Thus: **Ich lobE, du lobEST, er lobE, wir lobEN, ihr lobET, sie lobEN.** *Note: No* modification of root vowel. The Imperfect Subjunctive is the same as Imperfect Indicative (see page 139) but usually with modification of root vowels **ä, ö, ü**; and **-E** is added to the singular when there is no final **-E** in the Indicative. Thus: **ich spräche, ich würde** (from **WERDEN**), **ich hätte** (from **HABEN**).

As it is easily possible for the foreigner to avoid the Subjunctive altogether in speaking or writing, and he is likely to meet it most in reading, all that need be done until the language is known fairly well, is to be able to recognize it. The Present Subjunctive of **LOBEN** has been given. Here is the Past Subjunctive of the same Verb:

> **ich lobTE**
> **du lobTEST**
> **er lobTE**
> **wir lobTEN**
> **ihr lobTET**
> **sie lobTEN**

It will be seen that this is the same as the Past or Imperfect Indicative (page 139).

The other tenses of the Subjunctive are rarely used. But it is advisable to keep in mind the two fairly frequently occurring tenses of **SEIN**: *Present*—**ich sei, du seist, er sei, wir seien, ihr seiet, sie seien.** *Past*—**ich wäre, du wärest, er wäre, wir wären, ihr wäret, sie wären.**

PRACTICE: **ÜBUNG**

Sagen Sie es laut! Bitte sprechen Sie leise! Bleiben Sie hier! Halten Sie den Hut! Bleiben wir hier! Laufen wir schnell! Lassen Sie ihn den Koffer tragen! Lassen wir die Dinge gehen, wie sie wollen!

Gehen Sie nicht auf die Straße! Glauben wir es nicht! Fragen wir ihn nicht zweimal! Lassen Sie ihn nicht warten! Lassen wir es nicht geschehen! Entschuldigen Sie bitte!

Ich glaube es nicht. Er kommt heute nicht. Fahren Sie heute nicht? Die Kinder fragten uns nicht. Arbeiteten die Männer nicht? Wir sahen es nicht. Es regnete gestern nicht. Ich bin nicht im Theater gewesen. Haben Sie ihn nicht gelobt? Wir werden morgen nicht kommen. Ich hatte das nicht gehört. Er wurde nicht im Wagen gefahren. Hat man ihn gefragt? Hatten Sie das Geld nicht bekommen?—Ich hatte es nicht bekommen. Ich würde es auch nicht erhalten haben. Würden Sie die Geschichte nicht für wahr gehalten haben?

Hat er das Stück nie gesehen? Ich habe es auch nie gesehen. Rauchen Sie niemals?—Nein, ich rauche niemals. Kommt er niemals pünktlich? Sind Sie nie in einem Flugzeug gewesen? Er hatte das nie gehört. Das Wetter ist hier niemals so schön wie in Italien.

Glauben Sie, er habe Geld? Ich wünschte, er hätte es sofort gesagt. Wir denken, daß sie bald gehen. Sie sagten, sie kämen morgen wieder. Hofft er, daß man ihm den Mantel bald gebe? Würden Sie ihn fragen, ob er das Mädchen liebte?

Ich fragte ihn, ob das wahr sei. Sagen Sie ihm, daß ich nicht zu Hause sei. Er wollte wissen, ob jene Leute reich seien. Sie glauben, daß wir zufrieden seien. Er sagte, daß der Bote nicht gekommen wäre. Er dachte, Sie wären darüber ärgerlich. Sie nahmen an, daß wir ins Theater gegangen wären.

Radio and Amusements

das Radio, radio

der Radioapparat, wireless set

der Wetterbericht, the weather bulletin

die Nachrichten, news

der Knopf, knob, switch

die Wellenlänge, wavelength

das Programm, program

die Musik, music

die Tanzmusik, dance music

das Konzert, concert

anstellen, to switch on

abstellen, to switch off

ich werde das Radio abstellen, I'll switch off the radio

einschalten, to tune in

ich schalte Hamburg ein, I'm tuning in to Hamburg

der Sender, radio station

die Sendung, transmission

gut empfangen, to receive well
schlecht empfangen, to receive badly
hören, to hear
die Störung, interference
die Langwelle, long wave
die Mittelwelle, medium wave
die Kurzwelle, short wave
das Theater, theatre
die Kasse, box office
die Theaterkasse, theatre box office
die Oper, opera
das Lokal, local, *as in* das Tanzlokal, local (public) dance hall
das Restaurant mit Tanz, restaurant with dancing
das Café mit Musik, café with music
der Nachtklub, night club

das Kino, *or* Kinotheater, *or* das Lichtspielhaus, cinema (theatre)
die Vergnügung, amusement, pleasure
der Vergnügungspark, amusement park
der Fernsehapparat, television receiver
der Zoologische Garten, der Zoo, zoo
der Zirkus, circus
die Dame, das Damespiel, draughts
das Schach, das Schachspiel, chess
das Billard(-spiel), billiards
spielen, to play
sich amüsieren, to enjoy oneself, have fun
die Schallplattenmusik, music on records

Stellen Sie das Radio an. Switch on the radio.
Sie müssen den Knopf nach rechts drehen. You must turn the knob to the right.
Der Wetterbericht wird gerade gegeben. The weather report is just being given.
Danach gibt es Schallplattenmusik. After that there is music on records.
Schalten Sie auf Kurzwelle Münster ein. Tune in (to) Münster on short wave.
Von dort können wir Tanzmusik hören. From there we can hear dance music.
Der Empfang ist heute abend schlecht. The reception is bad to-night.
Man bekommt nichts als Störungen. One gets nothing but interference.

Was gibt es im Fernsehapparat? What is there on (the)
television?

**Erst eine Sendung aus einem Zirkus; dann aus dem Zoo
und einem Vergnügungspark.** First a transmission from a
circus; then from the Zoo and an amusement park.

Zum Schluß gibt es einige Akte aus einer Oper. Finally,
there are some acts of an opera.

**Wollen Sie mit mir Dame spielen oder vielleicht ein
Billardspiel?** Will you play draughts with me or perhaps a
game of billiards?

**Nein, lassen Sie uns lieber ins Kino gehen und danach in
einen Nachtklub.** No, rather let us go to the cinema and
afterwards to a night club.

So werden wir uns sicher gut amüsieren. So we certainly
shall amuse ourselves well (have a good time).

CONTINUOUS READING   Grimm's **MÄRCHEN**

HANS IM GLÜCK—2

„ **Pah, ich habe ja kein Pferd,"** entgegnete der Hans.
" *Pooh, I haven't got a horse," replied (our) Jack.*
„ **Dann aber trage ich auch einen schweren Klumpen auf**
" *But then I also carry a heavy lump on*
meiner Schulter.   Er ist zwar reines Gold, aber er drückt
my shoulder.   It is, however, of pure gold, but it presses (on)
mich furchtbar."
me terribly."

„ **Da wüßte ich schon, was du zu tun hättest,"** schlug
" *There I knew already what you had to do," suggested*
ihm der Reiter vor.   „ Wir wollen tauschen: du gibst mir
to him the horseman.   " Let us change: you give me
deinen schweren Klumpen und bekommst dafür mein
your heavy lump and you get for it my
Pferd."
horse."

„ **Schön!   Das ist ein Wort; wird gemacht!" sprach**
" *Fine!   That's a word;* * *it's done!" said*

                    * Now you're talking!

Hans voll Freude. „ Ich warne euch aber : der Klumpen
Jack   full   of   joy.   "But   I   warn   you: the   lump
ist verdammt schwer."   Der Reiter schwang sich aus dem
is   damned   heavy."   The   horseman   swung   himself   out   of   the
Sattel, nahm den Klumpen Gold und half Hans auf des
saddle,   took   the   lump   of   gold   and   helped   Jack   on   to   the
Pferdes Rücken.   Dann gab er ihm die Zügel in die Hände
horse's   back.   Then   he   gave   him   the   bridle   into   his   hands
und wies ihn an : „ Wenn es recht schnell gehen soll,
and   instructed   him: "If   you   want   to   go   pretty   fast,
mußt du , Hopplahopp ! ' rufen und mit der Zunge
you   must   call   'Hopplahopp!'   and   click   (with)   your
schnalzen."
tongue."

Hans ritt langsam dahin und war froh und vergnügt,
Jack   rode   slowly   away   and   was   glad   and   cheerful
daß es so gut ging.   Nach einer Zeit aber war es ihm
that   it   went   so   well.   After   some   time,   however,   it   was   still   too
doch zu langsam.   Er schnalzte daher mit der Zunge und
slow   for   him.   He   therefore   clicked   with   his   tongue   and
rief laut : „ Hopplahopp ! "
shouted : " Hopplahopp ! "

[*Contd. on page* 162.

§ 4. *Compound Tenses of Verbs—Verbs conjugated with* SEIN—
      Verbs with either SEIN *or* HABEN—*Practice—Sports—*
      Continuous Reading : Hans im Glück

In the TABLE on page 137 certain Tenses of the auxiliaries and
of **LOBEN,** *to praise* (a Weak Verb), were given.   They need
some explanation and extension.

The Compound Perfect Tense, or Past Perfect—**ICH HABE
GEHABT, ICH BIN GEWESEN, ICH BIN GEWORDEN,
ICH HABE GELOBT**—is more used in German than its English
equivalent *I have had, I have been,* etc.   In German it is often
used where we should use the Simple Past.   Thus: **ICH
HABE GELOBT,** literally *I have praised,* would in German be

used for *I praised* when it was a single act, especially one of recent occurrence.   Thus:

ALS ICH IHN SAH, HABE ICH IHN GELOBT.   When I saw him, I praised him.

The Pluperfect in German follows the same usage as in English:

ICH HATTE IHN GELOBT, I had praised him

There is in German as in English a Future Perfect Tense expressing the same idea: **ICH WERDE IHN GELOBT HABEN,** *I shall have praised him.*   The form is little used, but is given for reference:

ich werde gelobt haben, I shall have praised
du wirst gelobt haben, thou wilt have praised
er wird gelobt haben, he will have praised
wir werden gelobt haben, we shall, etc.
ihr werdet gelobt haben, you will, etc.
sie werden gelobt haben, they will, etc.

Sie werden gelobt haben, you will have praised

Similarly, there is a Conditional Perfect: **ICH WÜRDE GELOBT HABEN,** *I should, would have praised.*   This is made with the auxiliary **WERDEN** (the form **würde** being Imperfect Subjunctive) + the Past Participle of **LOBEN,** + **HABEN.**

Verbs Conjugated with **SEIN**: These Compound Tenses are not difficult, but care must be taken to use the right auxiliary with the principal Verb, as some Verbs take **HABEN** and some **SEIN.**

SEIN itself, and **WERDEN,** are both conjugated with **SEIN.** Also all intransitive Verbs and their compounds which denote *movement, change of place,* or *condition.*   This is a considerable number, and it is not possible to give them all here.   All Strong Verbs which take **SEIN** are marked in the Alphabetical List on pages 320-326.   Weak Verbs which take **SEIN** are indicated in the text.

Think of a Verb of movement and it will usually be found to take SEIN.

It is advisable to memorize at this stage the following common Verbs which take **SEIN:**

BLEIBEN, to remain

EILEN, to hurry

FAHREN, to go, travel in a conveyance

FOLGEN, to follow

GEHEN, to go

GESCHEHEN, to happen

KOMMEN, to come

LAUFEN, to run

STEIGEN, to go up, climb

STERBEN, to die

WACHSEN, to grow

VERBS WHICH TAKE EITHER **SEIN** OR **HABEN**: Certain Verbs of motion may be conjugated with either auxiliary, depending on the meaning. These should be noted:

REISEN, to travel

REITEN, to ride

RUDERN, to row

SCHWIMMEN, to swim

SEIN is used with these Verbs *when the destination is clear.* **HABEN** is used *when the activity is recreative.* Thus:

ICH BIN ANS ANDERE UFER GESCHWOMMEN. I have swum to the other bank (of the river).

MEIN BRUDER HAT DEN GANZEN MORGEN GERITTEN. My brother has ridden all morning (*for recreation, exercise*).

Some Verbs in their simple form which take **HABEN** may, when they acquire a separable or inseparable prefix (see **page** 172), take **SEIN.** Thus:

Ich HABE geschlafen, I have slept

Ich BIN eingeschlafen, I have fallen asleep

Other examples are **STEHEN,** *to stand*; **AUFSTEHEN,** *to stand up*; **TRINKEN,** *to drink*; **ERTRINKEN,** *to drown, be drowned.* Thus:

Ich habe getrunken. I have drunk

Der Knabe ist ertrunken. The boy has been drowned.

Apart from these fairly common instances, the learner will find guidance in the ALPHABETICAL LIST OF STRONG VERBS on pages 320-326.

PRACTICE: **ÜBUNG**

Wir haben große Freude daran gehabt. Der Knabe ist
gestern nicht in der Schule gewesen. Sind Sie krank gewesen?
—Ja, ich habe Fieber gehabt. Der Kaufmann ist schnell reich
geworden. Wir sind bei der Arbeit müde geworden. Haben
Sie kein Glück gehabt? Ich hatte zweimal eine Erkältung
gehabt. Er war früher arm gewesen. Sie waren alt geworden.
Ich habe ihn noch einmal gefragt. Die Frau hat ein Kind
bekommen. Wir haben die Reise dorthin nicht gemacht. Die
Äpfel sind vom Baum gefallen. Haben Sie das Neueste gehört?
Er hatte den Brief abgeschickt. Der Mann was zu Fuß gekom-
men. Er hat zwei Spatzen gesehen. Der Zug war schon
abgefahren. Hatten Sie das Buch gelesen? Wir hatten die
Freunde im Sommer besucht.

Ich werde ihn gesehen haben, bevor ich zurückkommen
werde. Werden Sie den Brief erhalten haben, bevor Sie aus
dem Hause gehen werden? Ich würde vorher gern mit Ihnen
gesprochen haben. Wir werden das Ziel nicht erreicht haben,
bevor es dunkel wird. Das Kind würde gern mit dem Ball
gespielt haben. Sie werden den alten Mann wohl gekannt
haben.

Ich bin heute zu Hause geblieben. Der Freund ist heute nach
London gereist. Wir sind auf den Bahnhof geeilt. Sind Sie
mit dem Wagen gekommen? Die Frau ist im Zug gefahren.
Der Knabe war schnell gelaufen. Der alte Herr ist gestorben.
Was ist geschehen? Die Bäume waren hoch gewachsen. Die
Hunde waren dem Jäger gefolgt.

Der starke Mann hat mit aller Kraft gerudert. Wir sind in
dem Boot ans Land gerudert. Er hat eine halbe Stunde im
Wasser geschwommen. Die Knaben sind von der Brücke bis
ans Schiff geschwommen. Haben Sie gestern eine Stunde
geritten? Die Bauern sind in die Stadt geritten. Hat er viel
gereist? Wir sind als Touristen nach Deutschland gereist.

Sports

der Sport, sport
der Alpensport, mountaineering
der Ski (*pl.* die Skier), ski(s)
das Skilaufen, ski-ing
der Schiedsrichter, referee
spielen, to play
das Spiel, game
der Spieler, player
der Gegner, opponent
der Wettkampf, match
der Gewinner ⎱ winner
der Sieger ⎰
gewinnen, to win
das Stadium, stadium
zählen, to count
die Punktzahl, score
der Meister, champion
das Handikap, handicap
die Olympischen Spiele, Olympic Games
das Golf, golf
schwimmen, to swim
der Golfschläger, golf-club
der Fußball, football
das Schlittschuhlaufen, skating
das Tennis, tennis
der Tennisplatz, tennis court
das Boxen, boxing
boxen, to box
das Rollschuhlaufen, roller-skating
schlittschuhlaufen; rollschuhlaufen-gehen, to go skating, roller-skating

die Skistöcke, ski-sticks
der Köcher, golf-bag
der Ball, ball
der Golfball, golf ball
das Eishockey, ice-hockey
der Hindernislauf, steeplechase
der Tennisschläger, tennis-racket
das Einzel, single (tennis)
das Doppel, double(s)
das gemischte Doppel, mixed double(s)
treiben, to be keen on (sport)
ich möchte gern spielen, I'd like a game
das Ergebnis, result
die Kabine, hut, cubicle
mieten, to hire
ein Fußballspiel sehen, to watch a soccer game
das Pferderennen, racing (horse-), races
auf den Fischfang gehen, to go out fishing
der Sportler, sportsman
die Mannschaft, team
das Schwimmbad, swimming-bath
das Fahrrad, bicycle
der Radfahrer, cyclist
rudern, to row
das Boot, boat
das Ruderboot, rowboat

Welchen Sport lieben Sie am meisten? Which sport do
you like best?

Ich spiele gern Tennis. I like to play tennis.

Ich denke, ich bin besser im Einzel als im Doppel. I
think I am better in (the) single(s) than in (the) doubles.

**Im Sommer gehe ich Schwimmen und im Winter Ski-
laufen.** In summer I go swimming and in winter ski-ing.

Manchmal gehe ich auch Schlittschuhlaufen. Sometimes
I also go skating.

Haben Sie gestern das Fußballspiel gesehen? Did you
see the game of soccer yesterday?

**Das Ergebnis muß für die „ B " Mannschaft hart gewesen
sein.** The result must have been hard for team " B ".

Aber die Entscheidung des Schiedsrichters war fair. But
the decision of the referee was fair.

**Die Olympischen Spiele fanden dieses Jahr in Australien
statt.** The Olympic Games took place in Australia this year.

Ich habe einige Wettkämpfe im Fernsehapparat gesehen.
I have seen some matches on (the) television.

**Vor allem haben mich ein Eishockeyspiel und ein Hinder-
nislauf interessiert.** Especially an ice-hockey game and a
steeple-chase interested me.

CONTINUOUS READING   Grimm's **MÄRCHEN**

HANS IM GLÜCK—3

Da setzte sich der Gaul in lebhaften Trab, und Hans
Then the horse started a lively trot and Jack
konnte sich nun nicht mehr im Sattel halten. Ehe er so
could not keep himself any longer in the saddle. Before he
recht zur Besinnung kam, war er abgeworfen und lag im
rightly (fully) realized it he was thrown off and lay in the
Straßengraben. Das Pferd rannte davon; aber ein Bauer
ditch. The horse ran away; but a farmer
hielt es auf, der daherkam und eine Kuh vor sich hertrieb.
*stopped it who was coming that way and (was) driving a cow
before him.*

Hans erhob sich und ging auf den Bauern zu.   „ Ich
Jack picked himself up and went towards the farmer.   " I
danke euch, Bauer, nun habe ich wieder meinen Gaul.
thank   you,   farmer,   now   I   have   my   nag   back.
Aber ich pfeife jetzt auf die ganze Reiterei, wenn ich kein
But I am fed up now with all riding since I haven't got a
anständiges Pferd habe.   Da lobe ich Eure Kuh.   Hinter
decent horse.   There I (must) praise your cow.   You can
der kann man gemächlich hergehen, ohne den Hals zu
walk   leisurely   behind   her   without   risking   your
riskieren, und hat oberdrein noch Milch, Butter und Käse,
neck,   and   besides   still   have   milk,   butter,   and   cheese
wenn man hungert.   Ich wollte, ich hätte so eine Kuh;
when   you're   hungry.   I   wish(ed)   I   had   such   a   cow;
Ihr seid da zu beneiden.“
you are to be envied."

„ Nun, mein Freund, dem Übel kann ich wohl abhelfen,“
" Well,   my   friend,   that   evil   I   can   perhaps   remedy,"
tröstete ihn der Bauer.   „ Wenn ich dir einen großen
the   farmer   consoled   him.   " If   I   can   do   you   a   great
Gefallen erweise, dann will ich dieses Pferd gegen die
favor,   then   I   will   exchange   this   horse   for
Kuh eintauschen.“
the cow."

„ Einverstanden,“ sagte Hans.   Der Bauer nahm den
" Agreed,"   said   Jack.   The   farmer   took   the
Gaul, und Hans erhielt die Kuh.
nag, and Jack the cow.

[*Contd. on page* 170.

§ 5. *Conjugation of a Strong Verb :* **TRAGEN—***Changes in Second and Third Person Singular—Conjunctions : Co-ordinating—Practice—Photography—Cartoon—Continuous Reading :* **Hans im Glück**

The principal parts of Strong Verbs most in use will be found on pages 188–9, 197–8, 209-11. Here is an example of a typical Strong Verb and the Conjugation of its tenses:

Infinitive : **TRAGEN,** to carry (*also* to bear *and* wear)

Present Participle : **TRAGEND,** carrying

Past Participle : **GETRAGEN,** carried

Present Tense Indicative	*Imperfect or Simple Past*
ich tragE, I carry	**ich trUg,** I carried
du trägST	**du trUgST**
er ⎫	**er,** etc., **trUg**
sie ⎬ **trägT**	
es ⎭	
wir tragEN	**wir trUgEN**
ihr tragT	**ihr trUgT**
sie tragEN	**sie trUgEN**
Sie tragEN, you carry	

Simple Future

ICH WERDE TRAGEN, I shall carry
du wirst, etc., **tragen**

Conditional

ICH WÜRDE TRAGEN, I should carry

Imperative

TRAGEN WIR *or* **lassen Sie uns tragen,** let us carry
TRAGEN SIE, (you) carry

Note the change from **a** to **ä** in the Second and Third Persons Singular of the Present. This kind of change and some others is quite usual in these persons of the Present singular. There is a certain regularity in the changes in Strong Verbs with the Root Vowel **-E.** There are three categories of these **-E** Root Strong Verbs:

I. Those with *short* **E** in the Root change it to **i** in the Second and Third Persons Singular Present Indicative. Thus:

SPRECHEN : ich sprEche, du sprIchst, er sprIcht

II. Those with *long* **E** in the root change it to **i e :**

LESEN, to read : **ich lEse, du lIEst, er lIEst**

III. A few **E**-Verbs have no vowel change in the Present :

GEHEN, to go : **ich gEhe, du gEhst, er gEht**

These changes are in the *singular only*.   In the plural the **E** is retained:

wir sprEchen, etc.
wir lEsen, etc.
wir gEhen, etc.

CONJUNCTIONS : A Conjunction is an indeclinable word used to connect sentences or parts of a sentence.   Thus :

you AND I
He was NEITHER a fool NOR a rogue.
He plays golf, BUT he plays it badly.
AND, NEITHER . . . NOR, BUT are Conjunctions.

German Conjunctions may conveniently be divided into two categories :

I. Those which do not alter the construction of the sentence they introduce.   These are co-ordinating Conjunctions.

II. Those which alter it, and then usually require the Verb to be placed at the end of the sentence.   These are subordinating Conjunctions.

Co-ordinating Conjunctions :

ABER, but, however
allein, but, yet (*rare*)
DENN, for
DOCH, jedoch, but, yet
JA, yes, indeed

NÄMLICH, as, since
ODER, or
SONDERN, but (*after a negative*)
UND, and

These are the " pure " Conjunctions, so called because they usually connect independent sentences.   Thus :

ER SPIELT FUSSBALL, ABER er spielt es schlecht.   He plays soccer, but he plays it badly.
ER IST KRANK UND der Arzt besucht ihn.   He is ill, and the doctor visits him.

DOCH, jedoch and (less common) **ALLEIN** are stronger words than **ABER.**
allein as an Adjective or Adverb means *alone.*

ER KAM ALLEIN, he came alone

SONDERN expresses *but* after a negative sentence, usually to contradict it:

Er ist nicht ein armer Mann, SONDERN ein reicher.
He is not a poor man but a rich one.

JA which, as an Adverb means *yes*, as a Conjunction is an emphatic word expressing *indeed* :

Ich schätze diesen Mann, JA ich bewundere ihn. I esteem this man, indeed I admire him.

There is a group of words with a similar function to that of the pure co-ordinating Conjunctions: they do not usually connect independent sentences each with its Verb, but connect parts of the independent sentence within itself. These are:

wie			as
sowie	⎫	⎧	and also
ebenso wie	⎬ = **UND** = ⎨		and likewise
wie auch	⎭	⎩	as well as

The following combinations of **als** or **wie** are often used as co-ordinating Conjunctions:

sowohl . . . als	⎫
sowohl . . . wie	⎬ both . . . and
ebenso . . . wie	⎭
wie . . . so	
nicht sowohl . . . als, not so much . . . as	
beide . . . und	⎫ both . . . and
beides . . . und	⎭
außer, except	
anstatt, instead of	
ausgenommen, except	
ohne, without	

Examples :

Er verkauft Bücher, Hefte WIE Bleistifte. He sells books, pamphlets, and pencils.
Er verkauft Bücher und Hefte SOWIE Bleistifte. He sells books and pamphlets and also pencils.

Er war verärgert $\begin{Bmatrix} \textbf{WIE AUCH} \\ \textbf{EBENSO WIE} \end{Bmatrix}$ **beleidigt.** He was annoyed $\begin{Bmatrix} \text{as well as} \\ \text{and likewise} \end{Bmatrix}$ offended.

Das Mädchen ist SOWOHL klug WIE schön. The girl is both intelligent and beautiful.

Er hat EBENSO viel Glück WIE Verstand. He has as much luck as understanding.

Ich verbrannte BEIDES, Brief und Umschlag. I burned both letter and envelope.

Er beantwortete ALLE Fragen AUßER der letzten. He answered all questions except the last (one).

ANSTATT Geld bekam er gute Worte. Instead of money, he received fine words.

As these words do not affect Word-order, they do not need special attention but should be learnt as vocabulary.

The subordinating Conjunctions will be dealt with later (Lesson VII, § 2).

PRACTICE: **ÜBUNG**

Trägt der Bote den Koffer? Die Frau trägt schöne Kleider. Ich trug gestern keinen Mantel. Die Männer trugen schwere Steine. Möchten Sie diesen Hut tragen? Ich werde ihn nicht tragen. Bitte tragen Sie diesen Brief zur Post! Der Vater hat den Knaben auf dem Arm getragen. Die Mädchen hatten Schuhe aber keine Strümpfe getragen. Würde die Dame die Handtasche selbst tragen? Ich würde die Schuhe getragen haben, wenn sie sauber gewesen wären.

Sprechen Sie deutsch? Ich spreche und lese deutsch. Mein Bruder spricht und liest französisch. Wir werden die Zeitung lesen. Der Knabe saß auf der Bank, ein Buch lesend. Jener Schüler liest nicht gut deutsch. Gehen wir heute nachmittag spazieren? Der Mann geht schnell über die Straße. Haben Sie eine gut gehende Uhr?

Diese Frau spricht nicht englisch, aber sie kann französisch sprechen. Mein Freund ist ebenso groß wie ich. In jener Bar können wir Bier wie auch Wein bekommen. Im Zoologischen Garten sind Löwen sowie Tiger. Hat er geschlafen anstatt zu arbeiten? Der Diener hatte alles zum Bahnhof getragen ausgenommen den schweren Koffer. Gehen wir langsam über die

Brücke ohne zu laufen. Haben Sie beides getan, die Blumen geholt und den Stuhl in den Garten getragen? Ich habe dieses wie auch jenes getan.

Photography

die Kamera, camera
die Kleinbildkamera, miniature camera
die Schmalfilmkamera, cine-camera
der Film (die Filme), film(s)
der Rollfilm, roll film
der Farbfilm, colour film
entwickeln, to develop
vergrößern, to enlarge
der Abzug, die Abzüge, print(s)
das Papier, paper
das Glanzpapier, glossy paper
mattes Papier, matt paper
möglichst bald, as soon as possible
fertig, ready
das Blitzlicht, flash-light
der Filter, filter
das Negativ, die Negative, negative(s)
Entwickeln Sie bitte diese Negative. Please develop these negatives.

Machen Sie einen Abzug von jedem Negativ. Make one print from each negative.
Ich möchte eine Vergrößerung. I'd like an enlargement.
einlegen, to load (a camera)
Bitte legen Sie einen Film ein. Please put a film in.
die Dunkelkammer, dark room
die Linse, lens
nicht ordentlich, out of order
in Ordnung, in order
Können Sie meinen Apparat in Ordnung bringen? Can you put my camera in order?
der Apparat, general word for camera
funktionieren, to function, work
die Photohandlung, camera shop, photo supply shop
die Aufnahme, photograph
die Momentaufnahme, snapshot

Wo ist die nächste Photohandlung? Where is the nearest photo supply shop?
Wollen Sie bitte diesen Film entwickeln und von jedem Negativ einen Abzug machen. Will you please develop this film and make a print from each negative.
Soll es auf Glanzpapier sein? Must it be on glossy paper?

Ja, und von diesen zwei Photos machen Sie bitte Vergrößerungen auf mattem Papier. Yes, and from these two photos please make enlargements on matt paper.

Könnte ich sie möglichst bald haben? Could I have them as soon as possible?

Wünschen Sie einen neuen Rollfilm für Ihre Schmalfilmkamera? Do you want a new roll of film for your movie camera?

Ja, wollen Sie den Film gleich einlegen. Yes, would you put the film in immediately (now).

LACHEND INS WOCHENENDE

„Ja, ja, das verstehe ich schon. Ich begreife nur nicht, wie man ein viereckiges Bild mit einer runden Öffnung bekommt."

Gestern habe ich mit meinem Apparat einige Blitzlichtaufnahmen gemacht. Yesterday I took some flash-light photos with my camera.

Er funktioniert jetzt nicht mehr ordentlich. It is now somehow out of order.

Einen Augenblick, bitte! A moment, please.

Ich will damit erst in die Dunkelkammer gehen und die Filmrolle herausnehmen. I'll first go with it into the dark room and take out the roll of film.

Wollen Sie einmal nachsehen, ob die Linse in Ordnung ist. Would you just see (examine) whether the lens is in order.

CONTINUOUS READING   Grimm's **MÄRCHEN**

HANS IM GLÜCK—4

Vergnügt trieb er das Tier vor sich her und freute sich
Cheerfully he drove the animal in front of him and was pleased
über den schlauen Handel. „ Ein Stück Brot werde ich
about   the   crafty   deal.   " I shall get a piece of bread
überall bekommen. Dazu esse ich Butter und Käse; und
everywhere.   With it I'll eat butter and cheese ; and
wenn ich Durst habe, trinke ich frische Milch. Aha, das
when I am thirsty I'll drink fresh milk.   Ah, that
wird ein feines Leben sein!" Als er an ein Wirtshaus
will be a fine life."   When he came to an inn,
kam, band er die Kuh an einen Haken, trat in die Gaststube
he tied the cow to a hook, entered the guest-room
und aß seine mitgenommenen Brote auf. Für seine
and ate the pieces of bread he had with him.   For his
letzten Groschen * kaufte er sich ein Glas Bier. Dann trieb
last small coin he bought himself a glass of beer.   Then he drove
er seine Kuh dem Dorf seiner Mutter zu.
his cow towards his mother's village.

Er kam dabei gegen Mittag durch eine öde Heide, die
By noon he then came over (through) a deserted heath which
sich sehr weit hinzog. Da wurde er durstig, und die
stretched very far.   He became thirsty, and his
Zunge klebte ihm am Gaumen. „ Jetzt ist es Zeit! Ich
tongue was parched in his mouth. " Now's the time! I'll
will meine Kuh melken," brummte Hans vor sich hin.
milk   my   cow,"   Jack   murmured   to   himself.
Er band die Kuh an einen Baum und legte seine Ledermütze
He tied the cow to a tree and placed his leather cap
unter das Euter.   Aber wie er auch das Euter bearbeitete,
under the udder.   But however much he belabored the udder,

* **der Groschen = 10 Pfennige** (see page 69).

es kam kein Tropfen Milch heraus.   Er war ganz unge-
no   drop   of   milk   came   out.   He   was   quite   clumsy
schickt dabei.   Da holte die Kuh mit dem Hinterfuß aus
at   it.   Thereupon   the   cow   lifted   a   hind   foot
und versetzte ihm einen starken Hieb vor den Kopf, daß
and   struck   a   heavy   blow   against   his   head   (so)   that
er lang niederstürzte und bewußtlos liegen blieb.
he fell down full length and remained lying unconscious.

[Contd. on page 179.

LESSON VI

§ 1. *Compound Verbs: Separable and Inseparable Prefixes—The Inseparable Prefixes and Meanings—List and Examples—Practice—Tobacco and Cigarettes, etc.—Continuous Reading:* **Hans im Glück**

TAKE the whole of this Lesson slowly. It is highly important, all of it. Review again and again until it is known, but first be sure that you understand before you memorize.

Nearly all German Verbs can change or expand their meaning by placing another word before them to make a compound Verb. Thus:

KOMMEN, to come ; **ZURÜCKKOMMEN,** to come back

The word **ZURÜCK,** is used as a prefix. When **ZURÜCK-KOMMEN** is conjugated, the **ZURÜCK** is separated from it and placed after it. Thus: **ich komme zurück,** *I come back.* In this event, the prefix is *separable.*

But there is a small group of prefixes that are *inseparable*: they never leave the Verb to which they are attached. As the inseparable prefixes are fewer in number than the separable, and their use is straightforward, it is better to become acquainted with them first. Then all other prefixes may be regarded as separable. Inseparable prefixes are unaccented: stress is on the root syllable of the Verb: **BESCHRE*I*BEN.**

INSEPARABLE PREFIXES: These are: **BE-,ENT- (EMP-** before **f),*** **ER-, GE-, VER-, WIDER,†** **ZER-,** and usually **MIß-.**

Note well :

(*a*) These are *never* separated from the Verb.

(*b*) They are *un*stressed.

---

* As in **empfinden,** *to feel, perceive.*
† Do not confuse **WIDER,** *against*, with **WIEDER,** *again*, which is a separable prefix.

(c) Verbs made with them do *not* take **GE-** in their Past Participles.

Example:

SCHREIBEN, to write; **BESCHREIBEN,** to describe

Present: **ich schreibe—ich beschreibe.**

Past: **ich schrieb—ich beschrieb.**

Compounds: **ich habe geschrieben—ich habe beschrieben.**

Rule: **An Inseparable Verb follows exactly the conjugation of its simple Verb. BESCHREIBEN** as above, and **BEKOMMEN,** *to come by, to get, receive.* **Ich bekomme, ich bekam, ich habe bekommen.**

MEANINGS OF INSEPARABLE PREFIXES: They have *or have had,* each one of them, a meaning or significance which could be pinned down to an English equivalent, often an exact meaning. Unfortunately it is not now always possible to do so, and therefore the safest rule for the English-speaking learner is to **LEARN EACH INSEPARABLE VERB WITH ITS COMMONEST MEANING,** which is always given in this text. Nevertheless, what follows should help as general indications of meanings of the inseparable prefixes:

BE- is related to the Preposition **BEI,** and usually indicates *around, on all sides of.* Consider the following:

DENKEN, to think; **BEDENKEN,** to consider, ponder = " think round something "

GREIFEN, to seize; **BEGREIFEN,** to grasp (mentally), to understand (well)

ENT- (EMP-)

(a) Originally **ant-** = Greek ANTI = *against, toward,* a meaning still found in some words:

SPRECHEN, to speak; **ENTSPRECHEN,** to answer, correspond to

(b) more often it indicates *separation, removal, withdrawal* or *depriving,* as in:

KOMMEN, to come; **ENTKOMMEN,** to escape (from)

EHREN, to honour; **ENTEHREN,** to dishonour (take away honour)

WICKELN, to wind, wrap up

ENTWICKELN, to unfold, to develop (photos)

ER-, *from within out, out from, completion of a process,* as :

DENKEN, to think ; **ERDENKEN,** to think out, evolve
FINDEN, to find ; **ERFINDEN,** to find out, discover
PRESSEN, to press ; **ERPRESSEN,** to extort,
to blackmail
WECKEN, to wake ; **ERWECKEN,** to awaken, arouse, excite

GE-

(*a*) *collection* or *union,* as in :

RINNEN, to run, flow ; **GERINNEN,** run together, curdle,
coagulate
FRIEREN, to freeze ; **GEFRIEREN,** to freeze up, to congeal

(*b*) **GE-** also indicates *the entrance into a state or condition,* as :

HORCHEN, to hearken ; **GEHORCHEN,** to hearken (*with
obedience as a result*), to obey

VER-   This is a frequently recurring prefix with so many and such
varied meanings that they cannot always be clearly defined.   The
indications for **VER-** come under three broad headings, each with
sub-headings.

I. (*a*) The commonest meaning is that of *away from, forth,* as in :

REISEN, to travel ; **VERREISEN,** to journey forth
JAGEN, to hunt, chase ; **VERJAGEN,** to chase away

(*b*) The idea of *away* often develops into *intensification* or *completion* as in :

BLÜHEN, to bloom ; **VERBLÜHEN,** to cease blooming
BLUTEN, to bleed ; **VERBLUTEN,** to bleed to death

II. Under this heading **VER-** (*a*) expresses ideas of *movement
outwards, or forward* to a goal, as in :

BEUGEN, to bend ; **VERBEUGEN,** to bow to
SPRECHEN, to speak ; **VERSPRECHEN,** to promise

(*b*) The forward movement often leads to one of *protecting,
concealing, refusing,* or *hindering* as :

ANTWORTEN, to answer ; **VERANTWORTEN,** to answer
for, to account for
FECHTEN, to fight, to fence ; **VERFECHTEN,** to fight for

(*c*) Or to the idea of *going beyond, excess,* as :

SCHLAFEN, to sleep ; **VERSCHLAFEN,** to oversleep

III. Or to *encircling, covering,* as :

HÜLLEN, to wrap ; **VERHÜLLEN,** to wrap up well

IV. (*a*) Under this rather vague heading come the more or less
concrete ideas of I, II, and III, fading into the abstract as :

BLEIBEN, to remain ; **VERBLEIBEN,** to remain long, to the
end
LESEN, to read ; **VERLESEN,** to read out (*a roll of names*),
to sort out
FOLGEN, to follow ; **VERFOLGEN,** to pursue, follow up

(*b*) A *change into a state* indicated by some Noun or Adjective.

ARM, *poor*. And so: **VERARMEN,** *to grow poor.*

BILLIG, cheap; **VERBILLIGEN,** to reduce the cost
DICK, thick; **VERDICKEN,** to thicken
GOTT, God; **VERGÖTTERN,** to deify

(c) A *fusion or union*, as in:

SCHMELZEN, to melt; **VERSCHMELZEN,** to blend, fuse
WACHSEN, to grow; **VERWACHSEN,** to grow together

V. **VER-** *converts intransitive Verbs into transitives*, as:

LACHEN, to laugh; **VERLACHEN,** to deride
FLUCHEN, to swear; **VERFLUCHEN,** to curse, damn

WIDER-, *against*, English *re-* or *back*, as:

SPRECHEN, to speak; **WIDERSPRECHEN,** to contradict
HALLEN, to sound; **WIDERHALLEN,** to echo, resound
RUFEN, to call; **WIDERRUFEN,** to call back, to retract, repeal

ZER-, *asunder, separation, scattering*, as:

BRECHEN, to break; **ZERBRECHEN,** to break in pieces
FLIEßEN, to flow; **ZERFLIEßEN,** to melt away
SCHNEIDEN, to cut; **ZERSCHNEIDEN,** to cut up, carve

MIß- = English *mis-, failure, error, falsity*, as:

DEUTEN, to interpret; **MIßDEUTEN,** to misinterpret
GÖNNEN, to be glad of, approve; **MIßGÖNNEN,** to begrudge
VERSTEHEN, to understand; **MIßVERSTEHEN,** to misunderstand

What has been stated above is neither exhaustive as regards the examples that could be given nor in regard to the very considerable number of inseparable Verbs. In many instances, only the inseparable Verb is now used, the original simple Verb having fallen out of use. It is desirable, first, to understand *how* these inseparable Verbs are made, *how* they work, and *the main ideas behind each prefix*. Second, the words given as examples should be memorized, each one in its simple form, and then with the prefix. Third, each time a new Verb with an inseparable prefix is met an attempt should be made to work out its meaning with the aid of this list, and the result checked with a dictionary, and *the Verb and meaning memorized*. See also page 265 *et seq.* for Word-building in general.

Practice : ÜBUNG

Er beschrieb seine Reise.   He described his journey.

Haben Sie den Brief geschrieben?   Have you written the letter ?

Ich habe das Bild beschrieben.   I have described the picture.

Er denkt an seine Schwester.   He thinks of his sister.

Er bedenkt den Vorschlag.   He ponders over the proposition.

Er erdenkt einen Plan.   He thinks out a plan.

Begreifen Sie das Problem?   Do you grasp the problem ?

Er spricht deutsch.   He speaks German.

Die Erzählung entspricht den Tatsachen.   The tale corresponds to the facts.

Der Sohn widerspricht seinem Vater.   The son contradicts his father.

Der Meister verspricht Hans einen guten Lohn.   The master promises Jack a good reward.

Kamen die Freunde?   Did the friends come ?

Entkamen die Feinde?   Did the enemies escape ?

Die Freunde sind gekommen und die Feinde entkommen.   The friends have come and the enemies escaped.

Das Volk ehrt den Künstler.   The people honor the artist.

Diebstahl entehrt den Mann.   Theft dishonors the man.

Sie wickeln die Wolle zu einem Ball.   They wind the wool into a ball.

Ich werde die Photos entwickeln.   I shall develop the photos.

Er hat den Draht auf die Rolle gewickelt.   He has wound the wire on the roll.

Das Kind ist gut entwickelt.   The child is well developed.

Werden Sie den Weg finden?   Will you find the way ?

Sie erfinden eine Geschichte, nicht wahr?   You make up a story, don't you ?

Er hat den Ring gefunden.   He has found the ring.

Er hat eine neue Methode erfunden.   He has discovered a new method.

Der Bursche erpreßte Geld von ihm.   The fellow extorted money from him.

Die Mutter weckte das Kind. The mother woke the child.

Jesus erweckte die Toten. Jesus awakened the dead.

Das Blut gerinnt. The blood coagulates.

Fleisch gefriert bei niedriger Temperatur. Meat freezes at low temperature.

Wir horchten auf die Geräusche. We hearkened to the sounds.

Wir gehorchten den Gesetzen. We obeyed the laws.

Ich werde mit dem Zug reisen. I shall travel by train.

Ich werde morgen verreisen. I shall journey forth to-morrow.

Der Jäger hat den ganzen Tag gejagt. The hunter hunted all day.

Der Hund hat die Hühner verjagt. The dog chased away the hens.

Die Blumen blühen heute schön, aber morgen werden sie verblüht sein. The flowers bloom beautifully to-day, but to-morrow they will have ceased to bloom.

Mein Finger hat geblutet. My finger has bled.

Der Verwundete ist verblutet. The wounded man bled to death.

Er beugte das Knie. He bent the knee.

Er verbeugte sich vor dem Richter. He bowed before the judge.

Sie hat nicht geantwortet. She has not answered.

Sie hat ihre Tat selbst zu verantworten. She has herself to answer for her deed.

Ich habe lange geschlafen. I have slept long.

Gestern habe ich verschlafen. Yesterday I overslept.

Sie verhüllte ihr Gesicht. She covered her face.

Verbleiben Sie im Zimmer? Do you remain (long) in the room?

Ich habe das Buch gelesen. I have read the book.

Die Ankündigung wurde laut verlesen. The announcement was read out aloud.

Der Hund folgte seinem Herrn. The dog followed his master.

Der Hund verfolgte die Hasen. The dog pursued the hares.

Jene Leute sind verarmt.   Those people have grown poor.

Der Koch verdickte die Suppe mit Reis.   The cook thickened the soup with rice.

Die Eltern vergöttern ihr Kind.   The parents idolize (deify) their child.

Die Bäume wachsen nicht in den Himmel.   (The) trees do not grow to heaven.

Die Zweige sind verwachsen.   The branches have grown together.

Er lachte laut.   He laughed loudly.

Er verlachte den Toren.   He derided the fool.

Man soll nicht fluchen.   One should not swear.

Er verfluchte die Übeltäter.   He cursed the evil doers.

Der Staat hat den Vertrag widerrufen.   The state has revoked the treaty.

Sie brechen ihr Wort nicht.   They don't break their word.

Wir zerbrechen die Teller.   We break the plates in pieces.

Er hat die Schrift richtig gedeutet.   He has interpreted the scripture correctly.

Hat er mein Lob mißdeutet?   Has he misinterpreted my praise?

Verstehen Sie mich recht, und bitte mißverstehen Sie meine Worte nicht!   Understand me rightly, and please do not misunderstand my words!

Tobacco and Cigarettes, etc.

die Zigarre, cigar

das Zigarrengeschäft, der Zigarrenladen, cigar store

der Tabak, tobacco

die Tabakspfeife, tobacco pipe

die Zigarette(-n), cigarette(s)

englische, ⎤ English,
amerikanische ⎬ American
Zigaretten, ⎦ cigarettes

das Streichholz (-hölzer), match, matches

reinigen, to clean

der Pfeifenreiniger, pipe-cleaner

die Schachtel, packet (of cigarettes)

ich hätte gern . . . I'd like to have . . .

ich möchte . . . haben, I'd like to have . . .

offen, open

öffnen, to open

Sonntags öffnen, to open on Sundays

schließen, to shut

geschlossen, shut, closed

das Feuerzeug, lighter

der Brennstoff, lighter fuel

der Feuerstein, flint

der Docht, wick

Ist der Zigarrenladen Sonntags geöffnet? Is the tobacconist's open on Sundays?

Ich will in das Zigarrengeschäft gehen und ein paar Zigarren kaufen. I'll go to the tobacconist's and buy a couple of cigars.

Was soll ich für Sie mitbringen? What shall I fetch for you?

Ich möchte gern etwas Tabak für meine Pfeife haben. I'd like to have some tobacco for my pipe.

Und für meine Frau bringen Sie bitte eine Schachtel amerikanische Zigaretten und zwei Schachteln Streichhölzer. And for my wife, please bring a packet of American cigarettes and two boxes of matches.

Außerdem brauche ich Brennstoff für mein Feuerzeug und habe einen Feuerstein und einen neuen Docht nötig. Apart from that I require some fuel for my lighter and need a flint and a new wick.

CONTINUOUS READING   Grimm's **MÄRCHEN**

HANS IM GLÜCK—5

In diesem Augenblick kam ein Metzger daher, der auf
At this moment a butcher passed by who had
einem Schubkarren ein junges Schwein hatte.
a young pig on a wheel-barrow.

„ Hallo, was ist dir denn passiert? " rief er laut und half
" Hello, what has happened to you then? " he called loudly and
Hans auf die Beine. Dann reichte der Metzger ihm einen
helped Jack on his legs. The butcher then gave him a
Trunk aus seiner Flasche und sagte: „ Da, trinke und
drink from his bottle and said: " There, drink and
erhol dich von dem Schreck! Die Kuh wird überhaupt
recover from the shock! The cow will not give any

keine Milch mehr geben, denn sie ist schon uralt und
more milk at all, because she is already (extremely) old and
taugt kaum mehr zum Ziehen, nur noch gut zum
hardly useful for pulling a cart, only good for being
Schlachten."
slaughtered."

„ Ei, ei, hm ja, Ihr habt recht. Wenn man solche Kuh
" Eh, maybe, yes, you're right. If one could slaughter such a
zu Hause abschlachten könnte! Aber nein, so altes
cow at home! But no, I wouldn't like such old
Fleisch mag ich nicht," meinte nun der Hans ganz ernst.
meat," Jack thought quite seriously.
„ Ja, wenn ich solch ein junges Schweinchen hätte, wie
" Yes, if (only) I had such a young little pig
das Eurige. Hm, das gibt prima Fleisch und feine
like yours. H'm, that (one) gives first-class meat and nice
Würste! "
sausages! "

„ Höre, lieber Hans," sagte der Metzger schmeichelnd,
" Listen, (my) dear Jack," the butcher said, flattering,
„ dir zuliebe würde ich tauschen. Du gibst mir die Kuh
" to please you I'm willing to change. You give me the cow
und erhälst dafür das Schwein."
and you'll get the pig."

„ Wahrhaftig, Ihr seid ein wahrer Freund, ich danke
" Indeed, you are a true friend, I thank
Euch! Hier habt Ihr die Kuh! " Und der Metzger gab
you! Here, have the cow! " And the butcher gave
ihm dafür den Strick des Schweines in seine Hand.
him for it the rope of the pig in his hand.

[Contd. on page 186.

§ 2. *Separable Verbs: Conjugation—List of Common Separable
Prefixes—Practice—Public Notices—Continuous Reading:*
Hans im Glück

Before proceeding to the Separable Verbs the learner must
make quite sure that he has the inseparable prefixes well in his

memory.   When this is certain, he may consider that every new Verb that is met which has *any other prefix* is a Separable Verb.

The separable part of a Verb must always be stressed.   Thus: **GEHEN,** *to go*; *AUSGEHEN,* *to go out*—stress on **AUS-.** (With the inseparables it is the *root* of the Verb and not the prefix that is stressed: **HA′LTEN,** *to hold*; **BEHAL′TEN,** *to retain, keep*).

The Separable Verbs are conjugated differently from the inseparables, and follow certain fixed rules:

I. In the Present and Past Tenses of both Indicative and Subjunctive, the prefix is detached and placed at the end of its clause.   Thus:

REISEN, *to travel*; *ABREISEN,* *to set out*
ICH REISTE AB, *I set out, I was setting out*

II. When **ZU** is used with the Infinitive, it is placed between the prefix and the Verb: **ABZUREISEN:**

Ich will abreisen (wollen does not need **ZU)**
Ich wünsche abZUreisen (wünschen requires **ZU)**

III. The **GE-** of Past Participles of separable Verbs is placed between the prefix and the Verb:

AUSGEHEN, to go out
ICH GING AUS, I went out
ICH BIN AUSGEGANGEN, I have gone out

IV. In the Imperative, the prefix goes to the end:

Gehen Sie AUS!   Go out!

V. In all other respects the Verb part of a Separable Verb is conjugated normally.   A Weak Verb follows the Weak Conjugation, a Strong Verb, the Strong, in accordance with the rules.   Thus:

Weak—

AUFMACHEN, to (make) open

Er macht die Tür auf.   He opens the door
Ich machte die Tür auf.   I opened the door
Sie hatte die Tür aufgemacht.   She had opened the door.

Strong—

SCHNEIDEN, to cut; **ABSCHNEIDEN,** to cut off
ICH SCHNITT AB, I cut off (past)
ICH HABE ABGESCHNITTEN, I have cut off

MEANING OF SEPARABLE PREFIXES: As with the inseparables, each separable prefix has a meaning, on the whole more clearly definable than most of the inseparable prefixes. When the separable prefix is a Noun there is seldom any difficulty about the meaning of the compounded Verb; and similarly when it is an Adjective. But when the prefix is an Adverb or a Preposition, one has to be careful.

It would not be either desirable or possible here to set out all the words used to make compound separable Verbs, but the learner must make himself thoroughly acquainted with the list which follows:

LIST OF COMMON SEPARABLE PREFIXES

Prefix	General Indications	Examples
AB-	Movement *downwards, off, away,* often with deterioration	**ABARBEITEN,** to wear out with work
AN-	*at, upon, on, onto,* expressing a rest or arrival at goal	**ANSTECKEN,** to put on, to fasten
AUF-	*up, open, arousing, restoration* to a previous state or condition	**AUFPACKEN,** to pack up
AUS-	*out, out of, cessation* of activity	**AUSSCHWITZEN,** to sweat out
BEI-	*by, aside, at the side of, nearness,* sometimes *hostility to*	**BEITRAGEN,** to (bring by) contribute
DA-, DAR-,	*there,* often with preposition (see page 237) as in **DAVON,** *thereof,* *therefrom,* **DARAN,** *thereto,* **DAHIN,** thither; etc.	**DARLEGEN,** to lay out, display, present
EIN-	*in, into*	**EINTRETEN,** to step into
EMPOR-	*up, upward*	**EMPORHEBEN,** to (heave up) raise
ENTGE-GEN-	*against, towards,* a move towards: **GEGEN,** in direction of	**ENTGEGENHAL-TEN,** to hold against
ENTZWEI-	*in two, apart*	**ENTZWEISCHLA-GEN,** to knock to pieces
FORT-	*onward, away, forth*	**FORTGEHEN,** to go away

Prefix	General Indications	Examples
HEIM-	home	HEIMKEHREN, to return home
HER-	motion towards the speaker	HERHOLEN, to fetch from afar
HIN-	motion from the speaker Compounds with HER- and HIN-: HERAB, HINAB, DA-HIN, motion towards, to that place, to it; DAHER, EIN-HER, along; HINTENAN, behind. And others similar.	HINABGLEITEN, to slide down
LOS-	loose, free, from, off (sudden movement)	SCHLAGEN, to strike, hit LOSSCHLAGEN, to begin battle
MIT-	with	MITTEILEN, to (divide with) make known
NACH-	after, in order of time, place	NACHLAUFEN, to run after
NIEDER-	down	NIEDERLEGEN, to lay down
OB-	above, on top, of duties or tasks	OBWALTEN, to prevail
VOR-	before, of time, also in compounds VORAN, VORAUS, in front of, beforehand	VORSCHIEBEN, to push forward (schieben, to push)
WEG-	away	WEGNEHMEN, to take away
WIEDER	again, afresh	WIEDERKOMMEN, to come again, return
ZU-	to, towards, active unceasing effort	ZUFÜHREN, to lead to
ZURÜCK-	back	ZURÜCKGEBEN, to give back
ZUSAM-MEN-	together	ZUSAMMENTRA-GEN, to carry together = to collect
ZUVOR-	before, ahead of (time, etc.)	ZUVORKOMMEN, anticipate
WEITER-	further, continuation of	WEITERTREIBEN, to drive on

The above separable verbs are made from Prepositions or Adverbs. Some Separable Verbs can be made up of Adjectives, as in TOTSCHLAGEN, to strike dead. Or Nouns, as in ACHT-GEBEN, to give (pay) attention, HAUSHALTEN, to keep house, TEILNEHMEN, to take part, etc.

☞ The general indications and significance of all these pre-fixes should be known. With a vocabulary of simple Verbs, and the prefixes, innumerable compounds are possible.

See Word-building, pages 265-267.

PRACTICE: ÜBUNG

Ist Ihr Freund gestern *abgereist*?—Nein, er *reist* heute *ab*, und seine Frau wird morgen *abreisen*. Wann sind Sie hier *ange-kommen*? Ich *kam* gestern *an*. Ich hoffte, schon früher *anzu-kommen*. Wir *schreiben* die Namen *auf*. Hat der Schüler die Lektion *aufgeschrieben*? Er *forderte* mich *auf*, etwas Geld *beizutragen*. Der Mann hat die Tatsachen *dargelegt*. *Treten* Sie bitte *ein*! Die Frau *trat ein*. Wir sind nicht *eingetreten*. *Ging* er *fort*? Sie bat uns, nicht *fortzugehen*. Ich bin *fort-gegangen*. Was *halten* sie ihm *entgegen*? Sie haben ihm nichts *entgegengehalten*. Das Mädchen *schlägt* den Teller *entzwei*. Warum hat es ihn *entzweigeschlagen*?

Holen Sie den Mann *her*! Er bittet mich, ihn *herzuholen*. Der Soldat ist aus dem Krieg *heimgekehrt*. Der Junge *fährt* mit dem Boot *los*. Er hatte vor, *loszufahren*. *Laufen* Sie ihm *nach*! Ich bin ihm *nachgelaufen*. *Teilte* er Ihnen seine Ankunft *mit*? Er hat sie mir *mitgeteilt*. Ich *legte* das Buch vor ihm *nieder*. Sie hatten es *niedergelegt*. Wer *ging* Ihnen *voraus*? Die Mädchen *gingen voraus*. Ich bat sie, *vorauszugehen*. Sie sind mir *vorausgegangen*. *Nehmen* Sie ihm das Messer *weg*! Es ist besser, es ihm *wegzunehmen*. *Kommen* Sie bald *wieder*? Er ist schnell *wiedergekommen*.

Hörte er aufmerksam *zu*? Wir haben gern *zugehört*. Sie *tragen* Holz *zusammen*. Es ist nicht leicht, alles *zusammen-zutragen*. *Führt* dieser Weg *weiter*? Ich hoffe, ein solches Leben *weiterzuführen*. Wann *gibt* er das Buch *zurück*? Er hat es schon *zurückgegeben*. Er ist uns *zuvorgekommen*.

Geben Sie bitte *acht*! Ich habe nicht *achtgegeben*. *Nehmen* Sie am Kurs *teil*? Ich *nahm* daran *teil*. Es war gut, daran *teilzunehmen*. Die Feinde *schlagen* einander *tot*. Haben sie einander *totgeschlagen*?

Public Notices

ANSCHLAG, Notice

EINTRITT FREI, Admission Free

. . . VERBOTEN, . . . Forbidden

BADEN VERBOTEN, Bathing Forbidden

ZUTRITT VERBOTEN, Entrance Forbidden

RAUCHEN VERBOTEN, Smoking Forbidden

RAUCHER, Smoker, Smoking

VORSICHT . . . Beware of . . .

ACHTUNG! Look Out!

GEFÄHRLICH, Dangerous

BAHNÜBERGANG, Level Crossing

LANGSAM FAHREN, Drive Slowly

PARKPLATZ, Parking Place

GARAGE, Garage

TANKSTELLE, Petrol Station, Gasoline Station

HALTESTELLE, Stopping-place

NACH RECHTS, To the Right

NACH LINKS, To the Left

Licht ausschalten! Light Out!

FUßGÄNGER, Pedestrians

WARTESAAL, Waiting-room

Notbremse, Alarm Signal

Speisesaal, Dining-room

HALLE, Lounge

Reserviert, Reserved

BESETZT, Engaged

NOTAUSGANG, Emergency Exit

AUSGANG, Exit

EINGANG, Entrance

BADEZIMMER, Bathroom

Kalt, Warm, Cold, Hot

ABORT, TOILETTE, W.C., Lavatory

Schreibzimmer, Writing-room

ZU VERMIETEN, To let

Möbliertes Zimmer, Furnished room

ZU VERKAUFEN, For Sale

FRISCH GESTRICHEN, Wet Paint

AUF; OFFEN, Open

GESCHLOSSEN, Closed

von . . . bis . . . from . . . to

GEÖFFNET, Open

HERREN, MÄNNER, Gentlemen, Men

DAMEN, FRAUEN, Ladies, Women

ZIEHEN, Pull

DRÜCKEN, Push, Press

GIFT! Poison

Äußerlich !   External   Use   **ARZT,** Doctor
Only   **Zahnarzt,** Dentist
APOTHEKE, Chemist, Drug-   **PFÖRTNER,**   Janitor,   Care-
store   taker

Learn these words as vocabulary.

CONTINUOUS READING   Grimm's **MÄRCHEN**

HANS IM GLÜCK—6

Hans zog zufrieden weiter und dachte mit Freude daran,
Contentedly Jack continued his journey and thought with joy
daß ihm bisher alles nach Wunsch gegangen sei.   Wie er
that so far everything had gone according to wish.   As he
so gemütlich weiter wanderte, kam ein Bursche des
thus   wandered   on   leisurely,   a   fellow   came   along
Weges, der eine schöne weiße Gans unter dem Arm trug.
who   carried   under   his   arm   a   nice   white   goose.
Der gesellte sich zu ihm, weil er mit ihm den gleichen
He   walked   beside   him   because   he   was   going   the   same
Weg hatte.   Sie sprachen von allerhand, um sich die Zeit
way.   They   talked   about   all   kinds   of   things   to   pass
zu vertreiben, und Hans erzählte ihm auch von seinem
the   time,   and   Jack   also   told   him   of   his
maßlosen Glück, wie er immer so vorteilhaft getauscht
tremendous   luck,   how   he   had   always   bartered   so   profitably.
hatte.   Der Bursche sagte zu ihm : „ Die Gans bringe ich
The   fellow   said   to   him :   " I   am   taking   the   goose
zu einer Kindtaufe.   Hebe einmal !   Sie ist ungewöhn-
to   a   christening.   Lift   it   once !   It's   un-
lich schwer.   Wenn man in diesen Braten beißt, muß
usually   heavy.   When   one   bites   into   such   a   roast,   one
man sich den Mund zweimal wischen, weil das Fett
has   to   wipe   one's   mouth   twice,   because   the   fat
überquillt."
flows over."
Hans nahm die Gans mit beiden Händen.   „ Wirklich
Jack   took   the   goose   with   both   hands.   " Really,

hat die ein Gewicht! Aber mein Schwein ist doch noch
what   a   weight!   But   my   pig   is   bigger
größer und wird einen ebenso fetten Braten liefern."
still and will give just as fat a roast."

Da machte der junge Bursche große Augen; er sah sich
Thereupon the young fellow opened his eyes wide; he looked round
scheu nach allen Seiten um und sagte dann mit leiser
timidly   to   all   sides   and   then   said   in   a   low
Stimme: „Höre, mein Lieber, mit deinem Schwein hat
voice: "Listen,   my   dear,   with   your   pig   there's
es wohl eine eigene Bewandtnis, denk ich . . ."
something peculiar, I think . . ."

[Contd. on page 193.

§ 3. *Essential Strong Verbs in Groups—Group I—Practice—*
Emergencies—Continuous Reading : **Hans im Glück**

Turn to page 163, Lesson V, § 5, and refresh your memory
regarding a typical " Strong " Verb: **TRAGEN.** There are no
really " irregular " Verbs in German as there are, for example,
in French or Spanish. German Verbs are of three kinds of
Conjugation: " Weak ", which are conjugated in accordance
with definite principles that can be learnt; " Strong ", which
means that the root vowel changes in the Simple Past (or Imperfect) Tense and in the Past Participle; and a few Verbs which,
for convenience, are called " Mixed ", because, like the Weak
Verbs, they take **-TE** and **GE- . . . T,** in the Imperfect and Past
Participle and change the root vowel (these are given on page 210).
Therefore, one must first know thoroughly the principles for con-
jugating Weak Verbs and the " Mixed ", which can easily be learnt.
The " Strong " verbs are not difficult, but as there are many of
them, and some are among the commonest Verbs in the language,
one should differentiate between those which must be mastered
for everyday use and those which can be relegated to a list for
reference. The latter should be as complete as possible, because
it must contain a number of Verbs which serve as " roots " for
many words, though some are hardly ever used by themselves.

To begin with, one must become well acquainted with what

are called here " Essential Strong Verbs ". For purposes of learning they are divided into Groups in accordance with the changes in the root vowel in the Imperfects and Past Participles. Note also that throughout all the Strong Verbs there are certain vowel changes which occur in the singular of the Present Indicative, Second and Third Persons. As the Second Person Singular is little used by the foreigner, and is best learnt by experience, it is not given here: the Third Person is in everyday use and must be known. Most Strong Verbs modify the root vowels **a, o, u,** in the Second and Third Persons Singular of the Present Tense.

☞ In the pages which follow take each Group separately for memorizing, and do not go on to the next until you know it fairly well. Come back to these lists again and again until you know the parts of each Verb. They have to be known! Hundreds of compound Verbs are made from them. They tell which auxiliary to use with them.

On pages 320-326, a full Alphabetical List of Strong Verbs is given *for reference.* It is as complete as is ever likely to be necessary: like the " *All-Purposes* " Vocabulary at the end of the book it is of permanent value. When you come upon a Strong Verb listed in it, memorize the parts. It is unnecessary to attempt to memorize this whole list of Strong Verbs as one task.

ESSENTIAL STRONG VERBS IN GROUPS
GROUP I: IMPERFECT IN -a-

Infinitive e, i, ie	Third Person Present	Imperfect a	Past Participle e	
SEHEN	er sieht	sah	gesehen	to see
GEBEN	er gibt	gab	gegeben	to give
GESCHEHEN *	es geschieht	geschah	geschehen	to happen
LESEN	er liest	las	gelesen	to read
ESSEN	er ißt	aß	gegessen	to eat
FRESSEN	er frißt	fraß	gefressen	to feed
MESSEN	er mißt	maß	gemessen	to measure
VERGESSEN	er vergißt	vergaß	vergessen	to forget
TRETEN	er tritt	trat	getreten	to tread
BITTEN	er bittet	bat	gebeten	to ask, beg
SITZEN	er sitzt	saß	gesessen	to sit
LIEGEN	er liegt	lag	gelegen	to lie

* Conjugate with **SEIN.**

Infinitive	*Third Person Present*	*Imperfect*	*Past Participle*
e, o		a	o
BEFEHLEN	er befiehlt	befahl	befohlen	to command
EMPFEHLEN	er empfiehlt	empfahl	empfohlen	to recommend
STEHLEN	er stiehlt	stahl	gestohlen	to steal
GEBÄREN	er ge-bIERT(-ärt)	gebar	geboren	to give birth
SPRECHEN	er spricht	sprach	gesprochen	to speak
BRECHEN	er bricht	brach	gebrochen	to break
ERSCHRECK-EN *	er erschrickt	erschrak	erschrocken	to be frightened
TREFFEN	er trifft	traf	getroffen	to meet, hit
STERBEN*	er stirbt	starb	gestorben	to die
GELTEN	er gilt	galt	gegolten	to be worth
HELFEN	er hilft	half	geholfen	to help
SCHELTEN	er schilt	schalt	gescholten	to scold
VERDERBEN	er verdirbt	verdarb	verdorben	to spoil
WERFEN	er wirft	warf	geworfen	to throw
NEHMEN	er nimmt	nahm	genommen	to take
KOMMEN *	er kommt	kam	gekommen	to come

i		a	o
BEGINNEN	er beginnt	begann	begonnen	to begin
GEWINNEN	er gewinnt	gewann	gewonnen	to win
RINNEN	er rinnt	rann	geronnen	to run, flow
SCHWIMMEN	er schwimmt	schwamm	geschwommen	to swim
SINNEN	er sinnt	sann	gesonnen	to meditate
SPINNEN	er spinnt	spann	gesponnen	to spin

i		a	u
BINDEN	er bindet	band	gebunden	to bind
FINDEN	er findet	fand	gefunden	to find
SINKEN *	er sinkt	sank	gesunken	to sink
TRINKEN	er trinkt	trank	getrunken	to drink
GELINGEN *	es gelingt	gelang	gelungen	to succeed
RINGEN	er ringt	rang	gerungen	to struggle, wring
KLINGEN	er(es)klingt	klang	geklungen	to sound. (bell)
SINGEN	er singt	sang	gesungen	to sing
SPRINGEN *	er springt	sprang	gesprungen	to spring
ZWINGEN	er zwingt	zwang	gezwungen	to force

* Conjugate with **SEIN.**

Practice: ÜBUNG

Was gibt es Neues? Wir gaben dem Postboten die Briefe.
Ich sah einen schönen Vogel. Welchen Film haben Sie heute
gesehen? Es geschieht ein Unglück. Wann ist das Unglück
geschehen? Der Schüler liest im Buch. Sie lasen die Zeitung.
Er hat viel gelesen. Die Frau ißt den Apfel. Wir aßen gestern
Erdbeeren. Haben Sie schon gegessen? Der Vogel frißt aus
der Hand. Die Katze fraß die Maus. Mißt er den Stoff für
das Kleid? Sie vergaß ihren Regenschirm. Der Herr tritt in
das Zimmer. Der Junge ist in den Schmutz getreten. Ich
habe ihm auf den Fuß getreten. Ich bitte um Verzeihung. Er
bat um Geld. Wir haben ihn mehrmals gebeten. Sie saßen auf
der Bank. Ich habe dort gesessen. Das Kind liegt im Bett.
Wie lange hat es da gelegen? Ein Buch lag auf dem Tisch.
    Der Herr befiehlt dem Hund. Er hat es streng befohlen.
Der Kellner empfahl uns diesen Wein. Der Rabe stiehlt ein
Stück Käse. Was hat der Dieb gestohlen? Die Frau gebar ein
Kind. Sie hat drei Kinder geboren. Er spricht fließend
deutsch. Wovon sprachen die Leute? Wir haben mit ihm
gesprochen. Er bricht ein Bein. Das Glas brach in seinen
Händen. Das Mädchen erschrickt sehr leicht. Ich bin über
den Fall erschrocken. Trifft er heute seinen Freund? Ich
traf ihn gestern. Im letzten Monat haben wir ihn oft getroffen.
Wir alle müssen sterben. Sein Vater starb vor kurzem. Wann
ist er gestorben? Der Wein verdirbt nicht. Sie haben uns die
Freude verdorben. Ich warf einen Stein ins Wasser. Der
Junge hat den Ball geworfen. Nimmt sie das Kind an die
Hand? Er nahm das Geld. Wir haben die Blumen genommen.
Die Schüler kamen aus der Schule. Wir sind in die Stadt
gekommen.
    Der Frühling beginnt im März. Ich begann früh mit der
Arbeit. Die Ferien haben begonnen. Wer wird den Kampf
gewinnen? Dieser Junge gewann den Wettlauf. Die Alliierten
haben den Krieg gewonnen. Das Pferd rann schnell. Die
Fische sind davongeschwommen. Ich sann lange darüber nach.
    Hans band die Kuh an das Tor. Ich finde es nicht. Fand

er seinen Hut? Wir haben ihn im Zimmer gefunden. Das Schiff sank in drei Minuten. Wie viele Boote sind bei dem Sturm gesunken? Trinken wir ein Glas Bier! Ich habe nichts getrunken. Dieses gelingt ihm gut. Gelang es dem Dieb zu entkommen? Es ist ihm nicht gelungen. Er rang mit aller Kraft um seine Freiheit. Es klingt nicht schön. Es hat laut aus dem Wald geklungen. Das Mädchen sang mit heller Stimme. Was für ein Lied hat sie gesungen? Springen Sie in das Auto! Er sprang auf den Stuhl. Der Hund ist ins Wasser gesprungen. Wir zwangen sie nicht. Sie haben uns gezwungen, mit ihnen zu gehen.

Emergencies

der Unfall(-älle), accident, mishap(s)

ein schwerer Unfall, serious accident

ein leichter Unfall, slight accident

der Zusammenstoß, collision

überfahren werden, to be run over

bewußtlos, unconscious

rufen, to call

der Krankenwagen, ambulance

der Schutzmann, policeman

verletzt, hurt, injured

unverletzt, uninjured, not hurt

besser gehen, to feel better

der nächste Arzt, nearest doctor

verbunden haben, to have dressed

Schmerzen haben, to have a pain

verbrannt, burnt

gebrochen, broken

zerschnitten, cut

der Schnitt, cut

einen schlimmen Schnitt haben, to have a bad cut

das Jod, iodine

die Wunde, wound

sich schwach fühlen, to feel faint

das Riechsalz, smelling salts

der Schmerz, pain

der Kopfschmerz, headache

der Halsschmerz, sore throat

die Influenza, influenza

im Bett bleiben, to stay in bed

gesund, all right, healthy

der Kasten, box, case

holen, to bring, fetch

kochendes Wasser, boiling water

die künstliche Atmung, artificial respiration

besorgen, to obtain for, get for

gestoßen, bruised
Es tut mir weh, it hurts me
die Pflegerin, nurse
telefonieren, to telephone,
  nach, to, for
der Verband, bandage

der Verbandkasten, first-aid
  box, case
Holen Sie Hilfe, bitte.
  Please bring help.
ertrinken, to drown
empfehlen, to recommend

(See also under *Chemist's and Drug Store,* p. 199)

Ist ein Unfall passiert?   Has an accident happened?

Es gab auf der Straße einen Zusammenstoß.   There was a collision on the road.

Ist jemand überfahren worden?   Was somebody knocked down?

Der Fahrer des Autos ist bewußtlos.   The driver of the car is unconscious.

Aber die Frau im Wagen ist unverletzt.   But the woman in the car is not hurt.

Wo wohnt der nächste Arzt?   Where (lives) is the nearest doctor?

Ein Schutzmann hat schon nach einem Krankenwagen telefoniert.   A policeman has already telephoned for an ambulance.

Der Mann hat einen schlimmen Schnitt am Arm.   The man has a bad cut on his arm.

Er hat starke Schmerzen.   He has (is in) great pain.

Die Frau fühlt sich schwach.   The lady feels faint.

Haben Sie in dem Verbandkasten Riechsalz?   Have you got some smelling salts in the first aid box?

Geben Sie mir etwas Jod für die Schnittwunde.   Give me some iodine for the cut.

Der Verletzte muß einige Tage im Bett bleiben und eine Pflegerin haben.   The injured man must stay in bed several days and have a nurse.

Er wird sich bald wieder gesund fühlen.   He will feel all right again soon.

Tut es Ihnen noch weh?   Does it still hurt you?

Jemand ist ertrunken.   Somebody is drowned.

Holen Sie schnell Hilfe!   Fetch help quickly!

Wenden wir künstliche Atmung an! Let's apply artificial respiration!

Der Mann kann vielleicht gerettet werden. The man can perhaps be saved.

Continuous Reading   Grimm's **MÄRCHEN**

HANS IM GLÜCK—7

. . . „ **In dem Dorf, durch das ich eben kam, ist dem**
. . . " *In the village through which I just passed,* a
Bürgermeister ein Schwein aus dem Stall * gestohlen
pig has been stolen from the burgomaster's
worden. Ich fürchte sehr, du hast da das Schwein des
pigsty. I'm much afraid that you've got there the burgo-
Bürgermeisters. Und wenn sie dich mit dem Schwein
master's pig. And if they catch you with the pig,
erwischen, dann ist der Teufel los. Zum mindesten wirst
then the devil (is) will be (let) loose. At least they'll clap
du in ein finsteres Loch gesteckt, wo Mäuse und Ratten
you in a dark hole where rats and mice
sich gute Nacht sagen."
bid each other good night."

Dem guten Hans sträubten sich langsam die Haare zu
Our good Jack's hair began to stand on end.
Berge. „ O weh, lieber Freund, hilf mir nur rasch aus
" *Alas, dear friend, help me quickly out of*
der Not!" bat er den Burschen. „ Du kennst hier alle
the calamity!" he implored the fellow. " *You know all*
Wege und wirst den Knechten sicher entkommen. Nimm
the roads here, and will surely escape his men. Take
rasch mein Schwein und gib mir dafür die Gans."
my pig at once and give me the goose for it."

„Wahrhaftig, du dauerst mich," tat der Bursche ver-
" *Really, I feel pity for you," the fellow pretended cun-*

---

* **der Stall,** *stable, stall, place for an animal.* Thus:

der Hühnerstall, hen-coop	**der Schafstall,** sheep-pen
der Hundestall, dog-kennel	**der Schweinestall,** pigsty
der Kuhstall, cow-house	

schmitzt. „ Ich will mich deiner erbarmen. Gib rasch
ningly. " *I   will   take   pity   on   you.   Give   me*
das Schwein her. Hier hast du meine Gans. Und nun
the pig quickly. Here take (have) my goose. And now,
lebe wohl! "
farewell! "

Der Bursche nahm das Schwein am Strick und führte
The   fellow   took   the   pig   by   the   rope   and   led
es rasch in einen Seitenweg hinter Hecken und Büsche.
it   quickly   into   a   side   path   behind   hedges   and   bushes.
Hans aber war froh, daß er auf so gute Art das Schwein
But   Jack   was   glad   that   he   got   rid   of   the   pig
losgeworden war, und schritt mit der Gans unter dem
in such a good way, and stepped out with the goose under his
Arm pfeifend vor Freude zu.
arm, whistling for joy.   [*Contd. on page* 201.

§ 4. *Reflexive   Verbs—Models:* **SICH SETZEN** *and* **SICH
FREUEN**—*The Passive of Verbs*—**MAN**—*Impersonal Verbs
—Impersonal Forms with Accusative or Dative—Essential
Strong Verbs*—contd.: *Group   II—Practice—Chemist's—
Continuous Reading:* **Hans im Glück**

REFLEXIVE VERBS : (See page 99 for Reflexive Pronouns). A
Verb is said to be " reflexive " when the action is suffered by or
" reflected " back on the subject. Thus: *I wash myself.* In
German there are many Verbs of a similar nature to " *to wash
oneself* ", which is **SICH WASCHEN.** They are conjugated like
ordinary Verbs *plus* the required Reflexive Pronoun. To take
another example:

(*a*) **SICH SETZEN,** to seat oneself, sit.
        ich setze mich, I sit, seat myself, etc.
        du setzt dich
        er ⎫
        sie ⎬ **setzt sich**
        es ⎭
        wir setzen uns

> ihr setzt euch
> sie setzen sich
> Sie setzen sich

Imperfect : **ich setzte mich,** I sat, etc.
Compound Perfect : **ich habe mich gesetzt**
Pluperfect : **ich hatte mich gesetzt**
Future : **ich werde mich setzen**
Imperative : **setze dich, setzen Sie sich**

Be careful not to confuse the Reflexive Pronoun **SICH,** etc., with **SELBST,** *self,* the latter being an emphatic word :

Er setzte sich, he seated himself, sat down
Er SELBST setzte sich, he HIMSELF sat down

(*b*) But in German there is another kind of Reflexive Verb, a kind that *by its own nature* is reflexive *in form* yet does not represent a reflexive action. For example :

SICH FREUEN, to be glad

ICH FREUE MICH, I am glad, etc.

DU FREUST DICH
ER FREUT SICH
WIR FREUEN UNS
IHR FREUT EUCH
SIE FREUEN SICH

Past : **ICH FREUTE MICH**
Future : **ICH WERDE MICH FREUEN,** etc.
Imperative : **FREUEN SIE SICH!** *Be glad!*

Note : All reflexive verbs in German are conjugated with **HABEN.**

ICH HABE MICH GEFREUT, I have been glad

Similarly :

sich beeilen, to hasten
sich fürchten (vor), to be afraid (of)
sich verirren, to go astray
sich wundern (über + Acc.), to be surprised (at)

sich erinnern, to remember
sich irren, to be mistaken
sich nähern (Dat.), to approach

THE PASSIVE OF VERBS: The passive of all verbs is formed with **WERDEN.**

Thus:

> **ICH WERDE GELOBT,** I am praised (or being praised)
> **ICH WURDE GELOBT,** I was praised
> **ICH WERDE GELOBT WERDEN,** I shall be praised, etc.

The past participle of **WERDEN** used in this sense is **WOR-DEN:**

> **ICH BIN GELOBT WORDEN** (not **geworden**), I have been praised

The learner should be able to recognize the passive though he need seldom use these forms.

MAN is more often used instead of the true passive form (see page 125). There are few passives which cannot be turned into the active form with **MAN.**

IMPERSONAL VERBS: So called because they are used only in the Third Person Singular with **ES,** *it,* for subject, or in the Infinitive. Some of the commonest deal with the weather:

ES BLITZT (it lightens), there's lightning

ES DONNERT, there's thunder

ES DUNKELT, it's getting dark

ES FRIERT, it's freezing

ES HAGELT, it's hailing

ES REGNET, it's raining

ES SCHNEIT, it's snowing

ES TAUT, it's thawing

ES, *it,* with the Third Person Singular or Plural of a Verb corresponds to our " *there* ", as in:

> **ES WAR EIN MANN,** there was a man. **ES SIND ZWEI MÄNNER,** there are two men
> **ES KOMMT EIN KNABE,** there comes a boy
> **ES FEHLT EIN BLEISTIFT,** there's a pencil missing
> **ES FEHLEN ZWEI BLEISTIFTE,** there are two pencils missing

For time:

> **ES IST DREI UHR,** it's three o'clock. (*See page 67.*)

Weather :

ES IST WARM, KALT, it's warm, cold, etc.

General Purposes :

ES GIBT, there is, there are
ES GIBT NICHTS NEUES, there's nothing new, no news
ES WIRD KRACH GEBEN, there will be a row
ES GAB EINEN MANN, there was a man

IMPERSONAL FORMS WITH OBJECT IN ACCUSATIVE OR DATIVE :

Accusative	*Dative*
ES ÄRGERT MICH, I'm vexed	**ES FEHLT IHM,** he's short
ES FREUT MICH, I'm pleased	of . . .
ES FREUT IHN, he's glad	**ES SCHEINT MIR,** it seems
ES HUNGERT MICH ⎱ I'm hun-	to me
gry,	**ES IST MIR KALT,** I'm cold
ES DURSTET MICH ⎰ thirsty	**ES GEHT UNS GUT,** we're
ES WUNDERT UNS, we wonder	well
	ES TUT MIR LEID, I'm sorry

These common phrases are given as examples to illustrate the
form. Many more could be given, but these must be known.

ESSENTIAL STRONG VERBS—*contd.*
GROUP II : IMPERFECT IN **i, ie**

Infinitive	Third Person Present	Imperfect	Past Participle	
ei		**i**	**i**	
GREIFEN	er greift	**griff**	gegriffen	to grasp
KNEIFEN	er kneift	**kniff**	gekniffen	to pinch
PFEIFEN	er pfeift	**pfiff**	gepfiffen	to whistle
GLEITEN *	er gleitet	**glitt**	geglitten	to glide
REITEN *	er reitet	**ritt**	geritten	to ride
STREITEN	er streitet	**stritt**	gestritten	to dispute
LEIDEN	er leidet	**litt**	gelitten	to suffer
SCHNEIDEN	er schneidet	**schnitt**	geschnitten	to cut
BEIßEN	er beißt	**biß**	gebissen	to bite
REIßEN	er reißt	**riß**	gerissen	to tear
STREICHEN	er streicht	**strich**	gestrichen	to pass through
GLEICHEN *	er gleicht	**glich**	geglichen	to resemble
SCHLEICHEN	er schleicht	**schlich**	geschlichen	to slink
WEICHEN *	er weicht	**wich**	gewichen	to yield

* Conjugate with **SEIN.**

Infinitive	Third Person Present	Imperfect	Past Participle	
ei		**ie**	**ie**	
SCHREIBEN	er schreibt	schrieb	geschrieben	to write
BLEIBEN*	er bleibt	blieb	geblieben	to remain
REIBEN	er reibt	rieb	gerieben	to rub
TREIBEN	er treibt	trieb	getrieben	to drive
MEIDEN	er meidet	mied	gemieden	to shun
SCHEIDEN *	er scheidet	schied	geschieden	to part
WEISEN	er weist	wies	gewiesen	to show
SCHEINEN	er scheint	schien	geschienen	to shine, seem
SCHWEIGEN	er schweigt	schwieg	geschwiegen	to be silent
STEIGEN *	er steigt	stieg	gestiegen	to climb
LEIHEN	er leiht	lieh	geliehen	to lend
VERZEIHEN	er verzeiht	verzieh	verziehen	to forgive
SCHREIEN	er schreit	schrie	geschrie(e)n	to shout
a, o, au, ä, u, ei		**ie, i**	**a, o, au, u, ei**	
FALLEN *	er fällt	fiel	gefallen	to fall
HALTEN	er hält	hielt	gehalten	to hold
SCHLAFEN	er schläft	schlief	geschlafen	to sleep
BRATEN	er brät	briet	gebraten	to roast, fry
RATEN	er rät, ratet	riet	geraten	to advise, counsel
BLASEN	er bläst	blies	geblasen	to blow
LASSEN	er läßt	ließ	gelassen	to let, leave
FANGEN	er fängt	fing	gefangen	to catch
STOSSEN	er stößt	stieß	gestoßen	to push
LAUFEN *	er läuft	lief	gelaufen	to run
HAUEN	er haut	hieb	gehauen	to hew, cut, thrash
HÄNGEN	er hängt	hing	gehangen	to be hanging
hängen†	er hängt	hängte	gehängt	to hang (something)
RUFEN	er ruft	rief	gerufen	to call, to call out
HEISSEN	er heißt	hieß	geheißen	to be called, named

* Conjugate with SEIN.
† A Weak Verb, often confused with the Strong.

Practice : ÜBUNG

Setzen Sie sich bitte! Wir setzten uns auf die Bank. Das
Kind freute sich über das Geschenk. Ich hatte mich darüber
nicht gefreut. Erinnern Sie sich an diese Frau? Er hat sich
an jenes Ereignis erinnert. Wir fürchteten uns vor dem Hund.
Wird er sich vor dem Tode fürchten? Bitte beeilen Sie sich

etwas! Der Bote hatte sich sehr beeilt. Die Feinde näherten sich der Stadt. Ich habe mich im Walde verirrt. Wir werden uns über den Erfolg nicht sehr wundern.

Hat es geblitzt? Es blitzte und donnerte viel. Gegen Abend dunkelt es. In England regnet es oft. Friert es draußen? Es hat gehagelt und geschneit. Hoffentlich wird es bald tauen.

Es war ein König in Thule. Es kamen drei Weise aus dem Morgenland. Es haben drei Messer gefehlt. In diesem Monat ist es wärmer. Es gab gestern kaltes und nasses Wetter. Wird es morgen besser sein?

Gibt es viel zu tun? Es hat einen guten Film gegeben. Es gibt in diesem Garten schöne Blumen. Was wird es zu essen geben?

Es hat mich gefreut; es hat ihn aber sehr geärgert. Glauben Sie mir, es tut mir furchtbar leid! Hat es Sie sehr gewundert? Es scheint mir das Richtige. Es fehlt ihm Geld. Es fehlen dem Kassierer hundert Mark. Wie geht es Ihrer Frau? Es ging ihr in letzter Zeit nicht gut.

Er griff nach dem Seil. Der Jäger hat ein Lied gepfiffen. Er ritt auf einem Esel. Die beiden Männer haben laut gestritten. Litt der Kranke große Schmerzen? Ich schrieb einen Brief. Wir haben uns die Hände gerieben. Warum mied er seinen Freund? Er ist im Guten von uns geschieden. Sie haben geschwiegen. Das Kind hat geschrien. Wie hieß jener Mann? Der Fahrer hielt seinen Wagen an. Haben Sie gut geschlafen? Er läßt Sie schön grüßen. Wir haben sie in Ruhe gelassen. Mit Speck fängt man Mäuse. Der Knabe ist auf die Straße gelaufen. Wir riefen die Kinder herbei. Dem Hunde hing die Zunge aus dem Halse.

Chemist's, Drug Store

die Apotheke, chemist's, drug store
das Abführmittel, laxative
die Borsäure, boracic acid
säurefrei, free from acid
das Aspirin, aspirin

das Chinin, quinine (*pronounce* **ch = k**)
das Fruchtsalz, fruit-salt
etwas für . . . geben, to give something for . . .
die Verstopfung, constipation

der **Durchfall,** diarrhœa

das **Fieber,** fever

die **Erkältung,** cold

fieberisch, feverish

die **Brusterkältung,** chest cold

der **Magenschmerz,** stomach-ache

der **Zahnschmerz,** toothache

der **Sonnenbrand,** sunburn

abholen, to call for

der **Puder,** powder

die **Puderquaste,** powder puff

das **Mundwasser,** gargle, mouth wash

die **Nagelbürste,** nail-brush

die **Nagelfeile,** nail file

der **Nagellack,** nail varnish

der **Nagellackentferner,** nail-varnish remover

die **Salbe,** ointment, pomade

die **Rasierklingen,** razor blades

die **Seife,** soap

das **Magenpulver,** stomach powder

das **Öl,** oil

das **Haaröl,** hair-oil

der **Rasierpinsel,** shaving-brush

Kölnisch Wasser, *eau de Cologne*

das **Rezept,** prescription

herstellen (or **machen**), to make up (a prescription)

das **antiseptische Mittel,** antiseptic

die **Haarwäsche,** shampoo

der **Ohrenschmerz,** ear-ache

die **Mückenstiche,** mosquito bites

etwas zum Einreiben, something to rub in

das **Augenwasser,** eye-lotion

der **Lippenstift,** lipstick

die **Pille(n),** pill(s)

die **Rouge,** rouge

die **Binden,** sanitary towels

die **Sonnenbrandsalbe,** sunburn salve

die **Schlaftabletten,** sleeping-tablets

der **Kamm,** comb

die **Watte,** cotton-wool

die **Brille,** pair of spectacles

die **Sonnenbrille,** sunglasses

Ich habe mehrere Toilettensachen nötig. I need several toilet articles.

Gehen wir in eine Apotheke. Let's go to a chemist's.

Ich möchte einen Lippenstift und Puder haben. I'd like to have a lipstick and some powder.

Wünschen Sie auch ein gutes Augenwasser? Do you want also a good eye-lotion?

Geben Sie mir Nagellack und Lackentferner. Give me some nail varnish and varnish remover.

Ich brauche ein Paket Watte, ein Fläschchen Kölnisch Wasser und eine Flasche Haaröl. I need a packet of cotton-wool, a small bottle of *eau de Cologne* and a bottle of hair-oil.

Ich leide an Verstopfung. I suffer from constipation.

Geben Sie mir bitte ein Abführmittel. Please give me a laxative.

Können Sie mir etwas für meinen Sonnenbrand geben? Can you give me something for my sunburn?

Hier ist eine Sonnenbrandsalbe. Here is a sunburn salve.

Haben Sie etwas zum Einreiben gegen Mückenstiche? Have you something to rub in against mosquito bites?

Nehmen Sie diese Salbe. Take this ointment.

Ich habe eine starke Erkältung mit Fieber. I've got a nasty cold with fever.

Wollen Sie Schlaftabletten haben? Do you want sleeping-tablets?

Was empfehlen Sie mir gegen Magenschmerzen? What do you recommend against stomach-ache?

Nehmen Sie dieses Magenpulver. Take this stomach powder.

Ich möchte einen Rasierpinsel und ein halbes Dutzend Rasierklingen haben. I'd like to have a shaving-brush and half a dozen razor blades.

CONTINUOUS READING   Grimm's **MÄRCHEN**

HANS IM GLÜCK—8

. . . „ **Ich bin doch ein rechter Glückspilz,"** * **sagte**
. . . " *I am really a lucky fellow,"* said *Jack,*
Hans vergnügt vor sich hin, „ ich habe wieder einen recht
pleased with himself, " *I again made a rather*
vorteilhaften Tausch gemacht. Der gute Braten, hm,
advantageous exchange. The good roast, h'm, then

* **der Pilz** = *mushroom, fungus.* Here **ein rechter Glückspilz** means *a very lucky devil.*

dann das viele Fett; das reicht ein Vierteljahr aufs Brot,
the rich fat; that will do a quarter of a year (for spreading) on bread
und nicht zuletzt die schönen, weißen Federn für ein
and not last (there are) the lovely white feathers for a
Kopfkissen, auf dem ich ruhen werde wie im Paradies.
pillow   on   which   I   shall   rest   as   in   Paradise.
Da wird meine Mutter aber eine große Freude haben."
And my mother (too) will have a great joy."

   Als er durch das letzte Dorf kam, stand auf dem Markt-
   When he came to the last village, a scissors-grinder was
plaz   ein   Scherenschleifer.   Sein   Rädchen   schnurrte
standing   in   the   market-place.   His   wheel   buzzed
fleißig, und der Mann sang dazu:
industriously, and the man sang to it:

>   **„ Ich schleife die Schere und drehe geschwind,**
>   *" I grind the scissors and spin the wheel,*
>   **Und hänge mein Mäntelchen nach dem Wind! "**
>   *And hang my coat to the wind! "*

Hans stellte sich zu ihm und sah seiner hurtigen Arbeit
Jack   stood   close   by   and   watched   his   quick   work.
zu.   Dann sagte er: „ Euch geht es wohl zum Besten,
Then   he   said: " You   must   be   very well   off,
Scherenschleifer, weil Ihr so lustig singt."
(Mr.) Grinder, for you sing so cheerfully."
   „ Tut sich, " sagte der Mann und lachte. „ Das Hand-
   " Right," said   the   man   and   laughed.   " My   trade
werk hat einen goldenen Boden.   Ein guter Schleifer hat
has   a   golden   base.   A   good   grinder   always   has
immer die Tasche voll Geld.   Sage, wo hast du die
his   pocket   full   of   money.   Tell   me   where   have   you
schöne Gans gekauft? "
bought the lovely goose? "

[Contd. on page 208.

§ 5. *Adverbs and their Uses—Irregular Comparisons—Adverbs and Word-order—Common Adverbs and Inversion—Practice— Stationery, Newspapers, Books—Continuous Reading :* **Hans im Glück**

An Adverb is a word used to qualify or describe any part of speech except a Noun or Pronoun. Thus: I *greatly* admire my friend Jones. He is *justly* proud. The car went *partly* into the water. I am *much* obliged. The words *greatly, justly, partly,* and *much* are Adverbs.

It is time now to review Adjectives, pages 23 and 59.

Most German Adjectives can be used as Adverbs without any change in form: that is, the Adjective also serves as an Adverb.

Der Mann ist ⎱		**Der Mann kommt früh**
Die Frau ist ⎬ **SCHÖN**		**Die Frau singt schön**
Das Kind ist ⎰		**Das Kind bleibt still**

When there is comparison, the Adverb follows the forms of the corresponding Adjective. Thus :

Er kam früh, he came soon, early
Er kam früher, he came sooner, earlier
Er kam am frühesten, he came soonest, earliest

AM + the ending **-(E)STEN** is the commonest form for the superlative. But **AUFS** + the ordinary adjectival superlative is often used. Alternatively, **-STENS** without **AUF**.

Adjective : **stark,   stärker,** ⎰ **der stärkste,** (the) strongest
             strong   stronger ⎱ **am stärksten** ⎱
Adverb :   **stark   stärker   aufs stärkste** ⎬ most
             strongly more strongly **stärkstens** ⎰ strongly

Note that **AUFS** is only used with an Adverb, and that the ending **-STENS** is entirely an adverbial ending :

AM SCHÖNSTEN = either Adjective or Adverb form
AUFS SCHÖNSTE = Adverb with **AUFS**
SCHÖNSTENS = Adverb only

Similarly:

EHESTENS, at the earliest
HÖCHSTENS, at the highest
MEISTENS, at the most

In a principal sentence an Adverb must never be placed between the subject and the Verb, as often happens in English. Thus, in German one does not say " I often go " but always " I go often ": **ICH GEHE OFT.**

NOCH, *yet*, *still*, *more*, always precedes the word it qualifies, Thus:

Sind Sie NOCH hier? Are you still here?
Geben Sie mir NOCH ein Glas Milch. Give me one more glass of milk.
SEHR, much (*intensity*): **SEHR BELIEBT,** much loved
VIEL, much (*quantity*): **VIEL GELD,** much money

GERN, *willingly* = *with pleasure*. With a Verb it expresses *like to*. Thus:

Ich spreche GERN deutsch. I like to speak German.

IRREGULAR COMPARISONS: As with Adjectives, there are some irregular comparisons which must be memorized:

BALD, soon; **EHER,** sooner; **AM EHESTEN,** soonest
SEHR, very; **HÖCHST,** extremely; **AM HÖCHSTEN,** highest
VIEL, much; **MEHR,** more; **AM MEISTEN,** most
WOHL, well; **BESSER,** better; **AM BESTEN,** best
GERN, willingly; **LIEBER,** rather; **AM LIEBSTEN,** best
WENIG, little; **WENIGER,** **MINDER,** less; **AM WENIGSTEN, AM MINDESTEN,** least

ADVERBS AND WORD-ORDER: When an Adverb begins a sentence (in German it then expresses emphasis on that word), the Verb must be placed before the subject—that is, inversion takes place. This is consistent with the general rule (for which

see pages 90, 284) that when any word but the subject begins a
sentence there must be inversion. Thus:

> **Gestern SAH ICH ihn.** Yesterday I saw him
> **Am Morgen ⎱ ARBEITETE ICH.** In the morning I
> **Morgens   ⎰** worked

COMMON ADVERBS AND INVERSION: The Adverbs in the list
which follows are very often used at the beginning of a sentence
and should be known:

ALSO, thus, so	**je . . . desto,** the . . . the
AUCH, also	**JETZT ⎱** now
außerdem, besides	**NUN ⎰**
BALD, soon	**KAUM,** hardly, scarcely
DANN, then	**nicht nur . . . sondern auch,**
DA, then, because	not only . . . but
dagegen, on the other hand	**NOCH,** nor, yet, still
DAHER ⎱ therefore	**SO,** so, thus, therefore
DARUM ⎰	**SONST,** otherwise
deshalb, on that account	**WEDER . . . NOCH,** neither . . .
DOCH ⎱	nor
dennoch ⎬ however, yet	**ZWAR,** indeed, truly
jedoch ⎰	
ENTWEDER . . . ODER, either	
. . . or	

PRACTICE: ÜBUNG

Der Baum ist hoch gewachsen. Er hat schwer getragen. Wir
glauben das gern. Sie fragten ihn vergeblich. Ist der Wein
sauer geworden? Der Junge ist schnell gelaufen. Der Freund
kam spät. Wir werden noch oft darüber sprechen. Sind Sie
heute früh aufgestanden?

Es ist leichter gesagt als getan. Der Hund hat immer lauter
gebellt. Sie sind noch höher gesprungen. Kam der Zug
früher oder später an? Er ist aufs tiefste beleidigt. Wir haben
meistens keine Zeit. Der Junge ist höchstens zwölf Jahre alt.
Haben Sie die Rechnung genauestens geprüft? Sie lehnten es
aufs heftigste ab. Ich danke Ihnen bestens für Ihren Brief.
Waren Sie sehr erfreut? Er wird viel darüber gelesen haben.
Essen Sie gern Kirschen? Befindet sich Ihre Mutter wohl?
Danke, es geht ihr besser. Kommen Sie bald wieder? Ich

habe mehr gelacht als geweint.   Er hat heute weniger gearbeitet als gestern.   Ich glaubte ihm sehr wenig.   Welche Blumen liebt sie am meisten?   Er geht lieber ins Theater als ins Kino.   Also sprach Zarathustra.   Außerdem hat er großes Glück gehabt.   Bald wird der Zug ankommen.   Dann schwieg ich. Daher gibt es keinen Streit mehr.   Doch bevor wir ins Haus gehen, klingeln wir.   Entweder waren sie nicht zu Hause oder schliefen sie.   Jetzt ist es Zeit aufzustehen.   Kaum waren wir in das Boot gestiegen, da fuhr es ab.   So konnte es geschehen, daß das Kind ins Wasser fiel.   Weder hat sie geschrieben noch telefoniert.   Sonst aber fühlt er sich wohl.

Stationery, Newspapers, Books

die Zeitung, newspaper

die Zeitschrift, magazine

das Schreibmaterial, writing material(s)

der Schreibblock, writing-pad

das Löschpapier, blotting-paper

der Briefumschlag, (-äge), envelope(s)

die Ansichtskarte, picture post card

die Postkarten, post cards

das Briefpapier, writing-paper

die Tinte, ink

der Bleistift, pencil

das Ersatzblei, refill (of lead)

der Füllfederhalter, fountain pen

der Bindfaden, string, twine

der Siegellack, sealing-wax

der Taschenplan, pocket map, plan

das Buch, book

die Karte, map

das Notizbuch, note-book

das Anhängeschild, luggage label

das Tagebuch, diary

die Buchhandlung, bookshop

der Roman, novel

ein Taschenwörterbuch, a pocket dictionary

ein Wörterbuch (deutsch-englisches, englisch-deutsches), dictionary

die Ausgabe, edition

eine gebundene Ausgabe, a bound edition

eine geheftete Ausgabe, a paper-cover edition

Romane auf englisch, auf deutsch, novels in English, German die Biographie, biography

eine billige Ausgabe, a cheap edition

die Übersetzung, translation

etwas in einfachem Deutsch, something in simple German

der neueste Roman, the latest novel

von, by (of a writer)

Hier ist die Abendzeitung. Here's the evening paper.

Kaufen Sie auch eine gute Zeitschrift! Buy also a good magazine.

Ich möchte einen Schreibblock, zwei Bogen Löschpapier und ein Dutzend Umschläge. I'd like a writing-pad, two sheets of blotting-paper, and a dozen envelopes.

Geben Sie mir Tinte für meinen Füllfederhalter. Give me some ink for my fountain pen.

Haben Sie schöne Ansichtskarten von der Stadt? Have you some nice picture post cards of the town?

Dieser Taschenplan ist sehr nützlich. This pocket map is very useful.

Ich möchte in der Buchhandlung den neuesten Roman eines modernen Schriftstellers kaufen. I'd like to buy the latest novel of a modern writer in the bookshop.

Ich empfehle Ihnen eine Biographie von Stefan Zweig. I recommend (you) a biography by Stefan Zweig.

Möchten Sie eine geheftete oder eine gebundene Ausgabe? Would you like a paper-cover or a bound edition?

Gibt es davon auch eine englische Übersetzung? Is there also an English translation?

Ich brauche ein gutes deutsch-englisches Taschenwörterbuch. I need a good German-English pocket dictionary.

Packen Sie diese Bücher ein und geben Sie mir etwas Bindfaden. Wrap up these books and give me some string.

HANS IM GLÜCK—9

. . . „ Die habe ich nicht gekauft," gab Hans Auskunft,
. . . " *I have not bought it,*" *Jack informed him,*
„ sondern gegen ein Schwein eingetauscht."
" *but exchanged* (*it*) *for a pig.*"

„ Und das Schwein? "
" *And the pig?* "

„ Das habe ich für eine Kuh bekommen."
" *I got it for a cow.*"

„ Und die Kuh? "
" *And the cow?* "

„ Die habe ich für ein Pferd eingehandelt."
" *I bartered it for a horse.*"

„ Und das Pferd? "
" *And the horse?* "

„ Dafür habe ich einen Klumpen Gold, so groß wie
" *For that, I've given a lump of gold, as big as*
meinen Kopf, gegeben."
my head."

„ Und das Gold? " Der Schleifer war sehr wißbegierig.
" *And the gold?* " *The grinder was very inquisitive.*
„ Ei, das war der gerechte Lohn für sieben Jahre Dienst! "
" *Eh, that was the just reward for seven years' service!* "

„ Da hast du sehr klug gehandelt," lobte ihn der
" *You've acted very wisely,*" *the grinder praised*
Scherenschleifer. „ Wenn du es noch fertig bringst,
him. " *If you* (*continue*) *bringing off that*
daß dir das Geld in der Tasche klimpert, dann ist dein
you'll have money clinking in your pocket, then your luck is
ganzes Glück gemacht."
made complete."

„ Hm," meinte Hans nachdenklich, „ das wäre nicht
" *H'm,*" *Jack reflected thoughtfully,* " *that wouldn't be*
übel; nur weiß ich nicht, wie ich das anfangen soll."
bad; only I don't know what to do about it."

[*Contd. on page* 213.

LESSON VII

§ 1. *Essential Strong Verbs*—contd.: *Group III—Verbs of "Irregular" or Mixed Conjugation—Practice—Barber's, Hairdresser's—Continuous Reading:* **Hans im Glück**

WITH what follows in this Section you come to the end of the Strong and Mixed Verbs that are likely to be of most practical use. It is hardly to be expected that you will remember them all, but you should at least be able to recognize them when you meet them. Until you know them well, make it a point to revise not only a Verb you may not know, but all in its Group. After a time you will find that they go with a swing, so that when you meet, say, **HEBEN**, *to lift*, you will immediately think of **HOB, GEHOBEN**, and of **er hebt**. Have patience and persist!

ESSENTIAL STRONG VERBS—*contd.*
GROUP III: IMPERFECT IN o, u

Infinitive	Third Person Present	Imperfect	Past Participle	
ie		o	o	
FLIEGEN *	er fliegt	flog	geflogen	to fly
BIEGEN	er biegt	bog	gebogen	to bend
VERBIETEN	er verbietet	verbot	verboten	to forbid
FLIEHEN *	er flieht	floh	geflohen	to flee
FRIEREN	er, es friert	fror	gefroren	to freeze
SCHIEBEN	er schiebt	schob	geschoben	to shove, push
VERLIEREN	er verliert	verlor	verloren	to lose
WIEGEN	er wiegt	wog	gewogen	to weigh
FLIEßEN *	er fließt	floß	geflossen	to flow, run
GIEßEN	er gießt	goß	gegossen	to flow, pour
SCHLIEßEN	er schließt	schloß	geschlossen	to shut, lock
SCHIEßEN	er schießt	schoß	geschossen	to shoot
KRIECHEN*	er kriecht	kroch	gekrochen	to creep
RIECHEN	er riecht	roch	gerochen	to smell, reek
ZIEHEN	er zieht	zog	gezogen	to pull, draw

* Conjugate with **SEIN**.

209

Infinitive	Third Person Present	Imperfect	Past Participle	
e, ö, ü, au		o	o	
HEBEN	er hebt	hob	gehoben	to lift, heave
FECHTEN	er ficht	focht	gefochten	to fight, fence
FLECHTEN	er flicht	flocht	geflochten	to twist, plait
QUELLEN	er quillt	quoll	gequollen	to spring, gush from
SCHMELZEN †	er schmilzt	schmolz	geschmolzen	to melt, smelt
SCHWELLEN *	er schwillt	schwoll	geschwollen	to swell
SCHWÖREN	er schwört	schwor	geschworen	to swear
LÜGEN	er lügt	log	gelogen	to tell a lie
BETRÜGEN	er betrügt	betrog	betrogen	to betray, deceive
SAUGEN	er saugt	sog	gesogen	to suck
SAUFEN	er säuft	soff	gesoffen	to swill, guzzle
a		u	a	
GRABEN	er gräbt	grub	gegraben	to dig
FAHREN *	er fährt	fuhr	gefahren	to travel, ride
LADEN	er lädt, ladet	lud	geladen	to load
SCHLAGEN	er schlägt	schlug	geschlagen	to strike, beat
TRAGEN	er trägt	trug	getragen	to carry, wear
WASCHEN	er wäscht	wusch	gewaschen	to wash
WACHSEN *	er wächst	wuchs	gewachsen	to grow (wax)
BACKEN	er bäckt	buk, backte	gebacken	to bake

* Conjugate with SEIN.
† Also with SEIN.

VERBS OF "IRREGULAR" OR MIXED CONJUGATION
GROUP IV: IRREGULAR OR MIXED CONJUGATION

Infinitive	Third Person Present	Imperfect	Past Participle	
e		a	a, e	
BRENNEN	er brennt	brannte	gebrannt	to burn
KENNEN †	er kennt	kannte	gekannt	to know
NENNEN	er nennt	nannte	genannt	to name, call
RENNEN *	er rennt	rannte	gerannt	to race, run
SENDEN	er sendet	sandte sendete	gesandt gesendet	to send
WENDEN	er wendet	wandte wendete	gewandt gewendet	to turn, turn about

* Conjugate with SEIN.
† English Verb *to know* can be translated by two German Verbs: **KENNEN,** which is the equivalent of *to be* (or *become*) *acquainted with,* and **WISSEN,** which is *to know and understand.* There is a difference

Infinitive i, e	Third Person Present	Imperfect a, i, u	Past Participle a, u	
BRINGEN	er bringt	brachte	gebracht	to bring
DENKEN	er denkt	dachte	gedacht	to think
WISSEN	er weiß	wußte	gewußt	to know
STEHEN	er steht	stand	gestanden	to stand, stop
GEHEN *	er geht	ging	gegangen	to go, walk
TUN	er tut	tat	getan	to do
MAHLEN	er mahlt	mahlte	gemahlen	to grind, mill
SALZEN	er salzt	salzte	gesalzen	to salt
SPALTEN	er spaltet	spaltete	gespalten	to split

which must be observed, as in the two French equivalents *connaître* and *savoir*. Thus: **Ich kenne Herrn Schmidt,** *I know Mr. Smith*, and **Ich weiß was ich weiß,** *I know what I know = I know for certain.* Always remember to use **kennen** for *to know* somebody. **Wissen** will meet most other instances.

* Conjugate with **SEIN**.

Practice: **ÜBUNG**

Die Vögel flogen auf das Dach.   Mit welchem Flugzeug sind Sie geflogen?   Er bog den Draht zu einem Haken.   Der Vater verbot dem Sohn zu lügen.   Wir haben es ihm streng verboten. Flieht er vor dem Feind?   Sie sind aus der Stadt geflohen.   Es fror in der Nacht.   Der Arbeiter hat den Wagen geschoben. Wieviel wiegt das Paket?   Ich habe es nicht gewogen.   Er verlor viel Geld.   Haben Sie etwas verloren?

Der Rhein fließt langsam.   Sie hat Tee in die Tasse gegossen. Er schloß das Fenster.   Haben Sie den Brief geschlossen?   Im Stall roch es nicht gut.   Die Pferde haben den Wagen gezogen.

Er hob seine Hände hoch.   Die Mädchen haben Kränze geflochten.   Der Fluß schwillt an.   Der Schnee ist geschmolzen. Er schwor, nicht zu lügen.   Er hat nicht gelogen.   Betrog der Händler ihn?   Das Schaf säuft die Milch.   Die Bauern gruben im Felde.   Er ist schnell gefahren.   Ich habe den Jungen nicht geschlagen.   Der Bäcker hat den Kuchen gebacken.   Die Mutter wusch ihr Kind.

Die Kerzen brannten hell.   Wir haben ein Paket gesandt. Haben Sie jenen Mann gekannt?   Ich nannte meinen Namen.

Hat er das Buch gebracht? Wir hatten nichts Böses gedacht. Weiß er die volle Wahrheit? Sie hat es nicht gewußt. Die Freunde sind spazieren gegangen. Der Mann spaltete Holz.

Barber's, Hairdresser's

das Haarschneiden, hair-cut
das Rasieren, shave
das Shampoonieren, shampoo
kurz, short
halblang, medium
kämmen, to comb
bürsten, to brush
die Massage, massage
stutzen, to trim
im Nacken, round the neck
an den Ohren, round the ears
die Brillantine, brillantine
absengen, to singe
das Haarwasser, hair tonic, lotion
schneiden, to cut
abschneiden, to cut from
mit der Schere, with scissors
mit der Maschine, with machine
der Föhn, dryer (*lit.* south wind)

die Barbierstube, barber's shop
der Friseur, hairdresser (ladies). **Die Friseuse** (fem.)
legen, to set
die Wellen, waves
die Dauerwelle, permanent wave
die Wasserwelle, the set
die Locken, curls
mit Wellen und Locken, waved and curled
nicht zu kurz, not too short
nichts von oben, nothing from the top
nur an den Seiten und hinten, only the back and sides
der Scheitel, parting
bitte kein Öl, no oil, please
die Haare schneiden lassen, to have a hair-cut
die Haarnadeln, hairpins
das Haarnetz, hair net
das Waschen und Legen, wash and set

Ich möchte einen Haarschnitt. I'd like a hair cut.
Wollen Sie es mit der Schere oder der Maschine geschnitten haben? Do you want to have it cut with scissors or with the machine?
Schneiden Sie es mit der Maschine im Nacken und an den Seiten. Cut it with the machine on the neck and sides.

Wollen Sie das Haar abgesengt haben? Do you want to have your hair singed?

Beim Damenfriseur. At the ladies' hairdresser's.

Ich möchte mein Haar gewaschen und eine Wasserwelle haben. I should like to have my hair shampooed and set.

Meine Freundin hätte gern eine Dauerwelle. My friend would like a permanent.

Tragen Sie den Scheitel immer auf der rechten Seite? Do you have the parting always on the right?

Geben Sie mir eine Massage und legen Sie mein Haar in Locken. Give me a massage and set my hair into curls.

Es ist nötig, das Haar gründlich zu kämmen und zu bürsten. It is necessary to comb and brush the hair thoroughly.

Soll ich es mit dem Föhn trocknen? Shall I dry it with the hand-dryer?

Möchten Sie Ihr Haar gebleicht oder lieber gefärbt haben? Would you like to have your hair bleached or preferably dyed?

Verkaufen Sie Haarnetze und ein gutes Haaröl? Do you sell hair nets and a good hair-oil?

CONTINUOUS READING   Grimm's **MÄRCHEN**

HANS IM GLÜCK—10

. . . „ **Das will ich dir verraten,"** sagte der Mann, „ **Du**
. . . "*That I will tell you*," *said the man*, "*you*
mußt ein Scherenschleifer werden. Dazu gehört eigent-
must become a scissors-grinder. For that you really
lich nichts weiter als ein guter Schleifstein. Das andere
need nothing else but a good grindstone. All the rest
kommt dann schon von selbst. Sieh, hier habe ich einen
then comes by itself. Look, I've got an older
älteren. Er ist aber noch ganz gut. Wohlan, wenn du
one here. But it is still quite good. Well, if you
mir die Gans gibst, dann will ich dir dafür den schönen
give me the goose, (then) I will let you have the fine
Stein überlassen. Willst du das tun? "
stone for it. Will you do that? "

Hans nickte freudig zustimmend: „ Wie könnt Ihr nur
Jack gladly   nodded   his   consent: " How   can   you
noch fragen? Freilich will ich das; denn dann werde
even ask?   Of   course,   I   will;   for   then   I   shall
ich der glücklichste Mensch auf Erden sein. Habe ich
be   the   happiest   man   on   earth.   If   I   have
immer Geld in der Tasche, dann brauch ich mich ums
money always in my pocket, (then) I need no longer worry
tägliche Brot nicht mehr zu sorgen." Damit reichte er
about   my   daily   bread."   Therewith   he   gave   the
dem Schleifer die Gans und erhielt von ihm den alten
goose   to   the   grinder   and   received   from   him   the   old
Schleifstein. Darauf sagten sie einander: „ Auf Wieder-
grindstone.   Thereupon they said to each other " Till we meet
sehen! "
again! "

„ Wahrhaftig, ich muß in einer Glückshaut * geboren
" Really, I must have been born under a lucky
sein," murmelte Hans begeistert vor sich hin, als er
star," Jack muttered enthusiastically to himself as he
weiterging, „ alle meine Wünsche gehen prompt in
walked   on,   " all   my   wishes   promptly   find
Erfüllung." Unverdrossen wanderte er weiter und ver-
fulfilment."   Undaunted   he   wandered   farther   and   gradu-
spürte allmählich großen Hunger; auch wurde er müde,
ally began to feel very hungry; he also became tired,
denn es ging gegen Mittag. Er hatte aber seinen Vorrat
for it was almost noon. But he had already eaten
bereits aufgegessen. . . .
up his provision(s). . . .

[Contd. on page 219.

* literally: *in a lucky skin.*

§ 2. *Subordinating Conjunctions—List and Use—Word-order-Examples—Practice—*RHEINDAMPFSCHIFFAHRT*—Continuous Reading:* Hans im Glück (end of)

SUBORDINATING CONJUNCTIONS (see page 165): As the subordinating Conjunctions affect word-order, they require special attention. The following are of frequent occurrence and must be known:

ALS, when (past)	**OBGLEICH, OBWOHL,** although
BEVOR, EHE, before	
BIS, until	**SEIT, SEITDEM,** since
DA, as = since (because)	**SOBALD (ALS),** as soon (as)
DAMIT, in order that	**SO OFT (ALS),** as often (as)
DAMIT NICHT, in order not	**SOLANGE (ALS),** (as long as)
DASS, that	**WÄHREND,** while, during
FALLS, in case	**WENN,** if, when, whenever
INDEM, as = while	**WIE,** as = in the same manner as
NACHDEM, after	
OB, whether, if = whether	**WEIL,** because

As most of these are in very common use, it is advisable to know how they affect word-order. First take two simple straightforward sentences:

> **ES IST WAHR.**   It is true.
> **ER IST KRANK.**   He is sick, ill.

Now insert **DASS**; making them one sentence:

> **Es ist wahr, DASS er krank IST.**

Or:

> **ER FRAGTE MICH.**   He asked me.
> **ICH WAR DORT.**   I was there.
> **Er fragte mich, OB ich dort WAR.**   He asked me whether I was there.

And:

> **Warten Sie, BIS ich fertig BIN.**   Wait until I'm ready.

WENN expresses *when* or *if*:

> **Ich werde ihn fragen, WENN ich ihn SEHE.** I'll ask him when, whenever, if I see him.

Note that **WANN** is *when* when it refers specifically to time. Thus:

> **KOMMEN SIE, WANN SIE WOLLEN.** Come at the time you wish.

But:

> **KOMMEN SIE, WENN SIE WOLLEN.** Come IF you wish, whenever you wish (if you should so wish).

ALS, *when* : usually refers to a past occasion:

> **ALS ICH DAS HAUS KAUFTE,** when I bought the house
> **ALS ICH DIESEN BRIEF SCHRIEB,** when I wrote this letter

ALS = *but* after **NICHTS.**

> **NICHTS ALS BIER,** nothing but beer
> **NICHTS ALS BUTTERBROT,** nothing but bread and butter

(For **ALS,** *than*, see page 61.)

And note these:

> **ENTWEDER . . . ODER,** either . . . or
> **WEDER . . . NOCH,** neither . . . nor

SOWIE is used to avoid repeating **UND** :

> **ICH HATTE WEIN UND BIER SOWIE TEE ZU TRINKEN.**

Examples of the Use of Subordinating Conjunctions:

ICH BESUCHTE IHN, ALS ER KRANK WAR. I visited him when he was ill.

DENKE $\left\{ \begin{array}{l} \textbf{BEVOR} \\ \textbf{EHE} \end{array} \right\}$ **DU HANDELST !** Think before you act !

ER SCHRIEB DEN BRIEF, $\left\{ \begin{array}{l} \textbf{EHE} \\ \textbf{BEVOR} \end{array} \right\}$ **ER DAS HAUS VER-LIESS.** He wrote the letter before he left the house.

ER LIEF, BIS ER GANZ MÜDE WAR. He ran until he was quite tired.

SIE RIEF LAUTER, DA ER ES NICHT GEHÖRT HATTE. She called louder as (since) he had not heard it.

SIE ARBEITEN, DAMIT SIE GELD VERDIENEN. They work in order to earn money.

GEBEN SIE IHM DAS BUCH, FALLS ER KOMMEN SOLLTE. Give him the book in case he should come.

ER DANKTE IHR, INDEM ER IHR BLUMEN GAB. He thanked her while (as) he gave her flowers.

DAS KIND SCHLIEF, NACHDEM ES GEGESSEN HATTE. The child slept after it had eaten.

ICH FRAGTE IHN, OB ER ES VERSTANDEN HÄTTE. I asked him whether he had understood it.

ER HOB DEN SACK, OBWOHL ER SCHWER WAR. He lifted the bag although it was heavy.

ER GING NACH HAUSE, SOBALD ES ZU REGNEN BEGANN. He went home as soon as it started to rain.

DER REICHE WURDE GELOBT, WEIL ER ETWAS GUTES GETAN HATTE. The rich (man) was praised because he had done something good.

WÄHREND ER IM KINO WAR, STAHL JEMAND SEINE UHR.* While he was in the movie, somebody stole his watch.

WENN ICH IHN SEHE, WERDE ICH IHN FRAGEN.* If (When) I see him, I'll ask him.

Practice: ÜBUNG

Hans sah seine Mutter wieder, als er zu Hause angekommen war. Er sagte mir den Preis, bevor ich es kaufen wollte. Ehe ich weggehen konnte, war das Tor geschlossen. Werden Sie warten, bis ich Zeit haben werde? Sie ging zum Arzt, da sie Fieber hatte. Wir wollen die Tür schließen, damit wir nicht gestört werden. Seien Sie vorsichtig, daß Sie nicht fallen!

* Note that the word-order is also affected when the subordinate clause precedes, as in the last two examples. See also Word-order page 285.

RHEINDAMPFSCHIFFAHRT

Tarif-kilometer ab Köln	Richtung **MAINZ**		Täglich 1. Juli bis 9. September	**FAHRPLAN**

<table>
<tr><th>Tarif-kilometer ab Köln</th><th colspan="2">Richtung</th><th>Schnellfahrt</th><th></th></tr>
<tr><td>50</td><td>Düsseldorf Rathausufer</td><td>r * ab</td><td></td><td></td></tr>
<tr><td>32</td><td>Düsseldorf-Benrath</td><td>r</td><td></td><td>Niederrhein</td></tr>
<tr><td>10</td><td>Leverkusen-Wiesdorf</td><td>r</td><td></td><td>30. Juli bis 6. September</td></tr>
<tr><td>0</td><td>Köln Frankenwerft</td><td>l † an / ab</td><td>6.30</td><td>Jeden Montag, Dienstag und Donnerstag</td></tr>
<tr><td>9</td><td>Porz</td><td>r</td><td></td><td></td></tr>
<tr><td>16</td><td>Wesseling</td><td>l</td><td></td><td></td></tr>
</table>

	Richtung MAINZ		Schnellfahrt	
30	**Bonn** gegenüber Rheingasse	l	8.50	
39	Bad Godesberg (N.- u. Oberdollendorf)	l	9.20	
42	Königswinter (Sieben-	r	9.35	
48	Bad Honnef Insel Grafenwerth gebirge)	r	9.52	
53	Unkel (Rheinbreitbach)	r		
57	Remagen (Bad Neuenahr, Ahrtal)	l	10.23	
62	Linz (Westerwald, Bad Kripp)	r	10.39	
69	Bad Niederbreisig (Bad Hönningen)	l	11.05	
71	Brohl (Laacher See, Eifel)	l		
79	Andernach	l	11.50	
84	Neuwied (Rengsdorf)	r	12.10	
92	Engers (Heimbach, Sayn)	r		
100	**Koblenz**	l	an 13.25 / ab 13.35	
105	Niederlahnstein (Bad Ems,	r	13.58	
107	Oberlahnstein Stolzenfels)	r		
112	Braubach (Marksburg)	r		
121	Boppard (Hunsrück)	l	15.03	
124	Kamp-Bornhofen (Feindl. Brüder)	r		
137	St. Goarshausen (Lorelei)	r		F
137	St. Goar (Rheinfels, Lorelei)	l	16.03	
145	Oberwesel (Schönburg)	l		
150	Kaub (Pfalz, Gutenfels)	r		
154	Bacharach (Stahleck, Steeg)	l	16.58	
157	Lorch (Wispertal)	r		
157	Niederheimbach (Sooneck)	l		
166	Aßmannshausen (Rheinstein)	r	17.45	
170	**Bingen** (Bad Kreuznach, Münster a. St.)	l	18.07	
172	Rüdesheim (Niederwald)	r	18.20	
175	Geisenheim (Johannisberg, Mariental)	r		
180	Ingelheim	l		
182	Oestrich (Winkel)	r		
185	Hattenheim (Haligt., Eberbach)	r		
187	Eltville (Schwalbach, Schl'bad)	r	19.20	
195	Wiesbaden-Biebrich	r	20.00	
200	**Mainz** Halleplatz	l	an 20.20 / ab	
212	Rüsselsheim	ab		
225	Frankfurt (M) Untermainbrücke	an		

Niederrhein
30. Juli bis 6. September
Jeden Montag, Dienstag und Donnerstag

	Rheinabwärts		
	82	84	86
Düsseldorf ab	)14.30	)17.30	)19.45
D.-Kaiserswerth ab	)15.03	)18.00	)20.18
K.-Uerdingen an	)15.30	—	)20.45
			Abend-fahrt

	Rheinaufwärts		
	81	83	85
K.-Uerdingen ab	)15.45	—	)20.50
D.-Kaiserswerth ab	)16.30	)18.15	)21.30
Düsseldorf an	)17.20	)19.05	)22.20

Fahrplan der Strecke Düsseldorf—Königswinter siehe Seiten 11 u. 13

AUSKÜNFTE

durch Reisebüros, die Agenturen an den Schiffslandeplätzen und die Direktion der

KÖLN - DÜSSELDORFER RHEINDAMPFSCHIFFAHRT

Köln - Frankenwerft 15

Ruf 21 25 44

Telegr.: Dampfschiffahrt

* **r** = **rechtsrheinisch,** on the right bank of the Rhine.
† **l** = **linksrheinisch,** on the left bank of the Rhine.

Falls es regnen wird, will er zu Hause bleiben. Sie fühlten sich besser, nachdem sie geruht hatten. Wissen Sie, ob er den Brief erhalten hat? Wir waren spazieren gegangen, obgleich wir wenig Zeit hatten. Die Freunde blieben zusammen, seit sie in der Stadt angekommen waren. Ich werde telefonieren, sobald ich im Hotel sein werde. Das Haus brannte, während die Bewohner auf dem Lande waren. Ich werde froh sein, wenn ich den Ring wiederfinde. Sie tranken viel Bier, weil es sehr warm war.

CONTINUOUS READING   Grimm's **MÄRCHEN**

HANS IM GLÜCK—11

. . . **Nirgends war ein Haus zu sehen, in dem er**
. . . *Nowhere was a house to be seen in which he*
Nahrung bekommen konnte. So kam er nur mühsam
could get some food. So he proceeded only
vorwärts. Der Stein drückte ihn sehr. Kaum konnte er
wearily. The stone pressed (on) him greatly. He could hardly
sich bis zu einem Brunnen schleppen, an dessen Wasser
drag himself to a well, with the water
er sich laben wollte. Damit er aber den kostbaren Stein
of which he wanted to refresh himself. In order that he might not
nicht beschädigte, wenn er sich auf den Brunnenrand
damage the precious stone when sitting down on the edge of the
setzte, legte er ihn neben sich. Als er sich dann bückte,
well, he placed it beside him. While bending down
um zu trinken, stieß er versehentlich an den Stein. Der
to drink, he happened to knock against the stone. It
rutschte, bekam das Übergewicht und plumpste klat-
slid, lost its balance, and fell splash-
schend ins Wasser. Gurgelnd verschwand der Stein in
ing into the water. Gurgling, the stone disappeared in
der Tiefe.
the depth.

Zuersı sah er bestürzt in den Brunnen, dann aber er-
At first he looked alarmed into the well, but then his
hellte sich sein Gesicht.
face brightened up.

„ Ach," rief er begeistert aus, „ was bin ich doch für ein
" Ah," he called out enthusiastically, " what a lucky chap
Glückspilz ! Nun bin ich von dem Stein befreit, ohne
I am ! Now I am relieved of the stone, and
daß man mir einen Vorwurf machen kann. Jetzt brauche
nobody can blame me for it. Now I need not
ich mich nicht mehr so abzuschleppen, wenn ich weiter-
carry so heavily any more when I continue my
gehe. Ich bin wahrhaftig der Hans im Glück ! "
way. I am really the Jack in luck ! "

Sprach's,* sprang munter auf und wanderte be-
So said, he jumped up merrily and wandered on-
schwingten Schrittes weiter, bis er glücklich zu Hause bei
ward with easy steps until he happily arrived at his
seiner Mutter ankam.
mother's home.

* Sprach's = sprach es.

ENDE

§ 3. *Nouns of Foreign Origin—Proper Nouns—Proper Nouns*
  with Article — Practice — Menu on Rhine Steamers —
  Reading: **Nietzsche: Kurze Denksprüche**

The general tendency is to assimilate into German forms all
words of foreign origin. This applies to words from Latin and
Greek as well as to words taken from modern languages. Although the majority of these words are now so far germanized
that only German endings are found, there are some in common
use which retain their foreign form in the plural. Of these, the
following should be known:

	Plural	*Also*
DAS BILLETT, ticket	**DIE BILLETS**	**DIE BILLETTE**
DAS EXAMEN, ex-amination	**DIE EXAMENS**	**DIE EXAMINA**
DER TUNNEL, tunnel	**DIE TUNNELS**	**DIE TUNNEL**

And note:

	Plural
das Coupé, compartment	**die Coupés**
der Leutnant, lieutenant	**die Leutnants**
das Portemonnaie, purse	**die Portemonnaies**
das Porträt, portrait	**die Porträts**
das Sofa, sofa	**die Sofas**
der Sport, sport	**die Sports**

A few Nouns ending in **-al** add **-ien**:

das Material	**die Materialien**
das Mineral	**die Mineralien**

A few ending in **-um** change to **-en**:

das Museum, museum	**die Museen,** museums
das Studium, study	**die Studien,** studies

PROPER NOUNS:

Rule: In general, when a Proper Noun stands by itself it takes **-s** in the Genitive and remains unaltered in other singular cases. This holds good for masculine as well as for feminine Proper Nouns. In the plural, both masculines and feminines take **-s** throughout, the same for Christian as for surnames. Thus:

	Mascs.	*Fem.*	*Surname*
N.	**Heinrich**	**Erna**	**Schmidt**
G.	**Heinrichs**	**Ernas**	**Schmidts**
D.	**Heinrich**	**Erna**	**Schmidt**
A.	**Heinrich**	**Erna**	**Schmidt**
Plurals throughout }	**HEINRICHS**	**ERNAS**	**SCHMIDTS**

There are some exceptions to this general rule:

1. Masculine Proper Nouns which end in a hissing sound (**s-, -ß, -z, -tz, -x, -sch**) form the Genitive singular by adding **-ENS** and the plural, with **-EN** otherwise throughout. Thus:

FRITZ   *Gen.:* **FRITZENS**   *Plural:* **FRITZEN**

2. Feminine Proper Nouns ending in **-E** take **-NS** in the Genitive singular and **-N** in the plural throughout:

LUISE   LUISE*NS* (also **LuisES**)   *Plural:* **LuisEN**

3. In many instances, which are learnt from experience, it is possible to form a second plural with **-E.** Thus: **Heinriche.** This is sometimes preferable, as in **die Auguste.**

The Dative singular in **-(E)N** has become antiquated:

Fritzen, Luisen

PROPER NOUN WITH ARTICLE: This remains unaltered throughout singular and plural, because the Article indicates the case:

der Heinrich	der Fritz
des Heinrich	des Fritz
dem Heinrich	dem Fritz
den Heinrich	den Fritz

Plural: **die HEINRICHE**   **die FRITZEN**

And note:

der Herr Schmidt	die Herren Schmidt
des Herrn Schmidt	der Herren Schmidt
dem Herrn Schmidt	den Herren Schmidt
den Herrn Schmidt	die Herren Schmidt

Similarly:

die Frau Schmidt, without change throughout
das Fräulein Schmidt, without change throughout (no **-S** in *Genitive singular*)

PRACTICE: **ÜBUNG**

Wir kauften drei Billette. Die Schüler fürchteten die Examina. Dieser Zug fährt durch zwei Tunnel. Die Porträts dieses Malers sind gut. Wir saßen auf den weichen Sofas. Die

Turn to page 224.

KLEINER AUSZUG
DER REICHHALTIGEN SCHIFFS-SPEISE- UND GETRÄNKEKARTE

		DM
Tasse Kaffee:	oder Glas Tee mit Zucker und Sahne (oder Zitrone)	0.59
	Kännchen Kaffee oder Tee, sonst wie vor.....................	1.18
	(auf Schnell- und Expreßschiffen 0.64 bzw. 1.27)	
	Obstkuchen .... **0.55**, Teekuchen	0.65
	Feste Torte (Wiener, Mailänder, Makronen od. dergl.)	0.75
	Buttercreme-, Sahne-, Holl. Kirschtorte oder dergl.	0.85
	Speise-Eis, Portion mit 2 Waffeln	0.64
	Eisbecher mit Früchten	1.25
Fleischbrühe:	oder Tagessuppe, Brötchen...................................	0.45
	mit Ei, Brötchen	0.80
Schnittchen:	Frischwurst (in Personenfahrt)	0.73
	Plock-oder Zervelatwurst	1.00
	Schinken oder Braten	1.36
	Käse (Holländer oder Schweizer)	0.91
	Bockwurst (100 g), Brötchen	1.18
	desgl. mit Kartoffelsalat und Brötchen	1.45
	3/2 Russische Eier, Mayonnaise, garniert auf Kartoffelsalat........	1.50
Tageskarte:	Fleischgericht, Kartoffeln und Beilage (in Personenfahrt)........	1.82
MITTAGSTISCH:	Suppe, Fleisch, Gemüse, Kartoffeln und Nachtisch..............	3.00
	dasselbe mit Vorspeise od. Fischzwischengericht	4.20
	(auf Schnell- u. Expreßschiffen DM 3.15, mit Vorspeise DM 4.40, m. Fischzwischengericht DM 5.25)	
	Weitere preiswerte Fleisch-, Fisch- und Eierspeisen nach der reichhaltigen Karte.	
GETRÄNKE:	**1 Flasche Bier** erster Brauereien, ½ l.	0.82
	Doppelkorn (2 cl)	0.41
	Marken-Steinhäger (2 cl)	0.59
	Qualitäts-Weinbrand (2 cl)	0.82
	Mineralbrunnen ½ l od. Limonade ½ l od. Apfelsaft ½ l	0.50
	Weine eigner Kellereien, reiche Auswahl............ 1/1 Fl. ab	3.50
	1/2 Fl. ab	1.95
	(Für Private: Bitte Sonderpreisliste anfordern!)	
	Schaumweine (einschl. Steuer) .... 1/1 Fl. ab	7.00

Bedienungszuschlag 10% — **Änderungen vorbehalten**

Als „ schwimmende Gaststätten" stehen unsere Schiffe seit jeher im besten Ruf. Die Schiffs-restaurateure, die als selbständige Unternehmer die Wirtschaftsbetriebe in eigener Verantwortung führen, berücksichtigen gern besondere Verpflegungswünsche, z. B. von Reisegesellschaften, Jugendgruppen usw. Niemand ist zu einem Verzehr verpflichtet; auch wer sich selbst verpflegt, ist stets ein willkommener Gast.

A typical Menu on one of the Rhine steamers (1956).

Vocabulary:

das Kännchen Tee, pot of tea
Teekuchen, tea cake
Plockwurst, a hard sausage
Bockwurst, " bock " sausage
Beilage, extras
Doppelkorn, double whisky
die Sonderpreisliste, special price list

Obstkuchen, fruit cake
Feste Torte, plain tart
Zervelatwurst, dried sausage
Fleischgericht, meat dish
die reichhaltige Karte, copious menu
der Bedienungszuschlag, supplement for service

Abbreviations: **bzw., beziehungsweise,** respectively. **od., oder,** or. **u., und,** and. **dergl., dergleichen,** similar (to). **Cl., Classe,** class. **Fl., Flasche,** bottle. **einschl., einschließlich,** inclusive(ly). **z.B., zum Beispiel,** for example. See page 313 for some Common German Abbreviations.

Mineralien werden aus der Erde geholt. In den Museen gibt es schöne Bilder. Haben Sie Ihre Studien beendet?

Dieses ist Ernas Buch. Ich habe Heinrich Geld gegeben. Die drei Fritzen sind gekommen. Haben Sie Luisens Bruder gesehen? Wir waren in Schmidts Garten. Ich habe einen Band von Friedrich Schillers Gedichten. Er las einen Roman von Thomas Mann. Wir trafen Herrn Robert Braun. Da lief der Hund des Herrn Meier. Sind Sie der Nachbar des Herrn Schultz? Ich bin Schultzens Nachbar. Wir haben es den Herren Schmidt und Schultz mitgeteilt. Ist dieses der Hut des Fräulein Schmidt? Ich habe Frau Schultz gesprochen. Er ging mit Frau Schultz spazieren. Die beiden Fräulein Schmidt sind hier. Das Büro der Herren Schmidt & Schultz.

NIETZSCHE: KURZE DENKSPRÜCHE

Tief sein und tief scheinen. Wer sich tief weiß, bemüht sich um Klarheit; wer der Menge tief scheinen möchte, bemüht sich um Dunkelheit. Denn die Menge hält alles für tief, dessen Grund sie nicht sehen kann: sie ist so furchtsam und geht so ungern ins Wasser. (173)

TO BE PROFOUND AND TO SEEM PROFOUND. Who knows himself (as) profound, tries hard for clarity; he who to the crowd would like to seem profound tries hard for obscurity. For the crowd thinks of as deep that of which it cannot see the bottom: it is so timid and goes so unwillingly into the water.

Lachen. Lachen heißt: schadenfroh sein, aber mit gutem Gewissen. (200)

LAUGHING. Laughing means: to be malicious, but with good conscience.

Kritik der Tiere. Ich fürchte, die Tiere betrachten den Menschen als ein Wesen ihresgleichen, das in höchst gefährlicher Weise den gesunden Tierverstand verloren hat,—als das wahnwitzige Tier, als das lachende Tier, als das weinende Tier, als das unglückselige Tier. (224)

ANIMALS' CRITICISM. I fear (that) animals consider man as a being like themselves that in the most dangerous way has lost the sound animal understanding,—(regarding him) as the insane animal, (as) the laughing animal, (as) the weeping animal, (as) the unfortunate animal.

Originalität. Was ist Originalität? Etwas sehen, das noch keinen Namen trägt, noch nicht genannt werden kann, ob es gleich vor aller Augen liegt. Wie die Menschen gewöhnlich sind, macht ihnen erst der Name ein Ding überhaupt sichtbar. Die Originalen sind zumeist auch die Namengeber gewesen. (261)

ORIGINALITY. What is originality? To see something that as yet bears no name, cannot be named, although it lies before all (our) eyes. As men usually are, it is first the name that makes a thing generally visible to them. Original people have also mostly been the name-givers.

Ohne Eitelkeit. Wenn wir lieben, so wollen wir, daß unsere Mängel verborgen bleiben,—nicht aus Eitelkeit, sondern weil das geliebte Wesen nicht leiden soll. Ja, der Liebende möchte ein Gott scheinen, und auch dies nicht aus Eitelkeit. (263)

WITHOUT VANITY. When we love, then we wish that our shortcomings remain concealed—not out of vanity, but because the loved person must not suffer. Indeed the lover would like to seem a God, and this also not out of vanity.

Note : Friedrich Nietzsche (1844–1900), German philosopher and writer. The above are from his **Die Fröhliche Wissenschaft,** the numbers refer to the sections thereof.

§ 4. *Surnames—Christian Names—Diminutives—Lists for Reference—Practice—Visiting—Reading :* **Premieren**

German surnames present no difficulties, nor do Christian names as regards declension and general use. But in German there are many Christian and other names which either have no equivalent in English or one that is not always easy to recognize.

It is best to be acquainted with the commonest.   Here is a short list for reference:

Adalbert, Ethelbert
Andreas, Andrew
Bartholomäus, Bartholomew
Bernhard, Bernard
Brigitte, Bridget
Eberhard, Everard
Erich, Eric
Ernst, Ernest
Eugen, Eugene
Franz, Francis, Frank
Gerold, Gerald
Gerhard, Gerard
Gottfried, Geoffrey, Godfrey
Hinz und Kunz, Tom, Dick, and Harry (phrase)

Jakob, James, Jacob
Karl, Charles
Kasperle und Rätchen, Punch and Judy
Lorenz, Lawrence
Ludwig, Lewis
Magda, Madeleine, Madge
Marianne, Mary Anne
Moritz, Maurice
Reinhold, Reginald
Rüdiger, Ro(d)ger
Rudolf, Ralph
Ruprecht, Robert, Rupert
Vincenz, Vincent

DIMINUTIVE CHRISTIAN NAMES: These not only follow the normal rules (see page 255) but also have variants.   Furthermore, with some of them the rule about gender is not always observed. For instance, one may say either **die** or **das Gretel,** *little Margaret.*   On the whole, they do not cause much trouble, except that many of them bear little or no resemblance to the word from which they derive.   Here is a short list for reference:

Ännchen, Annie
Beate, Trixie
Ditha, Edith, Edie
Dorette, Dorchen, Dorie, Dolly
Edi, Edu, Teddy
Flora, Flo, from Florence (also **Florchen**)
Hans, Jack, Johnny
Hanne, Hannchen, Jane, Jenny
Heinz, Heini, Harry, Hal
Jettchen, Jette, Harriet
Julchen, Jill

Käte, Kätchen, Kate, Katy
Klaus, Nick
Lieschen, Elschen, Bessie, Betty
Malchen, Amy
Mieze, May
Resel, Terry
Röschen, Rosie
Tildchen, Tilde, Maud
Trude,   Trudchen,   Trudel, Gertie
Willi, Willy, Willie, Bill

The list could easily be extended, but these indicate some of the variants.

Note that, when diminutives are used, familiarity is implied, which means that it might then be more apt to use the familiar form of the Verb.   Until the learner has become accustomed to this, it would be better avoided.

Practice : ÜBUNG

Andreas Hofer war ein Held. Sein Name ist Bernhard.
Kennen Sie ein Buch von Adalbert Stifter? Sie heißt Magda.
Prinz Ruprecht von Bayern. Das können Sie Hinz und Kunz
erzählen! Gottfried von Bouillon war ein Ritter. Unser Kind
wird Kätchen genannt. Er schreibt an seine Freundin Dorchen.
„ Liebes Julchen," sagte er schmeichelnd zu ihr. Der Vater
kam mit seinem Sohn, dem kleinen Heinz. Sind dies Ännchens
Schuhe? Hänsel und Gretel waren im Garten. Hat er das
Buch dem Klaus oder der Beate gegeben? Wir haben das Spiel
„ Kasperle und Rätchen " gesehen. Die Mutter besuchte uns
mit dem schönen Lieschen. Sind dieses Trudel Schmidts Bälle?
Er unterschrieb seinen Brief „ Ihr Freund Ludwig ".

Visiting

der Besuch (-e), visit(s)

die Karte, visiting card

einige Tage verbringen, to spend a few days

abholen, to call for, bring

zusammen amüsieren, to enjoy each other's company

gestatten, to permit

wohnen, to live, dwell

aufsuchen, to look up

sehr gern, very much

wiedersehen, to see again

sich bemühen, to trouble one's self

die Adresse notieren, to note the address

ich freue mich sehr, Sie kennen gelernt zu haben. I'm so glad to have met you.

das Empfehlungsschreiben von . . ., letter of introduction from . . .

Mit Vergnügen, with pleasure

sich zu Hause fühlen, to feel at home

Was soll ich anziehen? What shall I wear?

ein wundervoller Abend, a wonderful evening

vorstellen, to introduce

Gestatten Sie, dass ich vorstelle, permit me to introduce

Mein Freund Schmidt läßt Sie bestens grüßen, my friend Schmidt sends you best regards

vielmals danken, to thank very much

wiederkommen, to come again

Auf Wiedersehen, au revoir; till we meet again

in guter Gesundheit antreffen, to find (someone) well

ich würde lieber, I would rather

Herr Schmidt hat seine Karte abgegeben. Mr. Schmidt has left his visiting card.

Er will uns einen Besuch machen. He wants to pay us a visit.

Gestatten Sie, daß ich mich vorstelle. Permit me to introduce myself.

Ich freue mich sehr, daß Sie uns aufsuchen. I am very pleased that you look us up.

Ich hatte mir Ihre Adresse notiert. I had noted your address.

Bitte nehmen Sie Platz. Please take a seat.

Ich habe hier ein Empfehlungsschreiben von unserem gemeinsamen Freund, Herrn Müller. I have (here) a letter of introduction from our mutual friend, Mr. Müller.

Er läßt Sie bestens grüßen. He sends you best regards.

Danke sehr; er hat versprochen, einige Tage mit uns zusammen zu verbringen. Thank you so much; he promised to spend some days together with us.

Ich hoffe, Sie fühlen sich hier zu Hause. I hope you feel at home here.

Ich danke Ihnen vielmals für den wunderschönen Abend. (I) thank you very much for the wonderful evening.

Es freut mich, auch Ihre Frau Gemahlin kennen gelernt zu haben. I am so glad to have met your wife also.

Kommen Sie bald wieder. Do come again soon.

Ich würde lieber sehen, daß Sie auch einmal zu mir kämen. I'd rather that you came to see me some time.

PREMIEREN

Akademietheater

Der „ Biberpelz "

Vor mehr als 6o Jahren, als er entstand,[1] war Gerhart Hauptmanns „ Biberpelz " eine beißende [2] Satire auf den dünkelhaften Bürokratentyp der Wilhelminischen Ära. Das Treiben [3] einer Diebesbande, die einen kostbaren Biberpelz [4] entwendet,[5] wurde vom Dichter nur gezeigt, um den Amtsvorsteher [6] von Wehrhahn [7] bloßzustellen.[8] Der zieht es vor,[9] auf harmlose Bürger, die er verdächtigt, „ Demokraten " zu sein, Jagd zu machen, statt die Diebstähle aufzuklären.[10] Er wird sogar, ohne es zu merken, zum Komplicen der Diebe, die ihn an der Nase herumführen.[11] Theo Lingen zeichnet diese Type meisterlich präzis [12] und demaskierend.[13]

Der Mutter Wolff, die die Diebstähle organisiert, um ihre Familie über Wasser zu halten, kann man nicht böse sein. Hauptmann gab ihr so herzhaft-mutterwitzige,[14] gutmütigresolute Züge, daß man sie lieb haben muß. Gar,[15] wenn Käthe Dorsch sie spielt. Sie macht das hinreißend [16] echt, man glaubt ihr die „ Temperatur " (womit sie ihr Temperament meint).

Ulrich Bettacs Regie verwandelt [17] die Satire in humoristische Detailmalerei. Aber das Menschliche der Typen tritt klar hervor, lebendig wie eh und je.[18]

From : **DIE WOCHENPRESSE**

Wien, 9. Juni 1956

NOTES

Translation of difficult words :

PREMIERE(N), first night(s)

[1] **entstehen,** to come into existence
[2] **beißend,** biting
[3] **das Treiben,** activity
[4] **der Biberpelz,** beaver fur
[5] **entwenden,** to steal
[6] **der Amtsvorsteher,** chief of office
[7] **von Wehrhahn** (name)
[8] **bloßstellen,** to expose
[9] **vorziehen,** to prefer
[10] **aufklären,** to clarify
[11] **an der Nase herumführen,** to lead by the nose
[12] **präzis,** exactly
[13] **demaskierend,** revealing
[14] **mutterwitzig,** with mother wit
[15] **gar,** quite so
[16] **hinreißend,** enchantingly
[17] **verwandeln,** to transform
[18] **eh und je,** as ever

§ 5. *Various Methods of Practice: Exercises—Situations—Reading Matter—Newspapers, etc.—Text with Translation—Radio and Radio Stations: List—Exclamatory Phrases—Advertisements for Amusements*

By this time you should have a general grasp of important principles and a fair vocabulary of useful Words and Phrases. Hitherto much of your Practice (**Übung**) has been based on the grammar of the relative Section of each Lesson, with matter for recapitulation from time to time. This is a useful moment for stocktaking, so go back, turning over the pages of the Practice material, and test your knowledge. How much do you remember? Wherever there is something you have forgotten, look it up and refresh your memory. Then go on to the " Situations " with their vocabulary and again test your knowledge. Have you kept a note-book? The tests will indicate whether you need one before proceeding farther. Jot down everything you have forgotten, and keep this by you for constant revision. Go over the Reading Matter, covering up the Translation, and see how much you *easily* understand. All this is important, because from now your reading matter will be *Adult Reading* : that is to say, it will consist of passages of German written by German writers for adult German Readers, and has not been specially prepared (like **Hans im Glück**) for foreign learners. You will be provided with extracts from newspapers and other items of living German and, apart from the extracts from a famous novel to be found in the next two Lessons, for which a literal translation is given, you will be expected to work out—with the aid of some explanatory notes— the meaning of all these pieces. This should encourage you to obtain, whenever or wherever possible, newspapers and magazines in German ; and read them to the best of your ability. Illustrated publications are useful, because the pictures help you to memorize the new words to be found in the captions, etc.

RADIO AND RADIO STATIONS : You should by now be able to follow broadcasts and get the gist of what you hear, unless it is difficult or technical matter. Here is a List of Radio Stations which broadcast in German:

LIST OF RADIO STATIONS

GERMANY

Bavaria : München
  Bayrischer Rundfunk (187; 375 m.)
Nord-West-Deutscher Rundfunk
  Hamburg (309 m.)
  Münster (199 m.)
  Hannover (189 m.)
  Köln (93.3 m.) (U.K.W.) *
Frankfurt (506 m.)
Berlin
  RIAS (303; 407 m.)
  East Zone (287.6 m.)

Südwest-Funk (195; 295 m.)
Bremen (221; 278 m.)
Stuttgart (522 m.)

AUSTRIA
  Wien (293; 388 m.)

SWITZERLAND
  Beromünster (567 m.)
  Sottens (393 m.)

SAARLAND   Saarbrücken
  (211 m.)

LUXEMBURG   (1293 m.)
  (49.26 m. U.K.W.)

* To the wavelength of some German Stations is added: U.K.W. or UKW = Ultra-Kurz-Welle (*ultra-short-wave*).

CHANGES IN WAVELENGTHS

Note : Radio Stations sometimes change their wavelengths. It may therefore be advisable to look them up from time to time, or to apply to the nearest German, Austrian, or Swiss Consulate for the latest information.   This can often be found in publications which deal with international radio broadcasting.

INTERJECTIONS AND EXCLAMATORY PHRASES : An exhaustive list is neither possible nor necessary. Nor need all that are given below be memorized, though it is advisable to learn those in capitals. The English equivalents are generally approximates:

ACH ! Ah ! Oh !

Leider ! Unhappily !

HOCH !
Hurra ! } Hurrah !

SO ! ACH SO !   Indeed !
  Really ?

DANKE.   Thanks.   No
  thanks.

Entschuldigen Sie. Excuse me.

Verzeihen Sie. Pardon.

ALSO DOCH! Well I never!

AU! Expresses physical pain.

BRAVO!
GUT! } Splendid! Fine!
Sehr gut!

Quatsch! Bosh! Rubbish!

SCHÖN! Excellent! Fine!

BITTE (ich bitte). Please...

Bitte um Verzeihung! I beg your pardon.

*Bitte! Don't mention it.

Bitte sehr! To introduce a contradiction, or to take exception to something.

Bitte, bitte! Please do. Go ahead!

Bitte! Please may I pass?

Bitte schön! Please help yourself.

WIRKLICH? Really? Is that so?

Allerdings! Of course.

Unerhört! Scandalous!

STIMMT! Right! OK.

DOCH, yes (*after a negative*)

Ausgezeichnet! Magnificent!

Na so! There you are!

Nanu . . .? What on earth . . .?

NATÜRLICH! Naturally, of course!

Um so besser! So much the better!

Bestimmt! Surely!

Du meine Güte! Gracious me! Heavens!

HALLO! Hallo!

WIE, BITTE? What did you say? What's that? (*on the phone, for instance*)

AUF WIEDERSEHEN! Till we meet again. Au revoir.

Ach wo! Impossible!

Da haben wir's! That's done it!

ACHTUNG!
Passen Sie auf! } Look out!

These exclamatory phrases are very useful for the novice. With them he can express his interest, surprise, annoyance, etc., without the need for long speeches.

No special Practice (**Übung**) is necessary with this Section. If the learner follows the advice given on page 230, he will have sufficient to do, and he should not proceed farther until satisfied that he has a good grasp of most of the material given up till now. But he should *know* all the above Exclamatory Phrases in capitals as many of them are of everyday utility.

* The tone of the voice varies with the use of **bitte** to express words not stated. This can be learnt by experience.

ANZEIGEN Advertisements for Amusements

KONZERTDIREKTION DR. RUDOLPH GOETTE
Freitag, 4. Mai, Musikhalle, 20 Uhr
BRAILOWSKY
spielt Chopin
u. a. Polonaise B-Dur, Ballade As-Dur, Sonate H-Moll
DM 2,—bis 6,—
Theaterkasse Gerdes (45 33 26), bek. Vorverkaufsstellen
und (soweit vorrätig) an der Abendkasse

Montag, 7. Mai, Musikhalle, 20 Uhr
Gershwin-Konzert
Rhapsody in Blue, Amerikaner in Paris, Porgy and Bess u. a.
Sondra-Bianca (New York) **Klavier** — MGM-Records-Orchester
Leitung: Hans-Jürgen Walther
Karten 1,50—5,50 bei Gerdes (45 33 26), Vorverkaufsstellen u. Abendkasse

VATERLAND Varieté-Revue - Tägl. 16.15 und 20.30 - 33 01 55
Yvonné Carré, W. Meyen, Yonal, E. Merz u.v.a.

„Die Heiden sind prüde" Peter Ahrweiler's „rendezvous" Neuer Wall 54
Täglich 21 Uhr Hamburgs literarisches Cabaret Tel. 34 05 61

FAUN: Orchester Cha-Cha-Cha — sensationell

Continental am Hbf., sbds. ab 20 Uhr **Konzert u. Tanz**
sonntags ab 16.30 Uhr
Räume für Konferenzen und Festlichkeiten mietefrei

● **Hirte** Orchester Beauvais **TANZABENDE** ●
Eintritt frei

MALKASTEN
TÄGLICH BIS 2 UHR - KÜNSTLERLOKAL - PAPENHUDER STRASSE

HEIN TEN HOFF
empfiehlt sein **Klublokal mit Saal** für
Familien-, Vereins- u. Betriebsfeste
(20 bis 400 Personen)

Saseler Chaussee 254 — Ruf 60 90 64 — **Doppelte Bundeskegelbahn**

LESSON VIII

§ 1. *Prepositions—List: With Accusative or Dative, with Dative, with Accusative — Examples — Practice — Reading:* **Der Streit um den Sergeanten Grischa**

A PREPOSITION is a word which usually indicates position or direction. It is placed with a Noun or Pronoun to make clear its relation with some other word. In English the Prepositions are placed before their Nouns or Pronouns, but in German some Prepositions may be placed after. *In, to, at,* and other words listed below are Prepositions.

As Nouns and Pronouns are inflected in German, it is convenient to classify German Prepositions in accordance with the case or cases which must go with them, cases because some German Prepositions may "govern" more than one case, with different meanings in accordance with the case. Thus:

The Dative: usually expresses the idea of being *stationary* or *remaining*; or *motion within* the confines of the place.

The Accusative: usually answers the question *Where to, whither?* It expresses *direction*.

Examples:

Dative

ICH SITZE AUF DER BANK. I'm sitting on the bench.

ER SCHLÄFT IN DEM ZIMMER. He's sleeping in the room.

SEINE SCHUHE STEHEN VOR DER TÜR. His shoes are (stand) in front of the door.

ZWISCHEN DEN GÄRTEN IST EIN GRABEN. Between the gardens is a ditch.

Accusative

ICH GEHE AUF DIE STRAßE.   I'm going on to the
street.

ER REIST IN DIE STADT.   He travels to the town.

ER STELLT DEN STUHL VOR DIE TÜR.   He puts the
chair in front of the door.

ER FIEL ZWISCHEN ZWEI STÜHLE.   He fell between
two chairs (stools).

You have already met many of the Prepositions to be listed.
Now they should all be *memorized* so that, whenever you meet
or have to use one of these words, you will be conscious that it
entails a Noun or Pronoun in the correct case.   Examples have
been given of how the same Preposition works with Dative or
Accusative.   Here are some examples of Prepositions with the
Genitive:

WÄHREND DES WINTERS KAM ICH NACH HAUSE.
During the winter I came home.

DIESSEITS DES FLUSSES IST EIN HAUS.   This side of
the river (there) is a house.

JENSEITS DER GRENZE IST DEUTSCHLAND.   On
that side of the frontier is Germany.

**DIE ELTERN SIND IHRER KINDER WEGEN IN
SORGE.**   The parents are anxious (in anxiety) on account
of their children.

TROTZ SEINER KRANKHEIT IST ER STARK.   In spite
of his illness he is strong.

In the last two examples, note that **WEGEN** can be placed
either before or after **ihrer Kinder,** and **TROTZ** may also take
the Dative instead of the Genitive.   To come back again to the
Dative, which some learners find most difficult to grasp in regard
to Prepositions, when in doubt ask yourself whether it is a
question of *WHERE?* or *TO WHERE?*   If the answer is

where, use the Dative. If it is *to where*, use the Accusative. Thus:

> **Wo sind wir?** Where are we?
> **Wir sind in DER** (*Dative*) **Stadt.** We're in the town. (*Rest.*)
> **Wohin gehen wir jetzt?** Where are we going to now?
> **Wir gehen in DIE** (*Accusative*) **Stadt?** We're going into the city. (*Direction.*)

But:

> **WIR SPAZIEREN IN** *DER* **STADT AUF UND AB.** We're walking up and down in the city.

The dative is used here because the motion is within the confines of the city.

List of Prepositions

1. *With Accusative OR Dative*

ÜBER, over, across (*not touching*)
AUF, on, on to
UNTER, under
VOR, before, in front of
HINTER, behind

NEBEN, beside (*not touching*)
AN, on, at, against
IN, in, into
ZWISCHEN, between

2. *With the Dative*

AUS, out of
AUßER, outside, besides
BEI, by, at, near
BINNEN, within
Entgegen, against
GEGENÜBER, opposite, facing
GEMÄß, in accordance with

MIT, with
NACH, after
nebst, samt, along with
SEIT, since
VON, of, from, by
ZU, to
ZUWIDER, contrary to

3 *With the Accusative*

DURCH, through
ENTLANG, along (*also Dative*)
FÜR, for
GEGEN, against

OHNE, without, less (*so much*)
UM, round, about, at (*of time*), for
WIDER, against

4. *With the Genitive*

(*a*) **ANSTATT, STATT,** in- **WÄHREND,** during, while
    stead of   **WEGEN,** on account of
TROTZ, in spite of

(*b*) **diesseits,** this side of   **kraft,** by virtue of
    jenseits, that side of   **laut,** according to
    außerhalb, outside of   **halber,** on account of
    innerhalb, inside of   **ungeachtet,** notwithstanding
    oberhalb, above   **unbeschadet,** without preju-
    unterhalb, below   dice to
    unweit, not far from   **um . . . willen,** for the sake of

(*a*) are frequently used Prepositions. (*b*) are in the nature of Adverbs but are quite often used as Prepositions.

MITTEN, *in the middle of*; **BIS,** *to, as far as*, are Adverbs which can be used alone or with a Preposition. Thus:

ICH FAHRE BIS LONDON. I'm travelling as far as London.

Ich wartete bis Mittag. I waited until midday.

Wir warteten bis Montag. We waited until Monday.

ICH SASS MITTEN IN DEM ZIMMER. I sat in the middle of the room.

Mein Vater kam BIS AN die Grenze. My father came right to the frontier.

CONTRACTIONS: PREPOSITION + ARTICLE: The Definite Article can often be contracted with a preceding Preposition of one syllable, very often with **DEM** (*masculine* and *neuter* Dative) and **DAS** (*neuter* Accusative), ZUR for **zu der** is the only feminine contraction permissible. Note the following:

AM = an dem   **IM = in dem**
ANS = an das   **INS = in das**
AUFS = auf das   **VOM = von dem**
BEIM = bei dem   **ZUM = zu dem**
FÜRS = für das

DA *and* **DAR** *with Prepositions*: **DA,** *there*, **DAR** before a vowel, are commonly found with Prepositions to make the equivalent of our *thereby, therewith, thereafter, thereupon, thereto*, and many words for which we have no " *there-* combination ". *Examples*: **dabei, dadurch, dafür, dagegen, dahinter, danach, daneben, davon, dawider, dazu, dazwischen, daran, darauf, daraus, darin, darob, darüber, darum, darunter.** These are easily recognizable.

WO *and* **WOR** *with Prepositions :* Similarly **WO,** *where,* **WOR-** before a vowel, are used to make the equivalent of our " *where-* combinations " such as *whereby, whereto, whereat,* etc., and the German compounds are also easily recognizable : **wobei, wodurch, wofür, wogegen, wohinter, womit, wonach, woneben, wovon, wovor, wozu, wozwischen, worauf, woraus, worin, worüber, worum, worunter.** Be careful to distinguish between **WARUM,** *why?* and **worum,** which means *for which, for what.* Examples :

> **WARUM sprechen Sie?** Why do you speak ?
> **DAS, WORUM ICH BITTE,** that for which I ask

The examples which have been given illustrate pitfalls in the use of German Prepositions, but do not exhaust them. For the rest, the Prepositions are among the most frequently used words in the language, and their use in general is best learnt from reading and listening to German speakers.

It is important to know all the Prepositions given here as Vocabulary. That is the first step towards mastery. The examples should also be memorized.

Experience shows that, in the use of the Prepositions, the English-speaking learner—because English is so simple in this respect—finds most difficulty in making the distinctions which, in German, call for Dative or Accusative in accordance with the meaning to be expressed. The rules have been stated on page **234,** but what follows should clarify them further. Always remember: Dative for *rest,* Accusative for *motion.* Thus :

Place Person	*To*	*Rest*	*From*
house, home	**nach Hause**	**zu Hause**	**von Hause**
First Person	**zu mir**	**mit mir** (with) **bei mir** (near)	**von mir**
church (within)	**in die Kirche**	**in der Kirche**	**aus der Kirche**
field (surface)	**auf das Feld**	**auf dem Felde**	**von dem Felde**
bridge (near)	**an die Brücke** **nach der Brücke**	**an der Brücke**	**von der Brücke**
cities, towns	**nach Paris**	**in Paris** **zu Paris**	**von Paris**
countries	**nach England**	**in England**	**aus England**

aus London { from
belonging to } London
von London, coming from London

Note : The rules stated on page **234** are for those Prepositions which can take either Dative or Accusative, but note that they need not apply to those which are limited to only one case. Thus :

AUS DER KIRCHE KOMMEN, to come out of the church
VON DEM FELDE KOMMEN, to come from the field
ZU MIR KOMMEN, to come to me

In other words, these Prepositions must always have their own case, whether the meaning is *rest* or *motion*.

In the Reading Matter, always look carefully at the Prepositions and note how they are rendered.

Practice : ÜBUNG

Wir gingen in das Zimmer und setzten uns auf das Sofa.   Ein Buch liegt auf dem Tisch.   Der Hund läuft über die Straße. Über dem Eingang hängt eine Lampe.   Das Mädchen schläft in der Kammer unter dem Dach.   Am Brunnen vor dem Tore steht ein Baum.   Perlen vor die Schweine werfen.   Ich ging neben ihm.   Jack legte die Mütze neben sich.   Er klopfte an die Tür.   Das Bild hängt an der Wand.

Die Jahre zwischen den beiden Weltkriegen.   Außer ihm war niemand da.   Ich gehe bei schönem Wetter mit meinem Freund spazieren.   Er wohnt gegenüber dem Rathaus.   Seit drei Tagen ist er krank.   Ist dieses der Weg zum Bahnhof ?   Wir liefen durch den Regen.   Sie dankt für die Blumen aufs herzlichste. Er rennt mit dem Kopf gegen die Wand.   Statt der Mutter erschien die Tochter.   Während der Nacht hat es geschneit. Jenseits des Berges ist ein See.   Er wohnt außerhalb der Stadt.

Der Kinder wegen ist sie nicht gekommen.   Er tut das um der guten Sache willen.   Mitten im Fluß ist eine Insel.   Gehen Sie ins Theater ?   Holen wir Brot vom Bäcker !   Zum Schluß sagte er ja.   Ich kann es Ihnen beim besten Willen nicht sagen.

Was haben Sie dafür bezahlt ?   Er verläßt sich darauf.   Ich weiß nichts davon.   Wir wollen darüber sprechen.   Womit kann ich Ihnen dienen ?   Er sagte, worum es sich handelte. Ist das etwas, worauf man rechnen kann ?

Der Streit um den Sergeanten Grischa

Roman von Arnold Zweig

The Case of Sergeant Grischa, a famous German novel of the 1914–18 War, first published by Arnold Zweig in 1927, is a masterly account of a Russian sergeant who was prisoner of the Germans, escaped, took a false name, was recaptured, and, under his false name, tried for espionage, of which he was not guilty. He was found guilty, condemned to death, and finally executed. It is a moving story of a gross miscarriage of justice, and the struggle for a man's life. The style is vigorous, direct, and seldom presents difficulties. The Extracts which follow are given a literal translation to help the learner. A literary translation by Eric Sutton was published by Hutchinson International Authors in 1947. It is much freer than what is given here.

I. *Der Plan*

Es gibt nicht zwei Leute, die dem ehemaligen Sergeanten und jetzigen Gefangenen Nummer 173, Grischa Iljitsch Paprotkin, irgendeine Bitte abschlagen würden oder einem seiner Befehle widersprächen . . . Sergeant Grischa aber ist in Wologda zu Haus, weit hinten im Nordosten des mächtigen russischen Gebildes, und sucht er Frau und Kinder, muß er sie jenseits der russischen Front finden. Das ist sein Plan. Er wird den Deutschen fortlaufen ; er hält es nicht mehr aus. Mit dem Beginn des neuen Jahres, mit der Bestätigung vielfacher Gerüchte ist eine Unruhe in sein Herz getreten ; langsame, schwerfüßige Gedanken haben sich Morgen für Morgen mächtiger in seinem Kopfe eingestellt : nach Hause. Er hat allzu lange ausgeharrt. Zwischen den Stacheldrähten, zwischen den karierten Befehlen der verrückten Deutschen, die aus Angst dem Menschen nicht einmal mehr Freiheit zum Atmen lassen, sondern ihm am liebsten noch befehlen würden : jetzt atme ein, jetzt atme aus, jetzt schneuz dir die Nase, jetzt geh auf die Latrine—zwischen den enggepferchten Schlaflagern in den Baracken, zwischen diesen stieräugigen Scharen von Vorgesetzten, zwischen all dem ist für ihn zum Atmen nicht mehr Raum. Er ist jetzt sechzehn

Monate ihr Gefangener, und er wird es keinen neuen Morgen mehr sein. Heute nacht wird er seinen Weg zurück zu Marfa Iwanowna antreten und zu seiner kleinen winzigen Jelisawjeta, die er noch nicht gesehen hat.

TRANSLATION:
The Plan

There are not two people who, the former sergeant and now Prisoner Number 173, Grischa Ilyitsh Paprotkin, any request would deny, or (who would) disobey one of his orders. . . . But Sergeant Grischa has his home in Vologda, far behind the north-east of the mighty Russian formation, and if he is seeking (his) wife and children, must find them on the other side of the Russian front (line). That is his plan. He would run away from the Germans; he could not bear it any longer. With the beginning of the new year, with the confirmation of manifold rumours, a kind of unrest had entered his heart; slow, heavy-footed thoughts had day after day more strongly fixed themselves in his head: (he must go) home. He had delayed far too long. Between the barbed wire, the ever-changing orders of the daft Germans, who from fear hardly any more allowed men freedom to breathe, but would almost order: now breathe in, now breathe out, now wipe the (your) nose, now go to the latrine—what with the crowded sleeping-quarters in the barracks, the staring crowds of superiors, there was for him no longer breathing space. He had been their prisoner for sixteen months, and he would not be it for another new day. That (very) night he would set out on his way back to Marfa Ivanovna and to his little tiny Yelisavyeta, whom he had not yet ever seen.

[*Contd. on p.* 247.

§ 2. *Word-building—Some General Indications—Nouns I*: *General Examples—Long Words—Practice—Reading*: **Sergeant Grischa**

You have seen (page 50) and by many examples given throughout the Course that the German language has a remarkable capacity for compounding new words from simple elements. Hitherto you have learnt the new compound words, mostly simple ones and easily understood, as they have arisen and as vocabulary. In the sections which follow will be outlined the general principles on which new words are compounded from various elements. These principles must first be understood and then known. New words in large type must be learnt.

With the grammar already given, and a grasp of these important principles, a vast reading vocabulary becomes open to the student. There are about 2,500 simple or "elemental" words and roots in German which form the basis of the wider vocabulary of compound words. Nearly all these "basic" words are given in the Vocabulary at the end of the book, or in the grammar: especially among the Strong Verbs listed in Lessons VI and VII. Hence, although there will be much that is new in the pages which follow, there will also be many very important basic words which are already familiar.

A clear distinction must be made between **simple** and **compound words.** Resemblances between English and German are a great help in this. For example:

Simple Words:

> **der Garten,** garden   **das Gemüse,** vegetables
> **das Tier,** animal

Compound Words:

> **der Gemüsegarten,** vegetable garden
> **der Tiergarten,** zoological garden (" animal garden ")

Note well that the determining factor in the new compound is placed *first*. Also (as noted on page 50 in the Declension of Nouns) that the Gender of the new compound word and the Declension thereof follow that of the *last* component if this is a Noun.

Sometimes a compound is used as the determining factor in a further compound Noun. For example:

> **die Kirche,** church   ⌐ **der Turm,** tower, steeple
> **die Glocke,** clock

> **der KIRCHTURM,** church tower
> **die KIRCHTURMGLOCKE,** church-tower clock

Thus, if you know these three simple words, you can make two new compounds from them. Again, take:

ober, over ; **der Bürger,** citizen ; **der Meister,** master

der BÜRGERMEISTER, " master citizen " = mayor

der OBERBÜRGERMEISTER, " over mayor " = English Lord Mayor

Here the Preposition **ober** dominates, or determines, the new sense.

Hitherto in the Course you have been allowed to see for yourself how compound words are made, and this may seem rather haphazard. But there is system and method in compounding and making *derivatives* from words known. You may now set about a study of system and method and in some (though not exhaustive) detail. What is given from here to page 278 is worth careful consideration, and should be constantly reviewed. Let us begin with Nouns, which are highly important :

NOUNS : I. New Nouns can be made with a Noun + another Noun or Nouns :

die Tür, door ; **der Schlüssel,** key ; **das Haus,** house

DER HAUSTÜRSCHLÜSSEL, the house-door-key

Some very long words result from this process, many of them fairly common :

die LEBENSVERSICHERUNGSGESELLSCHAFT, life insurance company

Lebens, Genitive of **das Leben,** *life*

Versicherung, a Compound Noun made up from the Adjective **sicher** with prefix **ver-** (intensification) and ending **-ung** (feminine noun-ending), all meaning *insurance.*

Gesellschaft, made up from **Gesell,** *companion, co-partner,* to which is added the feminine noun-ending **-schaft,** corresponding to the English ending *-ship,* the whole word meaning *company*

And here is another :

die DAMPFSCHIFFAHRTSAKTIENGESELLSCHAFT, steam-ship journey(ing) joint-stock-company = Joint-Stock Steam Navigation Company

You will see from these examples that a very long word in German is no great cause for alarm. If all its constituent parts are known, it becomes easy to understand in most instances. If you do not know already the parts, look them up in a dictionary, list their meanings, which will generally make things clear. Many common Compound Nouns will be found set out in full in a good dictionary. Here a warning may be given:

WARNING: GERMAN–ENGLISH DICTIONARIES PROVIDE ONLY A FRACTION OF THE COMPOUND WORDS POSSIBLE IN GERMAN. IT IS THEREFORE DESIRABLE: (*a*) TO BE FAMILIAR WITH THE GENERAL PRINCIPLES OF WORD-BUILDING AS GIVEN HERE; AND (*b*) TO HAVE A GOOD VOCABULARY OF THE BASIC WORDS AND ROOTS USED IN WORD-BUILDING.

German literature, reviews, and newspapers provide the practice and experience required in this highly important aspect of the language.

PRACTICE: ÜBUNG

Do not attempt, on your own initiative, to make new Compound Words. The best way to become familiar with them is by hearing and by reading. Hearing does not always help, unless you already know the root words. If you should happen to be with a German speaker who uses an unfamiliar compound, you can always ask him to explain, and that should provide the key—providing you know the meaning(s) of the components! Read, read, read—this is the answer. And read *anything*: even reading Advertisements is a help, which explains why some are given in these pages. But *reading a long work* is undoubtedly best, and that is why the gripping novel **Der Streit um den Sergeanten Grischa** has been introduced here. When you have finished the Extracts, try to obtain a copy of the original German of the whole book. You will find to your delight that you understand most of it, and that the meaning of hundreds of Compound Words you have not hitherto met will become clear. Meanwhile, here are some fairly common Compound Nouns which you ought to understand. Guessing is not recommended,

except when the meaning seems to be obvious.   Then you may
take a chance.

Examples of Compound Words

die Post, mail
das Postamt, Post office
das Hauptpostamt, Main Post office
der Postbote, postman
der Hilfspostbote, assistant postman
die Straße, street
die Hauptstraße, main street
die Hauptverkehrstraße, main thoroughfare
die Nebenstraße, side street
der Hof, court yard
die Bahn, railway
der Bahnhof, station
der Hauptbahnhof, central station
die Bahnhofswirtschaft, station restaurant
die Bahnhofstraße, station road
der Bahnhofsvorsteher, station master
der Güterbahnhof, freight station
das Buch, book
das Lehrbuch, text-book
die Buchhandlung, bookshop
der Buchhändler, bookseller
die Buchhändlervereinigung, booksellers' association
die Schrift, script
der Schriftsetzer, typesetter, compositor
der Schriftsetzerlehrling, apprentice compositor
der Schriftsteller, author
der Schriftleiter, editor
die Zeitschrift, periodical
die Zeitschriftenhandlung, magazine stand (shop)
das Kind, child
die Kindtaufe, christening
die Kinderkrankheit, infants' disease
der Kindergarten, kindergarten
das Glückskind, lucky child

der Tisch, table
das Tischtuch, table cloth
der Schreibtisch, writing desk
die Schreibtischlampe, writing-desk lamp
der Tag, day
der Alltag, everyday
alltäglich, daily
der Feiertag, holiday
das Tagebuch, diary
die Tagereise, day's journey
die Liebe, love
die Liebschaft, love affair
der Liebesbrief, love letter
die Liebesgöttin, Goddess of Love
Liebesgöttinnenpalast, Palace of the Goddesses of Love

DEUTSCHER
WETTERDIENST

20.7.1956

Heiter bis wolkig

Vorhersage fürs Wochenende:

Heiter bis wolkig, mäßige auf Nord drehende Winde, Mittagstemperatur um 22°, im Binnenlande zunächst noch Neigung zu örtlichen Gewitterschauern.[1]

Wetterlage: Das über Mitteldeutschland liegende Gewittertief schwächt[2] sich allmählich ab, während das über dem Nordmeer liegende Hoch sich nach England verlagert.[3]

Temperaturen Freitag, 24 Uhr: In Hamburg + 12, Cuxhaven + 16, Lüneburg + 14, Hannover + 15, Lübeck + 13 Grad. Relative Luftfeuchtigkeit[4] in Hamburg: 94 Proz. Barometerstand: 1011,0 Millibar = 758,3 Millimeter. Tendenz: steigend.

NOTES

[1] **der Gewitterschauer,** thunderstorm with rain.
[2] **es schwächt sich ab,** it decreases.
[3] **es verlagert sich,** it shifts.
[4] **die Luftfeuchtigkeit,** air humidity.

Sergeant Grischa—2

Ein Ausbrecher

Waggons, die fertig beladen mitten im Walde stehen, sollen der Vorschrift gemäß bewacht werden. Aber wo kein Kläger ist, wer wird da richten? In einer warmen, erleuchteten Stationsbaracke, wellblechgedeckt und gut verschalt, spielt es sich, wenn man zu dreien sitzt und etwas zu rauchen hat, wunderbar Skat, zumal man sich ja Tee kochen kann und drei Rumrationen, sparsam gebraucht, ziemlich vielen Großzuschuß ergeben. Wer mit Küchenbullen Freundschaft hält, hat auch immer Zucker.

Ein Mensch klettert in einen Güterwagen ziemlich leicht, sofern er oben offen ist. In einer Höhle, einer von Holz umkapselten, harzriechenden Röhre, streckt er sich lang aus, nachdem er kieferne Stempel, kurze Bohlen mit einem Einschnitt an jedem Ende, über sich wieder sorgfältig zurechtgerückt hat; streckt sich aus und lacht, lacht laut los, durch und durch geschüttelt, schweißdurchtränkt das Hemd, fliegend an allen Gliedern in einer engen kantigen Rinne, die einem Sarge gleicht. Er liegt hart. Viel Bewegung kann er sich nicht machen. Aber er lacht, und seine Augen mögen in der Finsternis glänzen wie die eines ausgebrochenen, lange gefangenen Panthers.

TRANSLATION :

An Escaper

Waggons which stand loaded in the forest must be guarded in conformity with the order. But where there is no prosecutor, who will pass judgment? In a warm, lighted station-shed, with corrugated iron roof and well lined with boards, when three sit together and have something to smoke, a wonderful (card) game of Skat is played, especially if you can make yourself tea, and three rum-rations sparingly used yield a tolerably generous contribution. Whoever maintains friendship with the cook has always sugar also.

A man was climbing into a freight car easily enough, in that it was open on top. In a cavity, a resin-smelling tube, encased in wood, he stretched himself out at length, after he had carefully pulled back again some fir props, short planks with a groove at each end ; stretched himself out and laughed loud and freely, shook with laughter through and through, his shirt wet through with sweat, shivering in all his limbs in *a narrow, sharp groove that resembled a coffin. He lay hard. He could not make himself move much. But he laughed, and his eyes must shine * in the darkness like those of an escaped, long imprisoned panther.*

[*Contd. on p. 253.*

§ 3. *Compound Words—contd.—Nouns II: Derivatives—Endings* **-ER, -LER, -NER,** *and* **-IN**—*Feminine Ending* **-E**—*Ending* **-EL** *for means, instrument*—**-LING, -UNG, -HEIT, -KEIT, -SCHAFT, -TUM**—*Prefixes* **GE-, UR-, UN-** *and* **MIß**—*Newspaper Extract—Reading:* **Sergeant Grischa**

NOUNS II: New Nouns are made by adding certain endings to the *root* of another word. Such new compounds are, strictly, *derivatives.* Root + Ending = Derivative.

1. Masculine Endings: **-ER**   **-LER**   **-NER**
   Feminine Endings: **-ERIN**   **-LERIN**   **-NERIN**

When the masculine ends in **-ER,** meaning a person engaged in the function or activity expressed in the root-word, it usually takes **-IN** to express the feminine. Thus:

SPRECHEN, to speak; **SPRECHER,** speaker, announcer (radio); **SPRECHERIN** (*fem.*)

ARBEITEN, to work; **ARBEITER,** worker; **ARBEITERIN** (*fem.*)

die KUNST, art, skill; **der KÜNSTLER,** artist; **die KÜNSTLERIN** (*fem.*)

REDEN, to speak; **die REDE,**† speech; **der REDNER,**

speaker, orator; **die REDNERIN** (*fem.*)

2. Feminine ending **-E**: often with modification:

GROß, big; **die GRÖßE,** size, bigness
WARM, warm; **die WÄRME,** warmth
LIEBEN, to love; **die LIEBE,** love

---

* Note that the Historical Present Tense is more used in German than in English. " shine " is literal, but we should usually say " have shone ".

† See 2 below.

The names of inhabitants are made from many place-names by adding **-E,** and feminine **-IN** to the root (found by discarding the **-en** ending):

> **das PREUßEN,** Prussia ; *root :* **Preuß-**
> **der PREUße,** the Prussian (*m.*) ; **die PREUßIN,** the Prussian (*fem.*)
>
> See pages 82-83.

3. Ending **-EL,** mostly masculine, usually indicates a *means* or *instrument* :

> **SCHLIESSEN,** to shut, lock (*root vowel* **-ie** *changed to* **ü**) ; **der SCHLÜSSEL,** key
> **DECKEN,** to cover ; **der DECKEL,** lid
> **HEBEN,** to lift, raise ; **der HEBEL,** lever
> **GURTEN,** to gird ; **der GÜRTEL,** belt

4. Ending **-EI,** always feminine, often expresses a *business* and occasionally has a contemptuous connotation :

> **BACKEN,** to bake ; **der BÄCKER,** baker ; **die BÄCKEREI,** bakery
> **SPIELEN,** to play ; **der SPIELER,** player ; **die SPIELE-REI,** playing
> **SCHMEICHELN,** to flatter ; **der SCHMEICHLER,** flatterer ; **die SCHMEICHELEI,** flattery

5. Ending **-LING,** always masculine, often indicates a person who is *small*, *young*, or *held in contempt* :

> **JUNG,** young ; **der JÜNGLING,** young fellow, youngster
> **FEIGE,** cowardly ; **der FEIGLING,** coward, cowardly fellow

6. Ending **-UNG,** always feminine, usually indicates the *outcome* or *result* of an activity ; often corresponds to English *-ing* :

> **ERFINDEN,** to invent ; **die ERFINDUNG,** invention
> **ERKÄLTEN,** to cool down ; **die ERKÄLTUNG,** catching cold (**die Kälte,** cold)

RECHNEN, to calculate, reckon, count; **die RECH-NUNG,** reckoning, bill

KLEIDEN, to clothe; **die KLEIDUNG,** clothing

REGIEREN, to rule, govern; **die REGIERUNG,** government, regime

7. Endings **-HEIT** (**-KEIT** after **-ch, -ig, -r**) always feminine, indicates an Abstract Noun or a *totality* (English: *-hood, -head*):

der MENSCH, man, human being; **die MENSCHHEIT,** mankind, humanity in general

das KIND, child; **die KINDHEIT,** childhood

der GOTT, God; **die GOTTHEIT,** godhead, divinity

KLUG, clever, sensible; **die KLUGHEIT,** cleverness

BÖSE, bad, evil; **DIE BOSHEIT,** malice, spite (*Note:* drops modification)

DANKBAR, thankful; **die DANKBARKEIT,** thankfulness

RÜHRIG, active, stirring; **die RÜHRIGKEIT,** activity

8. Ending **-SCHAFT,** always feminine, indicates a *collectivity,* or a relation*ship* among several people:

der BÜRGER, citizen, townsman; **die BÜRGERSCHAFT,** citizenry, townsfolk

der FREUND, friend; **die FREUNDSCHAFT,** friendship

der GESANDTE, envoy, legate; **die GESANDTSCHAFT,** legation

der BOTE, messenger; **die BOTSCHAFT,** embassy (office)
Note: **der BOTSCHAFTER,** ambassador (*fem.* **-erin**)

9. Ending **-TUM,** always neuter (except **der Irrtum, der Reichtum,** *error, wealth*) and usually indicates an *abstract idea* (English: *-dom*):

der Christ, Christ, Christian; **das Christentum,** christianity; *but:* **die CHRISTENHEIT,** Christendom

der KÖNIG, king; **das KÖNIGTUM,** kingdom

der FÜRST, prince; **das FÜRSTENTUM,** principality

10. PREFIXES: **GE-** often indicating *a concentration of*, **UR-** indicating *great age*, *antiquity*, *the primitive*, and **UN-,** like *un-* in English, to indicate the opposite. (**UN-** *may* mean intensification!)

> **der Berg,** mountain; **das GEBIRGE,** mountains, mountain mass, massif
>
> **SCHWATZEN,** to chat; **das GESCHWÄTZ,** chatter
>
> **die Schwester,** sister; **die GESCHWISTER,** brothers and sisters
>
> **der BUSCH,** bush, shrub; **das GEBÜSCH,** bushes, coppice
>
> **der SCHREI,** cry, scream; **das GESCHREI,** cries, tumult
>
> **SAGEN,** to say; **die URSAGE,** primitive tradition
>
> **SCHREIBEN,** to write; **die URSCHRIFT,** original writing (of a document)
>
> **SPRECHEN,** to speak; **die URSPRACHE,** original language, text
>
> **der WALD,** wood, forest; **der URWALD,** primeval forest
>
> **der DANK,** thanks; **der UNDANK,** ingratitude
>
> **die MENGE,** crowd; **die UNMENGE,** mass, great number, dense crowd

And similarly **MIß-** more or less corresponds to English *mis-*:

> **das VERSTÄNDNIS,** understanding; **das MIßVERSTÄNDNIS,** misunderstanding
>
> **die GUNST,** favor; **die MIßGUNST,** grudge, envy
>
> **der BRAUCH,** use, usage; **der MIßBRAUCH,** misuse

PRACTICE: ÜBUNG

Die Arbeiter und Arbeiterinnen verließen nach der Arbeit die Fabrik. In diesem Geschäft waren viele Käufer und Käuferinnen. Maler und Musiker sind Künstler. Der Tischler macht Stühle und Tische. Was hat der Schmeichler mit seiner Schmeichelei erreicht? Mit einem Hebel kann man schwere Säcke heben.

Ich habe eine starke Erkältung bei der großen Kälte bekommen. Gute Kleidung ist teuer. Die Regierung des Fürstentums Monaco. Die ganze Menschheit leidet unter Kriegen.

Mit Klugheit erzielt man mehr als mit Bosheit und Dummheit.
Die Freundschaft der drei Jünglinge ist schön.   Der englische
Botschafter und die amerikanische Botschafterin in Rom.
Er beging einen schweren Irrtum.   Das hohe Gebirge liegt
im Norden des Königtums.   Er wurde durch das Geschrei der
Schüler und Schülerinnen im Hofe gestört.   Im Urwald Afrikas
gibt es eine Unmenge wilder Tiere. Von diesem Dokument ist
die Urschrift im Museum aufbewahrt.   Rechnet er mit dem
Undank der Welt?   Hier liegt ein kleines Mißverständnis vor.
Der Mißbrauch wird bestraft.

Tierdrama im Zirkuswagen

Tigerin „ Judith " schwebte in Lebensgefahr

Eigener Bericht

P. Lüneburg, 21. Juli

Unbemerkt vom Publikum spielte sich in einem Raubtierwagen des Zirkus Krone in Lüneburg ein Tierdrama ab.[1] Die sechsjährige Tigerin „ Judith ", die Mutterfreuden entgegensah,[2] schwebte [3] in Lebensgefahr.

Bisher war bei „ Judith " immer alles glatt [4] gegangen. Diesmal jedoch stimmte etwas nicht. Das Tier schrie pausenlos. Ein Auto wurde nach Hannover geschickt, um von der Klinik der Tierärztlichen Hochschule Dr. Brasse und zwei Assistenten zu holen. Die Veterinäre machten ernste Gesichter.[5] „ Judith " lag apathisch in einer Ecke ihres Wagens.

Der Tigerwagen wurde mit dicken Strohpolstern ausgelegt. „ Judith " bekam einen leichten Ätherrausch.[6] Dann wurde die Geburt eingeleitet.[7] Zwei Tigerbabys waren im Mutterleib gestorben, aber das dritte stieß [8] kurz vor Mitternacht den ersten Tigerschrei in die Welt.

„ Es war eine schwierige Geburt für alle. Wir haben nicht gedacht, daß wir das wertvolle Tier retten könnten ", sagte Dr. Brasse. Das Tigerbaby soll „ Luna " oder „ Luno " nach der Schutzgöttin [9] Lüneburgs heißen.

NOTES

[1] **abspielen,** to take place
[2] **Mutterfreuden entgegensehen,** to look forward to motherhood
[3] **in Lebensgefahr schwebte,** her life was in danger
[4] **glatt,** smoothly
[5] **Gesichter** (plur.), faces
[6] **der Ätherrausch,** narcosis
[7] **einleiten,** to initiate, prepare
[8] **stieß,** past tense of: **stoßen,** to thrust
[9] **die Schutzgöttin,** tutelary goddess; patron

SERGEANT GRISCHA—3

Der Waggon

Grischa hatte seine Flucht nicht ausgeklügelt; das Leben bestätigt umständliche Berechnungen selten, sprunghaft und willkürlich geht es mit jeder Stunde um, seinen Gesetzen gemäß, und wer weise ist, richtet sich nach Willkür. Er hatte gelegentlich, hie und da, bei den Bahnmannschaften und den Zugbegleitern behutsam vorgefühlt, wohin solch ein Wagen das viele Holz bringe, das sie herrichteten; wie der Bahnhof heiße, auf dem die Wagen, zu neuen Zügen verteilt, auseinanderglitten gleich den Geschicken von Menschen, die sich nach einer Zeit der Gemeinsamkeit trennen müssen; nach welcher Himmelsrichtung etwa diese Ladungen rutschen. Zur Front fuhren alle, und die Front zog sich in einer mannigfaltigen, gebeulten Linie zwischen Dünaburg und den Österreichern östlich hin, den Leib des heiligen Rußland mit einem scheußlichen Riß nordsüdwärts durchschneidend. Zwar galt ihm gleich, an welcher Stelle er den Übergang zwischen den Gräben bewerkstelligte; doch aber walteten auch hier Unterschiede. Er konnte—er mußte sogar auf dem kürzesten Wege ans Ziel kommen suchen, der Entdeckung und der Nahrung wegen. . . . Er hatte Decken und Zeltbahn bereits marschfertig aufgeschnallt aber wußte weder, wo er sich befand, noch eine Himmelsrichtung. Er belud sich mit seinem Rucksack, dann sprang er im vollen Bewußtsein großer Gefahr in drei, vier Sätzen über die Straße. . . .

Vorn an der Bude der drei Eisenbahnsoldaten, die diese Weiche verwalteten, standen die Bremser und der Lokomotivführer des Zuges und tranken heißen „ Kaffee ".

TRANSLATION :

The Freight Car

Grischa had not thought out his escape with care; life seldom approves (our) detailed reckonings, by fits and starts, and in a self-willed manner it treats every hour, according to its (own) laws, and whoever is wise conforms with arbitrariness. He had carefully felt (sounded) from time to time beforehand the railwaymen and train staffs.

whither a freight car was carrying so much timber, that they prepared; what was the name of the station at which the freight cars, detached to new trains, were slipping away like destined men who after a time of companionship must part; enquiring in which direction these loads were going (sliding). They all were travelling to the front, and the front dragged in a bent, bulging line between Dünaburg and the Austrians to the east, cutting through the body of Holy Russia in a horrible gash. It was all the same to him at which point he achieved the crossing between the trenches; though even in this there were differences. He could—indeed he must try to get by the shortest way to his goal, because of (possible) discovery and (shortage of) food. . . . He had already bundled blankets and tarpaulin ready for the march, but neither knew where he was nor in what direction to turn, he loaded himself with his rucksack, and then he sprang fully knowing (of the) great danger and in three or four strides was over the road.

In front of the hut of the three railway soldiers who looked after this siding, stood the brakesmen and the engine-driver of the train, drinking hot " coffee ".

[Contd. on p. 258.

§ 4. *Nouns*—contd.: *Endings* **-SAL**, **-NIS**—*Abstract Nouns from Verbs: three kinds—Diminutives* **-CHEN** *and* **-LEIN**—*Adjectives: from Noun plus Adjective—Prefixes—Suffixes—Practice—Reading:* **Sergeant Grischa**

NOUNS—*contd.*: 11. Ending **-SAL,** nearly all neuters, indicating *intellectual or moral abstract ideas* :

> **SCHICKEN,** to send (*old meaning*: to dispose); **das SCHICKSAL,** destiny
>
> **SCHEUEN,** to shun, shrink from; **die Scheu,** awe, fright; **das SCHEUSAL,** monster
>
> **MÜHEN,** to trouble; **die Mühe,** pains; **das** or **die MÜHSAL,** hardship

12. Ending **-NIS** plural **-NISSE,** feminines and neuters, also indicating *intellectual or moral abstract ideas* :

> **ERLAUBEN,** to permit; **die ERLAUBNIS,** permission
>
> **BEDÜRFEN,** to need, want; **das BEDÜRFNIS,** need, want
>
> **BEKENNEN,** to admit, confess; **das BEKENNTNIS,** confession (religious)

13. A group of abstract Nouns derived from Verbs and indicating *the action implied in the Verb*. These are of three kinds, one masculine, two feminine:

(*a*) Usually ending in a consonant, mostly masculine monosyllables, and having the plural in **-e**, root vowel modified. Examples:

der Schlag, blow, stroke, *from* **SCHLAGEN,** to strike
der SCHUß, shot, *from* **SCHIEßEN,** to shoot, fire
der LAUF, race, running, *from* **LAUFEN,** to run

Plurals: **die Schläge, die Schüsse, die Läufe.**

(*b*) Feminines ending **-E**, plural **-N**:

die PFLEGE, care, *from* **PFLEGEN,** to take care of
die Sprache, language, *from* **SPRECHEN,** to speak
die GABE, gift, *from* **GEBEN,** to give

(*c*) Feminines ending **-t**, plural **-en**:

die FAHRT, journey, *from* **FAHREN,** to travel
die FLUCHT, flight, *from* **FLIEHEN,** to flee (*not to be confused with* **fliegen,** to fly)
die LAST, burden, load, *from* **LADEN,** to load

The chief difficulty in these is the gender, for which the only safe rule is to learn the Article with the Noun. There is another difficulty: the Nouns so made may take on a meaning which is either remote from the Verb or but slightly related to it. Example: **der ZUG,** which means *the drawing*; *pulling*, or *draught* but commonly means *the train* (railway). In Compound Nouns made with **ZUG** the meaning is expanded to include many ideas which are not easy to recognize as connected with the original word:

der UMZUG, procession   **der GESICHTSZUG,** feature (of the face)

14. Endings **-CHEN** and **-LEIN** indicating *diminutives*, always neuter.

das HAUS, house; **das HÄUSLEIN,** *or* **das HÄUSCHEN,** little house, maisonette
die Frau, woman, lady; **das FRÄULEIN,** girl

Diminutives of Christian names often have a form ending in
-el instead of -chen :

Hänsel = Hänschen   **Gretel = Gretchen**

Word-building with :

II. ADJECTIVES: 1. They can be made by combining a Noun
with an Adjective to make a new Adjective with a special meaning:

> **die KIRSCHE,** cherry; **ROT,** red: **KIRSCHROT,**
> cherry-red
> **das KIND,** child; **die KINDER,** children; **REICH,** rich:
> **KINDERREICH,** rich in children
> **die SEE,** sea; **KRANK,** sick: **SEEKRANK,** seasick

Or by Adjective + Adjective:

> **BLAU,** blue; **GRAU,** grey: **BLAUGRAU,** bluish grey
> **SCHLECHT,** bad; **GELAUNT,** tempered: **SCHLECHT-**
> **GELAUNT,** ill-tempered
> **GROß,** big, great; **der MUT,** spirit, courage: **GROß-**
> **MÜTIG,** courageous, magnanimous

And similarly:

GROßJÄHRIG, of age   **GROßSPRECHERISCH,**
GROßSPURIG, very arrogant   boastful
  (**spurig,** haughty)   **GROßSTÄDTISCH,** of a great
                                      city

2. By *prefixing* one of the following: **all-, erz-, hoch-, über-,**
wohl-, ur-.

> **ALL-,** all, in every sense: **ALLMÄCHTIG,** almighty
> **ERZ-,** arch, to a high degree: **ERZDUMM,** very stupid
> **HOCH,** high, intensive, super: **HOCHFEIN,** superfine;
> **HOCHMÜTIG,** overbearing; **HOCHROT,** intense red
> **ÜBER-,** over, above: **ÜBERMÜTIG,** excessively merry.
> **der EIFER,** zeal; **EIFRIG,** zealous; **ÜBEREIFRIG,**
> over-zealous. **ÜBERGROß,** over-big. **ÜBERLAUT,**
> over-loud, top of one's voice

WOHL-, well, very much: **WOHLWEISE,** very wise; **WOHLBEKANNT,** well known

UR-, extremely: **URALT,** primeval; **URKRÄFTIG,** extremely strong; **URPLÖTZLICH,** very sudden; **URSÄCHLICH,** being the cause of

Note: These prefixes represent equivalents to the comparatives or superlatives of the simple words, and are used usually for greater intensity or for an intensity in an accrued quality. See page 251, Nouns.

3. By certain endings or suffixes, as follows:

-VOLL	**-LOS**	**-REICH**	**-ERN**	**-EN**	**-IG**
-LICH	**-ISCH**	**-SAM**	**-HAFT**	**-BAR**	

and the prefixes **UN-** and **MIß-,** equivalents of *un-* and *mis-*.

As a great number of Adverbs have the same forms as their Adjectives (see page 203), it will be realized that a knowledge of the indications of these endings to Nouns and Verbs (or to roots thereof) provides a key to an extensive vocabulary. It is therefore advisable to learn the indications and examples given below:

(a) **-VOLL,** full of; **die Gefahr,** danger: **GEFAHRVOLL,** dangerous

-LOS, less, without: **GEFAHRLOS,** without danger

-REICH, rich in; **der Fisch,** fish: **FISCHREICH,** rich in fish

-ERN, made of; **das Holz,** wood: **HÖLZERN,** wooden

-EN, made of; **das Gold,** gold: **GOLDEN,** gold, golden

Practice: **ÜBUNG**

Dieses Scheusal ist recht harmlos. Haben Sie die Erlaubnis bekommen? Die Menschen haben viele Bedürfnisse. Er spricht die deutsche Sprache fehlerlos. Der Zug kam pünktlich an. Der feierliche Umzug geht durch die Straßen der Stadt. Das Hündlein und das Kätzchen spielen miteinander. Das Kindlein hält einen Ball in den Händchen.

Sie sehen gelblichgrün im Gesicht aus. Sind Sie seekrank? Der Lehrer ist heute schlechtgelaunt. Jener wohlbekannte Mann ist sehr großmütig. Die kleinstädtischen Leute sind übereifrig bei der Arbeit. Die ursächliche Absicht des Täters war nicht schlecht. Liebevoll begrüßte er seine Frau. Ist der Fluß fischreich? Die Fahrt ist nicht gefahrlos. Sie hatte einen goldnen Ring am Finger. Ein silberner Teller stand auf dem Tisch. Der „ Eiserne Vorhang ". Mühsam schleppte Jack sich weiter. Die Kirschen sind noch unreif. Mißmutig legte er das Buch weg. Ich tue es nicht ungern. Der Plan wird mißlingen.

Sergeant Grischa—4

Babka

Ungläubig auf seine beiden Arme gestützt, sah Grischa auf Babkas Gesicht hinab, das zwischen seinen Fäusten lag und in einem bitteren Blick der Augen leuchtete. „ Mußt du jedem auf die Nase binden, wer du bist? Kommen jetzt nicht schockweise Überläufer durch die Stellungen, russische Soldaten, die genug haben, heim wollen wie du zu Frau und Kind? Nur daß ihre Dörfer hier liegen auf der deutschen Seite, nicht drüben im großen Rußland, dem Mütterchen. In der Baracke verwahre ich Hose und Rock von Ilja Pawlowitsch Bjuschew, der hier mit mir war und starb ; wir kriegten ihn nicht mehr auf die Beine. Seine Marke, wie ihr sie um den Hals tragt, liegt in der Schublade dort im Tisch. Kappen sie dich und hast du Pech, sagst du einfach, Ilja Pawlowitsch Bjuschew seist du aus Antokol, vom 67. Schützenregiment, 5. Kompanie, und willst nach Hause zu deinem Mütterchen ; durch die Stellung kämst du, ein Überläufer. Und alles ist in Ordnung. Schlimmstenfalls stecken sie dich in ein Lager wieder und forschen nach, und bis dahin gebe ich der alten Frau Bescheid, Natascha Pawlowa Bjuschew in ihrem Häuschen. Sie sagt, was wir wollen. Nun, Soldat, Idiot? "

Über Grischas rundes Gesicht zog allmählich aus den Schatten der Qual ein immer breiteres Lachen ; stolzes Bewundern verengerte seine schrägen Augen und öffnete sie wieder.

Translation :

Babka

Incredulous, propped on both his arms, Grischa looked down on Babka's face, which lay between his fists, and in her eyes shone a bitter gleam. " Must you tell everybody to their face (nose) who you are? Don't all kinds of deserters come now through the (army) positions, Russian soldiers who have (had) enough (and) want to go home like you to wife and child? Only that their villages lie here on the German side, not over there in great Russia, the little Mother. In the shed I keep (the) trousers and coat of Ilya Pavlovitch Byuschev, who was here with me and died; we got him no more on his legs.* His (identity) disc, which like you (all) he wore round his neck, lies there in the drawer in the table. If they nab you and you have bad luck, say simply you are Ilya Pavlovitch Byuschev (you are) from Antokol, of the 67th Rifle Regiment, 5th Company, and you want to go home to your little mother; through the position you came, a deserter. And all's in order. At the worst they stick you in a camp again and enquire about you, and until then I give the old lady information, Natasha Pavlova Byuschev in her little house. She says whatever we wish. Now, soldier, silly fool? "

Over Grischa's round face came an ever-broadening smile out of the shadows of torment; proud admiration closed his slanting eyes and opened them again.

[Contd. on p. 263.

§ 5. *Adjectives*—contd.: *Endings* **-IG, -LICH, -ISCH, -SAM, -HAFT, -BAR**—*Adverbs*—*Practice*—*Newspaper Extracts*— *Reading:* **Sergeant Grischa**

(b) **-IG** having the quality of ; the activity of

die Kraft, strength ; **KRÄFTIG,** strong
der Zorn, anger ; **ZORNIG,** angry, angry with
gefallen, to please ; **GEFÄLLIG,** pleasing
abhängen, to depend ; **ABHÄNGIG,** dependent (on)

(c) **-LICH,** activity of, aptitude for ; -ish

hindern, hinder, prevent ; **HINDERLICH,** hindering, preventing, cumbersome
nachdenken, ponder, reflect ; **NACHDENKLICH,** pensive

* We gave up trying to cure him.

begreifen, grasp, comprehend ; **BEGREIFLICH,** comprehensible

kaufen, to buy ; **KÄUFLICH,** for sale, venal

das Kind, child ; **KINDLICH,** childish

krank, ill, sick ; **KRÄNKLICH,** sickish, sickly

(*d*) **-ISCH (-erISCH),** tendency or aptitude for ; *-some, -ish, -al, -ful*

der ZANK, quarrel ; **ZÄNKISCH,** quarrelsome

spotten, to mock ; **der Spott,** mockery ; **SPÖTTISCH,** ironical, mocking

das SPIEL, game, play ; **SPIELERISCH,** playful

-isch is the suffix used to describe *people of*, the *inhabitants of*, and as an adjectival ending for proper names :

der Grieche, the Greek ; **GRIECHISCH,** Greek (*Adj.*)

der Franzose, Frenchman ; **FRANZÖSISCH,** French (*Adj.*), etc., etc., see page 83.

(*e*) **-SAM,** with the quality of ; our endings *-al, -ous, -some*

sparen, to save ; **SPARSAM,** economical, sparing

die Furcht, fear ; **FURCHTSAM,** timorous

die Mühe, pains, trouble ; **MÜHSAM,** troublesome

(*f*) **-HAFT,** with the quality of ; *-ing, -ful*

nähren, to nourish ; **NAHRHAFT,** nourishing

dauern, to last, endure ; **DAUERHAFT,** lasting, durable

die Scham, shame ; **SCHAMHAFT,** shameful

(*g*) **-BAR,** with the possibility of, quality of ; *-ful, -able*

trinken, to drink ; **TRINKBAR,** drinkable

die Frucht, fruit ; **FRUCHTBAR,** fruitful

der Dienst, service ; **DIENSTBAR,** serviceable

die Ehre, honour ; **EHRBAR,** honorable

III. ADVERBS: Adverbs also can be formed from words other than Adjectives by similar methods to those which apply to other words:

(*a*) by adding the suffix **-S** to certain words.

(*b*) to make Adverbs of manner by adding the endings—

> **-WEISE,** *English*—wise
> **-MAßEN,** extent, measure
> **-WÄRTS,** -wards, direction of
> **-LINGS,** tendency, manner

Examples:

(*a*) **ALLERDINGS,** indeed
JENSEITS, other side of
MEISTENS, mostly
NACHTS, by night
RECHTS, to the right
LINKS, to the left
RINGS, round about, around
TEILS, in part, partly

(*b*) **AUSNAHMSWEISE,** exceptionally
GLÜCKLICHERWEISE, happily, in a happy manner
KREUZWEISE, crosswise
PAARWEISE, by couples
EINIGERMAßEN, to some extent
FOLGENDERMAßEN, to the following extent
HEIMWÄRTS, homeward(s)
SEEWÄRTS, seaward
RÜCKLINGS, backwards
RITTLINGS, astride

PRACTICE: **ÜBUNG**

Er lernt diese Übung spielerisch. Ich habe dauerhafte Schuhe gekauft. Er wurde zornig, als er das sah. Die kräftigen Pferde ziehen den Wagen. Die Kolonien sind von England abhängig. Der Mann wurde bei der Nachricht sehr nachdenklich. Im

Geschäft gibt es käufliche Waren. Es ist ein kränkliches Kind. Er machte spöttische Bemerkungen. Der sparsame Kaufmann hat viel Geld. Die eßbaren Pilze sind nahrhaft. Ist die griechische Geschichte tragisch? Sie trinken französischen Wein. Sprechen Sie spanisch? Die englisch–amerikanische Freundschaft ist dauerhaft. Der ehrbare Bürger lebt friedlich.

Er hat das allerdings behauptet. Meistens treffen Sie ihn zu Hause. Wir schlafen nachts. Teils stehen die Bäume diesseits und teils jenseits des Grabens. Rings um den Hof ist eine hohe Mauer. In Deutschland fährt man rechts und in England links. Ausnahmsweise ist er einigermaßen zufrieden. Sie kamen glücklicherweise bald zurück. Der Satz lautet folgendermaßen: Fährt dieses Schiff heimwärts?

Newspaper Extracts

RUNDBLICK

Vater und Tochter stürzten vom Fahrrad. Das war Ecke Moorburger und Stader Straße in Harburg. Die dreijährige Karin K. geriet [1] dabei mit der linken Hand in die Speichen.[2] Das erste Glied eines Fingers wurde ihr abgerissen.[3] Vater Hans K. blieb unverletzt.

Drei Möwen [4] machen noch keinen Herbst. Damit tröstet sich [5] Frau Braese aus der Isestraße. Jedes Jahr zählt sie genau 42 Möwen als Stammgäste auf den umliegenden [6] Dächern. Die Gäste kommen sonst im Herbst. Diesmal sind aber schon drei eingetrudelt.[7] Sie wollen sich wohl die besten Plätze sichern.

Das gibt's nur einmal: Der Inhaber [8] eines Zeitungskiosks an der Lübecker Straße stellt auf seine Zeitungsstapel [9] ein Kästchen mit neuen Kämmen. Ein Zettel ermuntert [10] die Kunden: ,, Bei Bedarf [11] bedienen Sie sich bitte kostenlos ''.

In der Manege [12] eines kleinen Wanderzirkus in St. Pauli kam der zehnjährige Lothar P. mit der elektrischen Leitung in Berührung. Er wurde mit inneren Verletzungen ins Krankenhaus gebracht.

NOTES

[1] **sie geriet,** she happened to get
[2] **die Speichen,** spokes
[3] **abgerissen,** torn off
[4] **die Möwe,** sea-gull
[5] **sich trösten,** to console oneself
[6] **umliegend,** neighboring
[7] **eintrudeln,** to trundle, to roll in
[8] **der Inhaber,** proprietor
[9] **der Zeitungsstapel,** pack of newspapers
[10] **ermuntern,** to encourage
[11] **bei Bedarf,** if required
[12] **die Manege,** menagerie

Sergeant Grischa—5

Das Urteil

„ Sonst noch was, Tagesprogramm ? " fragte Exzellenz von Lychow. „ Russen schießen," sagte er plötzlich wieder, indem er sich mit einer leise schütternden Hand ein Streichholz entzündete und eine große braune Zigarre zu rauchen begann. „ Hast du eine Ahnung, Paul, wieviel Tote die da drüben im ganzen bis jetzt haben ? "

Der Oberleutnant wußte es nicht.

„ Ich auch nicht," sagte von Lychow. „ Aber wenn es elfhunderttausend Mann sind, dann sind es wenig. Großer Gott," setzte er halb murmelnd hinzu. „ Mit elfhunderttausend Mann hätten wir Anno Siebzig ganz Frankreich in die Tasche gesteckt. Und das allein jetzt drüben ex . . ." Er nickte vor sich hin. Dann wieder gegenwärtig: ob es sonst noch etwas gäbe ?

Paul Winfried entnahm der Mappe ein Urteil, das ihm vom Kriegsgericht der Division gestern abend zur Unterschrift zugestellt worden war, und legte es schweigend vor den Chef. Der General der Division, einer selbständigen Kampfgruppe, steht als oberster Gerichtsherr in Stellvertretung des Kaisers, der in diesem Zusammenhang Gottes und Schicksals Anteil verwaltet. Von Lychow vertiefte sich in das Schriftstück, Todesurteil gegen einen Spion, einen gewissen Ilja Pawlowitsch Bjuschew schuldig befunden, sich spionierend unbestimmte Zeit hinter der deutschen Front umhergetrieben zu haben. Er runzelte seine weißen schmalen Augenbrauen, und statt den Halter zu ergreifen, den Oberleutnant Winfried ihm hinhielt, schob er das Blatt zurück und sagte: „ Nein, danke schön, noch mehr tote Leute heute früh, das paßt mir nicht. Wer hat die Verhandlung geleitet ? "

Mit einem Blick auf die Unterschriften des Aktenstückes sagte Leutnant Winfried: „ Kriegsgerichtsrat Posnanski."

„ Posnanski," wiederholte der General, „ ein zuverlässiger Mann . . . Ich will ihn zum Vortrag haben . . . Und was hast du heute noch ? "

Translation :

The Sentence

" *Anything else (on the) daily program?* " *asked (His) Excellency von Lychow.** " *Russians to shoot," said he suddenly and lit a match with a slightly shaking hand and began to smoke a big brown cigar. " Have you an idea, Paul, how many dead there are in all up to now over there?* "

The (senior) lieutenant did not know (it).

" *I also (do) not (know)," said von Lychow. " But if it's eleven hundred thousand men, then it's an understatement. Good God," he added, half muttering. " With eleven hundred thousand men in the year '70 (1870) we'd have put the whole of France in our pocket. And now that only over there . . ." He nodded to himself. Then back again (asked) if there was anything else.*

Paul Winfried took from the portfolio a judgment from the Divisional Court-Martial that had been sent to him yesterday evening for signature, and laid it silently before the Chief. The General of the Division, an independent fighting group, stands as the highest legal authority in representation of the Kaiser (Emperor), who in this connection administers God's and destiny's part. Von Lychow buried himself in the document, a sentence of death on a spy, a certain Ilya Pavlovitch Byuschev found guilty of spying for an indefinite time behind the German front (line). He wrinkled his white thin eyebrows, and instead of seizing the fountain-pen which Lieutenant Winfried was offering him, pushed the sheet (of paper) back and said: " No, thanks very much, no more dead people so early to-day, that doesn't suit me. Who conducted the proceeding(s)? "

With a glance at the signature on the legal document, Lieutenant Winfried said: " War Advocate Posnanski."

" *Posnanski," repeated the General. " A reliable man . . . I'll have a discussion with him. . . . And what else (besides) have you to-day?* "

* Von Lychow, *the General in command.*

[*Contd.* on page 269.

LESSON IX

§ 1. *Word-building: Verbs—Compound and Derivative—Practice
—Newspaper Extract—Reading:* **Sergeant Grischa**

VERBS can be made in various ways and, in many instances, the
new Verbs made from other words are, strictly, not compound
words but derivatives. Nevertheless, as we are dealing with the
German system of Word-building, it is helpful for the learner to
consider the various ways in one comprehensive treatment.

IV. VERBS: New Verbs are made from other words:

(*a*) Sometimes by putting words together and adding the
verbal ending **-EN** or **-N. der TRAB,** trot. Thus:
traben, *to trot, to step* (of a horse); **HOCHTRABEN,** *to
step high* (*be a high stepper*), from which there is the Adjective
hochtrabend, with the meaning *high-stepping* (as of a
horse) and also *pompous, bombastic, high falutin(g).*

(*b*) With the Prefixes (Inseparable and Separable) listed
in Lesson VI, §§ 1 and 2, which should constantly be reviewed, as they are a very important part of the system of
Word-building.

(*c*) See Nouns II, 13 (*a*) on page 255. The verbal ending
-EN or **-N** is added to the root word as in the example
quoted in (*a*), **der TRAB, trabEN.**

(*d*) By using Adjectives and adding the verbal ending **-EN**
or **-N** to the root word.

(*e*) By using the root of an original Verb and then, by
some slight change in the root vowel (modification of **a, o,
u, au,** or a change in **i** or **e**), and sometimes a change of
consonant, making the new Verb. For example: **hangen,**
to hang, to be hanging (a Strong Verb, intransitive, Imperfect
hing, Past Participle, **gehangen**) and **hängen,** *to hang
something* (a Weak Verb with **hängte, gehängt**).

(*f*) By using the suffix **-EL + -N** (verbal ending), this suffix immediately following the root. This change imparts a kind of diminutive effect as, for example: **LACHEN,** *to laugh* : **LÄCHELN,** *to smile.*

It would be possible to give a large number of such built-up words to exemplify these principles, but this is hardly necessary—such Verbs are continually being found in almost every kind of reading matter. What is given below is merely for the purpose of helping to drive these useful principles home:

(*a*) **der Rat,** advice ; **der Schlag,** blow, stroke ; **SCHLAGEN,** to strike: **RATSCHLAGEN,** to take council with

das Rad, wheel ; **brechen,** to break : **radebrechen,** to break on the wheel

RADEBRECHEN is often used in the sense of *to murder a language.* Thus:

Mein Bruder radebricht das Deutsch, My brother speaks awful German (i.e. he " breaks it on the wheel " !)

(*b*) See Lesson VI, §§ 1 and 2, for examples. Here it may be noted that the Prefixes **BE-, ENT-, ER-, VER-** and **ZER-** are in common use in senses akin to those implied in some common English Prefixes:

decken, to cover ; **bedecken,** to deck out, *be*deck

das Haupt, head ; **enthaupten,** to *be*head

denken, to think ; **erdenken,** to *e*volve (*by thought*), produce, *con*struct, etc.

bieten, to bid ; **verbieten,** to *for*bid

das Glied, member, limb ; **zergliedern,** to *dis*member

(*c*) See Nouns II, 13 (*a*), (*b*), (*c*), page 255. This is a large category, and a very encouraging one for the learner. It may be subdivided into two main categories: (1) Verbs made directly from the simple Noun ; (2) Verbs that derive from the Noun but have **-EN** or **-N** added to its adjectival form when this ends in **-IG.** Thus:

(1) **das Feuer,** fire; **FEUERN,** to set on fire
   die Arbeit, work; **ARBEITEN,** to work
   der Schneider, tailor; **SCHNEIDERN,** to do tailoring
   (*Note:* **SCHNEIDEN,** to cut)
   der Hammer, hammer; **HÄMMERN,** to hammer

[*Contd. on p.* 270.

PRACTICE: **ÜBUNG**

Sentences with Compounds

Hat er nicht hochtrabende Ideen? Der Angeklagte wurde freigesprochen. Die Männer beratschlugen lange.

Ich begleitete die Frau. Er begab sich nach Hause. Wir beginnen unsere Arbeit. Die Ärzte behandeln die Kranken. Er wurde des Geldes beraubt.

Der Südpol wurde vor vielen Jahren entdeckt. Ich entfernte mich von der Stadt. Entschuldigen Sie bitte! Die Gefangenen sind entkommen. Es entspricht der Wahrheit.

Er erdachte eine Lüge. Haben Sie das Neuste erfahren? Dieses ergibt sich von selbst. Hat er den Brief erhalten? Der Vater ermahnt seinen Sohn. Wir erreichten das Ziel. Sie haben den Berg erstiegen.

Eintritt streng verboten! Die Nachricht verbreitet sich im Dorf. Haben Sie schöne Ferien verbracht? Er verdient viel Geld. Die Tage und Wochen vergehen schnell. Wir verlassen morgen das Haus. Er verschloß das Geld im Schrank. Sie verschweigt ihm nichts.

Ich zerriß den Brief. Das alte Schloß ist zerfallen. Das Mädchen zerbrach den Teller. Er hat eine Vase zerschlagen. Der Knochen ist zersplittert. Die halbe Stadt wurde im Krieg zerstört. Er zergliederte den Satz.

Newspaper Extract

Hamburger Fremdenblatt

Die Sportseite[1]

Almut und der Speer

Almut Brömmel, die kürzlich als erste Deutsche im Speerwurf [2] 50 m erreichte (50,73 m), ist ein Allerweltsmädel.[3] Im Kriege wurde sie mit den Eltern von Makranstädt bei Leipzig nach Müncheberg in Oberfranken verschlagen. Studienrat [4] Dr. Brömmel war selbst ein guter Könner mit dem Speer und wirft heute noch mit seiner Tochter um die Wette. Die Mutter, unter ihrem Mädchennamen Herzog ehemals Deutsche Meisterin im Brustschwimmen, hätte natürlich lieber gesehen, wenn Almut auf ihren Pfaden wandelte. So war es kein Wunder, daß die heute 21-jährige ihre ersten Jugendmeistertitel im Brustschwimmen und Kunstspringen [5] errang,[6] ehe sie zur Leichtathletik überwechselte.

Mit 17 Jahren baute die hochbegabte [7] Almut ihr Abitur. An der Universität München studiert das 1,76 m große Mädel nun Englisch, Deutsch und Geschichte. Schöngeistige [8] Bücher, fremde Länder und die Archäologie haben es ihr ebenso angetan wie der Sport. ,, Schade, daß der Tag nur 14 Stunden hat ", sagt Almut, ,, wann soll man da nur studieren, musizieren, nähen,[9] lesen und trainieren. Zehn Stunden brauche ich bestimmt für Schlaf."

Almut spielt Klavier, Geige [10] und Flöte, am liebsten Bach und seine Brandenburgischen Konzerte. Auch mit Malerei und Tierplastiken hat sie sich schon versucht. Beim Jugendwettbewerb [11] vor den Olympischen Spielen in Helsinki holte sich Almut einen Preis. Dafür durfte sie als begeisterte Zuschauerin [12] dieses große Fest miterleben. Nun aber lockt Melbourne, wo Almut diesmal als Olympiakämpferin mitmachen wird.

NOTES

[1] Sports page
[2] **der Speerwurf,** spear throwing
[3] **das Allerweltsmädel,** girl capable of everything
[4] **der Studienrat,** title of high school teacher
[5] **das Kunstspringen,** gymnastic jumping
[6] **sie errang,** she gained
[7] **hochbegabt,** highly gifted
[8] **schöngeistig,** aesthetic, literary
[9] **nähen,** to sew
[10] **die Geige,** violin
[11] **Jugendwettbewerb,** junior sports competition
[12] **die Zuschauerin,** spectator (female)

SERGEANT GRISCHA—6

Der Kriegsgerichtsrat liest . . .

Der Kriegsgerichtsrat Dr. Posnanski sieht weiß aus wie der Bogen dienstlichen Papieres, der jetzt in seiner Hand hin und her schwankt. Dann gibt er dem Oberleutnant einen leisen Wink. Winfried versteht: „ Sie sind der Bjuschew? "

Grischa, aufgeregt, mit einem Atem, den er sich erst der Brust entpressen muß: „ Mein Gott," sagt er russisch und meldet russisch: „ Ilja Pawlowitsch Bjuschew, Sergeant, siebenundsechzigstes Schützen-Regiment, fünfte Kompanie, zur Stelle." . . .

Dann räuspert sich der Kriegsgerichtsrat und schickt sich an, zu verlesen, was Absatz für Absatz der Dolmetsch ins Russische übertragen soll. Vorher aber kommandiert Oberleutnant Winfried wie vor einer Meldung seinem höchsten Herrn gegenüber: „ Kompanie, stillgestanden! " . . .

Und mit seiner Zivilstimme, der er vergeblich Gleichmut oder Festigkeit zu geben sich bemüht, kurz, von Atemnot behackt, liest der Kriegsgerichtsrat:

„ Im Namen seiner Majestät des Kaisers: Auf Grund der Verordnung E.V. Nr. 14/211 wird der Überläufer Ilja Pawlowitsch Bjuschew, nach eignem Geständnis der Spionage überführt, am dritten Mai 1917 zum Tote verurteilt. Gegen dieses Urteil, das mit der Verkündung rechtskräftig wird, steht dem Verurteilten Berufung nicht zu. Die Vollziehung regelt ein Befehl der Ortskommandantur, der der Verurteilte hiermit übergeben wird. Mervinsk, am vierten Mai 1917.

Von Lychow, General der Infanterie."

TRANSLATION:

The Judge-Advocate reads . . .

The (War) Judge Advocate Dr. Posnanski looked as white as the sheet of service papers in his portfolio, which now moved to and fro in his hand. Then he gave the Lieutenant a slight nod. Winfried understood: " You are Byuschev? "

Grischa, excited, with a breath which he had first to press out from his chest: " *My God,*" *he said in Russian and repeated in Russian:* " *Ilya Pavlovitch Byuschev, Sergeant, sixty-seventh Rifle Regiment, Fifth Company, present . . .*"

The Judge Advocate cleared his throat and set himself to read over what paragraph by paragraph the interpreter had to translate into Russian. But first Lieutenant Winfried gave order as if before an announcement (to be made before) his commander-in-chief: " *Company, Attention!* " *. . .*

And in his civilian voice, which he with equanimity or firmness vainly tried to control (steady), in short, breathless tones, the Judge Advocate reads:

" *In the name of His Majesty the Kaiser: In accordance with Order E.V.No. 14/211, deserter Ilya Pavlovitch Byuschev, after his own confession of espionage (was) convicted, (and) on the 3rd of May 1917 sentenced to death. Against this judgment (sentence), which with this announcement becomes effective, there is no appeal by the condemned. The fulfilment will be by order of the local commandant's office, to whom the condemned man will be handed over. Mervinsk, 4th May, 1917.*

Von Lychow, Infantry General."

[Contd. on p. 274.

§ 2. *Word-building: Verbs*—contd.—*Practice*—*Newspaper Items*—*Reading:* **Sergeant Grischa**

Contd. from page 267.

(2) **die Sünde,** sin ; **sündig,** sinful ; **SÜNDIGEN,** to sin
 die Kraft, strength ; **kräftig,** strong ; **KRÄFTIGEN,** to strengthen

(*d*) Excepting (*c*) (2) above, most Verbs made from Adjectives are made from the simple Adjectival root-form:

reif, ripe ; **REIFEN,** to ripen
offen, open ; **ÖFFNEN,** to open

Generally speaking, when a Verb is made from an Adjective the Verb is one of

BEING or *BECOMING* or *MAKING* (*INTO*)

Thus:

siech, sickly	**SIECHEN,** to be sickly	= *BEING*
krank, ill	**KRANKEN,** to be ill	„
faul, rotten (*also* lazy)	**FAULEN,** to putrify, rot	= *BECOMING*
trocken, dry	**TROCKNEN,** to dry	„
tot, dead	**TÖTEN,** to kill	= *MAKING*
besser, better	**BESSERN,** to improve	„
voll, full	**FÜLLEN,** to fill	„

(*e*) This is also a group in which the new Verbs are easily recognizable and not difficult to learn:

> **trinken,** to drink; **tränken,** to make drink, give to drink (*as in " watering " a horse*)
>
> **fallen,** to fall; **fällen,** to fell (*as of a tree*)
>
> **springen,** to spring; **sprengen,** to scatter, to explode (*as of a mine*)
>
> **saugen,** to suck; **säugen,** to suckle

(*f*) Further examples:

> **klingen,** to sound; **KLINGELN,** to ring, tinkle
>
> **husten,** to cough; **HÜSTELN,** to cough a little

It would somewhat strain the mental effort to include in this category a group of miscellaneous Verbs which might just as well come into some other. Perhaps it is best to consider them merely as representing a " type of Verb " which, by certain changes in root-vowel, and/or of a consonant or consonants, acquires a meaning *related to* that of the original, and usually indicates some kind of *intensification* in the action of the original Verb. Thus:

> **schneiden,** to cut; **schnitzen,** to carve
> **sich beugen,** to bow; **sich bücken,** to stoop
> **plagen,** to plague, torment; **placken,** to torture
> **raufen,** to pluck; **rupfen,** to fleece
> **ziehen,** to draw; **zücken,** to twitch, palpitate
> **schwingen,** to swing; **schwenken,** to flourish, shake
> **hängen,** to hang; **henken,** to hang (*on the gallows*)
> **rücken,** to push; **rutschen,** to glide
> **schlucken,** to gulp; **schluchzen,** to sob
> **quaken,** to quack; **quatschen,** to talk twaddle, bosh

Practice: ÜBUNG

Sie sündigten im Tempel. Ein kaltes Bad wird uns kräftigen. Die Äpfel reifen am Baum. Öffnen Sie das Fenster! Krankt er an Tuberkulose? Die Kartoffeln faulen im Keller. Die Soldaten töteten ihre Feinde im Krieg. Er wird sich schnell bessern. Das Glas war halb gefüllt. Der Bauer tränkte seine Pferde. Sie fällen Bäume im Walde. Die Katze säugt ihre Jungen. Wir klingelten an der Tür. Sie hüstelt etwas. Er bückte sich schnell. Die Frau rupfte die Gans. Vor Freude schwenkte er das Taschentuch. Beim Wiedersehen hat sie tief geschluchzt. Sie quatschten heute viel.

Newspaper Items

Ponton gegen Brücke

Deutsche Presse-Agentur-ap-up

Basel, 21. Juli

Ein furchtbares Ende hat der Ausflug [1] des schweizerischen ,, Pontoniervereins Rheinfelden '' auf dem Oberrhein genommen. Die 31 Klubmitglieder, ausnahmslos erfahrene Wassersportler, wollten zum Bodensee. In der Nähe von Trübbach stieß ihr Ponton gegen einen Brückenpfeiler [2] und brach in zwei Teile. Elf Ausflügler fanden wahrscheinlich den Tod, während zwanzig geborgen [3] werden konnten.

Nach dem Bericht eines Augenzeugen [4] waren auf dem Ponton genügend Schwimmwesten [5] und Rettungsringe [6] vorhanden. Das Unglück ereignete sich jedoch so schnell, daß niemand von den Rettungsgeräten [7] Gebrauch machen konnte. Ein Teil der Verunglückten [8] trieb auf eine Sandbank. Bisher konnte nur ein Toter geborgen werden.

Notes

[1] **der Ausflug,** excursion
[2] **der Brückenpfeiler,** bridge pillar
[3] **geborgen,** rescued
[4] **der Augenzeuge,** eye-witness
[5] **die Schwimmweste,** swim vest
[6] **der Rettungsring,** life-belt
[7] **die Rettungsgeräte,** implements for life-saving
[8] **der Verunglückte,** casualty

Minister auf dem Dach

Deutsche Presse-Agentur

Kassel, 21. Juli

Zur Eröffnung der modernsten Hochgarage der Bundesrepublik ist der hessische Minister für Arbeit, Wirtschaft und Verkehr, Gotthard Franke, mit einem Hubschrauber [9] auf dem Dach des fünfstöckigen [10] Gebäudes gelandet. Die Hochgarage kann 350 Fahrzeuge aufnehmen. Die ein- und ausfahrenden Kraftfahrzeuge gelangen auf einer ,, doppelgängigen Spindel " [11] bis in das höchste Stockwerk bei nur fünf bis sechs Prozent Steigung.[12]

NOTES

[9] **der Hubschrauber,** helicopter
[10] **ein fünfstöckiges Gebäude,** a five-story building

[11] **die doppelgängige Spindel,** double-way spindle
[12] **die Steigung,** elevation

Großfeuer in Berlin

Von unserer Berliner Redaktion

n. Berlin, 21. Juli

Die Explosion eines Transformators hat im Siemens-Kabelwerk Berlin ein Großfeuer ausgelöst.[13] Kilometerweit sichtbare Rauchpilze [14] standen über dem Brandherd,[15] der von der Feuerwehr [16] mit zehn Löschzügen [17] bekämpft wurde. Der S-Bahn-Verkehr auf der Strecke, die an dem Werk vorbeiführt, mußte unterbrochen werden. Der Führer eines S-Bahn-Zuges hatte als erster den Brand beobachtet und ihn gemeldet.

NOTES

[13] **auslösen,** to arouse, to start
[14] **der Rauchpilz,** smoke mushroom

[15] **der Brandherd,** focus of fire
[16] **die Feuerwehr,** fire brigade
[17] **der Löschzug,** fire engine

Suche nach Gipfelkreuz [1]

Associated Press

Graz, 21. Juli

Das große Gipfelkreuz auf dem fast 3000 Meter hohen Dachstein, das im Jahre 1947 errichtet worden war, ist spurlos [2] verschwunden. Es ist noch nicht geklärt, ob ein Bosheitsakt [3] vorliegt oder ob das Kreuz durch einen Blitzschlag [4] aus seiner Verankerung [5] gerissen und in die Tiefe geschleudert [6] worden ist. Das Kreuz war in einen großen Felsblock einbetoniert und durch mehrere Drahtseile gesichert. Unter dem Gipfel wurde eines dieser Sicherungsseile [7] gefunden.

NOTES

[1] **das Gipfelkreuz,** summit cross
[2] **spurlos,** without trace
[3] **der Bosheitsakt,** act of malice
[4] **der Blitzschlag,** lightning stroke

[5] **die Verankerung,** mooring (anchorage)
[6] **schleudern,** to sling
[7] **das Sicherungsseil,** safety rope

Sergeant Grischa—7

Rückverwandlung

Durch die hölzerne Tür seiner Zelle, den Mund, daß man ihn hört, dicht an den Spalten und Fugen, ruft Grischa : „ Ruf den Leutnant! Bring den Leutnant! Um deiner Seligkeit willen den Leutnant zurück! "

In der Zelle, auf der Pritsche, in Schweiß gewaschen, grau, sitzt Grischa, die Hände auf den Knien, und weiß nur eins : daß er den Bjuschew loswerden muß, den Bjuschew, der zum Tode bestimmt zu sein scheint, den sie ja jetzt wieder einmal erschießen wollen, und der er gar nicht ist. Sofort den Bjuschew loswerden! Und als Grischa Iljitsch Paprotkin, ausgebrochener Gefangener Nummer hundertdreiundsiebzig der Gefangenenkompanie zwei, Holzverarbeitungslager Nawarischkij, sein eigenes Selbst zurückerlangen ; das duldet keine Sekunde Aufschub. Etwas will nicht, daß er in fremdem Kleide entwische. Etwas will, daß er für seine Schuld seine Strafe auf sich nehme. „ Jeder seins ", heißt die Parole. Er ist es ja gar nicht, den sie verurteilt haben! Sofort muß das Gericht dies wissen. Erschießen, ihn! Lachen verscheucht den Tod. Auch diesmal dieses verfluchte Vieh Bjuschew, dem er erlauben wollte, ihn zu fressen, er, Grischa Iljitsch, Sergeant! Nein, Teufel, weg mit dir! Und halb befreit, halb im Krampfe schlägt er die Hände zusammen wie damals und lacht. Er ist es ja gar nicht! Er ist ja gerettet! Ohaha, und nun mach Beine!

So kam das Lachen des Gefangenen Bjuschew zustande.

Translation :

Retransformation

Through the wooden door of his cell, (with) his mouth (so) that they would hear, close against the splits and joints, Grischa shouted: " Call the Lieutenant! Bring the Lieutenant! For your salvation, get the Lieutenant back here! "

In the cell on the plank bed, bathed in sweat, grey, Grischa sat, his hands on his knees, and knowing only one (thought) : that he must get rid of (the) Byuschev, who seemed to have been destined to death, (and) whom they wanted to shoot again, and who he is not at all. Get rid of Byuschev at once! And as Grischa Ilyitch Paprotkin, escaped prisoner No. 173 of Prison Company (No.) two, (of) Timber Labor Camp Navarishkii to get back his own self: this must not brook a second's delay. Something willed that he should not slip away in another's clothes. Something willed that he should take his punishment for his own guilt (offence). " Every man to his own," says the watch-word. He was not at all (the man) whom they had sentenced! Justice must know this at once. Shoot—him! Laughing scares away death. This time also this cursed beast Byuschev, whom he wanted to allow to devour him, Grischa Ilyitch, Sergeant! No, (you) devil, away with you! And half relieved, half convulsed, he beat his hands together as before and laughed. He's not that man at all! He's now saved! Ha-ha! And now hurry up!

So the laughter of the prisoner Byuschev came about.

[Contd. on page 280.

§ 3. *Building up a Vocabulary*—BINDEN **and** KOMMEN: *Groups—Practice with a Dictionary—News Items:* MINIATUREN—*Reading:* **Sergeant Grischa**

This Section is devoted to the question of building up a vocabulary by learning German words in accordance with their groups, and from their original simple words or roots.

A good dictionary is essential here (for advice on this, see page 299). But you must always remember that, under a common word, you will find compound words or derivatives which you may seldom meet elsewhere. Furthermore, you may *not* find under a common or root-word all the compounds which stem from it. The examples given below are for the purpose of showing you how to set out *for learning purposes* a vocabulary springing from **BINDEN**, *to bind*, and **KOMMEN**, *to come*: two fruitful root-words.

BINDEN, to bind	**BAND**	**geBUNDen**
die Binde, band, bandage, sling	**das Band,** string, bond (blood)	**der Bund,** league, union
die Bindung, bond, tie	**die Bande,** band, gang	**das Bündel** ⎱ truss, **das Bund** ⎰ bundle
die Verbindung, union, connection	**der Verband,** medical dressing	**der Ausbund,** pattern, paragon
	der Einband, binding	**das Bündnis,** alliance
	der Band, volume	

Add compound Verbs made with prefixes:

anbinden, to fasten   **aufbinden,** tie up   **abbinden,** to untie
einbinden, to bind   **entbinden,** to free   **losbinden,** to unbind
umbinden, tie round   **unterbinden,** to tie   **vorbinden,** to tie on
zubinden, to tie up   under   **(sich) verbünden,** to
zusammenbinden,   ally oneself
to tie together

And Compound Nouns with the **bind, band,** or **bund** root either before or after another word: Here are a few examples:

der Buchbinder, bookbinder
die Halsbinde, necktie
das Bindemittel, link, connection, cement
der Bindestrich, hyphen
das Bindewort, conjunction
der Bindfaden, string

der Prachteinband, choice binding
die Bandschleife, knot (of ribbons, etc.)
die Bandwaren, ribbons
der Bandwurm, tapeworm

das Schlüsselbund, bunch of keys
der Bundesgenosse, confederate
die Bundesgenossenschaft, confederacy
der Bundesstaat, federal state
die Bundesverfassung, federal constitution

Although this does not exhaust the possibilities of this one word **BINDEN,** it gives a fair picture of them. The learner may wish to make a more limited selection, so the everyday Verb **KOMMEN,** *to come*, **ich KAM, ich bin GEKOMMEN** may be selected as an example.

It will be noted that the new words made from it do not keep to the vowels of the simple Verb, but include **u** and **ü**:

Nouns

DAS EINKOMMEN, income
DER NACHKOMME, descendant
DAS UNTERKOMMEN, shelter
DIE NACHKOMMENSCHAFT, offspring, issue
DAS VORKOMMNIS, event, occurrence
DIE ZUVORKOMMENHEIT, politeness
DAS WILLKOMMEN, welcome
DIE ABKUNFT, origin, descent
DIE ÜBEREINKUNFT, agreement
DIE ZUKUNFT, future

DER ZUKÜNFTIGE, future husband, fiancé
DIE ANKUNFT, arrival
DAS HERKOMMEN, tradition
DIE HERKUNFT, origin

Verbs

ANKOMMEN, to arrive
BEKOMMEN, to come by, obtain
ENTKOMMEN, to escape
ENTGEGENKOMMEN, to meet, treat kindly
ÜBEREINKOMMEN, to agree
UNTERKOMMEN, to find shelter, obtain a position
VERKOMMEN, to go to seed, to the dogs
ZUVORKOMMEN, to be beforehand, prevent

Adjectives and Adverbs

WILLKOMMEN, welcome
ABKÖMMLICH, able to get away
HERKÖMMLICH, traditional
ZUKÜNFTIG, future

NOTE: MANY WORDS GIVEN IN THESE PAGES TO ILLUSTRATE WORD-BUILDING WILL NOT BE FOUND IN THE VOCABULARY AT THE END OF THE BOOK, THOUGH MOST OF THE SIMPLE OR ROOT-WORDS ARE GIVEN THERE. SEE ALSO *"WARNING"* ON PAGE 244.

Finally, the learner must not regard the treatment given in these pages to Word-building as exhaustive. It sets out main principles and exemplifies them, and should provide means of access to thousands of new words that can be made from those given in the Course and will be found in reading matter. For those who intend to pursue the study of German further, it should be regarded as a useful practical introduction to Word-building, and not as a final statement.

Note: It is not safe to make up new words yourself, but you should always take note of every new compound or derivative word met in reading.

PRACTICE :

If you have a Dictionary (German–English),* even a small one, you can expand on the method of word-learning described above, and do so almost indefinitely.   Thus, when you come upon a new word in reading, look it up and note its compounds, making a group similar to that of **BINDEN** or **KOMMEN**.   This you will have to do long after you have finished the Course, if you wish your vocabulary to be up to the miscellaneous reading matter you must deal with in pursuing your studies.   If you haven't yet a Dictionary, just **note down every new Compound Word with its meaning,** and this will meanwhile serve a similar purpose.   German has a large vocabulary, a fact which must be recognized and dealt with.   Wide reading, listening to Radio, and practice with German speakers provide the answers.

* See pages 299 –300.

SOME RECAPITULARY SENTENCES BASED ON §§ 1, 2, AND 3

Sie bedeckte ihr Gesicht.   Wir werden gern mitarbeiten.   Er hat mehrere Schüsse abgefeuert.   Wollen Sie schon weggehen?   Das Glas ist heruntergefallen.   Wir denken, bald wiederzukommen.   Der Hund wurde festgebunden.   Sie haben die Ratten totgeschlagen.   Ein Mann wurde mit dem Auto überfahren.   Müssen wir hier aussteigen?   Werden die Vereinigten Nationen in dieser Frage übereinstimmen?

Das Kind lächelte uns an.   Er kränkelt schon lange.   Der Junge schnitzte mit dem Messer.   Ich bin auf der Straße ausgerutscht.   Sie sind ihm scharf entgegengetreten.   Er hat die Fehler verbessert.   Ich will mir die Hände trocknen.

Ich gebe ihm das Buch.   Er dankt für die Gabe.   Wir begeben uns in den Saal.   Sie vergab ihm den Irrtum.   Er ist ein begabter Knabe.   Der Bote hat einen Brief abgegeben.   Ich wollte ihm das Geld zurückgeben.   Er wird es mir wiedergeben.   Die Gefangenen wurden freigegeben.   Hier ist die Ausgabe für Postpakete.   Ist Ihre Angabe richtig?   Das Ergebnis ist gut.   Dieser Mann ist sehr freigebig.   Es ist nicht vergeblich.

Miniaturen

Philip, Herzog von Edinburg, konstruierte ein von elektrischen Drähten durchzogenes Filz-Tischtuch für die königliche Jacht „ Britannia ". An das Stromnetz angeschlossen, versorgt [1] es an jeder Stelle die daraufgestellten elektrischen Leuchter mit Strom.

Dr. Lajos Vetoe, Oberhaupt der evangelisch-lutherischen Kirche Ungarns, kam in Begleitung des Budapester Theologen Professor Dr. Kramer zu einem mehrtägigen [2] Besuch in die Sowjetzone.

Felix von Eckardt, Bundespressechef, verbringt seine ersten Sommerferien nach der Rückkehr in die Bundeshauptstadt auf der Insel Sylt.

Jawaharlal Nehru, indischer Ministerpräsident, hat Bundeskanzler Dr. Adenauer ein Danktelegramm für die herzliche Aufnahme in der Bundesrepublik übersandt.

Edmund Forschbach, ehemaliger Leiter des Presse- und Informationsamtes der Bundesregierung, befindet sich noch immer auf Urlaub, ohne zu wissen, welche neue Verwendung [3] für ihn vorgesehen ist.

Kosovska-Mitrovica, Mitglied der jugoslawischen Volkstanzgruppe, die gegenwärtig in Nizza gastiert,[4] hat mit einem Operettensäbel zwei Männer verletzt und in die Flucht geschlagen. Die Männer gehörten der Exilbewegung „ Freies Serbien " an und hatten versucht, den Choreographen der Tanzgruppe zu entführen.[5]

Shigemitsu, japanischer Außenminister, wird sich zur Aufnahme der russisch-japanischen Friedensverhandlungen am 25. Juli mit einer Delegation nach Moskau begeben.

William Beemer, ehemaliger Friedensrichter von Reno, dem amerikanischen Hochzeits- und Scheidungsparadies,[6] hat in seiner einjährigen Amtszeit 93,000 Dollar an Heiratsgebühren [7] verdient. Um seinen Posten bewerben [8] sich vier Kandidaten.

NOTES

[1] **versorgt,** supplies
[2] **mehrtägig,** of several days
[3] **die Verwendung,** use, employment
[4] **gastieren,** to give a guest performance
[5] **entführen,** to abduct
[6] **das Hochzeits- und Scheidungsparadies,** marriage and divorce paradise
[7] **die Heiratsgebühren,** marriage fees
[8] **sich bewerben,** to apply

Sergeant Grischa—8

„ Gemacht ! "

So kam es, daß gegen fünf ein preußischer General und ein russischer Kriegsgefangener einander zu mustern Gelegenheit hatten. . . . . Inzwischen betrachtete Exzellenz den Mann, der für eine läßliche Schwindelei beinahe erschossen worden wäre. Grischa wußte mit der natürlichen Klugheit eines Mannes den richtig einzuschätzen, der da vor ihm stand. Es konnte nur ein sehr hoher Offizier sein, ein Arzt bestimmt nicht, sondern ein richtiger General, und er meldete in russischer Sprache, wie es der Dienst seines Heeres vorschrieb, indem er die vorschriftsmäßige Anrede: *wosche prewasschaditjelstwo* in die Luft des Zimmers schmetterte und auf russische Art dabei salutierte. „ Gelernt ist gelernt," sagte Exzellenz, auch ohne daß ihm der Dolmetsch erklärte, was vorging.

„ Ob du nun wirklich Paprotkin bist, mein Sohn, wird sich ja bald herausstellen," sagte er wohlwollend, und während der Dolmetsch auch seine Worte weitergab, ging zwischen den beiden Augenpaaren ein Strom hin und her. Grischa zuckte mit keiner Wimper. Zwischen der Farbe von Generalsaugen und der von Gefangenenaugen bestand fast kein Unterschied, konstatierte Dr. Posnanski im stillen ; die Natur oder Gott handelte hier geradezu aufrührerisch. . . .

„ Fragen Sie ihn mal, ob er uns nun die Wahrheit sagt," meinte er zum Dolmetsch. . . . Er beteuerte die Wahrheit zu reden. Er bereute, daß er es nicht von vornherein getan habe. Er wollte ja nichts anderes als nach Hause. . . . „ Eigentümliche Leute," sagte Excellenz. . . . Später rief der Kriegsgerichtsrat: „ Gemacht ! "

Translation :

It Comes Off!

Thus it came (about) that towards five o'clock a Prussian General and a Russian prisoner of war had the opportunity to size one another up. . . . Meanwhile (His) Excellency was looking at the man who had almost been shot for a pardonable trick. Grischa knew with the natural shrewdness of a (simple) man how to weigh up the one who stood before him. It could only be a very high officer, a doctor certainly not, but a real General, and he addressed him in (the) Russian language, as was by his duty prescribed, in which he gave him his title: "Voshe Prevasshadityelstvo" *resounded through the room and he saluted in the Russian manner. "What he has learnt, he has learnt," said (His) Excellency, even without the interpreter explaining what happened.*

" Whether you are now truly Paprotkin, my son, will soon be made clear," said he benevolently, and as the interpreter translated his words, between the two (men) both pairs of eyes gazed to and fro. Grischa did not move an eyelash. Between the color of the General's eyes and that of the prisoner's there was hardly any difference, Dr. Posnanski said to himself: Nature or God in this case worked something subversive. . . .

" Just ask him whether he tells us the truth," he said to the interpreter. . . . He swore that he spoke the truth. He regretted that he had not done so before. He wanted really nothing else but to go home. . . . " Strange people," said (His) Excellency. . . . Later the Judge Advocate shouted: " Done it! " *

[Contd. on page 288.

§ 4. *Word-order : General Rules—Direct Order—Inverted Order —Subordinate Clause Order—Further Remarks:* **NICHT—** *Practice—Quiz:* **50 FRAGEN—***Reading:* **Sergeant Grischa**

The order of words in a German sentence presents some difficulties for English-speaking learners, but the subject need not cause undue trouble if the method of learning given here is mastered.† German word-order depends largely on *emphasis* ; and on certain *grammatical principles*. Because German word-order differs from English, especially in long sentences, it has to be studied and practised until it is known. In the Practice and Reading the learner will already have become familiar with the principles to be observed. Now they can be set out so that they can be learnt, and kept for reference.

* Meaning that the general was convinced that Grischa was innocent of espionage.

† See pages 2 and 134: How to Study (Parts I and II).

For your purpose the most important kind of sentence is the direct statement, and in this the word-order is the *normal for all direct principal statements*. When Direct Order is known, and not before, the learner may proceed to (2) Inverted Order and then to (3) Subordinate Clause Order. These present fewer difficulties.

1. DIRECT WORD-ORDER

I SUBJECT *with* Qualifiers	II MAIN VERB *or* Auxiliary	III OBJECT PRONOUN(S) (1) *Direct Object* (2) *Indirect Object*
IV TIME ADVERB	V OBJECT NOUNS (1) *Indirect Object* (2) *Direct Object*	(VI) OTHER ADVERBS (1) *Of Manner* (2) *Of Place*
VII ADJECTIVE *used as* Predicate	VIII COMPLETION OF VERB (1) *Separable Particle* (2) *Past Participle* (3) *Infinitive*	

Notes: I. Subject With Qualifiers: Can be a Noun or a Pronoun, and if a Noun may have an Article and/or Adjective(s) qualifying it.

II. If a simple Verb, it comes here. If a Compound Tense of a Verb is necessary, its Auxiliary comes here.

III. Note that when two Pronouns are necessary, the Direct Object precedes the Indirect.

V. If there are Noun Objects, the Indirect precedes the Direct.

III and V. If there is a Noun and a Pronoun, the Pronoun comes first.

VI. An Adverb of Manner is placed before an Adverb of Place, if both are necessary.

VII. In the sentence *The girl looks beautiful*, " beautiful " is used predicatively. See page 26.

VIII. If an Auxiliary or the main part of a Separable Verb is used in II the Particle comes here, also the Past Participle or an Infinitive, whichever is necessary, and in that order.

This may seem a little complicated, because a sentence involving all the different words required would be a rarity. But the full word-order has to be given, because it is required to make all kinds of sentences. Some learners find that German word-order can be learnt quite easily by memorizing English sentences set out in the German order. Thus:

(1) *The good boy gives her the sugar.*
(2) *He has her the sugar given.*
(3) *He has her the sugar willingly given.*
(4) *He will her the sugar willingly give.*
(5) *He gave it to her.*
(6) *He gave it to her to-day.*
(7) *He gave it to her to-day willingly.*
(8) *He will to-morrow my sister this sugar willingly*
     I   II   IV   V(1)   V(2)   VI(1)
in the room give.
  VI(2)   VIII(3)

In German these sentences are:

(1) DER GUTE JUNGE GIBT IHR DEN ZUCKER.
(2) ER HAT IHR DEN ZUCKER GEGEBEN.
(3) ER HAT IHR DEN ZUCKER GERN GEGEBEN.
(4) ER WIRD IHR DEN ZUCKER GERN GEBEN.
(5) ER GAB IHN IHR.
(6) ER GAB IHN IHR HEUTE.
(7) ER GAB IHN IHR HEUTE GERN.
(8) ER WILL MORGEN MEINER SCHWESTER DIESEN ZUCKER GERN IM ZIMMER GEBEN.

Further examples:

    I   II   III   IV   VIII(3)
WIR WERDEN IHN SELTEN SEHEN
We shall seldom see him
DER JUNGE HAT ES IHM GEGEBEN
The boy has given it to him
DER JUNGE HAT IHM DAS BUCH GEGEBEN
The boy has given him the book
DAS MÄDCHEN SIEHT SCHÖN AUS (aussehen, separable)
The girl looks beautiful

Now take as illustration a sentence (admittedly an awkward one!) that follows Direct Word-order and is as full a one as is likely to be met:

I   II   IV   V(1)

ICH WERDE ÜBERMORGEN MEINER SCHWESTER

V(2)   VI(2)   VI(2)

IHREN HUT   GERN   IM BAHNHOFE

VIII(2)   VIII(3)

GEGEBEN   HABEN

I shall willingly (with pleasure) have given my sister her hat the day after to-morrow in the railway station.

These examples should all be memorized.   Some practice in making German sentences, following the word-order given above, plus listening to good speakers and reading good German, will bring mastery.

DIRECT WORD-ORDER, as explained above, embraces the majority of sentences of everyday life and in most reading matter.

EMPHASIS is expressed in German by putting the word to be emphasized *first* in the sentence.   This requires:

2. INVERTED ORDER, which has the Subject Pronoun or Noun immediately *after* the Verb or Auxiliary:

> **GESTERN GING ICH IN DEN GARTEN.**   *Yesterday* I went into the garden.

Direct Order:

> **Der Vater gab zu Weihnachten dem Kinde ein Buch.** The father gave the child a book at Christmas.

Inverted Order for Emphasis:

> **ZU WEIHNACHTEN GAB DER VATER DEM KINDE EIN BUCH.**   (It was) at Christmas the father gave the child a book.

In questions the Verb is placed first, the Noun or Pronoun comes after it:

> **GAB DER VATER DEM KINDE EIN BUCH ?**
> **IST DAS MÄDCHEN SCHÖN ?**

See also page 152.

3. SUBORDINATE CLAUSE ORDER: This Word-order applies to all dependent clauses in a sentence. It is the same as Direct Order except that the *dependent clause begins with a relative or a conjunction* followed by the subject, and at the end of the sentence the order is: (1) Past Participle; (2) Infinitive; and (3) Main Verb or Auxiliary, which is *last*. **All words between Direct Object Pronoun and Past Participle follow the rules for Direct Order.**

See Lesson VII, § 2, Subordinating Conjunctions. The same word-order applies when the word introducing the dependent clause is a Relative Pronoun. See page 106.

The most important thing to remember is that the Main Verb or Auxiliary is always relegated to the end of the sentence. There is always a " warning " in the form of a *Relative or Conjunction* to indicate that a change of word-order is necessary. Study the examples given on pages 106, 216-7.

The learner must be able to recognize this change of word-order in Subordinate Clauses and, when he wishes to use such a clause, be able to apply it correctly. It is possible (though undesirable except in the learning stage) to avoid such clauses in everyday speech.

4. FURTHER REMARKS ON WORD-ORDER: **NICHT:** The statement of Word-order on page 282 is a safe guide, but some learners tend to make mistakes even when they know it fairly well. This is often due to overlooking the fact that **nicht,** *not*, is an Adverb which is often lightly stressed and often well stressed. An example of this was given on page 152, but it may help if some further indications are given in regard to this important little word. **NICHT** *is an Adverb of Degree* and, like " Other Adverbs " in the statement on page 282, tends to stand at or near the end of the sentence, following Objects, Pronoun(s), or Noun(s). But as **NICHT** is so often lightly stressed, the tendency then is for it to be placed before a stressed word—which explains the example on page 152. This is a modern tendency, and is a question of emphasis and not of grammar. The same applies to **NIE, NIEMALS,** *never*. An Adverb modifying another Adverb stands before it: **Er ist sehr gut. Er spricht sehr gut deutsch.** Phrases used adverbially or predicatively occupy the same

place as the words which they represent (Adverbs or Adjectives as Predicates), which often causes confusion in the minds of some learners. Thus: *in the evening* = **abends** = Adverb of Time. The young man behaved *like a gentleman* : " like a gentleman " = adverbial phrase of manner. Place each accordingly in German.

Finally, the learner must be careful to distinguish a principal sentence from a subordinate sentence or clause which depends on it. The principal sentence makes a clear, direct statement, the subordinate in itself may not have any sharp meaning or any meaning at all without the principal sentence. This is a useful test.

As most of the sentences made by the learner will be principal direct statements, these finer points need not be mastered immediately. They will come by experience and by constantly referring to this Section on Word-order.

1. *Direct Word-order :*

Subject with Qualifiers	Verb Auxiliary	Objects (1) Indirect (2) Direct	Adverbial Qualifiers	Past Participle Infinitive Predicate
Der kleine Hund	bellt [1]	—	laut	—
Der treue Hund	begleitet	seinen Herrn	stets	—
Unser Hund	hat	das Haus	gut	bewacht
Unser Hund	wird	unser Haus	—	bewachen
Der bissige [2] Hund	darf	den Hof	am Tage nicht	verlassen
Der Koch	hat	dem Hund (1) einen (2) Knochen (2)	—	gegeben
Der treue Hund	dient	dem Menschen (1)	gern	als Freund

2. *Inverted Order :*

Begleitet der große Hund seinen Herrn?

Hat der große Hund seinen Herrn begleitet?

Plötzlich sprang der Hund ins Wasser.

Böse war der Hund, der das Kind biß.

Weil der große Hund gefährlich ist, muß er angebunden werden.

[1] from **bellen,** to bark.   [2] **bissig,** biting, snappy.

3. *Subordinate Clause Order :*

Er fürchtet,* daß er zu spät kommen wird.
Der Knabe sagte, daß er einen großen Hund gesehen hätte.
Ich fragte ihn, ob er mir helfen wollte.
Wenn ich den Schlüssel nur gefunden hätte !
Nachdem er gegessen hatte, ging er spazieren.

* Note that a subordinate clause in German is always preceded by a comma.

PRACTICE :

In every Lesson you have had Practice in Word-order, and your practice here consists in re-reading the German text of **Sergeant Grischa,** beginning on page 240, and studying the construction of the sentences. From time to time, take a sentence and analyse it, comparing its Word-order with that given in the Rules in this Section. Continue, until you feel confident that you know these Rules. Remember one thing: a skilled author may on occasion depart from a rule, but you will generally find that this is for style, often just for emphasis. You yourself must not depart from the Rules !

THINKING IN GERMAN : QUIZ

This should by now be easier. You may try the Quiz given below, but do not expect to get all items right! All the same, trying is excellent Practice. The Answers to all these questions will be found on page 298, at the end of § 5.

50 Fragen :

Literatur :

1 Wer schrieb die ,, Göttliche Komödie '' ?
2 Welcher Held der Literatur kämpfte gegen Windmühlen?
3 Wer schrieb ,, Grüne Blätter '' ?
4 Nennen Sie einen Roman von Dostojewski.
5 Nennen Sie einen Roman Gustave Flauberts.
6 Nennen Sie den Namen eines deutschen Dichters.

Religion:

7 Wie lautet das erste der zehn Gebote?
8 Welche ist die verbreiteste Religion in Pakistan?
9 Welche ist die verbreiteste Religion in Griechenland?
10 Wer verriet Jesus?
11 Nennen Sie drei Religionen außer dem Christentum.

Philosophie:

12 Nennen Sie einen Philosophen, der vor Platon gelebt hat.
13 Wer sagte: „ Ich denke, also bin ich " ?
14 Wer schrieb „ Also, sprach Zarathustra " ?
15 Welcher moderne Philosoph gilt als Begründer des Existenzialismus?
16 Nennen Sie den Titel eines Buches von Karl Marx.

Architektur:

17 Was ist ein Kapitäl?
18 Welcher Stil dominiert in den russischen Kirchen?
19 Nennen Sie zwei Arten griechischer Säulen.
20 Was ist der Parthenon?
21 An welchen Stil denken Sie, wenn Sie das Wort „ Kathedrale " hören?

Musik:

22 Nennen Sie den Titel einer Komposition von Debussy.
23 Was ist die Scala?
24 Nennen Sie den Namen eines bedeutenden zeitgenössischen Komponisten.
25 Wer komponierte „ Finnlandia " ?

[QUIZ *continued on page* 295.

SERGEANT GRISCHA—9

Aktenstück „ Bjuschew alias Paprotkin "

Grischa verließ den warmen Raum mit einem Gefühl von Straffheit und Glück, das ihm aus Augen und Haltung unhemmbar leuchtete. Nun war er wieder er selbst. Nichts mehr von Bjuschew, Gott sei dank; nichts als Paprotkin, Grischa Iljitsch, ging hier mit den alten Kameraden durch den Frühlingsdreck. Nun würde alles Erlittene abgewaschen werden wie der Schmutz von den Stiefeln heute abend, und nach einigen Wochen Wartens diese Sache wieder in Ordnung kommen.

Ihm war, als sei bis jetzt ein wesentlicher Teil seines Selbst wie ein Spiegelbild von ihm entfernt gewesen und wäre eben endlich, wie beim Zerschlagen eines trennenden Glases, wiederum mit ihm in eins geflossen. Heil und ganz ging er wieder unter die Menschen, und wenn seine Fröhlichkeit sich auch um vieles bedächtiger anfühlte, spürte er sich dafür doch auch erfahrener, gewichtiger. Seine Seele, erstarrt im militärischen Betrieb und erweckt durch das Lebendige der Flucht und das Tödliche jenes Urteilsstoßes, hatte begonnen zu altern, weiser zu werden. Er wußte es nicht, aber in der Art seiner Freude empfand er Veränderung.

Indessen umknotete Posnanski eigenhändig das Aktenstück „ Bjuschew alias Paprotkin " mit einem jener bunten Bindfäden, die zur Verpackung von Liebesgaben aus den Fabriken geschäfts- tüchtiger Unternehmer kommen und die, bei den Preußen sorgfältig gespart, wieder Verwendung finden müssen. Ein schwarz-weiß-rot gedrehtes Schnürband bündelte die ge- wichtigen Papiere.

TRANSLATION :

File " Byuschev *alias* Paprotkin "

Grischa left the warm room with a feeling of strength and happiness (luck) which shone unchecked in his eyes and bearing. Now he was again himself. No more of Byuschev, thank God; no other but Paprotkin, Grischa Ilyitch, was walking here with (his) old comrades through the spring muck. Now all sufferings would be washed away like the mud from his boots that evening, and after a few weeks of waiting this thing would come in order. It was to him as if until now an essential part of himself had been parted from him like a reflection in a mirror, and finally with smashing the glass, had been restored to him. Hale and whole he walked again among men, and even if his joy appeared to be much more thoughtful, he noted himself (to be) also more experienced, more important. His soul, benumbed in military routine and awakened through the living (experience) of the escape and the deadly blow of that sentence, had begun to grow older and wiser. He did not know it, but in the nature of his joy he discovered change.

Meanwhile Posnanski with his own hands tied round the file " Byuschev alias *Paprotkin " with one of those bright ribbons used for the packing of gift-parcels from the factories of clever business-men and which are put aside by the careful Prussians so that they can find another use. A black-white-and-red twisted lace made a bundle of the important papers.*

[*Contd. on page* 296.

§ 5. *Letter-writing: Formal and Informal—Examples of Correspondence—Quiz*—contd.: **50 FRAGEN**—*Sergeant Grischa End*—Answers to Quiz:

Letter-writing in German tends towards the formal, unless the correspondents are on very friendly terms. The learner ought not to overlook it as a way to practise the written language, and it should not be difficult to find a " pen-pal " for correspondence. To begin with, each correspondent will write in his or her own language, and later will write in the other's. Openings and endings are formalized as follows:

FORMAL OPENING: **Geehrter Herr!** Or **Sehr geehrter Herr!** Equivalent to *Dear Sir.* **Geehrte Frau! Geehrtes Fräulein! Geehrter Herr Schmidt! Geehrte Frau Schmidt! Geehrtes Fräulein Schmidt!** Or **Geehrtes Fräulein Ilse!** (geehrt, *honoured*).

A MODERATELY FAMILIAR OPENING: **Werter Herr Schmidt! Gnädige Frau Schmidt! Gnädiges Fräulein! Meine gnädige Frau!** (gnädig, *kind, gracious*). This is polite and friendly, and can be used on most occasions.

A FAMILIAR OPENING: **Lieber Karl! Liebe Ilse! Mein lieber Freund! Mein liebes Fräulein! Mein lieber Schmidt!**

ENDINGS FOR BUSINESS LETTERS:

> ... **und zeichnen**
> **mit Hochachtung,**

or simply: **Hochachtungsvoll,** equivalent of *Yours respectfully.* Or **Ihr Ergebener,** *Yours truly.* Or **Ergebenst,** *faithfully.*

A FORMAL ENDING FOR OTHER LETTERS: **Mit vorzüglicher Hochachtung** = With the highest respect = our *Yours sincerely.*

MODERATELY FAMILIAR AND POLITE: **Ihr ergebener ...** *Yours affectionately* = our *Yours ever* (ergeben, *devoted, at-*

tached).   This is a useful formula for friendly letters to a person
who has been met.

With best wishes, **Mit bestem Gruß**
With kind regards, **Mit freundlichen Grüßen**

The address is written:

> **Herrn** (singular) **A,**
> **Herren** (plural) **B & C.**
> **BERLIN, W.10**
> **Grillparzer str. 32.**

> **Frau, Fräulein A, B.**

Never omit a title: **Herrn Dr. Krause.**
For date see page 75.

SOME COMMON ABBREVIATIONS:

Dr. jur.   = **Doktor der Rechtswissenschaft** (juris-
                        prudence) = LL.D. = Dr. of Laws
Dr. med.   = **Doktor der Medizin** = M.D.
Dr. med. dent. = **Doktor der Zahnheilkunde** = Dr. of
                        Dentistry = Dental Surgeon, Dentist
Dr. phil.   = **Doktor der Philosophie** = D.Ph.
Dr.-Ing.   = **Doktor-Ingenieur** = Dr. of Engineer-
                        ing

The abbreviation **Dipl.** = *Diploma in*.

Dipl.-Ing. = Diploma in Engineering

All these are written *before* the name.

EXAMPLES OF CORRESPONDENCE IN GERMAN

I. Letter to a Bookseller : Formal

An die

Buchhandlung
Robert Peppmüller
Göttingen
Barfüßer Str. 19

Hameln,
Weserstraße 23.
den 3. September 1956.

Sehr geehrte Herren!

Ich möchte Sie bitten, mir ein Exemplar der „ Hausmärchen "
von Brüder Grimm, in einem vollständigen, illustrierten Band
zu besorgen.   Sollten Sie eine gute, nicht zu teure Ausgabe auf
Lager haben, wäre ich Ihnen verbunden, wenn Sie sie mir direkt
an meine obige Adresse zusenden würden.

Mit vorzüglicher Hochachtung!
(signed) *Hans Hoffmann*

TRANSLATION:

Dear Sirs,

I should like to ask you to obtain for me a copy of Hausmärchen
*by the Brothers Grimm, in a complete illustrated volume.   Should you
have a good, not too expensive edition, in stock, I would be obliged if
you mailed it direct to my above address.*

Yours faithfully,
(sgd.) Hans Hoffman

II. *Bookseller's Reply*

Herrn Hans Hoffmann
      Hameln
      Weserstraße 23   Göttingen, den 6. September 1956

Sehr geehrter Herr!
   In Beantwortung Ihrer geschätzten Anfrage vom 3. des Monats
teilen wir Ihnen mit, daß wir

Brüder Grimms ,, Hausmärchen "

in einer recht schönen, ungekürzten Ausgabe, in Ganzleinen
gebunden, zum Preise von DM. 12.50 vorrätig haben. Diese
ist jedoch nicht illustriert. Wenn Sir allerdings ein Werk mit
Illustrationen vorziehen, so können wir Ihnen ein solches auch
ohne große Verzögerung besorgen. Wir möchten Ihnen dann
die von der Droemerschen Verlagsanstalt herausgebrachte
Ausgabe empfehlen, die etwa DM. 16.– kostet.
   In Erwartung Ihrer festen Bestellung

zeichnen wir hochachtungsvoll
pp. ROBERT PEPPMÜLLER
R. Schmidt.

TRANSLATION :

Dear Sir,

   *In reply to your enquiry of the 3rd of (this) month, we wish to
inform you that we have in stock*

Brüder Grimms : HAUSMÄRCHEN

*in a beautiful, unabridged edition, full linen, price DM.12.50. This,
however, is not illustrated. So, should you prefer a volume with
illustrations, we could (also) obtain such a one without much delay.
We should like to recommend the edition published by Dromersche
Verlagsanstalt costing about DM.16.*

   In expectation of your definite order,

we are,
Yours truly, etc.

III. *Friendly Informal Letter : From an English Student to a*
" Pen Pal " in Germany.

Lieber Freund,

heute schreibe ich Ihnen mit einer besônderen Absicht.
Schon seit langer Zeit habe ich den Wunsch gehabt, einmal eine
Reise nach Deutschland zu machen. Nun hoffe ich, daß ich
diesen Plan bald verwirklichen kann. Sie können sich denken,
wie sehr ich mich freuen werde, Sie dann auch persönlich
kennenzulernen.

Ich wende mich daher mit einer Bitte an Sie. Könnten Sie
wohl eine gute und doch billige Pension in Ihrer Heimatstadt
für mich finden ? Oder vielleicht kennen Sie sogar eine nette
Familie, bei der ich als zahlender Gast wohnen könnte. Das
wäre natürlich noch schöner, besonders wenn ich Familienan-
schluß haben würde. Dabei hätte ich dann die beste Gelegenheit, in zwanglosen Unterhaltungen meine deutschen Sprach-
kenntnisse zu verbessern. Ich nehme an, daß es in Ihrer Stadt
auch Abendkurse gibt, an denen ich teilnehmen kann.—Ach, nun
hätte ich doch beinahe das Wichtigste zu erwähnen vergessen :
nämlich, daß ich beabsichtige, diese Ferienreise im Monat Juli
oder Anfang August auf etwa vierzehn Tage zu machen !

Haben Sie nicht auch einmal vor, nach England auf Besuch
zu kommen ? Ich lade Sie schon heute herzlich ein. Nur auf
eine Sache muß ich Sie gleich vorbereiten : Das Wetter ist bei
uns nicht so schön, wie es bei Ihnen ist. Es regnet in England
viel häufiger als auf dem Kontinent. Und es bleibt hier im
Sommer nicht lange Zeit warm. Wind, Regen und Sonnen-
schein wechseln beständig ab.

Nun, lieber Freund, haben Sie im voraus besten Dank für die
Mühe, die ich Ihnen bereite. Voll Ungeduld erwarte ich Ihren
nächsten Brief.

Mit vielen Grüßen,

Ihr

(*signature*)

PRACTICE

Read these Letters several times until you are familiar with the
phraseology.

QUIZ—*Contd. from page* 288.

50 Fragen

Bildende Kunst:

26 Wer malte das ,, Letzte Abendmahl '' ?
27 Welcher Maler der italienischen Renaissance war auch ein berühmter Bildhauer?
28 Nennen Sie den Namen eines englischen Malers des 19. Jahrhunderts, der wegen seiner Meeresbilder berühmt war.
29 Wer schuf den ,, Denker '' ?
30 Nennen Sie den Namen eines bekannten spanischen Malers.

Zu übersetzen aus Fremdsprachen:

31 Se verrà presto, lo vedrà.
32 Ich habe schon einen Brief an Sie geschrieben.
33 Por los Menos, voy a hacerlo si hay tiempo.
34 Prima luce et nostri omnes erant flumen transportati.
35 On voit toujours la même côté de la lune.

Geschichte:

36 Welcher General eroberte das antike Persien?
37 Wann wurde China Republik?
38 Nennen Sie den Namen einer an die Geschichte Südamerikas gebundenen Persönlichkeit.
39 und 40 Welchen Ländern gehörten Metternich und Cavour an?

Sozial- und Wirtschaftswissenschaften:

41 Wer schrieb ,, Wealth of Nations '' ?
42 Was ist der Malthusianismus?
43 Was versteht man unter ,, Laissez faire '' ?
44 Wer schrieb den ,, Contrat social '' ?
45 Nennen Sie ein Werk von Thomas Paine.

Naturwissenschaften:

46 Wie lautet das zweite thermo-dynamische Gesetz?
47 Wer war Pawlow?
48 Wer war der Schöpfer der Psychoanalyse?
49 Welches ist der größte Planet?
50 Was ist ein Gen?

Antworten Seite 298.

Sergeant Grischa—10

„ Nach Kenntnisnahme zurück "

Der Einlauf eines Tages, einer Woche bei der Justizabteilung schwillt ungeheuerlich. Die Kriminalität im Heere nimmt ständig zu. . . . . Inzwischen geht der Mensch, der lebendige Mensch, auf den von dem Aktenstück in der fernen Stadt Schatten fallen, gleichgültig tagaus, tagein seinen Beschäftigungen nach. Grischa, mit wachsamen Augen, erwartet den Ablauf seiner Verstrickung zuversichtlich. Der General hat ihn gesehen und er einem General standgehalten—zu Besorgnis kein Anlaß mehr, zumal da der Schreiber mit der Brille ihm versichert, die Untersuchungshaft, die er hier erleidet, kürze seine spätere Strafe mächtig. Überflüssige Esser kann sich im Krieg kein Gefängnis leisten. . . .

Zurückkehrend sah der Kriegsgerichtsrat von Lychow über ein Aktenstück auf seinem Schreibtisch gebeugt, die Arme aufgestützt.

„ Lassen Sie mich Exzellenz ganz kurz berichten——"

„ Es ist die Sache da, Paprotkin, mit dem Kriegsgefangenen."

„ Befehl ; Exzellenz erinnern sich ? "

„ Bin ganz im Bilde. Netter Kerl, sah aus wie—ich weiß nicht wer. Müßte mich sehr irren, wenn sein Gesicht nicht vorhin unter den Ordonnanzen gependelt hätte."

Posnanski erklomm den Gipfel des Unmilitärischen. „ Richtig ", sagte er und „ Pardon " und nahm der Exzellenz das Aktenstück aus den Fingern.

„ Der Sachverhalt war vollkommen klar. Einen Bjuschew, Überläufer, hatten wir verurteilt, ein Paprotkin, entwichener Gefangener, wurde rekognosziert und einwandfrei nachgewiesen. Die Akten gingen an Ober-Ost zur Ermittlung der Zuständigkeit. Folgendermaßen entscheidet die oberste Justizbehörde dieses Landes." Er ergriff einen der Mappe beigelegten Bogen mit schwarzen, ziemlich großen Maschinenbuchstaben und las vor :

„ Nach Kenntnisnahme zurück. In Übereinstimmung mit dem Herrn Generalquartiermeister ersucht der Oberbefehlshaber Ost, es bei dem einwandfrei gefällten Urteil des Kriegsgerichts der Division bewenden und den Verurteilen behufs

Vollstreckung der Todesstrafe auf dem üblichen Wege der Ortskommandantur Merwinsk zuführen zu lassen. . . ."

Der alte General klemmte das Monokel ins Auge und las sorgsam, indem er die Lippen dabei bewegte, Satz für Satz das Urteil nach. Mit volkommen höflicher Stimme sagte er dann in der Unbetontheit eines Gentleman: „ Wenn ich recht verstanden habe, wohnen wir hier einem Ausbruch von Weisheit bei." Leise, halb zwischen den Zähnen. „ Dieser Quatsch! " fügte er hinzu.

TRANSLATION:

" Noted and Returned "

The " in "-papers in one day, one week (reaching) the Department of Justice swelled enormously. Criminal offences in the army increased apace. . . . Meanwhile the man, the living man, upon whom fall the shadows of the case-file in the distant city, went on calmly day in and day out about his occupations. Grischa, with watchful eyes, was confidently awaiting the unravelling of his entanglement. The General had seen him and he had stood up to a General—there was no more cause for anxiety, especially as the clerk with the spectacles assured him (that) the detention undergone here would shorten his later punishment very much. No prison can do with superfluous eaters in time of war.

On his return the Judge Advocate saw von Lychow bending over a case-file on his desk, his arms propped up.

" Allow me, Excellency, to explain quite briefly——"

" It's the Paprotkin matter, the Prisoner of War."

" Right; Your Excellency remembers? "

" I have it all in my mind. A fine fellow, reminded me of—I don't know whom. I must be greatly mistaken if I haven't caught sight of his face among the orderlies."

Posnanski reached the peak of the unmilitary. " Right," he said and " Pardon " and took the file from the General's fingers.

" The (whole) matter is quite clear. One Byuschev, a deserter, we had sentenced, one Paprotkin, an escaped prisoner, was recognized and beyond dispute identified. The case went to Ober-Ost to find out the competent (court). What follows is (the) decision of the highest judicial authority of this country." He seized from the portfolio a sheet with black, rather big, typescript and read out:

" Noted and returned. In consultation with the Chief of General Staff, the Commander-in-Chief, East, requests that the sentence of the Division Court Martial be upheld, and that for the fulfilment of the penalty of death the condemned be delivered in the customary way to the local commander at Mervinsk. . . ."

The old General stuck (pressed) his monocle in his eye and read the judgment carefully, his lips moving (with the words), sentence by sentence. In a very polite voice he then said with the under-emphasis of a gentleman: " If I have rightly understood, we are present at an outburst of wisdom." Low, half between his teeth. " What rubbish! " he added.

ANSWERS TO QUIZ ON PAGES 287 AND 295.

Die Antworten:

1 Dante ● 2 Don Quijote ● 3 Walt Whitman ● 4 „ Brüder Kara-masow,“ „ Schuld und Sühne “ ● 5 „ Madame Bovary “ ● 6 Goethe, Schiller, Thomas Mann ● 7 Du sollst allein an einen Gott glauben ● 8 Der Islam ● 9 Griechisch-orthodox ● 10 Judas ● 11 Buddhismus, Konfuziuslehre, hebräische Religion ● 12 Sokrates, Heraclit ● 13 Descartes ● 14 Nietzsche ● 15 Jean Paul Sartre ● 16 „ Das Kapital “ ● 17 Ein Säulenabschluß ● 18 Byzantinisch ● 19 Dorisch, jonisch, korinthisch ● 20 Der Tempel der Athene auf der Akropolis ● 21 Gotik ● 22 La Mer ; L'après midi d'un faune ● 23 Mailands Opernhaus ● 24 Strawinsky, Schostakowitsch ● 25 Jan Sibelius ● 26 Leonardo da Vinci ● 27 Michelangelo ● 28 Constable, Turner ● 29 Rodin ● 30 Goya, El Greco, Velasquez ● 31 Wenn Sie rasch kommen, werden Sie ihn sehen ● 32–33 Wenigstens werde ich es tun, falls ich Zeit habe ● 34 Im Morgengrauen wurden alle die unseren zum Fluß befördert ● 35 Man sieht stets die gleiche Seite des Mondes ● 36 Alexander der Große ● 37 1912 ● 38 Simon Bolivar, Josè de San Martin ● 39 und 40 österreich und Italien ● 41 Adam Smith ● 42 Lehre von der Geburtenbeschränkung zur Hebung der Wohlfahrt ● 43 Ein Wirtschaftssystem, das ohne Regierungseingriff funktioniert (Freihandel) ● 44 Rousseau ● 45 Das Recht des Menschen, Das Alter der Vernunft ● 46 Beim Über-gang der Materie von einem Zustand in den anderen geht stets Energie verloren ● 47 Ein russischer Physiologe ● 48 Freud ● 49 Jupiter ● 50 Träger der Erbanlagen in den Keimzellen.

Quiz from **DIE WOCHEN-PRESSE**
(Wien)

Do not be disappointed if you do not get all answers right, because this is a general-knowledge test as well as a test of your German. After you have read the Answers, go back over the Questions and see how they fit. Unless you know Italian, Spanish, Latin, and French, you need not attempt Questions 31–35.

LESSON X

§ 1. *On Using a Dictionary—Some Useful Dictionaries—Other Reference Books—German for Science and Technology—Story:* **100 Dollar Verloren—***Reading: Nietzsche:* **DIE FRÖHLICHE WISSENSCHAFT**

THIS Lesson is devoted chiefly to informing you how best to benefit from this Course, which provides the fundamentals of German Grammar, a very practical vocabulary, and sufficient Practice and Reading Matter to provide a good grounding for all purposes. Your problems from now onwards are: (1) to become so familiar with all that is given in this book that it may become a part of yourself—a high ideal to be achieved by constant revision; (2) to expand this knowledge for your particular requirements.

Unless you are learning German for such simple purposes as holiday travel, or to enable you to get the gist of a newspaper or magazine in German, you will have to extend your knowledge of *words*, which are the raw material of the language. And German is rich in words. Even having completed the Course to your satisfaction, it is unlikely that you will pick up a newspaper or a book without finding a number of words that you do not know. Many who have a good knowledge of German and speak it fluently are accustomed to this experience, and have or should have available the indispensable dictionary. So, the first question to be settled is: *What kind of Dictionary?* Here are some hints which you may follow in accordance with your aims:

(1) *For a beginning, Langenscheidt's Universal* (pocket) *German–English and English–German Dictionary*—published in the United States, its possessions and territories, and the Philippine Islands, by Barnes & Noble, Inc.— should serve well. But if you prefer something bigger—

(2) *For General Use*, the excellent *Dictionary of German and English and English and German*, by Max Bellows, published by Longmans, Green & Co., London, New York, Toronto. This is perhaps the best all-round small dictionary for general use. It contains a summary of grammar and of the Verbs, regular and irregular, the Metric and the British–American Systems of Weights and Measures, and has the genders of German Nouns indicated by different types. German–English and English–German run alphabetically on the same page throughout. The Bellows' Dictionary has proved its worth and can be recommended. An up-to-date edition was published in 1956.

(3) *Bigger bi-lingual dictionaries :* There are several good ones, the smallest of which is Langenscheidt's SHORTER GERMAN dictionary, also published by Barnes & Noble, Inc., New York. It is a comprehensive (35,000 entries) German-English, English-German dictionary specially adapted to American usage, and gives information about grammar, weights and measures, etc., similar to Bellows, with current abbreviations.

A good book for the desk or library is Cassell's German Dictionary (German–English and English–German), which meets most requirements. Apart from the work to which reference will be made immediately, Cassell's is as good as any other dictionary of its size.

Finally, the most comprehensive and thorough work available is the *Muret–Sanders Encyclopedic Dictionary* in two volumes : I, English–German and II, German–English. This is a superb reference work and ideal for the person who fully intends to pursue German to an advanced level. Only translators are likely to require the English–German part. The German–English contains not only all of the living language that is ever likely to be required for reading in the literature, but also thousands of technical terms, colloquialisms, and slang expressions. It is published in the United States by Barnes & Noble, Inc., New York, in a newly revised edition.

From the above, the student will make his own choice, but one thing is certain: he *must* have *a* dictionary!

GRAMMAR: Easily the best reference German grammar in English is *A Grammar of the German Language*, by George O. Curme (second edition, New York, 1952). This is a work of over 600 pages, and answers every question of grammar that is likely to arise. For the prime essentials of grammar, tersely and simply presented, Eric Greenfield's *German Grammar*, published by Barnes & Noble, Inc., is recommended as a quick review. In German for Germans is the long-standing **DUDEN** (published by Bibliographisches Institut). It is not a bad idea, having finished the present Course, to run through the **DUDEN** and keep it for reference.

OTHER REFERENCE BOOKS: Each student will have his or her hobbies and special inclinations, and a host of excellent reference books are available in German. You should make a point of reading those of interest to you. Consult a bookseller who specializes in German books. Those interested in science and technology may require one or more volumes of the excellent series of polyglot technical dictionaries published by Langenscheidt KG. Verlag, Berlin-Schöneberg, and usually available in good bookshops.

Sooner or later those students who go beyond this Course, and whose knowledge of German is fairly sound, should have access to **DER SPRACH-BROCKHAUS—Das Deutsche Bildwörterbuch für Jedermann: Wortschatz und Rechtschreibung, Herkünfte, Sprach- und Stillehre, Mundarten und Fremdwörter, über 5400 Abbildungen und Übersichten.** This book is rather like the French *Nouveau Petit Larousse Illustré*. **Der Sprach-Brockhaus** is not expensive and is highly rewarding as a thoroughly up-to-date dictionary. It has been used in the preparation of GERMAN FOR ADULTS.

WHEN YOU LOOK UP A WORD IN YOUR DICTIONARY, DO NOT BE SATISFIED WITH ITS SIMPLE MEANING. STUDY THE VARIANT MEANINGS, AND ESPECIALLY THE COMPOUND OR DERIVATIVE WORDS THAT SPRING FROM IT.

Story   **ERZÄHLUNG**

100 DOLLAR VERLOREN!

Sie sind Reporter? " fragte der Dollarmann.

„ Bei der ‚ Sun-Sun-Post ' ", sagte Harper.

„ Was wollen Sie wissen? "

Harper überlegte [1] nicht lange.

„ Eigentlich nur eins: Wie sind Sie zu Ihren Millionen gekommen? "

Der Multimillionär lächelte, musterte sein Gegenüber und sagte: „ Ich will Ihnen antworten. Ich bin Millionär geworden, weil ich 100 Dollar verloren habe."

Harper stutzte.[2]

„ Verloren? "

„ Richtig. Ich war jung wie Sie und Buchhalter bei Mils. Eines Tages drückte mir Mils eine Postanweisung [3] und 100 Dollar in die Hand. Auf dem Wege zur Post verlor ich das Geld. Meine Stellung war in Gefahr. Aber in der Not hat der Mensch die besten Ideen! Die Idee, die ich hatte, bildete den Grundstock [4] zu meinen Millionen."

„ Welche Idee? "

„ Ich inserierte,[5] ‚ Junger Mann, 20 Jahre, ohne Eltern et cetera, hat 100 Dollar verloren und ist, wenn er sie nicht zurückgeben kann, im Begriff,[6] auch seine Stellung zu verlieren. Wer hilft Aermstem ' ? "

Harper fieberte.

„ Und Sie hatten Erfolg? Sie bekamen die 100 Dollar? "

„ Hundert? Am nächsten Tag hatte ich 682 Zuschriften [7] und 1269 Dollar 40 Cent. Ich gab die Postanweisung auf, brachte Mils den Abschnitt,[8] und machte mich selbständig. Reiste kreuz und quer [9] durch die Staaten. Inserierte in allen Zeitungen. Der Erfolg riß nicht ab. Mit dem Geld, daß ich erwarb, kaufte ich eine Fabrik. So fing ich an."

„ Interessant ", sagte Harper.

*

Als der Multimillionär am Tage darauf die „ Sun-Sun-Post " aufschlug, konnte er keinen Artikel über sich finden. Statt dessen entdeckte er in den Anzeigenspalten [10] eine Annonce mit der Ueberschrift: „ 100 Dollar verloren! " Der Text war sein Text.

Harper aber saß in seinem New Yorker möblierten [11] Zimmer und wartete auf den Erfolg seines Inserates.

Am vierten Tag kam ein Brief. Und das war alles, was Harper an Zuschriften auf sein Inserat erhielt. Der Brief stammte von dem Multi-

NOTES

[1] **überlegen,** to think over
[2] **stutzen,** to be startled
[3] **die Postanweisung,** money order
[4] **der Grundstock,** foundation
[5] **inserieren,** to advertise
[6] **im Begriff sein,** to be on the point of
[7] **die Zuschrift,** written reply, letter
[8] **der Abschnitt,** coupon
[9] **kreuz und quer,** criss-cross
[10] **die Anzeigenspalte,** advertisement column
[11] **möbliert,** furnished

millionär. Er lautete folgendermaßen: „ Ich bin sicher, daß Sie
keinen Erfolg haben werden.
Denn Sie haben drei Fehler gemacht. Der erste Fehler ist, daß
Sie mit der Idee eines andern Geld
machen wollen—man muß eigene
Ideen haben! Ihr zweiter Fehler:
Sie haben nicht einkalkuliert,[12] daß
die Welt sich ständig ändert—
heutzutage gibt es keine Menschen

mit Mitleid mehr! Der dritte
Fehler aber ist der schlimmste:
Sie haben kein Talent! Sonst
hätten Sie wissen müssen, daß kein
Millionär einem Reporter verrät,
wie er zu seinem Geld gekommen
ist, und daß man durch einen Job
allein nie zu Millionen kommt!—
Man muß nämlich auch einen
Kopf haben! "

Von Manfred Thomas

From: **WOCHENEND.**

Nürnberg (1956).

Note

[12] **einkalkulieren,** to take into account

NIETZSCHE

DIE FRÖHLICHE WISSENSCHAFT

Reiz der Unvollkommenheit.—Ich sehe hier einen Dichter, der,
wie so mancher Mensch, durch seine Unvollkommenheiten einen
höheren Reiz ausübt als durch alles das, was sich unter seiner
Hand rundet und vollkommen gestaltet,—ja, er hat den Vorteil
und den Ruhm viel mehr von seinem letzten Unvermögen als
von seiner reichen Kraft. Sein Werk spricht es niemals ganz
aus, was er eigentlich aussprechen möchte, was er gesehen haben
möchte: es scheint, daß er den Vorgeschmack einer Vision
gehabt hat, und niemals sie selber:—aber eine ungeheure
Lüsternheit nach dieser Vision ist in seiner Seele zurückge-
blieben, und aus ihr nimmt er seine ebenso ungeheure Bered-
samkeit des Verlangens und Heißhungers. Mit ihr hebt er
den, welcher ihm zuhört, über sein Werk und alle „ Werke "
hinaus und gibt ihm Flügel, um so hoch zu steigen, wie Zuhörer
nie sonst steigen: und so, selber zu Dichtern und Sehern geworden, zollen sie dem Urheber ihres Glückes eine Bewunderung,
wie als ob er sie unmittelbar zum Schauen seines Heiligsten und
Letzten geführt hätte, wie als ob er sein Ziel erreicht und seine
Vision wirklich gesehen und mitgeteilt hätte. Es kommt seinem
Ruhme zugute, nicht eigentlich ans Ziel gekommen zu sein.

From: The Joyful Wisdom

TRANSLATION : Charm of Imperfection.—*I see here a poet, who, like so many men, through his imperfections exercises a higher charm than through all that he rounds off and puts perfect under his hand—yes, he has the advantage and reputation more from his ultimate inability than from his abundant strength. His work never fully expresses what he would really like to express, what he would like to have seen: it seems that (as if) he has had the foretaste of a vision and never (of) itself: but a monstrous longing towards this vision has remained back in his soul, and out of this he takes his equal(ly) monstrous eloquence of desire and ravenous hunger. With (this vision) he lifts those who listen to him above his " Work " and all " Works " and gives them wings to rise as high as hearers never hitherto rose: and thus themselves becoming poets and seers, they render (as) his due an admiration to the originator of their happiness, as if he had led them at once to the sight of his holiest and ultimate (truths), as if he had achieved his goal and truly seen and shared his vision. It is good for his renown not to have reached his goal.*

Note : Nietzsche wrote **Die Fröhliche Wissenschaft** in 1882, just before he wrote **Also sprach Zarathustra.** The latter he regarded as his best and most important work, but it is rather too difficult for the learner at this stage. Not so **Die Fröhliche Wissenschaft,** which, though one of this author's best books, is not difficult reading. Nietzsche's ideas are more difficult than his language, as the above passage shows. He writes magnificent German, and for this reason, and the fact that all his works have been published in English, his prose is worth study by the learner whose mother-tongue is English.

§ 2. *Expanding One's Knowledge of German—What to read—List of Books—Reading in Gothic Type :* **Der Rattenfänger von Hameln** (" *The Pied Piper of Hamelin* ") **von Brüder Grimm**

Your knowledge of German, of the culture, and of the German-speaking countries generally, expands with reading, personal contacts, and listening to Radio. In regard to Radio and personal contacts, no further advice need be given. Reading is another matter, and here some advice can be given. First, in order to keep abreast not only of the language but also of " what is happening " in everyday life, it is advisable to read newspapers and magazines: and do not forget that German is the language used by very differing peoples—by Austrians, Swiss, and others. Find a newsagent or a shop which specializes in German-language periodicals and make your choice. Unless you are particularly interested in some special subject, choose something different each week or month and, until you can read with ease, develop the habit of looking up unknown words in the dictionary. This is rather laborious at first ; but if you persist for a few weeks or months, it all becomes easy.

The question of what books to read must in the end depend on individual taste, but in one direction considerable help of great utility is available. Innumerable British and American authors have been translated into German, and if Somerset Maugham, Huxley, Hemingway, or Graham Greene should be your choice, you will find books by all of them in German. Try one, and have the English text to help you along. Nothing is more encouraging for the novice than, having gone through a chapter with the aid of the original, to read over the German without it. And, having finished the book in this way, to read the whole work in German from the beginning. The same applies vice versa: there are in English translations of many excellent authors who write in German. But always remember that, generally speaking, " literary " translations tend to be " free ": the translator is often content to convey the gist of a sentence or passage without too close a regard for the literal meaning of the words. Indeed, this is sometimes unavoidable because of the difference in idiom of the two languages. When you feel that you can get out of this stage, begin to read German authors without any help other than that of the dictionary. And never be dismayed if a phrase, a sentence, or a paragraph defeats you. Forge ahead, come back to it later, and you may suddenly be enlightened.

German classical literature is rewarding, and some classical authors are easy to read. Begin with the Brothers Grimm, an example of whose pure, straightforward style will be found on page 149, a famous story from their **KINDER- UND HAUS-MÄRCHEN**. Many German books survive only in Gothic and you must become accustomed to it, for which purpose the alpha-bet and examples are given. If you are intent upon reading classical German literature, it is advisable to begin with an anthology which provides examples of the style of many authors; then select the author whose works you wish to read or study. Many anthologies are available, and a good one is **DAS MEIS-TERBUCH,** Herausgegeben von Hermann Hesse: it contains extracts from about forty authors. But, however much you may wish to read the classics, do not ignore the moderns, of whom the following may be mentioned: Gottfried Keller, **Der Grüne Heinrich;** Thomas Mann, **Der Zauberberg** (*The Magic Mountain*); Franz Kafka, **Der Prozess** (*The Trial*) and other works. Many others could be mentioned, but these should suffice for a beginning, and they are all first-rate. For guidance in regard to post-Second World War writers in general, a book-seller should be consulted. Here, only the novel is considered, as likely to be of most interest. But non-fiction ought not to be ignored, and in this the choice is wide.

Eine Bibliothek im kleinen

Die Reihe »REISEN UND ABENTEUER«

Reisebücher? Reisen tut man doch heute lieber selbst, und erforscht ist doch eigentlich längst alles? Eine solche Meinung wäre allerdings reichlich falsch. Es gibt nämlich noch viele Stellen auf der Erde, die noch niemals ein Mensch gesehen oder betreten hat: die gigantischen Gebirge und Gräben in der schwarzen Nacht der Ozeane, von deren Erforschung Beebe, der selbst hinabgestoßen ist, und de Latil erzählen; oder geheimnisvolle kilometerlange Höhlen, deren dramatische Bezwin-gung Tazieff lebendig werden läßt. Doch auch von Gegenden, die als weiße Flecke auf der Landkarte längst getilgt sind, wissen Forscher und Reisende noch viel Neues, Fesselndes und Interessantes zu berichten, das mit echten Abenteuern verbunden ist: Joslin, wie er den afrikanischen Medizinmännern entkam, oder Rittlinger von seiner unglaublichen Paddelfahrt im wilden Land der Kurden.

Beebe:	Auf Entdeckungsfahrt mit Beebe
Berset:	Nöis, der Großjäger von Spitzbergen
Brustat-Naval:	Lichter über dem Meer
Earl:	Krokodil-Fieber
Ellsberg:	Stärker als das Meer
Filchner:	Bismillah
Hanssen:	Der harte Weg
Hedin:	Abenteuer in Tibet
	Durch Asiens Wüsten
Helfritz:	Im Lande der Königin von Saba
Herdemerten:	Die weiße Wüste
Joslin:	Den Medizinmännern entronnen
Landt-Lemmél:	Wal frei
de Latil:	Vom Nautilus zum Bathyskaph
Pommier:	Jenseits von Thule
Rittlinger:	Faltboot stößt vor
Scott:	Letzte Fahrt
Tazieff:	Im Zauber der Korallenriffe
Trumbull:	34 Tage ohne Hoffnung

You may wish to become acquainted with the Gothic type or Fraktur. It will be seen that most of the letters resemble ours, but attention should be paid to the Gothic small **k,** the three Gothic forms for **s,** and the double letters. Do not confuse capitals **B** and **V.** Here are the two printed alphabets:

a	b	c	d	e	f	g	h	i
𝔞	𝔅	ℭ	𝔇	𝔈	𝔉	𝔊	𝔥	𝔍
ah	bay	tsay	day	ay	eff	gay	haa	ee
Aa	Bb	Cc	Dd	Ee	Ff	Gg	Hh	Ii

j	k	l	m	n	o	p	q	r
𝔍	𝔎	𝔏	𝔐	𝔑	𝔒	𝔓	𝔔	𝔑
yot	kaa	ell	emm	enn	o	pay	koo	err
Jj	Kk	Ll	Mn	Nn	Oo	Pp	Qq	Rr

ſ, s*	t	u	v	w	x	y	z	
𝔖	𝔗	𝔘	𝔙	𝔚	𝔛	𝔜	𝔷	
ess	tay	oo	fow	vay	ix	ipsilon	tzet	
Ss	Tt	Uu	Vv	Ww	Xx	Yy	Zz	

Note these double letters:

ch	ck	ß = sz	ss	tz
ch	ck	ß = sz	ss	tz

Der Rattenfänger von Hameln

Im Jahre 1284 ließ sich zu Hameln ein wunderlicher [1] Mann sehen. Er hatte einen Rock [2] von vielfarbigem, buntem Tuch an, weshalb er Bundting soll geheißen haben, und gab sich für einen Ratten= fänger [3] aus, indem er versprach, gegen ein gewisses Geld die Stadt von allen Mäusen und Ratten zu befreien. Die Bürger wurden mit ihm einig und versicherten ihm einen bestimmten Lohn. Der Rattenfänger zog demnach ein Pfeifchen [4] heraus und pfiff; da kamen alsobald [5] die Ratten und Mäuse aus allen Häusern hervorge= krochen und sammelten sich um ihn herum. Als er nun meinte, es wäre keine zurück, ging er hinaus, und der ganze Haufen folgte ihm, und so führte er sie an die Weser; dort schürzte [6] er seine Kleider und trat in das Wasser, worauf ihm alle die Tiere folgten und hineinstürzend ertranken.

Nachdem die Bürger aber von ihrer Plage befreit waren, reute [7] sie der versprochene Lohn, und sie verweigerten ihn dem Manne unter allerlei Ausflüchten, [8] so daß er zornig und erbittert wegging. Am 26. Juni auf Johannis und Pauli Tag, morgens früh sieben Uhr, nach anderen zu Mittag, erschien er wieder, jetzt in Gestalt eines Jägers erschrecklichen Angesichts [9] mit einem roten, wunder= lichen Hut, und ließ seine Pfeife in den Gassen hören. Alsbald kamen diesmal nicht Ratten und Mäuse, sondern Kinder, Knaben und Mägdlein vom vierten Jahr an in großer Anzahl gelaufen, worunter auch die schon erwachsene Tochter des Bürgermeisters war. Der ganze Schwarm folgte ihm nach, und er führte sie hinaus in einen Berg, wo er mit ihnen verschwand. Dies hatte ein Kindermädchen gesehen, das mit einem Kind auf dem Arm von fern nachgezogen war, danach umkehrte und das Gerücht in die Stadt brachte. Die Eltern liefen haufenweis [10] vor alle Tore und suchten mit betrübtem Herzen ihre Kinder; die Mütter erhoben ein jämmerliches Schreien und Weinen. Von Stund an wurden Boten zu Wasser und Land an alle Orte herumgeschickt, zu erkundigen, [11] ob man die Kinder oder auch nur etliche [12] gesehen, aber alles vergeblich. Es waren im ganzen hundertunddreißig verloren. Zwei sollen, wie einige

Notes

[1] **wunderlich,** strange
[2] **der Rock,** coat
[3] **der Rattenfänger,** rat-catcher, (Pied Piper)
[4] **das Pfeifchen,** little flute
[5] **alsobald,** forthwith
[6] **schürzen,** to tuck up
[7] **reuen,** to rue
[8] **die Ausflucht,** pretext
[9] **das Angesicht,** countenance
[10] **haufenweis,** in heaps
[11] **erkundigen,** to find out
[12] **etliche,** several

sagen, sich verspätet haben und zurückgekommen sein, wovon aber
das eine blind, das andre stumm gewesen, also daß das blinde den
Ort nicht hat zeigen können, aber wohl erzählen, wie sie dem
Spielmann [13] gefolgt wären, das stumme aber den Ort gewiesen,
ob es gleich nichts gehört. Ein Knäblein war im Hemd mitge-
laufen und kehrte um, seinen Rock zu holen, wodurch es dem Unglück entgangen; denn als es zurückkam, waren die anderen schon
in der Grube [14] eines Hügels, die noch gezeigt wird, verschwunden.

Jakob und Wilhelm Grimm.

NOTES

[13] **der Spielmann,** player
(musician)

[14] **die Grube,** pit, cave

Script

Die Lorelei.

Ich weiß nicht, was soll es bedeuten,
Daß ich so traurig bin,
Ein Märchen aus alten Zeiten,
Das kommt mir nicht aus dem Sinn.

Die Luft ist kühl und es dunkelt,
Und ruhig fließt der Rhein;
Der Gipfel des Berges funkelt
Im Abendsonnenschein.

(See page 142 for text.)

§ 3. *Idioms—Some Examples of Idioms—Newspaper Extract:—* **Bei gelbem Licht: ANHALTEN!**—*Test*: **Prüfen Sie Ihre Intelligenz—Auflösung**

An " idiom " is an expression consisting of words used in a special sense that is not clear from their root senses, and peculiar to the language in which it is expressed. Thus, in English we say " I am right " and in German **„ Ich habe recht "**; in English " I'm thirsty ", in German **„ Ich habe Durst "**. Similarly: **Ich habe unrecht,** *I'm wrong* ; **Ich habe Hunger;** *I'm hungry.* These are idioms.

German is rich in idioms, and you have already met some of the commonest. Idioms are best learnt by everyday conversation and reading: a good dictionary provides many, and there are some large collections of these troublesome phrases, but you need not attempt to learn idioms from lists. What is given below is merely to exemplify:

Mir ist heiß, I'm hot
Mir ist kalt, I'm cold
Ich habe es eilig, I'm in a hurry
Was heißt das? What does that mean?
Wie heißen Sie? What's your name?
Ich heiße Hans Schmidt. My name's Jack Schmidt.
Was ist los? What's the matter?
Was haben Sie? What's the matter with you?
Ich glaube ja, I believe so.
Beeilen Sie sich. Hurry up.
Es paßt uns sehr gut. It suits us very well.
Ich bedaure sehr. I'm very sorry.
Danke sehr. Thanks very much.
Wie sagt man das auf deutsch? How do you say that in German?

Bei gelbem Licht: Anhalten!

Darf ich noch? Muß ich anhalten? Jeder Autofahrer stellt sich diese Fragen, wenn er an einer Kreuzung mit Lichtsignalen das gelbe Licht aufleuchten [1] sieht. Der eine tritt mit kühnem Entschluß noch einmal auf den Gashebel,[2] der andere steigt in die Bremsen,[3] daß die Reifen singen. Was ist richtig? Polizeikommissar Klewe erläutert [4] hier, was man bei gelbem Licht tun darf und wie man sich verhalten [5] muß.

An Kreuzungen oder Einmündungen [6] bedeutet gelbes Licht nach Grün: „ Kreuzung räumen ",[7] für die sich nähernden Fahrzeuge: „ Anhalten! " Es ist lange Zeit zweifelhaft gewesen, ob das gelbe Licht für den sich der Lichtsignalanlage [8] nähernden Fahrzeugführer ein unbedingtes Haltegebot [9] darstellt. Sowohl aus der Formulierung des §2 der Straßenverkehrsordnung,[10] der dem Gebot „ Halt " des roten Farbzeichens das Gebot „ Anhalten " bei gelbem Licht gegenüberstellt, als auch aus der Tatsache, daß das gelbe Farbzeichen [11] ein nur kurzes, die Förderung des flüssigen Verkehrsablaufs bezweckendes [12] Ankündigungs- und Vorbereitungszeichen sein soll, zeigen deutlich, daß damit den Fahrzeugführern nicht ein unbedingtes „ Halt " geboten werden soll. Es soll ihnen vielmehr die Möglichkeit eingeräumt [13] werden, sich in ihrem Verhalten auf das folgende, durch rotes Licht gekennzeichnete „ Haltegebot " einzustellen.[14]

Ist es dem Fahrzeugführer aber unter Berücksichtigung [15] der Fahreigenschaften des Fahrzeuges und seiner dem Verkehr angepaßten Geschwindigkeit nicht mehr möglich, rechtzeitig [16] anzuhalten, kann ihm gegenüber das gelbe Farbzeichen nur den Sinn haben, mit der nach Verkehrslage und Leistungsfähigkeit des Fahrzeuges möglichen Geschwindigkeit in die Kreuzung oder Einmündung einzufahren und diese zu überqueren.[17] Damit soll allerdings nicht gesagt werden, daß ein absichtliches Beschleunigen [18] des Fahrzeuges

NOTES

[1] **aufleuchten,** to light up
[2] **der Gashebel,** accelerator
[3] **die Bremsen,** brakes
[4] **erläutern,** to explain
[5] **sich verhalten,** to behave
[6] **die Einmündungen,** junctions
[7] **räumen,** to give room, to clear
[8] **die Lichtsignalanlage,** light signal post
[9] **das Haltegebot,** stop signal
[10] **die Straßenverkehrsordnung,** traffic regulations
[11] **das Farbzeichen,** color signal
[12] **bezweckend,** effecting
[13] **einräumen,** to concede
[14] **sich einstellen,** to adapt oneself
[15] **unter Berücksichtigung,** in consideration
[16] **rechtzeitig,** well in time
[17] **überqueren,** to cross over
[18] **das Beschleunigen,** the acceleration

beim Aufleuchten des gelben Lichtes zulässig ist, um ein sonst noch mögliches Anhalten vor der Kreuzung zu vermeiden.

Um den Fahrzeugführern die rechtzeitige Orientierung über einen bevorstehenden Lichtwechsel [19] zu ermöglichen, hat die Firma Siemens ein Schaltgerät [20] entwickelt, das kurz vor Ende der grünen Phase zusätzlich [21] das gelbe Licht einschaltet. Für etwa zwei Sekunden leuchten dann also grünes und gelbes Licht gleichzeitig.

K. W. Klewe, Polizeikommissar

NOTES

[19] **der Lichtwechsel,** change of light

[20] **das Schaltgerät,** switch box
[21] **zusätzlich,** additional

Prüfen Sie Ihre *Intelligenz*

1. **Frage (Zeit 1 Minute):** Wer sprach vor fast vierzig Jahren die historischen Worte: „ Dieser Trip wird entweder zum größten Erfolg oder auch zur größten Tragödie der Weltgeschichte "?

2. **Frage (Zeit 30 Sekunden):** Darf ein Mann die Schwester seiner Witwe heiraten?

3. **Frage (Zeit 2 Minuten):** Fritzchen beantwortet gerade eine Frage und sagt: „ Ich ist . . .",

als der eintretende Schulrat ihn mit den Worten unterbricht:

„ Das heißt, ich bin ". Fritzchen begann von neuem und wiederholte: „ Ich ist . . .". Der Schulrat wurde ärgerlich und forderte energisch die Aussage „ ich bin ". Darauf hin stotterte Fritzchen: „ Ich bin ein persönliches . . ." Können Sie ein Wort hinzufügen, durch das Fritzchen recht bekommt?

4. **Frage (Zeit 1 Minute):** Eine Papierschneidemaschine soll in einer Sekunde einen Meter Papier von einer 200-Meter-Rolle abschneiden. Die Maschine ist genau eingestellt. Dennoch stellt man fest, daß sie 199 Sekunden benötigt, um die 200 Meter aufzuteilen. Wie ist das zu verstehen?

5. **Frage (Zeit 3 Minuten):** Können Sie aus nachstehenden Sätzen ein zusammengesetztes Hauptwort finden: „ Wer wie

der erste Teil des Wortes steht,
ist zu beneiden; den zweiten
Teil will jedermann zeigen, und
wer alle beide Teile hat, wird
gemieden "?

6. **Frage** (Zeit 2 Minuten): „ Gestern, war am Montag morgen,
und morgen, ist am Freitag gestern." Welcher Tag kann es
sein?

(Auflösungen auf Seite 314)

§ 4. *German   Abbreviations: List   for   Reference—Extract:*
BUNTE WELT—
Schillers erster wichtiger Brief an Goethe

Some Common German Abbreviations

Abbreviation	*Explanation*	*English Equivalent*
Abt.	Abteilung	*department*
AG.	Aktiengesellschaft	*stock company*
Bd., Bde.	Band (⸚e)	*volume(-s)*
Bez.	Bezirk	*district*
Co.	Compagnon, Companie	*partner, company*
d.h., d.i.	das heißt, das ist	*that is*
d.J.	dieses Jahres	*(of) this year*
d.M.	dieses Monats	*(of) this month, inst.*
DM.	Deutsche Mark	*German Mark*
do.	ditto	*ditto, do.*
einschl.	einschließlich	*inclusive, incl.*
ev.	evangelisch	*Protestant*
Fa.	Firma	*firm, Messrs.*
Forts.	Fortsetzung	*continuation; contd.*
Ges.	Gesellschaft	*company*
G.m.b.H.	Gesellschaft mit be-schränkter Haftung	*limited liability company, incorporated*
Hbf.	Hauptbahnhof	*main railway station*
hrsg.	herausgegeben	*published, pubd.*
i.allg.	im allgemeinen	*in general*
i.A.	im Auftrage	*by order*
I.G.	Interessengemeinschaft	*trust, cartel*
i.J.	im Jahre	*in the year*
Inh.	Inhaber	*proprietor*
Kap.	Kapitel	*chapter*
kath.	katholisch	*(Roman) Catholic*
Kl.	Klasse	*class*
lfde. Nr.	laufende Nummer	*current number*
Lkw.	Lastkraftwagen	*lorry, truck*
M.E.Z.	mitteleuropäische Zeit	*Central European Time*

Abbreviation	*Explanation*	*English Equivalent*
Mitropa	Mitteleuropäische Schlaf- und Speisewagen AG.	*Middle European Dining and Sleeping-car Co.*
nachm.	nachmittags	*in the afternoon*
n.Chr.	nach Christus	*after Christ;* A.D.
p.Adr.	per Adresse	*care of;* c/o
Pf.	Pfennig	*pfennig, coin*
PS.	Pferdestärke(n)	*horse-power;* h.p.
P.S.	postscriptum	P.S., *postscript*
S.	Seite	*page,* p.
s.; s.o.; s.u.	siehe; siehe oben, siehe unten	*see; see above; see below*
tägl.	täglich	*daily, per day*
u.	und	*and;* &
u.a.; u.ä.	und anderes, unter anderen; und ähnliche	*and other(s), among others; and the like*
usw.	und so weiter	*and so on; et cetera;* &c.
v.	von, vom	*of*
v.Ch.	vor Christus	*before Christ;* B.C.
v.H.	vom Hundert	*a hundred per cent;* 100%
vorm.	vormittags	*in the morning;* a.m.
W.E.Z.	westeuropäische Zeit	*West European (Greenwich) Time*
z.B.	zum Beispiel	*for example*
z.Hd.	zu Händen	*to care of,* c/o
z.Zt.	zur Zeit	*for the time being*

See also page 291, for professions, titles, etc.

Prüfen Sie Ihre Intelligenz. Auflösungen der Fragen

1. Frage : Der amerikanische Präsident Wilson, als er 1919 zur Friedenskonferenz nach Europa reiste.
2. Frage: Er dürfte, aber er lebt ja nicht mehr.
3. Frage: „. . . Fürwort ".
4. Frage: Die letzten zwei Meter ergeben sich durch einen einzigen Schnitt.
5. Frage: Hochmut.
6. Frage: Mittwoch.

BUNTE WELT
NEUESTE NACHRICHTEN

400 000 Kommunisten

Auf dem Kongreß der Kommunistischen Partei Frankreichs in Le Havre wurde gestern die Zahl der eingeschriebenen Parteimitglieder mit 429 653 angegeben. Michail Suslow vom Präsidium der sowjetischen KP überbrachte [1] die Grüße der „ russischen Genossen ".

Europatrip per Flugzeugträger [2]

90 Farmer aus USA haben von der Regierung einen Flugzeugträger gechartert. Alle sind begeisterte Amateur-Piloten. „ Ich sehe gar nicht ein ", sagte der Privatpiloten-Klubpräsident, „ warum wir beim Europatrip auf unsere Privatflugzeuge verzichten [3] sollen. Schließlich und endlich wollen wir doch auch etwas sehen für unser Geld—natürlich alles von oben."

Vier Kochbücher

Eine junge Braut aus Chikago hatte kurz vor der Hochzeit sechs Bücher aus einer Bibliothek gestohlen. Vier davon waren Kochbücher. Der Richter hatte ein Einsehen [4] und ließ es mit einer Verwarnung [5] bewenden.[6]

Motorroller-Studium

15 Sowjettechniker trafen gestern in Mailand ein. Sie wollen die Massenherstellung von Lambretta-Motorrollern [7] kennenlernen.

Chruschtschew im Ural

Sowjetparteisekretär Chruschtschew ist nach Swerdlowsk (Ural) geflogen. Er will sich bei einer Konferenz der Landarbeiter umsehen. Das meldete gestern Radio Moskau.

Sehnsucht nach dem Süden

Italien ist 1955 von 10 768 018 Ausländern besucht worden—eine Rekordziffer in der Geschichte des Landes. Deutschland stellte mit über 2,3 Millionen den größten Anteil der Italien-Besucher.

Bier-Demokraten

Bürgermeister Brummer von Koppenbach (Bayern) kennt seine Pappenheimer. Er wollte eine Bürgerversammlung abhalten und dabei die Einrichtungen der Demokratie plausibel machen. Damit es recht voll werde, ließ Brummer verkünden: „ Nach der Versammlung gibt es Freibier." [8] Alle, alle kamen.

Notes

[1] **überbringen,** to deliver
[2] **der Flugzeugträger,** aircraft carrier
[3] **verzichten auf,** to forego something
[4] **das Einsehen,** understanding
[5] **die Verwarnung,** warning
[6] **bewenden lassen,** to acquiesce
[7] **der Motorroller,** motorscooter
[8] **das Freibier,** free beer

Schillers erster wichtiger Brief an Goethe

Jena, den 23. Aug. 94

Man brachte mir gestern die angenehme Nachricht, daß Sie von Ihrer Reise wieder zurückgekommen seien. Wir haben also wieder Hoffnung, Sie vielleicht bald einmal bei uns zu sehen, welches ich an meinem Teil herzlich wünsche. Die neulichen[1] Unterhaltungen mit Ihnen haben meine ganze Ideenmasse in Bewegung gebracht, denn sie betrafen einen Gegenstand, der mich seit etlichen[2] Jahren lebhaft beschäftigt. Über so manches, worüber ich mit mir selbst nicht recht einig werden konnte, hat die Anschauung[3] Ihres Geistes (denn so muß ich den Totaleindruck[4] Ihrer Ideen auf mich nennen) ein unerwartetes Licht in mir angesteckt. Mir fehlte das Objekt, der Körper, zu mehreren spekulativen Ideen, und Sie brachten mich auf die Spur davon. Ihr beobachtender Blick, der so still und rein auf den Dingen ruht, setzt Sie nie in Gefahr, auf den Abweg zu geraten,[5] in den sowohl die Spekulation als die willkürliche und bloß sich selbst gehorchende Einbildungskraft[6] sich so leicht verirrt.[7] In Ihrer richtigen Intuition liegt alles und weit vollständiger, was die Analysis mühsam sucht, und nur weil es als ein Ganzes in Ihnen liegt, ist Ihnen Ihr eigener Reichtum verborgen; denn leider wissen wir nur das, was wir scheiden.[8] Geister Ihrer Art wissen daher selten, wie weit sie gedrungen[9] sind, und wie wenig Ursache sie haben, von der Philosophie zu borgen,[10] die nur von ihnen lernen kann. Diese kann bloß zergliedern, was ihr gegeben wird, aber das Geben selbst ist nicht Sache des Analytikers, sondern des Genies,[11] welches unter dem dunkeln, aber sicheren Einfluß reiner Vernunft nach objektiven Gesetzen verbindet.

NOTES

[1] **neulich,** recent
[2] **etliche,** several
[3] **die Anschauung,** perception
[4] **der Totaleindruck,** total impression
[5] **auf den Abweg geraten,** to get on the wrong track
[6] **die Einbildungskraft,** power of imagination
[7] **sich verirren,** to err, go astray
[8] **scheiden,** to analyse
[9] **dringen,** to penetrate
[10] **borgen,** to borrow
[11] **das Genie,** genius

§ 5. *Thinking in German:* KREUZWORT-RÄTSEL—LÖSUNGEN — *Alphabetical List of Strong and Irregular Verbs*

You have already had two tests of your ability to think in German: the QUIZ on pages 287, 295, and **die Prüfung** on page 312. Now you may try something more difficult: a cross-word puzzle (**ein Kreuzwort**). If you are not much good at cross-words in English, do not expect a good result in this test. But try it, nevertheless. In all these tests in German, the foreigner is handicapped by a lack of some knowledge which the average adult German would have. This is not to say that you may forthwith conclude that it is a waste of time to test yourself with them. Do your best, and, if you don't succeed, try again later. *These tests compel you to think in German,* and that is their value, whatever the results. The solution of this **Kreuzwort** will be found on page 319, and also that of the " Riddle ".

KREUZWORT

Waagerecht: 1 Gang im Bergwerk, 5 Baumteil, 7 Entgegnung, 11 verwesende Tierleiche, 12 Tabakliebhaber, 15 starkes Seil, 16 Beförderungsmittel, 18 Singstimme, 20 akadem. Titel (Abk.),[1] 21 Einsteins Werk, 22 Zeitmesser, 23 häufig, 24 Höhenzug in Braunschweig, 26 Teil des Rundfunkgerätes, 28 Waldgott, 29 Pensionär, 30 Zahl, 31 leichte Fußbekleidung.

Senkrecht: 1 urweltl. Kriechtier, 2 Liste, 3 Zeichen für Osmium, 4 hier siegte Friedrich d. Große 1757, 5 feuchte Niederung, 6 Gesamtheit der Kopfknochen, 7 Flächenmaß, 8 Fernsprecher, 9 rücksichtslos, 10 frz. Feldherr (1611–75), 13 Erdteil, 14 Metall, 16 Tierbehausung, 17 engl. Adelstitel, 18 finn. Schriftsteller (1861–1921), 19 leblos, 25 Zeichen für Mangan, 27 persönl. Fürwort. (ä = ein Buchstabe.)

[1] **Abk.** = **Abkürzung,** *abbreviation.*

RÄTSEL

Strom und Klang

In Nehrus Heimat rausche ich dahin,
Am Ufer herrliche Tempel stehen,
Heilig den Bewohnern ich bin,
Die Rettung in mir sehen.

Willst du sinnig nun vertauschen
Meiner Zeichen äußeren Rang,
So erstirbt der Wogen Rauschen
Und du lauschest anderm Klang.

Ob er tiefempfunden quillt,
Leise wie ein fromm' Gebet,
Ob er voll und mächtig schwillt,
Wie des Sturmes Brausen weht.

[Lösung auf Seite 319.]

Schaum aus allen Ecken

15jähriger wollte ein Flugzeug stehlen

Eigener Bericht

r. st. Hannover, 21. Juli

Aus „ Lust am Stehlen " beging der 15jährige Günther K. aus Hannover innerhalb kurzer Zeit 206 Einbrüche, Diebstähle und andere Straftaten. Günther, Sohn begüterter [1] und angesehener Eltern, fühlte sich zu Hause zu wenig beachtet [2] und führte die Einbrüche, wie der Leiter der einzigen in der Bundesrepublik bestehenden „ Jugendschutz-Dienststelle" [3] der Polizei in Hannover, Kurt Köhler, mitteilte, nur aus, um sich in seinem jugendlichen Tatendrang [4] irgendwie betätigen zu können.

Während Günther K.'s Eltern dachten, ihr Sohn schliefe, kletterte er aus dem dritten Stock an der Dachrinne [5] in die Tiefe und ging auf Diebesfahrt. Vor Morgengrauen [6] kam er auf die gleiche Weise wieder in sein Zimmer zurück, ohne daß jemand etwas merkte. Günther stahl alles, was ihm in die Hände kam. Er verschenkte den größten Teil seiner Beute oder tauschte sie bei Freunden ein.

Als er einmal auf dem Messegelände [7] ein Schweizer Sportflugzeug entdeckte, stieg er unbemerkt in den Pilotensitz und versuchte den Motor zu starten. Er verwechselte aber den Anlasser [8] mit der Feuerlöschanlage [9] und wurde innerhalb kürzester Zeit völlig in Schaum [10] eingehüllt. Polizeibeamte in der Nähe wurden aufmerksam und nahmen den Jungen fest.[11]

NOTES

[1] **begütert,** well-to-do.
[2] **beachtet,** taken notice of
[3] **Jugendschutz-Dienststelle,** Youth Protection Office
[4] **der Tatendrang,** eagerness to do deeds
[5] **die Dachrinne,** gutter (on roof)
[6] **das Morgengrauen,** dawn
[7] **das Messegelände,** exhibition ground
[8] **der Anlasser,** starter
[9] **die Feuerlöschanlage,** fire extinction apparatus
[10] **der Schaum,** foam
[11] **festnehmen,** to arrest

Kreuzwort : Lösung

Rätsel: Lösung

GANGES — GESANG

ALPHABETICAL LIST OF STRONG AND IRREGULAR VERBS

Those marked with one asterisk * are conjugated with SEIN.
Those with two asterisks ** take either SEIN or HABEN.
HEAVY TYPE indicates the most important.

Note: This list is comprehensive, and therefore includes some uncommon Verbs not given in either the lists in Lessons VI and VII or in the Vocabulary at the end. It is essentially a Reference List which should continue to be useful after the Course has been completed. The First and Third Persons Singular of the Present Tense in the last column should be noted. The Second Person Singular, with **-S** before the **-T**, is usually the same as the Third but is seldom required.

Infinitive	Imperfect	Past Participle	First and Third Singular Present Indicative
backen, *to bake*	backte (buk)	gebacken	ich backe, er backt *or* bäckt
befehlen, *to command*	befahl	befohlen	ich befehle, er befiehlt
befleißen (sich), *to endeavour*	befliß	beflissen	ich befleiße mich, er befleißt sich
beginnen, *to begin*	begann	begonnen	ich beginne, er beginnt
beißen, *to bite*	biß	gebissen	ich beiße, er beißt
bergen, *to hide, salvage*	barg	geborgen	ich berge, er birgt
*bersten, *to burst*	barst	geborsten	ich berste, er birst *or* berstet
besinnen (sich), *to reflect*	besann	besonnen	ich besinne mich, er besinnt sich
besitzen, *to possess*	besaß	besessen	ich besitze, er besitzt
betrügen,[1] *to deceive*	betrog	betrogen	ich betrüge, er betrügt
bewegen,[1] *to induce*	bewog	bewogen	ich bewege, er bewegt
biegen, *to bend*	bog	gebogen	ich biege, er biegt
bieten, *to bid, offer*	bot	geboten	ich biete, er bietet
binden, *to bind*	band	gebunden	ich binde, er bindet
bitten, *to ask, beg, request*	bat	gebeten	ich bitte, er bittet
blasen, *to blow*	blies	geblasen	ich blase, er bläst
*bleiben, *to remain*	blieb	geblieben	ich bleibe, er bleibt
braten, *to fry or roast*	briet	gebraten	ich brate, er brät *or* bratet
brechen, *to break*	brach	gebrochen	ich breche, er bricht
brennen, *to burn*	brannte	gebrannt	ich brenne, er brennt
bringen, *to bring*	brachte	gebracht	ich bringe, er bringt

Infinitive	Preterite	Past Participle	Present
denken, to think	dachte	gedacht	ich denke, er denkt
dingen,[2] to engage, hire	dang	gedungen	ich dinge, er dingt
dreschen, to thrash	drosch	gedroschen	ich dresche, er drischt
dringen, to press	drang	gedrungen	ich dringe, er dringt
dünken,[3] to seem	deuchte	gedeucht	es dünkt (deucht) mir or mich
dürfen, to be allowed	durfte	gedurft	ich darf, er darf
empfangen, to receive	empfing	empfangen	ich empfange, er empfängt
empfehlen, to recommend	empfahl	empfohlen	ich empfehle, er empfiehlt
empfinden, to feel	empfand	empfunden	ich empfinde, er empfindet
*erbleichen,[4] to turn pale	erblich	erblichen	ich erbleiche, er erbleicht
entrinnen, to escape	entrann	entronnen	ich entrinne, er entrinnt
erküren, to elect	erkor	erkoren	ich erküre, er erkürt
*erlöschen, to die out	erlosch	erloschen	ich erlösche, er erlischt
erschallen,[5] to resound	erscholl	erschollen	ich erschalle, er erschallt
erschrecken, to frighten	erschrak	erschrocken	ich erschrecke, er erschrickt
essen, to eat	aß	gegessen	ich esse, er ißt
**fahren, to ride (in a vehicle)	fuhr	gefahren	ich fahre, er fährt
*fallen, to fall	fiel	gefallen	ich falle, er fällt
fangen, to catch	fing	gefangen	ich fange, er fängt
fechten, to fight, fence	focht	gefochten	ich fechte, er ficht (fechtet)
finden, to find	fand	gefunden	ich finde, er findet
flechten, to plait	flocht	geflochten	ich flechte, er flicht or flechtet
*fliegen, to fly	flog	geflogen	ich fliege, er fliegt
*fliehen, to flee	floh	geflohen	ich fliehe, er flieht
*fließen, to flow	floß	geflossen	ich fließe, er fließt
fressen, to eat (of animals)	fraß	gefressen	ich fresse, er frißt
frieren, to freeze	fror	gefroren	ich friere, er friert
gären, to ferment	gor	gegoren	ich gäre, er gärt
gebären, to bear (child)	gebar	geboren	ich gebäre, sie gebärt (gebiert)
geben, to give	gab	gegeben	ich gebe, er gibt
*gedeihen, to thrive	gedieh	gediehen	ich gedeihe, er gedeiht

¹ Also: bewegen, bewegte, bewegt, to move.
² Also: dingen, dingte, gedingt.
³ Also: dünken, dünkte, gedünkt.
⁴ Also: erbleichen, erbleichte, erbleicht.
⁵ Also: erschallen, erschallte, erschallt.

Infinitive	Imperfect	Past Participle	First and Third Singular Present Indicative
gefallen, *to please*	gefiel	gefallen	ich gefalle, er gefällt
*gehen, to go	ging	gegangen	ich gehe, er geht
*gelingen, *to succeed*	gelang	gelungen	es gelingt
gelten, *to be valid, worth*	galt	gegolten	ich gelte, er gilt
*genesen, *to convalesce*	genas	genesen	ich genese, er genest
genießen, *to enjoy, eat*	genoß	genossen	ich genieße, er genießt
*geraten, *to turn out well*	geriet	geraten	ich gerate, er gerät
*geschehen, *to happen*	geschah	geschehen	ich geschehe, er geschieht
gewinnen, *to win*	gewann	gewonnen	ich gewinne, er gewinnt
gießen, *to gush, pour*	goß	gegossen	ich gieße, er gießt
gleichen, *to resemble*	glich	geglichen	ich gleiche, er gleicht
*gleiten, *to glide*	glitt	geglitten	ich gleite, er gleitet
glimmen, *to glimmer*	glomm	geglommen	ich glimme, er glimmt
graben, *to dig*	grub	gegraben	ich grabe, er gräbt
greifen, *to grasp*	griff	gegriffen	ich greife, er greift
haben, *to have*	hatte	gehabt	ich habe, er hat
halten, *to hold*	hielt	gehalten	ich halte, er hält
hangen,[1] *to be hanging*	hing	gehangen	ich hänge, er hängt
hauen, *to hew, cut*	hieb	gehauen	ich haue, er haut
heben, *to lift*	hob	gehoben	ich hebe, er hebt
heißen, *to be named, order*	hieß	geheißen	ich heiße, er heißt
helfen, *to help*	half	geholfen	ich helfe, er hilft
kennen, *to know*	kannte	gekannt	ich kenne, er kennt
*klimmen, *to climb*	klomm	geklommen	ich klimme, er klimmt
klingen, *to sound, ring*	klang	geklungen	ich klinge, er klingt
kneifen, *to pinch*	kniff	gekniffen	ich kneife, er kneift
*kommen, *to come*	kam	gekommen	ich komme, er kommt
*können, *to be able, can*	konnte	gekonnt	ich kann, er kann
*kriechen, *to creep*	kroch	gekrochen	ich krieche, er kriecht
laden, *to load*	lud	geladen	ich lade, er lädt *or* ladet
lassen, *to let, leave*	ließ	gelassen	ich lasse, er läßt
*laufen, *to run*	lief	gelaufen	ich laufe, er läuft
leiden, *to suffer*	litt	gelitten	ich leide, er leidet

leihen, *to lend*	lieh	geliehen	ich leihe, er leiht
lesen, *to read*	las	gelesen	ich lese, er liest
liegen, *to lie (situation)*	lag	gelegen	ich liege, er liegt
lügen, *to tell a lie*	log	gelogen	ich lüge, er lügt
mahlen, *to grind*	mahlte	gemahlen	ich mahle, er mahlt
meiden, *to shun*	mied	gemieden	ich meide, er meidet
melken, *to milk*	melkte, molk	gemolken	ich melke, er melkt
messen, *to measure*	maß	gemessen	ich messe, er mißt
mögen, *to like to*	mochte	gemocht	ich mag, er mag
müssen, *to be obliged to*	mußte	gemußt	ich muß, er muß
nehmen, *to take*	nahm	genommen	ich nehme, er nimmt
nennen, *to name*	nannte	genannt	ich nenne, er nennt
pfeifen, *to whistle*	pfiff	gepfiffen	ich pfeife, er pfeift
pflegen,² *to be in the habit of*	pflog	gepflogen	ich pflege, er pflegt
preisen, *to extol*	pries	gepriesen	ich preise, er preist
quellen, *to spring, gush from*	quoll	gequollen	ich quelle, er quillt
raten, *to counsel*	riet	geraten	ich rate, er rät (ratet)
reiben, *to rub*	rieb	gerieben	ich reibe, er reibt
reißen, *to tear*	riß	gerissen	ich reiße, er reißt
reiten, *to ride (a horse)*	ritt	geritten	ich reite, er reitet
*rennen, *to run, race*	rannte	gerannt	ich renne, er rennt
riechen, *to smell*	roch	gerochen	ich rieche, er riecht
ringen, *to wrestle*	rang	gerungen	ich ringe, er ringt
rinnen, *to flow, leak*	rann	geronnen	ich rinne, er rinnt
rufen, *to call, shout*	rief	gerufen	ich rufe, er ruft
salzen, *to salt*	salzte	gesalzen	ich salze, er salzt
saufen, *to swill*	soff	gesoffen	ich saufe, er säuft
saugen, *to suck*	saugte (sog)	gesaugt (gesogen)	ich sauge, er saugt
schaffen,³ *to create*	schuf	geschaffen	ich schaffe, er schafft
scheiden, *to separate*	schied	geschieden	ich scheide, er scheidet
scheinen, *to seem, shine*	schien	geschienen	ich scheine, er scheint

¹ *Note:* **hängen, hängte, gehängt,** to hang something.   ³ *Also:* **schaffen, schaffte, geschafft,** to work.

² *Also:* **pflegen, pflegte, gepflegt,** to nurse.

Infinitive	Imperfect	Past Participle	First and Third Singular Present Indicative
schelten, to scold	schalt	gescholten	ich schelte, er schilt
scheren, to shear	schor	geschoren	ich schere, er schert (schiert)
schieben, to push, shove	schob	geschoben	ich schiebe, er schiebt
schießen, to shoot	schoß	geschossen	ich schieße, er schießt
schinden, to flay	schund	geschunden	ich schinde, er schindet
schlafen, to sleep	schlief	geschlafen	ich schlafe, er schläft
schlagen, to beat, strike	schlug	geschlagen	ich schlage, er schlägt
*schleichen, to slink, sneak	schlich	geschlichen	ich schleiche, er schleicht
schleifen, to sharpen	schliff	geschliffen	ich schleife, er schleift
schleißen, to slit	schliß	geschlissen	ich schleiße, er schleißt
schließen, to lock, shut	schloß	geschlossen	ich schließe, er schließt
schlingen, to wind, twist	schlang	geschlungen	ich schlinge, er schlingt
schmeißen, to fling, "chuck"	schmiß	geschmissen	ich schmeiße, er schmeißt
schmelzen, to melt	schmolz	geschmolzen	ich schmelze, er schmilzt
schnauben, to snort	schnaubte (schnob)	geschnaubt (geschnoben)	ich schnaube, er schnaubt
schneiden, to cut	schnitt	geschnitten	ich schneide, er schneidet
schrauben, to screw	schraubte (schrob)	geschraubt (geschroben)	ich schraube, er schraubt
schreiben, to write	schrieb	geschrieben	ich schreibe, er schreibt
schreien, to scream, shout	schrie	geschrieen	ich schreie, er schreit
*schreiten, to stride	schritt	geschritten	ich schreite, er schreitet
schweigen, to be silent	schwieg	geschwiegen	ich schweige, er schweigt
*schwellen, to swell	schwoll	geschwollen	ich schwelle, er schwillt
**schwimmen, to swim	schwamm	geschwommen	ich schwimme, er schwimmt
schwinden, to shrink, dwindle	schwand	geschwunden	ich schwinde, er schwindet
schwingen, to swing	schwang	geschwungen	ich schwinge, er schwingt
schwören, to swear	schwor	geschworen	ich schwöre, er schwört
sehen, to see	sah	gesehen	ich sehe, er sieht
*sein, to be	war	gewesen	ich bin, er ist; wir, sie sind
senden, to send	sandte (sendete)	gesandt (gesendet)	ich sende, er sendet
sieden,[1] to boil	sott	gesotten	ich siede, er siedet
singen, to sing	sang	gesungen	ich singe, er singt
*sinken, to sink	sank	gesunken	ich sinke, er sinkt
sinnen, to ponder	sann	gesonnen	ich sinne, er sinnt

**sitzen, *to sit*	saß	gesessen	ich sitze, er sitzt
sollen, *ought to*	sollte	gesollt	ich soll, er soll
spalten, *to split*	spaltete	gespalten	ich spalte, er spaltet
speien, *to spit*	spie	gespieen	ich speie, er speit
spinnen, *to spin*	spann	gesponnen	ich spinne, er spinnt
spleißen, *to split*	spliß	gesplissen	ich spleiße, er spleißt
sprechen, *to speak*	sprach	gesprochen	ich spreche, er spricht
*sprießen, *to sprout*	sproß	gesprossen	ich sprieße, er sprießt
*springen, *to spring, leap*	sprang	gesprungen	ich springe, er springt
stechen, *to sting, stab*	stach	gestochen	ich steche, er sticht
stecken, *to stick*	stak, steckte	gesteckt	ich stecke, er steckt
**stehen, *to stand*	stand	gestanden	ich stehe, er steht
stehlen, *to steal*	stahl	gestohlen	ich stehle, er stiehlt
*steigen, *to ascend*	stieg	gestiegen	ich steige, er steigt
*sterben, *to die*	starb	gestorben	ich sterbe, er stirbt
*stieben, *to scatter*	stob	gestoben	ich stiebe, er stiebt
stinken, *to stink*	stank	gestunken	ich stinke, er stinkt
stoßen, *to push*	stieß	gestoßen	ich stoße, er stößt
streichen, *to pass, sweep through*	strich	gestrichen	ich streiche, er streicht
streiten, *to dispute*	stritt	gestritten	ich streite, er streitet
tragen, *to carry, wear*	trug	getragen	ich trage, er trägt
treffen, *to hit, meet*	traf	getroffen	ich treffe, er trifft
treiben, *to drive*	trieb	getrieben	ich treibe, er treibt
treten, *to tread, step*	trat	getreten	ich trete, er tritt
triefen,² *to trickle*	troff	getroffen	ich triefe, er trieft
trinken, *to drink*	trank	getrunken	ich trinke, er trinkt
trügen, *to deceive*	trog	getrogen	ich trüge, er trügt
tun, *to do*	tat	getan	ich tue, er tut
verbergen, *to conceal*	verbarg	verborgen	ich verberge, er verbirgt
verbieten, *to forbid*	verbot	verboten	ich verbiete, er verbietet
verderben, *to spoil*	verdarb	verdorben	ich verderbe, er verdirbt
verdrießen, *to vex*	verdroß	verdrossen	ich verdrieße, er verdrießt

¹ Also: sieden, siedete, gesiedet, to simmer.   ² Also: triefte, getrieft.

Infinitive	Imperfect	Past Participle	First and Third Singular Present Indicative
vergessen, to forget	vergaß	vergessen	ich vergesse, er vergißt
verlieren, to lose	verlor	verloren	ich verliere, er verliert
verzeihen, to forgive	verzieh	verziehen	ich verzeihe, er verzeiht
***wachsen**, to grow	wuchs	gewachsen	ich wachse, er wächst
wägen, to weigh, ponder	wog	gewogen	ich wäge, er wägt
waschen, to wash	wusch	gewaschen	ich wasche, er wäscht
weben,[1] to weave	wob	gewoben	ich webe, er webt
***weichen**, to yield	wich	gewichen	ich weiche, er weicht
weisen, to show	wies	gewiesen	ich weise, er weist
wenden,[2] to turn	wandte	gewandt	ich wende, er wendet
werben, to woo, enlist	warb	geworben	ich werbe, er wirbt
***werden**, to become	wurde (ward)	geworden	ich werde, er wird
werfen, to throw	warf	geworfen	ich werfe, er wirft
wiegen,[3] to weigh	wog	gewogen	ich wiege, er wiegt
winden, to wind	wand	gewunden	ich winde, er windet
wissen, to know	wußte	gewußt	ich weiß, er weiß
wollen, to want to	wollte	gewollt	ich will, er will
zeihen, to accuse	zieh	geziehen	ich zeihe, er zeiht
ziehen, to draw, pull	zog	gezogen	ich ziehe, er zieht
zwingen, to force, compel	zwang	gezwungen	ich zwinge, er zwingt

[1] *Also:* webte, gewebt.

[2] *Also:* wendete, gewendet. When Weak, means *to apply to.*

[3] *Also:* wiegte, gewiegt. When Weak, means *to rock, a cradle or a baby.*

"ALL PURPOSES" VOCABULARY

This list contains about 3,000 "basic" words useful for everyday purposes and for making many compound words. Some of the latter are not given in the main text of the book. It omits the more unusual Strong or Irregular Verbs given on pages 320-326; also numerals on page 66, and all but a few of the geographical names and adjectives on pages 82-3.

A

ab, off, away
abbrechen, to break off
der Abend, evening
abends, in the evening
das Abendessen, evening meal
das Abenteuer, adventure
aber, but
abfahren, to leave, set out
die Abfahrt, departure
abgeben, to give away (also, to register luggage)
abgehen, to go away
der Abgang, departure
abhängen (von), to depend (on)
abhelfen (*dat.*), to remedy
abholen, to fetch
abnehmen, to take from, decrease
der Abort, lavatory
die Abreise, setting out, leaving
abreisen, to leave (on a journey)
Abschied nehmen, to take leave
die Absicht, intention
die Abstimmung, vote, ballot
das Abteil, compartment, section, department
abwesend, absent
das Abzeichen, badge
achten, to respect, esteem
achten (auf), to mind, heed
die Achtung, attention, respect
die Adresse, address

der Affe, ape, monkey
ahnen, to suspect
ähnlich, like, similar
die Ähnlichkeit, similarity, resemblance
die Ahnung, foreboding, misgiving
all(-e), all
allein, alone
allerbeste, best of all
allerdings, of course, surely
allerlei, all kinds of
allgemein, general
als, when, as, than
also, thus, therefore, so
alt, old
das Alter, old age
die Ameise, ant
das Amt, office
amüsieren, to amuse
an, at, on
der Anblick, view, sight
andere (der, die, das), other
anderswo, elsewhere
anderthalb, one and a half
anerkennen, to acknowledge
der Anfang, beginning
anfangen, to begin
angenehm, pleasant
das Angesicht, face, countenance
der Angestellte, clerk, employee
angreifen, to attack
der Angriff, attack
die Angst, anxiety, fear, torment
ängstlich, anxious
anhalten, to stop at
anklagen, to accuse

die **Anklage,** accusation
ankommen, to arrive at
die **Ankunft,** arrival
der **Anlaß,** occasion
die **Anmut,** grace
anmutig, graceful
annehmen, to assume, accept
der **Anruf,** phone call
ansagen, to announce
der **Ansager,** announcer (radio)
anschauen, to look at
der **Anschluß,** junction, connection, union
ansehen, to look at
die **Ansicht,** view
der **Anspruch,** title, claim (to)
anstatt, instead of
anstellen, to appoint
der **Anteil,** share
die **Antenne,** aerial
die **Antwort,** answer
antworten, to answer
anwesend, present at
anziehen, to put on (clothes), attract
anziehen (sich), to dress oneself
der **Anzug,** suit, costume
anzünden, to light
der **Apfel,** apple
die **Apotheke,** chemist's, druggist's
der **Apotheker,** chemist, pharmacist
der **Apparat,** apparatus (radio, etc.)
die **Arbeit,** work
arbeiten, to work
der **Ärger,** annoyance
ärgerlich, annoying
ärgern (sich), to be vexed
arm, poor
der **Arm,** arm
die **Armbanduhr,** wrist watch
die **Armee,** army
die **Art,** kind, sort, species
artig, good, well-behaved
der **Artikel,** article
der **Arzt,** physician
der **Aschenbecher,** ashtray
das **Aspirin,** aspirin
der **Ast,** branch

der **Atem,** breath
atmen, to breathe
das **Atom,** atom
auch, also
auf, on, upon
der **Aufbau,** building on, superstructure, composition
der **Aufenthalt,** sojourn, stay
die **Aufgabe,** exercise, task
aufgehen, to rise (of the sun)
aufhalten (sich), to stay, sojourn
aufhören, to cease, stop
aufkleben, to affix
aufmachen, to open
aufmerksam, attentive
die **Aufmerksamkeit,** attention
aufrecht, erect, upright
aufregen, to excite
die **Aufregung,** excitement
aufrichtig, upright, honest
aufstehen, to rise
der **Auftrag,** order
aufziehen, to wind up (a watch)
der **Aufzug,** lift, elevator
das **Auge,** eye
der **Augenblick,** moment
aus, out (of)
ausbessern, to repair
ausbrechen, to break out
der **Ausbruch,** eruption
der **Ausdruck,** expression
ausdrücken, to express, utter
der **Ausflug,** outing, picnic
ausführen, to execute, carry out
der **Ausgang,** exit
ausgehen, to go out (for a walk)
ausgezeichnet, splendid, excellent
ausgleiten, to slip, slide
die **Auskunft,** information, news
Ausland (im), abroad (to be)
Ausland (ins), abroad (to go)
ausländisch, foreign
auslöschen, to extinguish
die **Ausnahme,** exception
ausruhen, to rest
die **Aussicht,** view, prospect
die **Aussprache,** pronunciation

aussprechen, to pronounce
die Ausstellung, exhibition
die Auswahl, choice, selection
der Auswanderer, emigrant
auswendig, by heart
das Auto, motor car
die Autobahn, super highway
der Autobus, motor omnibus
der Autofahrer, driver
außen, outside of (*adv.*)
außer (*dat.*), without, except

B

der Bach, stream, river
backen, to bake
der Bäcker, baker
das Bad, bath
baden, to bathe
der Bahnhof, station
der Bahnsteig, platform
bald, soon
der Ball, ball, dance
der Band, volume
das Band, ribbon
die Bank, bank, bench, seat
die Bar, bar (drinking)
der Bär, bear
der Baron, Baron
der Bart, beard
bauen, to build
der Bauer, farmer, peasant
die Bäuerin, farmer's wife
der Baum, tree
die Baumwolle, cotton
beabsichtigen, to intend
beantragen, to propose
beantworten, to answer
beauftragen, to order
der Becher, cup, beaker
bedauern, to regret, pity
das Bedauern, regret, pity
bedecken, to cover
bedeuten, to mean, signify
bedienen, to serve
bedienen (sich), to make use of
die Bedienung, service
die Bedingung, condition, stipulation
bedürfen, to need, require

beeilen (sich), to hasten, hurry
beeinflussen, to influence
beenden, to finish
befähigen, to enable
befehlen (*dat.*), to command, order
befinden (sich), to be (of health)
befördern, to promote, further
befreien, to release
begabt, gifted
begegnen (*dat.*), to meet
begeistert, enthusiastic
beginnen, to begin
begleiten, to accompany
die Begleitung, accompaniment
begraben, to bury
das Begräbnis, burial
begreifen, to comprehend, grasp
der Begriff, idea
begründen, to found, establish
begrüßen, to greet
behalten, to keep
bei, at, near
beide, both, the two
das Bein, leg
beißen, to bite
das Beispiel, example
zum Beispiel, for example
beistimmen (*dat.*), to agree
der Beitrag, contribution
bekannt, well-known
der, die Bekannte, acquaintance
beklagen (sich), to complain
bekommen, to get, receive, obtain
beleidigen, to offend
die Beleidigung, offence
beleuchten, to illuminate, light
beliebt, beloved, popular
belohnen, to reward
die Belohnung, reward
belustigen (sich), to amuse oneself
bemitleiden, to pity
bemühen (sich), to trouble, endeavour

das **Bemühen,** endeavour, trouble
das **Benzin,** gasoline
beobachten, to watch
bequem, comfortable
bereden, to persuade
bereit, ready, prepared
bereiten, to prepare
bereits, already
der **Berg,** mountain
bergab, downhill
bergauf, uphill
der **Bericht,** report
berichten, to report
der **Beruf,** profession
beruhigen, to calm
berühmt, famous, celebrated
beschädigen, to damage
der **Bescheid,** information
bescheiden, modest
beschließen, to decide
der **Beschluß,** resolution
beschreiben, to describe
die **Beschreibung,** description
besehen, to see, look at
besetzen, to occupy (a place)
besinnen (sich), to reflect, remember
der **Besitz,** possession, property
besitzen, to possess
der **Besitzer,** owner, proprietor
besonder(s), special(ly)
besorgen, to take care of
die **Besorgnis,** care, anxiety
besprechen, to review
besser, better
bestäubt, dusty
beste (der, die, das), best
bestehen (auf *acc.***),** to insist (on)
bestehen (aus), to consist (of)
bestellen, to order
bestimmt, definite, intended
bestrafen, to punish
der **Besuch,** visit
besuchen, to visit, pay a visit
beten, to pray, say one's prayer(s)
der **Beton,** concrete
der **Betrag,** amount
betragen (sich), to behave oneself
das **Betragen,** behaviour

der **Betrieb,** traffic, the works
betrinken (sich), to get drunk
der **Betrug,** fraud
betrügen, to deceive
das **Bett,** bed
die **Bettdecke,** blanket
betteln, to beg (for alms)
der **Bettler,** beggar
das **Bettuch,** sheet (bed)
beurteilen, to judge
bevor, before
bewachen, to guard, watch
bewaffnen, to arm
bewegen, to move, stir
die **Bewegung,** movement
der **Beweis,** proof
beweisen, to prove
bewerben (sich . . . um), to apply (for)
bewohnen, to inhabit
der **Bewohner,** inhabitant
bewundern, to admire
die **Bewunderung,** admiration
bezahlen, to pay
die **Bezahlung,** payment
bezaubern, to bewitch
der **Bezirk,** district
die **Bibel,** Bible
die **Bibliothek,** library
biegen, to bend
biegsam, flexible
die **Biene,** bee
das **Bier,** beer
bieten, to offer
das **Bild,** picture
die **Bildung,** education, formation
billig, cheap, fair
binden, to bind, tie
die **Birne,** pear; bulb (electric)
bis, till, until
ein bißchen, a little, a bit
der **Bischof,** bishop
die **Bitte,** request
bitte, please
bitten (um), to request, ask (for)
bitter, bitter
blasen, to blow
blaß, pale
das **Blatt,** leaf (newspaper)
blau, blue
das **Blei,** lead

bleiben, to stay, to remain
bleich, pale
bleichen, to bleach
der Bleistift, pencil
der Blick, look
blicken, to look
blind, blind
der Blitz, lightning
blitzen, to lighten, sparkle
der Blitzkrieg, lightning war
bloß, only
blühen, to bloom, be in bloom
die Blume, flower
das Blumenbeet, flower-bed
der Blumenkohl, cauliflower
das Blut, blood
die Blüte, blossom
der Boden, floor, ground
der Bogen, arch, bow
die Bohne, bean
bohren, to drill, bore
die Bombe, bomb
das Bonbon, sweet, candy
das Boot, boat
böse (auf), angry (with)
der Bote, messenger
die Botschaft, embassy
boxen, to box
die Bratkartoffeln, fried potatoes
brauchen, to need
braun, brown
brausen, to roar
die Braut, bride, fiancée
der Bräutigam, bridegroom, fiancé
brechen, to break
breit, broad, wide
die Bremse, brake
brennen, to burn
der Brennspiritus, methylated spirits
der Brief, letter
der Briefkasten, letter box
die Briefmarke, stamp
das Briefpapier, writing-paper
der Briefträger, postman
der Briefumschlag, envelope
der Briefwechsel, correspondence
die Brille, spectacles
bringen, to bring
das Brot, bread, loaf

der Bruch, break, rupture
die Brücke, bridge
der Bruder, brother
der Brunnen, fountain, well
die Brust, chest, breast
brüten, to breed
das Buch, book, quire
die Buche, beech tree
der Buchhändler, bookseller
die Buchhandlung, bookshop
bücken (sich), to stoop, bend
bügeln, to press, iron
der Bund, alliance, league
die Bundesrepublik, Federal Republic (of Germany)
das Bündnis, alliance
der Bunker, shelter; pill-box
bunt, colorful
die Burg, castle
der Bürger, citizen
das Büro, office
der Bursche, fellow
bürsten, to brush
die Butter, butter
das Butterbrot, bread and butter

C

das Café, café, coffee
der Charakter, character
der Chauffeur, chauffeur
der Chef, principal
die Chemie, chemistry
christlich, Christian
(der) Christus, Christ
v.Ch., B.C.
n.Ch., A.D.
der Club (also Klub), Club
der Cocktail, cocktail

D

da, there, then
da, as, because, since
dabei, at it, in doing so
das Dach, roof
dadurch, thereby, through it
dagegen, against it
daher, therefore, along
dahin, there, thither
damals, at that time, then
die Dame, lady

damit, with it (them)
damit, in order that
dämmern, to dawn, grow dark
die **Dämmerung,** dawn, dusk
der **Dampf,** vapor, steam
der **Dampfer,** steamer
der **Dank,** thanks
dankbar, grateful, thankful
die **Dankbarkeit,** gratitude
danken (*dat.*), to thank
dann, then, after that
dann und wann, now and then
daran, at it (them)
darauf, thereupon, on it (them)
daraus, out of it (them)
darin, in it (them)
der **Darm,** gut, intestine
darstellen, to represent
darüber, over it (them)
darum, therefore
darunter, under (below) it (them)
daß, that
das **Dasein,** existence
das **Datum,** date
die **Dauer,** duration
dauern, to last
der **Daumen,** thumb
davon, from it (them)
dazu, to it (them)
dazwischen, between it (them)
die **Decke,** cover, ceiling
decken, to cover, set a table
dehnen, to stretch
dein, thy
demokratisch, democratic
denken, to think
denken (sich), to fancy, imagine
das **Denkmal,** monument
denn, for, because
deshalb, therefore
deswegen, therefore
deutlich, distinctly
dicht, dense, thick
der **Dichter,** poet
dick, thick, stout
der **Dieb,** thief

dienen, to serve
der **Diener,** servant
der **Dienst,** service
der **Dienstmann,** porter
diesseits (*gen.*), on this side of
die **Diktatur,** dictatorship
das **Ding,** thing, gadget
direkt, direct
der **Direktor,** manager
doch, *intensifying word,* but, yet; also " *yes* " in reply to negative
das **Dogma,** the dogma
der **Doktor(-en),** doctor(s)
der **Dolmetscher,** interpreter
der **Dom,** cathedral
der **Donner,** thunder
donnern, to thunder
doppelt, double
das **Dorf,** village
die **Dorfschenke,** village inn
der **Dorn,** thorn
dort, there
dorthin, there (thither)
der **Drache,** dragon, kite
der **Draht,** wire
drahtlos, wireless
das **Drama,** drama
drängen, to urge, press
draußen, outside
drehen, to turn
die **Drehung,** threat
dreifach, threefold
dringen, to urge, press
dringend, urgent
das **Drittel,** one-third
drittens, thirdly
drohen (*dat.*), to threaten
drüben, yonder, over there
drucken, to print
drücken, to press
die **Druckerei,** printing works
die **Drucksache,** printed matter
dulden, to suffer, endure
dumm, stupid
dumpf, dull
dunkel, dark
die **Dunkelheit,** darkness
dunkelrot, crimson
dünn, thin, lean
durch, through, per, by
durchaus, throughout

durchaus nicht, by no means, not at all
durchfallen, to fail (in an exam)
der **Durchgang,** passage, gateway
dürfen, to dare, be allowed to
der **Durst,** thirst
dürsten, to thirst
durstig, thirsty
das **Dutzend,** dozen

E

eben, even, flat, level
eben, just now
die **Ebene,** plain
das **Echo,** echo
echt, genuine, real
die **Ecke,** corner
edel, noble
edelmütig, heroic, courageous
die **Ehe,** marriage
ehe, ere, before
eher, rather, sooner
die **Ehre,** honor
ehren, to honor
die **Ehrenbezeugungen,** honours
ehrlich, honest
die **Ehrlichkeit,** honesty
das **Ei,** egg
die **Eiche,** oak; measure
der **Eid,** oath
der **Eierkuchen,** omelette
der **Eifer,** zeal
die **Eifersucht,** jealousy, envy
eifersüchtig, jealous
eifrig, keen
eigen, own
die **Eigenschaft,** quality
eigentlich, really, in fact
das **Eigentum,** property
der **Eigentümer,** proprietor
die **Eile,** haste, hurry
der **Eimer,** bucket
ein(e), one, a, an
einander, each other
die **Einbahnstraße,** one-way street
einbilden (sich), to fancy, imagine

eindringen, to penetrate
der **Eindruck,** impression
einfach, single, simple
die **Einfachheit,** simplicity
einfältig, onefold, stupid
der **Einfluß,** influence
der **Eingang,** entrance
die **Einheit,** unit
einholen, to catch up
einig, at one (friendly terms)
einige, a few, some
die **Einkehr,** visit
einkehren, to call on
das **Einkommen,** income, revenue
einladen, to invite
die **Einladung,** invitation
einmal, once
einpacken, to pack
einsam, lonely
einschlafen, to fall asleep
einschläfern, to lull to sleep
einschreiben, to register (letters)
einsehen, to perceive
einst, once (upon a time)
einsteigen, to enter (car, train)
einstweilen, meanwhile
eintönig, monotonous
eintreten, to enter (a room)
der **Eintritt,** entrance, admission
die **Eintrittskarte,** card of admission
der **Einwanderer,** immigrant
einweihen, to dedicate
die **Einweihung,** dedication
einwilligen, to consent, agree
der **Einwohner,** inhabitant
die **Einzelheit,** detail
einzeln, single, individual
einzig, sole, only
das **Eis,** ice
das **Eisen,** iron
die **Eisenbahn,** railway
eitel, vain
die **Eitelkeit,** vanity
der **Elefant,** elephant
elektrisch, electric
das **Element,** element
das **Elend,** misery
die **Eltern,** parents

empfangen, to receive
empfehlen, to recommend
die **Empfehlung,** recommendation
empfinden, to feel
die **Empfindung,** feeling
empor, up
das **Ende,** end, final
enden, to end
endlich, at last
eng, narrow
der **Enkel,** grandson
entdecken, to discover
die **Entdeckung,** discovery
die **Ente,** duck
entfalten, to display, unfold
entfernen, to remove
entfernen (sich), to leave, go away
entfernt, distant, far off
die **Entfernung,** distance
entfliehen, to escape, elope
entgegen, towards
entgegnen, to reply, answer
entgehen, to escape
enthalten, to contain
enthalten (sich) (von), to abstain (from)
entschließen (sich), to resolve, decide
der **Entschluß,** resolution
entschuldigen, to excuse
entschuldigen (sich), to excuse (oneself)
die **Entschuldigung,** excuse
entstehen, to arise, grow
enttäuschen, to disappoint
die **Enttäuschung,** disappointment
entweder . . . oder, either . . . or
entwickeln, to develop (films)
entzücken, to delight
entzückend, charming, delightful
entzünden, to inflame
die **Entzündung,** inflammation
erbarmen (sich, *gen.***),** to pity
das **Erbarmen,** pity
der **Erbe,** heir

das **Erbe,** legacy, inheritance
erben, to inherit
die **Erbschaft,** legacy, inheritance
die **Erbse,** pea
die **Erde,** earth, globe, soil
ereignen (sich), to happen
das **Ereignis,** event
erfinden, to invent
die **Erfindung,** invention
der **Erfolg,** success
erfolglos, unsuccessful
erfolgreich, successful
erfüllen, to fulfil
die **Erfüllung,** fulfilment
ergänzen, to supplement
ergreifen, to seize, get hold of
erhaben, superior, sublime
erhalten, to receive
erheben, to raise
erheben (sich), to rise
erholen (sich), to recover
erinnern, to remind
erinnern (sich), to remember
die **Erinnerung,** remembrance, souvenir
erkälten (sich), to catch cold
die **Erkältung,** cold, chill
erkennen, to recognize
die **Erkenntnis,** recognition
erklären, to explain
die **Erklärung,** explanation
erkranken, to become ill
erkundigen (sich), to make enquiries
die **Erkundigung,** enquiry
erlauben (*dat.***),** to permit, allow
die **Erlaubnis,** permission
erleben, to experience
erlöschen, to extinguish
ermangeln (*gen.***),** to be short of
ermorden, to murder
ernennen, to appoint
ernst, earnest
die **Ernte,** crop, harvest
erreichen, to reach, get to
errichten, to erect
der **Ersatz,** substitute
erschaffen, to create
erscheinen, to appear (in sight)

erschrecken, to frighten
erschrecken, (sich) to be frightened
erst, not until, only
erst, first
erstaunen, to astonish
das Erstaunen, astonishment, surprise
erstaunt, astonished, surprised
erstens, firstly
der erstere, former
erstrecken, to extend
der Ertrag, profit
ertragen, to bear
ertränken, to drown
ertrinken, to be drowned
erwachen, to awaken
erwachsen, grown up
der Erwachsene, adult
erwähnen, to mention
erwarten, to expect
erweisen. to bestow
das Erz, ore
erzählen, to relate, tell
die Erzählung, tale, story
erziehen, to rear, educate
die Erziehung, education
der Esel, donkey
essen, to eat
das Essen, meal, repast
der Essig, vinegar
das Eßzimmer, dining-room
etliche, a few, some
etwa, about, approximately
etwas, something, anything
ewig, everlasting, eternal
das Exemplar, copy, specimen
die Expedition, expedition

F

die Fabrik, factory, works
der Fabrikant, manufacturer
das Fach, department, speciality
der Faden, thread
fähig, capable
die Fahne, flag
fahren, to drive (in a vehicle)
der Fahrer, driver
das Fahrgeld, fare
die Fahrkarte, ticket

der Fahrkartenschalter, ticket office
der Fahrplan, time-table
das Fahrrad, bicycle
der Fall, case, incident
fallen, to fall
falls, in case
der Fallschirm, parachute
der Fallschirmjäger, paratrooper
falsch, wrong
falten, to fold
die Familie, family
fangen, to catch
die Farbe, colour
färben, to dye
der Färber, dyer
fast, almost
faul, idle, lazy
die Faulheit, idleness, laziness
die Faust, fist
die Feder, pen, feather
das Federmesser, penknife
fehlen (dat.), to fail, miss
der Fehler, mistake, error
die Feier, festival, feast
feiern, to celebrate
der Feiertag, holiday
fein, fine
der Feind, foe, enemy
das Feld, field
der Fels(en), rock
das Fenster, window
die Ferien, holidays
fern, distant, far
die Ferne, distance
der Fernsehapparat, television set
das Fernsehen, television
fertig, ready
fest, firm, fixed
das Fest, the feast
feucht, damp, moist
das Feuer, fire
die Feuerwehr, fire brigade
das Fieber, fever
die Figur, figure
der Film, film, moving picture
der Filmschauspieler, film actor
finden, to find
der Finger, finger
finster, dark

die **Finsternis**, darkness
der **Fisch**, fish
der **Fischer**, fisher(man)
   flach, flat, even, smooth
die **Fläche**, surface
die **Flamme**, flame
die **Flasche**, bottle, flask
der **Fleck**, spot
das **Fleisch**, meat, flesh
der **Fleischer**, butcher
der **Fleiß**, diligence
   fleißig, diligent, industrious
   flicken, to mend
die **Fliege**, fly
   fliegen, to fly
der **Flieger**, aviator
   fliehen, to flee, escape
   fließen, to flow
   fließend, fluent(ly)
die **Flöte**, flute
die **Flotte**, fleet
die **Flucht**, flight, escape
   flüchtig, careless(ly)
der **Flug**, flight (of birds)
der **Flügel**, wing
der **Flughafen**, air port
der **Flugplatz**, airport
das **Flugzeug**, airplane
die **Flur**, fields
der **Fluß**, river
die **Flüssigkeit**, liquid
die **Flut**, flood
die **Folge**, consequence
   folgen (*dat.*), to follow
   folglich, consequently
   fort, forth, away
der **Fortschritt**, progress
die **Fotografie**, photo
die **Frage**, question
   fragen, to ask
die **Fraktur**, Gothic type
die **Frau**, Mrs., lady, woman
das **Fräulein**, Miss, young lady
   frech, impertinent, rude
die **Frechheit**, impertinence
   frei, free, at liberty
die **Freiheit**, liberty, freedom
   freilassen, to release
   freilich, certainly
   freisprechen, to acquit
   freiwillig, voluntary
   fremd, strange, foreign

   fressen, to eat (of animals)
die **Freude**, joy, pleasure
   freuen (sich), to be glad, to
   rejoice
der **Freund**, friend
   freundlich, friendly, kind
der **Friede**, peace
der **Friedhof**, cemetery
   frieren, to freeze, to be cold
   friert (es . . . mich), I am
   cold
   frisch, fresh, cool
der **Friseur**, barber
   froh, glad
   fröhlich, merry, cheerful
   fromm, pious, devout
die **Front**, battle front
der **Frosch**, frog
der **Frost**, frost
die **Frucht**, fruit
   früh, early
der **Frühling**, spring
das **Frühstück**, breakfast
   frühstücken, to breakfast
der **Fuchs**, fox
   fühlen, to feel
   führen, to lead
der **Führer**, leader, guide
   füllen, to fill
die **Füllfeder**, fountain pen
der **Funke**, spark
   funkeln, to sparkle
   für, for
die **Furcht**, fear, awe
   furchtbar, frightful
   fürchten, to be afraid (of), to
   fear
der **Fürst**, prince
das **Fürstentum**, principality
der **Fuß**, foot
der **Fußball**, football, soccer
der **Fußboden**, floor
der **Fußgänger**, pedestrian
der **Fußweg**, footpath
   füttern, to feed

G

die **Gabe**, gift, present
die **Gabel**, fork
der **Gang**, walk, speed, corridor
die **Gans**, goose

ganz, whole, entire, all
gänzlich, entirely
gar, very
gar nicht, not at all
die Garage, garage
die Garderobe, cloakroom
der Garten, garden
der Gärtner, gardener
das Gas, gas
der Gast, guest
das Gasthaus, hotel
der Gasthof, hotel
der Gastwirt, hotel proprietor
die Gattin, wife
das Gebäude, building
geben, to give
das Gebirge, mountain range
geboren, born, né(e)
der Gebrauch, use
gebrauchen, to make use of
die Gebrüder (*pl.*), brothers
gebunden, bound (of book)
die Geburt, birth
der Geburtstag, birthday
der Gedanke, thought
das Gedicht, poem
die Geduld, patience
geduldig, patient
die Gefahr, danger, peril
gefährlich, dangerous
gefallen (*dat.*), to please, like
der Gefallen, favor
gefälligst, please
der Gefangene, prisoner
das Gefängnis, prison, jail
das Gefühl, feeling
gegen, towards, against
das Gegenteil, contrary
(im) Gegenteil, on the contrary
gegenüber, opposite
geheim, secret
das Geheimnis, secret
gehen, to go
gehen (zu Fuß), to go on foot
das Gehirn, brains
das Gehör, hearing
gehorchen (*dat.*), to obey
gehören (*dat.*), to belong to
die Geige, fiddle, violin
geigen, to fiddle
der Geist, spirit

geläufig, fluent(ly)
gelb, yellow
gelblich, yellowish
das Geld, money
der Geldbeutel, purse
das Geldstück, coin
die Gelegenheit, opportunity
der Gelehrte, scholar
das Geleise, line (of rails)
gelingen (*dat.*), to succeed
geloben, to vow
das Gemälde, painting
gemein, common, vulgar
die Gemeinschaft, community
das Gemüse, vegetables
gemütlich, pleasant
genau, exact
der General, general
genesen, to recover (after illness)
die Genesung, convalescence
genießen, to enjoy
genug, enough
genügen, to suffice
genügend, sufficient
der Genuß, enjoyment
die Geographie, geography
das Gepäck, luggage
der Gepäckraum, (left) luggage room
der Gepäckschein, luggage ticket
der Gepäckträger, porter
der Gepäckwagen, luggage car
gerade, straight, just
gerade aus, straight on
das Gerät, apparatus, instrument
das Geräusch, noise
geräuschlos, noiseless
gerben, to tan, dress, curry
das Gericht, court (of justice)
gering, poor, meagre
geringste (der), the least
geringsten, nicht im, not in the least
gern, gladly
die Gerste, barley
der Geruch, smell, scent
das Gerücht, rumor
die Gesandtschaft, legation
das Geschäft, business, store
geschehen, to happen
das Geschenk, present, gift

die **Geschichte,** history, story
der **Geschmack,** taste
die **Geschwindigkeit,** speed
die **Geschwister** (*pl.*), brothers and sisters
die **Gesellschaft,** company
das **Gesetz,** law
das **Gesicht,** face
die **Gestalt,** form, shape
gestern, yesterday
gestorben, died, dead
gesund, healthy, wholesome
die **Gesundheit,** health
das **Getränk,** drink
das **Getreide,** corn, grain
die **Gewalt,** power
gewaltig, powerful
das **Gewehr,** rifle
die **Gewerkschaft,** trade union
das **Gewicht,** weight
gewinnen, to earn, win, gain
gewiß, certain, sure(-ly)
das **Gewissen,** conscience
das **Gewitter,** thunderstorm
gewöhnen (**sich**) (**an**), to accustom oneself (to)
die **Gewohnheit,** custom, use, habit
gewöhnlich, usually, generally
gießen, to pour, cast
das **Gift,** poison
der **Gipfel,** top, summit
das **Glas,** glass
glatt, flat, smooth
glauben, to believe
gleich, alike, same
gleich, immediately
gleichen, to resemble
gleichfalls, also, too
gleichgültig, careless
gleichschalten, to co-ordinate
die **Glocke,** bell
das **Glück,** happiness
glücklich, happy
gnädig, gracious, merciful
gnädige Frau } very
gnädiges Fräulein } polite forms
das **Gold,** gold
der **Gott,** God

das **Grab,** grave
der **Graben,** ditch, trench
graben, to dig, delve
der **Grad,** degree
die **Grammatik,** grammar
das **Gras,** grass
gratulieren (*dat.*), to congratulate
grau, grey
grausam, cruel
greifen, to seize, grasp
der **Greis,** old man
die **Grenze,** boundary, frontier
der **Griff,** handle
die **Grippe,** influenza
groß, big, tall, great, large
die **Größe,** size
die **Großeltern** (*pl.*), grandparents
die **Großmut,** generosity
großmütig, generous
die **Großmutter,** grandmother
der **Großvater,** grandfather
die **Grube,** pit
grün, green
der **Grund,** ground, reason
die **Gruppe,** group
der **Gruß,** greeting
grüßen, to greet, salute
das **Gummi,** rubber
die **Gunst,** favour
günstig, favorable
gut, good
das **Gut,** estate, property
die **Güte,** goodness, kindness
die **Güter** (*pl.*), goods
der **Güterzug,** goods train
gütig, kind

H

das **Haar,** hair
haben, to have
die **Habsucht,** greed
habsüchtig, greedy
der **Hafen,** harbor, port
der **Hafer,** oats
der **Hagel,** hail
hageln, to hail
der **Hahn,** cock, rooster
halb, half
die **Hälfte,** half

die **Halle**, large room, hall
der **Hals**, neck
das **Halsband**, neckband
das **Halstuch**, muffler, scarf
halten, to hold, keep
die **Haltestelle**, stopping place
das **Hammelfleisch**, mutton
der **Hammer**, hammer, mallet
hämmern, to hammer
die **Hand**, hand
der **Handel**, trade, commerce
das **Handgepäck**, hand luggage
der **Handschuh**, glove
die **Handtasche**, handbag
das **Handtuch**, towel
hangen, to hang, be hanging
hängen, to hang (*active*)
hart, hard
der **Hase**, hare
hassen, to hate, detest
häßlich, ugly
hauen, to hew, cut
häufig, often
das **Haupt**, head, chief
der **Hauptbahnhof**, main station (terminus)
der **Hauptmann**, captain
die **Hauptsache**, main thing
die **Hauptstadt**, capital (town)
die **Hauptstraße**, main street
das **Haus**, house
der **Hausmeister**, concierge, hall-porter, caretaker
Hause (nach), towards home
Hause (zu), at home
hausen, to house
die **Haut**, skin
heben, to lift, raise
die **Hecke**, hedge
das **Heer**, army
der **Heide**, pagan, heathen
die **Heide**, heath, meadow
heil, whole, intact
heilig, holy
das **Heim**, home
die **Heimat**, home, native place
das **Heimatdorf**, native village
das **Heimatland**, native country
der **Heimatort**, native place
die **Heimatstadt**, native town
das **Heimweh**, homesickness
die **Heirat**, marriage

heiraten, to marry
heiß, hot
heißen, to be called
heizen, to heat
der **Held**, hero
helfen (*dat.*), to help
hell, clear, bright
hellrot, light red, pink
das **Hemd**, shirt
die **Henne**, hen
der **Herbst**, autumn
der **Herr**, Mr., gentleman
Herr Ober, waiter
herrlich, splendid
herrschen, to rule
der **Herrscher**, ruler
hervorbringen, to produce
das **Herz**, heart
der **Herzog**, duke
das **Herzogtum**, duchy
das **Heu**, hay
heute, to-day
heute abend, this evening, to-night
heutzutage, now-a-days
hier, here
hierher, here (hither)
hiesig, local, of this place
die **Hilfe**, help
der **Himmel**, sky, heaven
hindern (an), to hinder, deter from
hinten, behind, in arrear
hinter, behind
der **Hintergrund**, background
hinterlassen, to leave (after death)
hin, to, there
hinrichten, to execute
hinübergehen, to cross (road)
hin und her, hither and thither (up and down)
hinzufügen, to add
der **Hirt**, shepherd
die **Hitze**, heat
hoch, high
der **Hochmut**, arrogance, pride
hochmütig, arrogant, haughty
höchstens, at most
die **Hochzeit**, wedding

der **Hof,** court, yard
hoffen, to hope
hoffentlich, (it is) to be hoped
die **Hoffnung,** hope
höflich, polite
die **Höhe,** height
hohl, hollow
die **Höhle,** cave, den, hole
holen, to fetch
das **Holz,** wood
der **Honig,** honey
hörbar, audible
horchen, to listen
hören, to hear
das **Horn,** horn, bugle
die **Hose,** trousers
das **Hotel,** hotel
hübsch, pretty
der **Hügel,** hill
hügelig, hilly
das **Huhn,** fowl, hen, chicken
der **Hühnerstall,** hen house
der **Humor,** humor
der **Hund,** dog
der **Hunger,** hunger
hungern, to hunger
die **Hungersnot,** famine
hungrig, hungry
der **Hut,** hat
hüten, to watch, guard
hüten (sich) (vor), to beware (of)
die **Hütte,** hut, cottage

I

die **Idee,** idea
ihm (*dat.*), to him
ihn (*acc.*)., him
Ihr, your
ihr, her, their
Ihrige (der, die, das), your
ihrige (der, die, das), theirs, hers
illustriert, illustrated
immer, always, ever
improvisieren, to improvise
in, in, into
indem, while
das **Individuum,** individual
die **Industrie,** industry
die **Infanterie,** infantry

der **Ingenieur,** engineer
der **Inhalt,** contents
innen, inside
das **Insekt,** insect
die **Insel,** island
intelligent, intelligent
interessant, interesting
das **Interesse,** interest
irdisch, earthly
irgend(-wo), some(where)
irgendwoher, from somewhere
irren (sich), to be mistaken, wrong
der **Irrtum,** error, mistake
isolieren, to isolate

J

ja, yes
die **Jacke,** coat (of a suit)
die **Jagd,** hunt, chase
jagen, to hunt
der **Jäger,** hunter
das **Jahr,** year
jahrelang, for years
die **Jahreszeit,** season
das **Jahrhundert,** century
jährlich, yearly, annually
jauchzen, to shout (with joy)
je, ever, apiece
je . . . je, the . . . the . . .
jedenfalls, in any case
jeder (-e, -es), each, every
jedermann, everybody
je . . . desto . . . , the . . . the
jedoch, however
jemals, ever
jemand, somebody, anybody
jenseits, on that side of, the other side of
jetzt, now
der **Jubel,** rejoicing
jubeln, to rejoice
der **Jude,** Jew
die **Jugend,** youth
jung, young
die **Jungfrau,** spinster, maiden
der **Jüngling,** youth, young man
jüngst, recently
der **Juwelier,** jeweller

K

das Kabel, cable
der Kaffee, coffee
   kahl, bare, bald, leafless
der Kahn, rowing boat
der Kai, quay
der Kaiser, emperor
die Kajüte, cabin
das Kalb, calf
das Kalbfleisch, veal
   kalt, cold
die Kälte, cold
der Kamerad, comrade, pal
der Kamin, chimney, fireside
der Kamm, comb
   kämmen, to comb
der Kampf, fight, match
der Kanal, channel
die Kanone, cannon
der Kanzler, chancellor
die Kapelle, band, orchestra
das Kapital, capital (money)
der Kapitän, captain (of a ship)
   kaputt, " broke ", " all in "
die Karte, card, ticket
die Kartoffel, potato
die Kaserne, barracks
die Kasse, cash-box, cash-desk
der Kassierer, cashier
der Kasten, box, cupboard
der Katholik, Catholic
   katholisch, catholic
die Katze, cat
   kaufen, to buy
der Käufer, buyer
der Kaufladen, shop
der Kaufmann, merchant
   kaum, hardly
die Kehle, throat
   kehren, to turn, to sweep
   kein, no, not any
   keiner (-e, -es), none
   keineswegs, by no means
der Keks, biscuit
der Kellner, waiter
   kennen, to know, be acquainted (with)
die Kenntnis, knowledge
der Kerl, fellow, " guy "
der Kern, pip, kernel, core
die Kerze, candle

der Kessel, kettle
die Kette, chain
der Kiefer, jaw
die Kiefer, fir tree, pine tree
das (der) Kilometer, kilometre
das Kind, child
das Kindlein, baby, little child
das Kinn, chin
das Kino, cinema
   kippen, to tip
die Kirche, church
die Kirchenuhr, church clock
der Kirschbaum, cherry tree
die Kirsche, cherry
das Kissen, cushion, pillow
die Kiste, case (wooden)
die Klage, complaint
   klagen, to complain
   klagen (über), to complain (of)
   klar, clear
die Klasse, class
das Klavier, piano
   kleben, to stick
der Klee, clover
das Kleid, dress
   kleiden (sich), to dress oneself
   klein, little, small
das Kleingeld, small change
die Kleinigkeit, trifle
das Klima, climate
die Klinge, blade
die Klingel, door bell
   klingen, to sound
   klopfen, to knock
das Kloster, convent, cloister
der Knabe, boy
   knapp, scarce
die Knappheit, scarcity
der Knecht, hired man
das Knie, knee
der Knopf, button, stud
der Koch, cook (m.)
   kochen, to cook
die Köchin, cook (fem.)
der Kognak, cognac
der Kohl, cabbage
die Kohle, coal
der Koffer, trunk, case
die Kolonie, colony
   kommen, to come

die **Kommode,** chest of drawers
der **König,** king
die **Königin,** queen
 königlich, royal, regal
das **Königreich,** kingdom
das **Königtum,** kingdom
 können, to be able
der **Konsonant,** consonant
der **Konsul,** consul
das **Konsulat,** consulate
der **Kontinent,** continent
das **Konto,** (bank) account
die **Kontrolle,** control
das **Konzert,** concert
der **Kopf,** head
das **Kopfweh,** headache
der **Korb,** basket
der **Korkzieher,** corkscrew
der **Körper,** body
der **Korridor,** corridor
das **Korn,** grain
 korrigieren, to correct
die **Kost,** food
 kostbar, costly, precious
 kosten, to cost
die **Kosten** (*pl.*), costs
die **Kraft,** strength
 kräftig, strong
der **Kraftwagen,** motor-car
das **Kraftwerk,** power station
der **Kragen,** collar
 krähen, to crow
 krank, ill, sick, diseased
das **Krankenhaus,** hospital
die **Krankheit,** illness
die **Krawatte,** tie
die **Kreide,** chalk
der **Kreis,** circle
der **Krem,** cream (for shaving, shoes, etc.)
das **Kreuz,** cross
 kriechen, to creep
der **Krieg,** war
das **Krokodil,** crocodile
die **Krone,** crown
 krumm, crooked, bent
die **Küche,** kitchen
der **Kuchen,** cake
der **Kuckuck,** cuckoo
die **Kugel,** bullet
die **Kuh,** cow
 kühl, cool

die **Kultur,** culture
die **Kunde** (*sing.*), news, information
 künftig, in future
die **Kunst,** art
der **Künstler,** artist
 künstlerisch, artistic
 künstlich, artificial
das **Kupfer,** copper
der **Kurs,** course; rate of exchange
die **Kurve,** curve
 kurz, short, brief
 kürzlich, recently
die **Kusine,** cousin (girl)
der **Kuß,** kiss
die **Küste,** coast
der **Kutscher,** cabman, driver

L

 lachen, to laugh
das **Lachen,** laughter
 lächeln, to smile
das **Lächeln,** smile
 laden, to load, invite
die **Laden** (*pl.*), shutters
der **Laden,** shop, store
die **Ladung,** load, cargo
die **Lage,** situation
das **Lager,** camp
 lahm, lame
 lähmen, to lame
das **Lamm,** lamb
die **Lampe,** lamp
das **Land,** country, land
 landen, to land
das **Landhaus,** country house
die **Landkarte,** map
die **Landstraße,** road
die **Landung,** landing
der **Landwirt,** farmer
die **Landwirtschaft,** agriculture
 lang, long (*dimens.*)
 lange, long (time)
die **Länge,** length
 längs, along
 langsam, slow(-ly)
 langweilen, to bore, tire
 langweilig, boring, tiring
die **Lärche,** larch tree
der **Lärm,** noise

lärmen, to make a noise
lassen, to let, allow
die Last, burden
der Lauf, course
laufen, to run
die Laune, humor, mood
die Laus, louse
lauschen, to listen
der Laut, sound, tone
laut, loud, noisy
lauten, to sound, run (of story)
läuten, to ring (of bells)
das Leben, life
leben, to live
die Lebensmittel (*pl.*), provisions
lecken, to lick
das Leder, leather
leer, empty
leeren, to empty
legen, to lay, put
lehren, to teach
der Lehrer, teacher, master
der Lehrling, apprentice
der Leib, body
leicht, light easy
der Leichtsinn, frivolity
leichtsinnig, frivolous
leid (tun) (*dat.*), to be sorry
das Leid, sorrow, pain
das Leiden, suffering
leiden, to suffer
leihen, to lend
das Leinen, linen
leise, low (tone)
leiten, to guide, lead
der Leiter, leader, guide
die Leiter, ladder
die Lektion, lesson
lenken, to direct
die Lerche, lark
lernen, to learn
das Lesebuch, text book, reader
lesen, to read
letzte, last
leuchten, to illuminate
die Leute (*pl.*), people
der Leutnant, lieutenant
das Licht, light
lieb, dear
das Liebchen, darling

die Liebe, love
lieben, to love
der Liebhaber, lover
lieblich, lovely, pleasant
liebreich, amiable, lovable
das Lied, song
liegen, to lie, be lying
die Limonade, lemonade
die Linde, lime tree, linden
die Linie, line
link, left
links, to the left
die Lippe, lip
die List, cunning, ruse
listig, cunning
das Liter, litre (*also* der)
das Lob, praise
loben, to praise, laud
lobenswert, praiseworthy, laudable
das Loch, hole
der Löffel, spoon
der Lohn, wages
lohnen, to reward
das Lokal, place (eating, drinking)
los, loose
lösen, to loosen, to take (a ticket)
der Löwe, lion
die Luft, air
die Luftpost, air mail
die Lüge, lie, falsehood
lügen, to tell a lie
der Lügner, liar
die Lunge, lung
die Lust, pleasure
Lust haben, to feel inclined
lustig, merry, cheery

M

machen, to make, to do
die Macht, power
mächtig, powerful
das Mädchen, girl
die Magd, maid servant
der Magen, stomach
der Magnet, magnet
das Mahl, meal, repast
die Mahlzeit, meal, repast
der Major, major
das Mal, time

malen, to paint
der Maler, painter
man, one (Fr. *on*)
mancher (e, es), many a
manchmal, sometimes
der Mangel, want, need
mangelhaft, wanting, short of
der Mann, man, husband
männlich, manly, masculine
der Mantel, overcoat
das Manuskript, manuscript
das Märchen, fairy tale
die Mark, German coin
die Marke, stamp, mark
der Markt, market
die Marmelade, marmalade, jam
marschieren, to march
die Maschine, machine
die Masern, measles
das Maß, measure
die Masse, mass, heap
das Material, material
die Mathematik, mathematics
die Matratze, mattress
der Matrose, sailor
matt, dull, flat
die Matte, mat
die Mauer, wall (outside)
das Maul, mouth (of an animal)
der Maurer, mason
die Maus, mouse
der Mechaniker, mechanic
die Medizin, medicine
das Meer, sea, ocean
das Mehl, meal (flour)
mehr, more
mehrere, several
mehrmals, several times
meiden, to avoid, shun
die Meile, mile
mein(e), my
meinen, to mean, think
meiner (e, es), mine
meinige (der, die, das), mine
die Meinung, opinion
meist, most (of)
meisten (am), most
meistens, mostly
der Meister, master (of trade)
melden, to report

die Meldung, report, despatch
die Melodie, melody
die Menge, crowd, lot
der Mensch, man (human being)
merken, to notice
merkwürdig, remarkable
messen, to measure
das Messer, knife
das Messing, brass
das Metall, metal
der Meter, meter
die Miete, rent
mieten, to hire, take (a house)
die Milch, milk
das Militär, army
die Million, million
minder, less
mindesten (zum), least
mindestens, at least
das Mineral, mineral
das Mineralwasser, mineral water
der Minister, minister (govt.)
die Minute, minute
das Mißverständnis, misunderstanding
mit, with
das Mitleid, sympathy
der Mitreisende, fellow traveller
der Mitschüler, fellow pupil
der Mittag, midday, noon
das Mittagessen, dinner
die Mitte, middle, center
das Mittel, means
das Mittelalter, Middle Ages
die Mitternacht, midnight
das Möbel, (piece of) furniture
mögen, to like to
möglich, possible
der Monat, month
monatlich, monthly
der Mond, moon
der Mondschein, moonlight
der Mord, murder
morden, to murder
der Mörder, murderer
die Mordtaten, murders
der Morgen, morning
morgen, to-morrow
morgen früh, to-morrow morning
das Motorrad, motorcycle

müde, tired
die Mühe, trouble
der Mund, mouth
die Münding, mouth (of a river)
das Münster, minster, cathedral
munter, cheerful, gay
das Museum, museum
die Musik, music
der Muskel, muscle
müssen, to have to, must
das Muster, pattern
müßig, idle
der Müßiggang, idleness
der Mut, spirit, courage
die Mutter, mother
die Mütze, cap, bonnet

N

nach, after, to (a place)
nachahmen, to imitate
der Nachbar, neighbor
nachdem, after
nachher, afterwards
nachlässig, careless
der Nachmittag, afternoon
nachmittags, in the afternoon
die Nachricht(-en), news
nächste, nearest, next
nächstens, shortly
die Nacht, night
der Nachteil, disadvantage
das Nachtessen, supper
das Nachtlokal, night club
die Nadel, needle
der Nagel, nail
nahe, near
die Nähe, vicinity, nearness
Nähe (in der), near
nähen, to sew
nähern (sich) (dat.), to approach
nähren (sich), to feed, nourish
die Nahrung, food
der Name, name
die Nase, nose
naß, wet
nässen, to wet
die Nation, nation
die Natur, nature

natürlich, natural(-ly)
der Nazi, Nazi (Nationalsozialist)
der Nebel, fog, mist
neben, beside, near
die Nebensache, secondary matter
neblig, foggy, misty
der Neffe, nephew
nehmen, to take
nein, no
nennen, to name, call
das Nest, nest
nett, pleasant, nice
das Netz, net
neu, new
das Neujahr, New Year
der Neujahrstag, New Year's Day
neulich, recently, newly
nicht, not
die Nichte, niece
der Nichtraucher, non-smoker
nichts, nothing, not anything
nie, never
nieder, down
niedrig, low
niemals, never
niemand, nobody
nimmer, never
nirgends, nowhere
noch, yet, still
der Norden, north
nördlich, northern
die Nordsee, North Sea
die Not, need, care
nötig, necessary, needful
notwendig, necessary, needful
null, zero
nun, now (well)
nur, only
die Nuß, nut, walnut
der Nußbaum, walnut tree
der Nutzen, use
nützen (dat.), to be of use, to be useful
nützlich, useful

O

ob, if, whether
das Obdach, shelter
oben, upstairs, above

die **Oberfläche,** surface
der **Oberkellner,** head waiter
   obgleich, although
   obschon, although
das **Obst,** fruit
der **Obstbaum,** fruit tree
der **Obstgarten,** orchard
   obwohl, although
der **Ochs,** ox
   oder, or
der **Ofen,** stove, oven
   offen, open
   offenbaren, to reveal, manifest
   öffentlich, open, public
der **Offizier,** officer
   öffnen, to open
die **Öffnung,** opening
   oft, often
   ohne, without
die **Ohnmacht,** faint, swoon
   ohnmächtig, fainting
   ohnmächtig werden, to faint
das **Ohr,** ear
das **Öl,** oil
der **Omnibus,** bus
der **Onkel,** uncle
die **Oper,** opera
das **Opfer,** victim, sacrifice
das **Orchester,** orchestra
   ordnen, to order, arrange
die **Ordnung,** arrangement
die **Orgel,** organ
der **Ort,** spot, place
der **Osten,** East
die **Ostern** (*pl.*), Easter
   östlich, eastern
die **Ostsee,** Baltic Sea
der **Ozean,** ocean, sea

P

das **Paar,** pair, couple
   paarweise, two and two, in couples, pairs
   packen, to pack, seize
das **Paket,** parcel
der **Palast,** palace
die **Panne,** puncture
der **Papagei,** parrot
das **Papier,** paper

der **Papst,** pope
der **Park,** park
die **Partei,** party (political)
das **Parterre,** ground floor
der **Pass,** passport
   passen (*dat.*), to suit, match
die **Paste,** paste (tooth)
der **Pate,** godfather
der **Patient,** patient
die **Patin,** godmother
die **Pause,** interval, rest
der **Pelz,** fur
die **Pension,** boarding-house
das **Pergament,** parchment
die **Person,** person
der **Personenzug,** passenger train
das **Petroleum,** petroleum
der **Pfad,** path
der **Pfeffer,** pepper
die **Pfeife,** pipe, whistle
   pfeifen, to whistle
der **Pfennig,** 100 Pfennig = 1 Mark
das **Pferd,** horse
die **Pfingsten** (*pl.*), Whitsuntide
der **Pfingstsonntag,** Whitsunday
die **Pflanze,** plant
   pflanzen, to plant
die **Pflaume,** plum
die **Pflege,** care
   pflegen, to be wont, nurse, cultivate
die **Pflicht,** duty
das **Pfund,** pound (lb. and £)
   pfundweise, by the pound
der **Philosoph,** philosopher
die **Philosophie,** philosophy
der **Photograph,** photographer
die **Photographie,** photography
der **Pilz,** fungus, mushroom
der **Plan,** plan
der **Planet,** planet
   platt, flat
der **Platz,** place, seat
   platzen, to burst
   plötzlich, suddenly
die **Pocken,** smallpox
der **Poet,** poet
der **Pol,** pole (magnetic)
   politisch, political
die **Polizei,** police
das **Polizeiamt,** police office

die **Polizeiwache**, police station
der **Polizist**, policeman
der **Portier**, (hotel) hall porter; caretaker
das **Porto**, postage
die **Post**, post, post office
das **Postamt**, post office
die **Postkarte**, postcard
der **Präsident**, president, chairman
der **Preis**, price
die **Presse**, press
  pressen, to press
der **Priester**, priest
  privat, private
die **Probe**, test, " tryout "
das **Produkt**, product
das **Programm**, program
der **Prophet**, prophet
der **Protestant**, protestant
  protestantisch, protestant
  prüfen, to test, examine
die **Prüfung**, test, examination
das **Pult**, desk
der **Punkt**, point, dot, period
die **Puppe**, doll
  putzen, to polish, shine

Q

die **Qual**, torment
  quälen, to torment, tease
der **Quatsch**, bunk
die **Quelle**, source, spring, well
  quer, slanting, athwart

R

der **Rabe**, crow, raven
die **Rache**, revenge
  rächen, to revenge
das **Rad**, wheel
der **Radfahrer**, cyclist
das **Radio**, radio
der **Rahm**, cream
  rasch, rapid, quickly
  rasieren (sich), to shave
die **Rasierklinge**, razor blade
das **Rasiermesser**, razor
die **Rast**, rest
  rasten, to rest
der **Rat**, advice, council, councillor

das **Rathaus**, town hall
der **Ratschlag**, advice, resolution
das **Rätsel**, riddle, puzzle
die **Ratte**, rat
  rauben, to rob, steal
der **Räuber**, robber
der **Rauch**, smoke
  rauchen, to smoke
der **Raucher**, smoker
der **Raum**, room
  rauschen, to rustle
die **Rebe**, vine
  rechnen, to reckon
die **Rechnung**, bill, invoice
  recht, right, just
  rechts, to the right
der **Rechtsanwalt**, lawyer
die **Rede**, speech
  reden, to talk, converse
der **Redner**, speaker
die **Regel**, rule
der **Regen**, rain
der **Regenschirm**, umbrella
  regieren, to rule, govern
die **Regierung**, government
  regnen, to rain
  regnerisch, rainy
  reiben, to rub
die **Reibung**, friction
  reich, rich
das **Reich**, empire
  reichen, to reach, hand
der **Reichtum**, wealth, riches
  reif, ripe, mature
  reifen, to ripen, mature
der **Reifen**, tire
die **Reihe**, line, series
  rein, clean, neat, pure
  reinigen, to clean
  reinlich, clean, tidy
die **Reise**, journey
der **Reisekoffer**, travelling trunk
  reisen, to travel
der, die **Reisende**, traveller
  reißen, to tear
  reiten, to ride (on horseback)
der **Reiter**, rider, horseman
der **Reiz**, charm
  reizen, to provoke, entice
  reizend, charming
der **Rekrut**, recruit
  rennen, to run

der **Rennplatz,** racecourse
die **Republik,** republic
reservieren, to reserve
das **Restaurant,** restaurant
retten, to rescue, save
der **Retter,** rescuer
die **Rettung,** salvage, rescue
die **Reue,** repentance
reuen, to rue, repent
das **Rezept,** prescription, recipe
der **Richter,** judge
richtig, right, correct
die **Richtung,** direction
riechen, to smell
der **Riese,** giant
die **Rinde,** bark (of a tree)
das **Rindfleisch,** beef
das **Rindvieh,** cattle
der **Ring,** ring, circle
der **Ringfinger,** ring-finger
der **Riß,** tear, gap
der **Ritter,** knight
der **Rock,** coat, skirt
die **Rocktasche,** coat pocket
roh, raw
das **Rohr,** tube
die **Rolle,** role
der **Roman,** novel
die **Rose,** rose
rot, red
röten, to redden, blush
rötlich, reddish
die **Rübe,** root (*as in*):
die **gelbe Rübe,** carrot ⎫
die **rote Rübe,** beet ⎬
die **weiße Rübe,** turnip ⎭
der **Rücken,** back
die **Rückseite,** back, reverse side
rückwärts, backward
der **Rückweg,** way back (home)
das **Ruder,** oar
das **Ruderboot,** rowing boat
rudern, to steer, row
der **Ruf,** call, shout
rufen, to call, shout
die **Ruhe,** rest, peace, repose
ruhen, to rest, repose
ruhig, calm, serene, quiet
der **Ruhm,** glory
rühmen, to praise
die **Rühreier,** scrambled eggs
rund, round

der **Rundfunk,** wireless (broad-casting)
rüstig, vigorous, alert
die **Rüstung,** armament

S

der **Saal,** room (large)
die **Sache,** thing, matter
der **Sack,** sack, bag
die **Sage,** legend, tale
sagen, to say, tell
die **Sahne,** cream (milk)
der **Salat,** salad
das **Salz,** salt
der **Same,** seed
sammeln, to collect
die **Sammlung,** collection
der **Sand,** sand
sanft, soft, gentle
die **Sanftmut,** gentleness
der **Sänger,** singer, bard
satt, tired, sick (of), satiated
sättigen, to satisfy
sauber, clean, tidy
sauer, sour
saugen, to suck
die **Schachtel,** small box
schade (wie . . .), what a pity, shame
schaden, to damage, injure
der **Schaden,** damage, injury
schädlich, harmful, injurious
das **Schaf,** sheep
der **Schäfer,** shepherd
schaffen, to work, get done
schaffen, to create
der **Schaffner,** guard (of a train) conductor (bus)
der **Schall,** sound
die **Schallplatte,** gramophone record
schalten, to switch gears
der **Schalter,** ticket office; switch
das **Schaltjahr,** leap year
schämen (sich) (*gen.*), to be ashamed of
die **Schande,** shame
die **Schar,** crowd, herd, pack
scharf, sharp
der **Schatten,** shade, shadow
schattig, shady

der **Schatz,** treasure
schätzen, to value, treasure
der **Schatzgräber,** treasure hunter
die **Schatzkammer,** treasury
schaudern, to shudder
schauen, to look, see
das **Schaufenster,** show window
der **Schaum,** froth, foam
schäumen, to foam, froth
die **Scheibe,** disk, slice
die **Scheide,** sheath
scheiden, to separate, depart
der **Schein,** appearance; certificate
scheinen, to seem, shine
der **Scheinwerfer,** searchlight
schelten, to scold
die **Schenke,** tavern, inn
schenken, to give (as a present)
die **Schere,** (pair of) scissors
der **Scherz,** joke, jest
scherzen, to joke, jest
scherzhaft, joking, jesting
die **Scheune,** barn
der **Schi(Ski)er,** ski-ing, -er
schi(ski)-laufen, to ski
schicken, to send
das **Schicksal,** fate, destiny
schieben, to shove, push
schief, crooked, wrong
schießen, to shoot
das **Schiff,** ship, boat
der **Schild,** shield
das **Schild,** signboard
schimpfen, to scold
der **Schimpfname,** nickname, bad name
der **Schinken,** ham
der **Schirm,** screen, umbrella
die **Schlacht,** battle, fight
schlachten, to slaughter
der **Schlaf,** sleep
der **Schlafanzug,** pyjamas
schlafen, to sleep
der **Schlafwagen,** sleeper, sleeping car
der **Schlafwagenplatz,** sleeping-berth
der **Schlag,** blow
schlagen, to strike, beat

die **Schlagsahne,** whipped cream
die **Schlagzeile,** headline
die **Schlange,** snake
schlank, slender, slim
schlau, sly, cunning
schlecht, bad
schließen, to lock, close
schlimm, bad
der **Schlitten,** sleigh
die **Schlittschuhe** (*pl.*), skates
schlittschuhlaufen, to skate
das **Schloß,** castle; lock
der **Schlosser,** locksmith
schluchzen, to sob
der **Schlummer,** slumber, sleep
schlummern, to slumber
der **Schluß,** end, conclusion
der **Schlüssel,** key
schmal, narrow
schmecken, to taste
die **Schmeichelei,** flattery
schmeichelhaft, flattering
schmeicheln, to flatter
der **Schmeichler,** flatterer
schmelzen, to melt
der **Schmerz,** pain
schmerzen, to pain, smart
schmerzhaft, painful
schmerzlich, painful, grievous
der **Schmied,** smith
die **Schmiede,** smithy
schmierig, greasy
der **Schmuck,** ornament
die **Schmucksachen,** jewellery
schmutzig, dirty
der **Schnabel,** beak
der **Schnaps,** brandy
die **Schnecke,** snail
der **Schnee,** snow
schneiden, to cut
der **Schneider,** tailor, cutter
schneien, to snow
schnell, quick(-ly), rapid(-ly)
die **Schnelligkeit,** speed
der **Schnellzug,** express train
der **Schnupfen,** common cold
die **Schnur,** string
die **Schokolade,** chocolate
schon, already
schön, beautiful, handsome
die **Schönheit,** beauty

der **Schornstein,** chimney
der **Schrank,** cupboard
die **Schraube,** screw
der **Schrecken,** terror, fright
    schrecklich, terrible, frightful
    schreiben, to write
die **Schreibfeder,** pen
der **Schreibfehler,** slip of the
    pen, mistake
das **Schreibheft,** exercise book,
    jotter
die **Schreibmaschine,** type-
    writer
    schreien, to cry, shout
    schreiten, to stride, step
die **Schrift,** writing
    schriftlich, in writing, in
    black and white
der **Schritt,** step, pace
der **Schuh,** shoe
der **Schuhmacher,** shoemaker
die **Schuld,** debt, fault, guilt
    schuldig, guilty
    schuldig (sein) (*dat.*), to owe
die **Schule,** school
der **Schüler,** schoolboy
die **Schülerin,** schoolgirl
die **Schulter,** shoulder
der **Schupo,** policeman, " cop ",
    " bobby "
die **Schürze,** apron
der **Schuster,** cobbler
der **Schuß,** shot
    schütteln, to shake
der **Schutz,** protection
der **Schutzmann,** policeman
    schwach, weak, feeble
die **Schwäche,** weakness, feeble-
    ness
die **Schwachheit,** weakness,
    feebleness
der **Schwager,** brother-in-law
die **Schwägerin,** sister-in-law
der **Schwamm,** sponge
der **Schwanz,** tail
    schwarz, black
    schwärzlich, blackish
der **Schwarzwald,** Black Forest
    schweigen, to be silent
das **Schweigen,** silence
das **Schwein,** pig
das **Schweinefleisch,** pork

die **Schwelle,** threshold
    schwellen, to swell
    schwer, heavy, difficult
die **Schwermut,** melancholy
    schwermütig, melancholy
das **Schwert,** sword
die **Schwester,** sister
    Schwieger-, -in-law
die **Schwiegereltern,** parents-
    in-law
    schwierig, difficult, awkward
die **Schwierigkeit,** difficulty
    schwimmen, to swim
    schwinden, to disappear,
    decrease
die **Schwindsucht,** consumption
    schwindsüchtig, consump-
    tive
    schwingen, to swing
    schwirren, to soar
    schwitzen, to perspire, sweat
    schwören, to swear
    schwül, sultry
der **See,** lake
die **See,** sea
die **Seele,** soul
die **Seereise,** sea voyage
das **Segelschiff,** sailing vessel
der **Segen,** blessing
    segnen, to bless
    sehen, to see
    sehnen (sich) (nach), to long
    (for), yearn
die **Sehnsucht,** yearning, longing
    sehr, very
    seicht, shallow
die **Seide,** silk
die **Seife,** soap
    sein, to be
    sein, his
    seinige (der, die, das), his
    seit (*dat.*), since
    seitdem, since
die **Seite,** side, page
    seither, since then
der **Sekretär,** secretary
der **Sekt,** champagne
    selbst, self, even
    selbständig, independent
    selten, seldom
    seltsam, strange, odd
das **Semester,** term (school)

senden, to send, broadcast
der Sender, transmitter
die Sendung, broadcast; consignment
der Senf, mustard
senkrecht, vertical
separat, separate
setzen, to set, put
setzen (sich), to sit down
sich, self (*reflexive*)
sicher, safe, sure
sichtbar, visible
das Sieb, sieve
die Siedlung, settlement
der Sieg, victory
singen, to sing
sinken, to sink
der Sinn, sense, mind
sitzen, to sit
die Skizze, sketch
skizzieren, to sketch
so, thus, in this way
die Socke, sock
das Sodawasser, soda water
das Sofa, sofa
sofort, at once, immediately
sogar, even
sogleich, at once, immediately
der Sohn, son
solcher (-e, -es), such
der Soldat, soldier
sollen, to be obliged to, must
der Sommer, summer
Sonder-, special- (+ noun)
sonderbar, strange, odd
sondern, but
die Sonne, sun
der Sonnenschirm, parasol
sonst, or, else, otherwise
die Sorge, care, worry
sorgen, to care
sorgfältig, careful
sparen, to save, economize
der Spargel, asparagus
der Spaß, joke, jest
spaßen, to joke, jest
spaßhaft, joking(-ly), jesting(-ly)
spät, late
der Spaten, spade
spätestens, at the latest

spazieren gehen, to walk, go for a walk
die Spazierfahrt, pleasure drive
der Spaziergang, walk
der Speck, bacon
die Speise, food
speisen, to dine
der Speisewagen, dining car
das Speisezimmer, dining room
die Spesen (*pl.*), freight, expenses
der Spiegel, looking glass, mirror
das Spiel, game, play
spielen, to play
der Spielplatz, playground
die Spielsache, toy, plaything
der Spinat, spinach
spinnen, to spin
der Spion, spy
spitz, pointed
der Sport, sport
spotten, to mock, jeer
die Sprache, language
sprechen, to speak
das Sprichwort, proverb
springen, to jump
der Spruch, saying
die Spur, trace
der Staat, state
die Stadt, town, city
der Stahl, steel
der Stall, stable
der Stamm, stem, trunk
der Stand, stand
stark, strong, firm
die Stärke, strength, power
statt, instead of
die Stätte, place
stattfinden, to take place
der Statthalter, governor
stattlich, handsome
der Staub, dust
staubig, dusty
staunen, to be astonished
stechen, to sting
stecken, to put (into pocket), to stick, to pin
die Stecknadel, pin
stehen, to stand
stehlen, to steal
steif, stiff
steigen (auf), to mount, ascend

steil, steep, precipitous
der Stein, stone
    steinern, of stone, stony
die Stelle, spot, place
    stellen, to put, place, set (a clock)
die Stellung, situation, position
    sterben, to die
der Stern, star
die Steuer, tax, duty, rate
das Steuer, rudder, helm
der Stiefel, boot
der Stift, tag, crayon
das Stift, institution
    still, calm, quiet
    stillen, to calm, satisfy
die Stimme, voice, vote
    stimmen, to tune, vote
    stinken, to stink
die Stirn, forehead, brow
der Stock, stick, storey (of house)
das Stockwerk, storey (of house)
der Stoff, stuff, material
    stolz (auf), proud (of)
der Stolz, pride
    stören, to disturb
die Strafe, punishment
    strafen, to punish
der Strand, beach, shore
die Straße, street
die Straßenbahn, streetcar
die Straßenecke, street corner
    streben, to strive
    streichen, to stroke
das Streichholz, match
der Streik, strike
der Streit, dispute, quarrel
    streiten, to dispute, quarrel
der Strich, stroke, dash
der Strom, river, stream; electric current
    strömen, to flow
die Strömung, current (of river)
der Strumpf, stocking
die Stube, parlour, sitting-room
das Stück, piece, fragment
der Student, student
    studieren, to study
das Studierzimmer, study (room)
das Studium, study, pursuit
der Stuhl, chair

stumm, dumb
stumpf, blunt, dull
die Stunde, hour
    stündlich, hourly
    stürzen, to rush, fall (rapidly)
    stützen, to support
    suchen, to seek, search, look for
der Süden, south
    südlich, southern
die Suppe, soup
    süß, sweet
die Süßigkeit, sweetness, sweets
die Symphonie, symphony
das Symptom, symptom
    synthetisch, synthetic

T

der Tabak, tobacco
der Tadel, blame
    tadellos, blameless
    tadeln, to blame
der Tag, day
    täglich, daily
das Tal, valley, dale
die Tanne, pine tree
die Tante, aunt
der Tanz, dance, ball
    tanzen, to dance
die Tapete, wallpaper
die Tasche, pocket
das Taschentuch, handkerchief
die Taschenuhr, pocket watch
die Tasse, cup
die Tat, deed, action
    tätig, active, alert
die Tätigkeit, activity
die Tatsache, fact
der Tau, dew
    taub, deaf
die Taube, pigeon
    taubstumm, deaf and dumb
    tauchen, to dive
der Taugenichts, good-for-nothing
    tauschen, to change, barter
das Tauwetter, thaw
das Taxi, taxi
die Technik, technics
    technisch, technical
der Tee, tea

der Teil, part, deal, share
teilen, to separate, share
die Teilnahme, sympathy
teilnehmen (an), to take part (in)
das Telegramm, telegram
das Telephon, telephone
telephonieren, to telephone
der Teller, plate
die Temperatur, temperature
das Tennis, tennis
der Tenor, tenor
der Teppich, rug, carpet
das Testament, last will, testament
teuer, dear, expensive
das Theater, theatre
der Theologe, theologian
das Thermometer, thermometer
tief, deep, profound
die Tiefe, depth
das Tier, animal, beast
die Tinte, ink
das Tintenfaß, ink-well
der Tisch, table
der Tischler, carpenter
das Tischtuch, table cloth
die Tochter, daughter
der Tod, death
die Toilette, toilet
der Ton, sound, tone
der Topf, pot
das Tor, gate
tot, dead
tötlich, fatal(-ly), mortal(-ly)
die Tour, tour
tragen, to carry, bear, wear
die Träne, tear
tränken, to water (animals)
der Transport, transport
die Traube, grape
trauen, to trust
die Trauer, mourning
trauern, to mourn
der Traum, dream
träumen, to dream
der Träumer, dreamer
träumerisch, dreamy
traurig, sad
treffen, to hit, meet
treiben, to drive, carry on
der Treibstoff, fuel (liquid)

die Treppe, staircase
treten, to step, tread
treu, faithful, true
die Treue, faithfulness
trinken, to drink
das Trinkgeld, tip
trocken, dry, withered
der Tropfen, drop
trotz, in spite of
der Trotz, defiance, spite
trotzen, to defy
trüb, dull, impure
die Trümmer (*pl.*), ruins
die Truppe(n), troop(s)
das Tuch, piece of cloth
die Tür, door
der Turm, tower, belfry
der Tyrann, tyrant

U

über, over, above
überall, everywhere
übereinstimmen, to agree
überhaupt, on the whole, indeed
überholen, overtake
überlassen, to leave to
überlegen, to reflect
die Überlegung, reflection
übermorgen, day after tomorrow
der Übermut, arrogance
übermütig, arrogant
übernachten, to stay the night
übernehmen, to take over
überraschen, to surprise
die Überraschung, surprise
überreden, to persuade
übersehen, to overlook
übersetzen, to translate
die Übersetzung, translation
überwältigen, to overpower
überwinden, to overcome
übrige (das), rest, what is left over
die Übung, exercise
das Ufer, shore, strand, beach
die Uhr, watch, clock
der Uhrmacher, watchmaker
das Uhrwerk, clockwork

um, about, round about
umarmen, to embrace
umfassend, comprehensive
umgeben, to surround
die **Umgebung,** surroundings, environs
umkehren, to turn round
umkommen, to perish
der **Umschlag,** envelope
umsonst, in vain
der **Umstand,** ceremony, fuss
umsteigen, to change (trains)
der **Umweg,** round about way, detour
umwenden, to turn over
umziehen, to remove
unabhängig, independent
unartig, naughty, badly behaved
unbegreiflich, incomprehensible
unbegründet, unjustified, unfounded
unbekannt, unknown
unbescheiden, immodest, rude
unbeschreiblich, indescribable
unbestimmt, undecided, indefinite
und, and
unerträglich, unbearable
der **Unfall,** accident
unfreundlich, unkind
die **Ungeduld,** impatience
ungeduldig, impatient
ungefähr, about, approximately
ungeheuer, immense, huge
ungestört, undisturbed
das **Unglück,** misfortune, accident
unglücklich, unhappy, unlucky, unfortunate
unglücklicherweise, unfortunately
die **Unglücksfälle,** accidents
das **Unheil,** misfortune
unhöflich, impolite
die **Uniform,** uniform
die **Universität,** university
das **Unkraut,** weeds

unmöglich, impossible
unrecht, wrong
unreif, unripe
unsichtbar, invisible
unten, below, downstairs
unter, under, below
unterbrechen, to interrupt
die **Unterbrechung,** interruption
untergehen, to set (of the sun)
unterhaltend, amusing
die **Unterhose,** drawers, pants
unterirdisch, subterranean
unternehmen, to undertake
das **Unternehmen,** undertaking
unterscheiden, to distinguish, to discriminate
der **Unterschied,** distinction, difference
unterschreiben, to subscribe, sign
die **Unterschrift,** signature
untersuchen, to examine, look into
die **Untersuchung,** examination
die **Untertasse,** saucer
die **Unterwäsche,** underclothes
der **Urlaub,** leave, furlough
die **Ursache,** cause
das **Urteil,** judgment, sentence
urteilen, to judge

V

der **Vater,** father
das **Veilchen,** violet
verachten, to despise
die **Verachtung,** scorn, disdain, contempt
veranlassen, to occasion
verändern, to change something
der **Verband,** bandage; association
verbergen, to hide, conceal
verbessern, to amend, improve, correct
die **Verbesserung,** correction, improvement
verbieten (*dat.*), to forbid
verbinden, to connect, units, join

die **Verbindung,** connection, alliance
verboten, forbidden
verbrannt, burnt, tanned
das **Verbrechen,** crime
der **Verbrecher,** criminal
verbreiten, to spread
verbrennen, to burn up
der **Verdacht,** suspicion
verdächtig, suspicious
verdächtigen, to suspect
verderben, to spoil
verdienen, to gain, earn, merit
der **Verdienst,** wages, earnings
das **Verdienst,** merit
verdrießen, to vex, annoy
vereinen, to unite, join
vereinfachen, to simplify
die **Vereinigten Staaten von Amerika** = U.S.A.
verfehlen, to miss
verfließen, to pass (of time)
verfolgen, to pursue
vergeben (*dat.*), to forgive
vergehen, to pass (of time)
vergessen, to forget
das **Vergnügen,** pleasure
verheiraten (sich), to get married
das **Verhör,** trial (in court)
verirren (sich), to lose one's way
verkaufen, to sell
der **Verkehr,** traffic
verkürzen, to shorten
verlangen, to desire, demand
verlängern, to prolong, lengthen
verlassen, to leave (a place)
verlassen (sich) (auf), to depend, to rely (on)
verlegen, to mislay
verlegen, embarrassed
die **Verlegenheit,** embarrassment, dilemma
verletzen, to hurt, injure
verlieren, to lose
verloben (sich), to get engaged
die **Verlobung,** engagement, betrothal

der **Verlust,** loss
vermeiden, to avoid, prevent
vermieten, to let (a room)
vermissen, to miss
vermuten, to presume, surmise
vernachlässigen, to neglect
verneinen, to deny
vernichten, to destroy
verpassen, to miss (a train)
verraten, to betray
verrechnen (sich), to err in calculation
versammeln (sich), to assemble
die **Versammlung,** meeting, assembly
verschaffen, to procure
verschieben, to postpone
verschieden, different
die **Verschiedenheit,** difference
verschließen, to lock up
verschreiben, to prescribe (medicine)
verschreiben (sich), to make a slip of the pen
verschwenden, to squander, waste
verschwinden, to disappear
versichern, to insure
verspäten (sich), to be late
die **Verspätung,** delay
versprechen, to promise
der **Verstand,** intelligence
verständig, sensible
verständlich, comprehensible
verstehen, to understand, comprehend
verstimmt, out of tune, in bad humour
der **Versuch,** attempt, trial
versuchen, to try, attempt
die **Versuchung,** temptation
verteidigen, to defend
der **Vertrag,** contract
das **Vertrauen,** confidence
vertreiben, to drive away
vertreten, to represent
der **Vertreter,** representative, agent

verursachen, to cause
die **Verwaltung,** administration
verwandt, related to, allied to
verweigern, to refuse
verwenden, to apply, use
verwunden, to wound
verzehren, to devour
verzeihen (*dat.*), to pardon
die **Verzeihung,** pardon
verzichten (auf), to renounce
die **Verzögerung,** delay
verzollen, to declare (at the Customs)
der **Vetter,** cousin
das **Vieh,** cattle
viel, much
viele, many
vielleicht, perhaps
das **Viertel,** quarter
das **Vierteljahr,** three months
die **Viertelstunde,** quarter of an hour
viertens, fourthly
die **Violine,** violin
das **Visum,** visa
der **Vogel,** bird
der **Vokal,** vowel
das **Volk,** people
der **Volkswagen,** people's car
voll, full, complete
die **Vollendung,** completion
völlig, fully, completely
von, from, of
vor, before, in front of
vorbehalten, to reserve
vorbei, past
vorbereiten, to prepare (lesson)
die **Vorbereitung,** preparation
vorgestern, day before yesterday
der **Vorhang,** curtain
vorlesen, to read to
der **Vormittag,** forenoon
vormittags, in the forenoon
vorn, in front
vornehm, distinguished
der **Vorrat,** provision
der **Vorschlag,** suggestion

die **Vorsicht,** caution, foresight
vorsichtig, careful, cautious
vorstellen, to present, introduce
die **Vorstellung,** performance
der **Vorteil,** advantage
vorüber, past
der **Vorwand,** pretext
vorwärts, forward
vorwerfen, to reproach

W

die **Waage,** balance, scales
wach, awake
die **Wache,** guard, sentinel
wachen, to watch, guard
der **Wachposten,** sentinel, guard
das **Wachs,** wax
wachsen, to grow
die **Wacht,** watch, guard
der **Wächter,** watchman, guard
die **Waffe,** weapon
der **Wagen,** carriage
wagen, to dare, venture
wägen, to weigh, balance
wählen, to elect, choose, to dial (phone)
wahr, true
währen, to last
während, during, while
die **Wahrheit,** truth
wahrnehmen, to perceive
wahrscheinlich, probably
der **Wald,** wood, forest
die **Wand,** wall (inside)
das **Wanderlied,** hiker's song, marching song
die **Wanderlust,** hiker's joy, joy of walking, roaming
wandern, to roam, wander
die **Wanduhr,** timepiece, clock
die **Wange,** cheek
wanken, to totter
wann, when
das **Wappen,** coat of arms
die **Ware,** ware, article
warm, warm
die **Wärme,** heat, warmth
warnen, to warn
die **Warnung,** warning
warten (auf), to wait for

der **Wartesaal,** waiting-room (railway)
das **Wartezimmer,** waiting-room (doctor's)
warum? why?
was, what
was . . . auch, whatever
die **Wäsche,** washing, laundry
waschen, to wash
das **Wasser,** water
die **Wasserflasche,** carafe
waten, to wade
wechseln, to change
wecken, to waken
der **Wecker,** alarm clock
weder . . . noch, neither . . . nor
der **Weg,** way, path
weg, away
wegen, on account of
weh tun, to hurt, to be sore
wehen, to blow (of wind)
wehmütig, melancholy
die **Wehr,** defence
wehren (sich), to defend (oneself)
weich, soft
weichen, to yield, give way
die **Weide,** pasture
weiden, to graze
weigern (sich), to refuse, object
weihen, to consecrate
die **Weihnacht,** Holy Night, Xmas Eve
die **Weihnachten** (*pl.*), Christmas
die **Weile,** while, time
der **Wein,** wine
der **Weinberg,** vineyard
weinen, to weep, cry
weise, wise
weisen, to point out, show
weiß, white
weit, far
der **Weizen,** wheat
welcher (e, es), which, that, who
die **Welle,** wave
die **Welt,** world, globe
das **Weltall,** universe
die **Weltanschauung,** ideology, view of life

die **Weltstadt,** city, metropolis
der **Weltteil,** continent
wenden, to turn (about)
wenig, little (quantity)
wenige, few
weniger, less
wenigstens, at least
wenn, if, when
wer, who
werden, to get, become
werfen, to throw
das **Werk,** work, opus
die **Werkstatt,** workshop
der **Wert,** value
wertlos, valueless
wertvoll, valuable
die **Weste,** waistcoat, vest
der **Westen,** West
die **Westentasche,** vest pocket
westlich, western
die **Wette,** bet
wetten, to bet, wager
das **Wetter,** weather
wichtig, important
die **Wichtigkeit,** importance
wickeln, to wrap
wider, against
widersprechen, to contradict
der **Widerspruch,** contradiction
der **Widerstand,** resistance
widerstehen, to resist, withstand
widmen, to devote
wie, how, as
wieder, again, back
wiederholen, to repeat
wiederholt, repeatedly
die **Wiege,** cradle
wiegen, to rock (cradle)
wiegen, to weigh
die **Wiese,** meadow, pasture
wild, wild
der **Wille,** will
die **Willenskraft,** will power
der **Wind,** wind, breeze
winken, to hint, beckon
der **Winter,** winter
wirklich, real(ly)
die **Wirkung,** effect
der **Wirt,** landlord, host

die **Wirtin,** landlady
die **Wirtschaft,** economy
das **Wirtshaus,** inn, tavern, pub
　　wischen, to dust, wipe
　　wissen, to know (Fr. *savoir*)
die **Wissenschaft,** science
　　wissentlich, knowingly
die **Witwe,** widow
der **Witwer,** widower
der **Witz,** joke
　　wo, where
　　wobei, whereby, by which
die **Woche,** week
　　wöchentlich, weekly
　　wodurch, whereby, through which
　　wogegen, against which
　　woher, where (from)
　　wohin, where (to)
　　wohl, well
　　wohnen, to dwell, live
die **Wohnung,** dwelling, flat
das **Wohnzimmer,** living room
die **Wolke,** cloud
die **Wolle,** wool
　　wollen, to wish, want
　　womit, wherewith, with which
　　woran, at which, whereat
　　worauf, whereon, on which
　　woraus, out of which
　　worin, wherein, in which
das **Wort,** word
das **Wörterbuch,** dictionary
　　wörtlich, literally, word for word
der **Wortschatz,** vocabulary
　　worüber, over (above) which
　　worunter, under which
die **Wunde,** wound
das **Wunder,** wonder, miracle
　　wunderbar, wonderful
　　wunderlich, curious, peculiar
　　wundern (sich), to wonder
　　wunderschön, wonderful(ly), beautiful(ly)
der **Wunsch,** desire, wish
　　wünschen, to desire, wish
　　wünschenswert, desirable
die **Würde,** dignity
die **Wurst,** sausage

die **Wurzel,** root
die **Wut,** rage, anger, ire
　　wüten, to rage

Z

　　zähe, tough
die **Zahl,** number
　　zahlen, to pay
　　zählen, to count
die **Zahlung,** payment
　　zahm, tame
der **Zahn,** tooth
der **Zahnarzt,** dentist
die **Zahnbürste,** toothbrush
die **Zahnpaste,** toothpaste
das **Zahnweh,** toothache
die **Zange** (*sing.*), tongs
der **Zank,** quarrel
die **Zänkereien,** quarrels
　　zart, soft, delicate
der **Zauber,** magic
die **Zehe,** toe
das **Zeichen,** signal
　　zeichnen, to sketch
　　zeigen, to show
der **Zeigefinger,** index finger
der **Zeiger,** hand (of clock)
die **Zeile,** line (printed)
die **Zeit,** time
die **Zeitung,** newspaper
das **Zeitwort,** verb
die **Zelle,** cell
das **Zelt,** tent
der, das **Zentimeter,** cm, 0·4 inch
　　zentral, central
　　zerbrechen, to break (glass, etc.)
　　zerreißen, to tear (to pieces)
　　zerschlagen, to smash
　　zerschneiden, to cut (to pieces)
　　zerstören, to destroy
der **Zettel,** scrap of paper, label
der **Zeuge,** witness
die **Ziege,** goat
der **Ziegel,** tile
　　ziehen, to pull, draw
das **Ziel,** aim, target
　　ziemlich, rather, pretty (*adv.*)
die **Ziffer,** cipher, figure

das **Zifferblatt,** dial
die **Zigarre,** cigar
die **Zigarrette,** cigarette
das **Zimmer,** room
das **Zimmermädchen,** chamber-maid
der **Zirkel,** compass
die **Zitrone,** lemon
zittern, to tremble
der **Zivilist,** civilian
der **Zoll,** toll, duty
das **Zollamt,** customs office
der **Zollbeamte,** customs official
zollfrei, free of duty
die **Zone,** zone
der **Zorn,** anger, wrath
zornig, angry
zu, to a (person)
das **Zubehör,** belongings
zubringen, to spend (time)
die **Zucht,** discipline
zucken, to tremble, quiver
der **Zucker,** sugar
zudecken, to cover
zuerst, at first
zufällig, by chance
zufrieden, pleased, satisfied

der **Zug,** train
zugeben, to admit, confess
zugleich, at the same time
zuhören (*dat.*), to listen to
die **Zukunft,** future
zuletzt, at last
zumachen, to close, shut
zunehmen, to increase
die **Zunge,** tongue
zürnen (*dat.*), to be angry
zurück, back
zurückkehren, to return
der **Zusammenhang,** context
die **Zusammenkunft,** meeting
der **Zuschauer,** spectator
zwar, indeed, to be sure
der **Zweck,** purpose
zweierlei, of two kinds
zweifach, twofold
der **Zweifel,** doubt
zweifeln, to doubt
zweitens, secondly
der **Zwerg,** dwarf
zwingen, to force, compel
zwischen, between
der **Zwist,** dispute
die **Zwistigkeiten** (*pl.*), disputes